'An important addition to the literature in victimology and legal studies, the book provides a comprehensive discussion of the interface between social science research on victims in justice proceedings and victim rights from a comparative perspective. Integrating findings from multi-jurisdictional approaches to the study of victims, victimization, and victim rights, it fills a void in the burgeoning victimological literature. Professor Kirchengast has meticulously assembled and analyzed case studies from different jurisdictions, legal systems, regional and international fori addressing victim rights, resulting in an impressive work that will serve well victimologists, legal scholars, and policy makers in efforts to advance crime victims' concerns and rights.'

Professor Edna Erez, Department of Criminology, Law and Justice,
University of Illinois at Chicago

'The nature and status of victim rights remains ill understood internationally. Tyrone Kirchengast brings full analytical rigour to shed a comparative and international light on this most topical issue. *Victimology and Victim Rights* is indispensable reading for anyone interested in the topic.'

Professor Frédéric Mégret, William Dawson Scholar, Faculty of Law,
McGill University, Canada Research Chair on the Law of
Human Rights and Legal Pluralism, 2006–2015

'This important new book traces how crime victims' rights have been expanding on often parallel (and sometimes different) tracks in various countries around the globe. It is a "must read" for anyone trying to understand emerging norms in victimology and victims' rights. It also offers a systematic view of victims' rights in both supra-national bodies such as the European Court of Justice as well as in domestic law in many countries around the world. The book fills an important gap by stepping back and taking a comparative view of what is one of the most important subjects in criminal law today.'

Professor Paul G. Cassell, Ronald N. Boyce Presidential Professor of
Criminal Law, University Distinguished Professor of Law,
S.J. Quinney College of Law at the University of Utah

'Kirchengast provides researchers with the status report on rights for victims of crime in the inquisitorial, adversarial and hybrid legal systems. It is an essential resource to getting victims the long overdue equitable access to justice across the world.'

Professor Irvin Waller, Faculty of Social Sciences, Department of
Criminology, University of Ottawa, author of *Rights for
Victims of Crime: Rebalancing Justice*

Victimology and Victim Rights

This book examines the international, regional, and domestic human rights frameworks that establish victim rights as a central force in law and policy in the twenty-first century. Accessing substantial source material that sets out a normative framework of victim rights, this work argues that despite degrees of convergence, victim rights are interpreted on the domestic level, in accordance with the localised interests of victims and individual states. The transition of the victim from peripheral to central stakeholder of justice is demonstrated across various adversarial, inquisitorial, and hybrid systems in an international context.

Examining the standing of victims globally, this book provides a comparative analysis of the role of the victim in the International Criminal Court, the *ad hoc* tribunals leading to the development of the International Criminal Tribunal for the former Yugoslavia and the International Criminal Tribunal for Rwanda, together with the Extraordinary Chambers of the Courts of Cambodia, Special Panels of East Timor (Timor Leste), and the Internationalised Panels in Kosovo. The instruments of the European Parliament and Council of Europe, with the rulings of the European Court of Justice, and the European Court of Human Rights, interpreting the European Convention of Human Rights, are examined. These instruments are further contextualised on the local, domestic level of the inquisitorial systems of Germany and France, and mixed systems of Sweden, Austria, and the Netherlands, together with common law systems, including England and Wales, Ireland, Scotland, USA, Australia, Canada, New Zealand, India, South Africa, and the hybrid systems of Japan and Brazil.

This book organises the authoritative instruments while advancing debate over the positioning of the victim in law and policy, as influenced by global trends in criminal justice, and will be of great interest to scholars of international law, criminal law, victimology, and socio-legal studies.

Dr Tyrone Kirchengast is a Senior Lecturer in the Faculty of Law at the University of New South Wales, Australia. He is admitted as a legal practitioner of the Supreme Court of NSW and is a solicitor and barrister of the High Court of Australia. His principal teaching and research interests are in criminal law and procedure and his publications focus on the integration of victim interests within criminal law. His recent work focuses on the role of victim impact statements in sentencing homicide offenders; the rise of victim lawyers and the integration of victims into adversarial proceedings; and victim rights as human rights under the European Convention on Human Rights and before the International Criminal Court. He has published widely on the integration of victims in the criminal trial and is the author of *The Victim in Criminal Law and Justice* (2006), *The Criminal Trial in Law and Discourse* (2010), *Criminal Law in Australia* (with L. Finlay, 2014), and *Victims and the Criminal Trial* (2016).

Victimology and Victim Rights

International comparative perspectives

Tyrone Kirchengast

Routledge
Taylor & Francis Group

LONDON AND NEW YORK

First published 2017
by Routledge
2 Park Square, Milton Park, Abingdon, Oxon OX14 4RN

and by Routledge
711 Third Avenue, New York, NY 10017

First issued in paperback 2018

Routledge is an imprint of the Taylor & Francis Group, an informa business

British Library Cataloguing in Publication Data
A catalogue record for this book is available from the British Library

Library of Congress Cataloging-in-Publication Data
Names: Kirchengast, Tyrone, 1978–
Title: Victimology and victim rights : international comparative perspectives / Tyrone Kirchengast.
Description: Abingdon, Oxon ; New York, NY : Routledge, 2017. | Includes bibliographical references and index.
Identifiers: LCCN 2016017843 | ISBN 9781472461834 | ISBN 9781317002291 (web) | ISBN 9781317002284 (epub) | ISBN 9781317002277 (mobipocket)
Subjects: LCSH: Victims of crimes—Legal status, laws, etc.
Classification: LCC K5572 .K57 2017 | DDC 345/.05046—dc23
LC record available at https://lccn.loc.gov/2016017843

ISBN 13: 978-1-138-60639-5 (pbk)
ISBN 13: 978-1-4724-6183-4 (hbk)

Typeset in Galliard
by Apex CoVantage, LLC

Contents

Abbreviations

2013 NSW Act	*Victims Rights and Support Act 2013* (NSW)
A Crim R	Australian Criminal Reports
ABCA	Alberta Court of Appeal
AC	Appeal Cases
ACHPR	African Commission on Human and Peoples' Rights
ACrHPR	African Charter on Human and Peoples' Rights
ACtJHR	African Court of Justice and Human Rights
ADRDM	American Declaration of the Rights and Duties of Man
AHRC	African Human Rights Court
AIR	All India Reporter
All ER	All England Law Reports
BOCSAR	Bureau of Crime Statistics and Research (NSW)
CAAF	Court of Appeals for the Armed Forces
Can	Canada
CAT	The Convention against Torture and Other Cruel, Inhuman or Degrading Treatment or Punishment
CCTV	Closed-Circuit Television
CEDAW	The Convention on the Elimination of All Forms of Discrimination against Women
CEU DVC	European Union, Directive of the European Parliament and of the Council 2012/29/EU, 25 October 2012, establishing minimum standards on the rights, support and protection of victims of crime, and replacing council framework decision 2001/220/JHA
CEU FD	European Union, European Council Framework Decision 2001/220/JHA, 15 March 2001, standing of victims in criminal proceedings
CICA	Commission to Inquire into Child Abuse
CIRCA	Cultural and Indigenous Research Centre Australia
CIS	Community Impact Statement
CLR	Commonwealth Law Reports
CPS	Crown Prosecution Service
Cr App R	Criminal Appeal Reports
CVRA	Crime Victim Rights Act
DCYA	Department of Children and Youth Affairs, Ireland.
ECCC	Extraordinary Chambers of the Courts of Cambodia
ECHR	European Convention of Human Rights

ECtHR	European Court of Human Rights
EHRR	European Human Rights Reports
EU	European Union
EUECJ	Court of Justice of the European Communities
EWHC	High Court of England and Wales
F 2d	Federal Reporter, Second Series
F 3d	Federal Reporter, Third Series
F Supp	Federal Supplement
HCA	High Court of Australia
HVSG	Homicide Victim Support Group (NSW)
IACHR	Inter-American Commission of Human Rights
IACtHR	Inter-American Court for Human Rights
ICC	International Criminal Court
ICCPR	The International Covenant on Civil and Political Rights
ICERD	The International Convention on the Elimination of All Forms of Racial Discrimination
ICMW	The International Convention on the Protection of the Rights of All Migrant Workers and Members of Their Families
ICRPD	The International Convention on the Rights of Persons with Disabilities
ICTR	International Criminal Tribunal for Rwanda
ICTY	International Criminal Tribunal for the Former Yugoslavia
IMT	International Military Tribunal
IMTFE	The International Military Tribunal for the Far East
Ind	India
IPK	Internationalised Panels in Kosovo
Ire	Ireland
Jpn	Japan
NATO	North Atlantic Treaty Organisation
NCPCR	National Commission for Protection of Child Rights
NGO	Non-Government Organisation
NPA	National Prosecuting Authority, South Africa
NSW	New South Wales
NSWCCA	New South Wales Court of Criminal Appeal
OJ	Ontario Superior Court of Justice
PJVC	The Declaration of Basic Principles of Justice for Victims of Crime and Abuse of Power
PRB	Prosecution Review Board, Japan
QB	Queens Bench Decisions
Qld	Queensland
RCIRCA	Royal Commission into Institutional Responses to Child Abuse
RPE ICC	Rules of Procedure and Evidence International Criminal Court
RRRVGV	Basic Principles and Guidelines on the Right to a Remedy and Reparation for Victims of Gross Violations of International Human Rights Law and Serious Violations of International Humanitarian Law
SA	South Australia
SASC	South Australia Supreme Court
SAVI Report	Report on the Sexual Abuse and Violence in Ireland
SCC	Supreme Court Cases (India)

Scot	Scotland
SPTL	Special Panels of East Timor (Timor Leste)
SthA	South Africa
TIAS	Treaties and Other International Acts Series
UKUT	Upper Tribunal (Administrative Appeals Chamber)
UN	United Nations
UNESC Guideline	Guidelines on Justice in Matters involving Child Victims and Witnesses of Crime
UNSC	United Nations Security Council
UNTAET	United Nations Transitional Administration in East Timor
UNTS	United Nations Treaty Series
US/USA	United States of America
USC	United States Code
UST	United States Treaty
Victims' Code	Code of Practice for Victims of Crime (England and Wales)
VIS	Victim Impact Statement
VLRC	Victorian Law Reform Commission
VPS	Victim Personal Statement
VVCI	Victoria's Vulnerable Children Inquiry
WDNC	Western District of North Carolina

International instruments

Charter of the International Military Tribunal – Annex to the Agreement for the Prosecution and Punishment of the Major War Criminals of the European Axis.

Council of Europe, Preventing and Combating Violence against Women and Domestic Violence, Treaty No. 210, in force 1 August 2014.

European Commission, DG Justice Guidance Document of December 2013 related to the transposition and implementation of Directive 2012/29/EU of the European Parliament and of the Council of 25 October 2012 establishing minimum standards on the rights, support and protection of victims of crime, and replacing Council Framework Decision 2001/220/JHA.

European Union, Council Decision 2015/1523 of 14 September 2015 establishing provisional measures in the area of international protection for the benefit of Italy and of Greece.

European Union, Council Decision 2015/1601 of 22 September 2015 establishing provisional measures in the area of international protection for the benefit of Italy and Greece.

European Union, Directive of the European Parliament and of the Council 2005/85/EC of 1 December 2005 on minimum standards on procedures in member states for granting and withdrawing refugee status.

European Union, Directive of the European Parliament and of the Council 2013/33/EU of the European Parliament and of the Council of 26 June 2013 laying down standards for the reception of applicants for international protection.

European Union, Council of Europe Framework Decision 2001/220/JHA, 15 March 2001, Standing of victims in criminal proceedings.

European Union, Directive of the European Parliament and of the Council 2004/81/EC of 29 April 2004 on the residence permit issued to third-country nationals who are victims of trafficking in human beings or who have been the subject of an action to facilitate illegal immigration, who cooperate with the competent authorities.

European Union, Directive of the European Parliament and of the Council 2011/36/EU of the European Parliament and of the Council of 5 April 2011 on preventing and combating trafficking in human beings and protecting its victims.

European Union, Directive of the European Parliament and of the Council 2011/93/EU on combating the sexual abuse and sexual exploitation of children and child pornography.

European Union, Directive of the European Parliament and of the Council 2011/99/EU of the European Parliament and of the Council of 13 December 2011 on the European protection order.

European Union, Directive of the European Parliament and of the Council 2012/13/EU of the European Parliament and of the Council of 22 May 2012 on the right to information in criminal proceedings.

European Union, Directive of the European Parliament and of the Council 2003/9/EC of 27 January 2003 laying down minimum standards for the reception of asylum seekers.

European Union, Directive of the European Parliament and of the Council, 2012/29/EU, 25 October 2012, establishing minimum standards on the rights, support and protection of victims of crime, and replacing council framework decision 2001/220/JHA.

European Union, Proposal for a Directive of the European Parliament and of the Council, 2011/0129 (COD), establishing minimum standards on the rights, support and protection of victims of crime.

Geneva Conventions (1864–1949) Geneva Convention for the Amelioration of the Condition of the Wounded and Sick in Armed Forces in the Field of 12 August 1949, 6 UST 3114, TIAS No. 3362, 75 UNTS 31; Geneva Convention for the Amelioration of the Condition of the Wounded, Sick and Shipwrecked Members of Armed Forces at Sea of 12 August 1949, 6 UST 3217, TIAS No. 3363, 75 UNTS 85; Geneva Convention Relative to the Treatment of Prisoners of War of 12 August 1949, 6 UST 3316, TIAS No. 3364, 75 UNTS 135; Geneva Convention Relative to the Protection of Civilian Persons in Time of War of 12 August 1949, 6 UST 3516, TIAS No. 3365, 75 UNTS 287.

United Nations (CAT) (1984) Convention against Torture and Other Cruel, Inhuman or Degrading Treatment or Punishment, resolution GA/RES/39/46 of the General Assembly 10 December 1984, in force 26 June 1987.

United Nations (CEDAW) (1979) The Convention on the Elimination of All Forms of Discrimination against Women, resolution GA/RES/34/180 of the General Assembly 18 December 1979, and in force 3 September 1981.

United Nations (ICCPR) (1966) International Covenant on Economic, Social and Cultural Rights, International Covenant on Civil and Political Rights and Optional Protocol to the International Covenant on Civil and Political Rights, resolution GA/RES/2200(XXI) A-C of the General Assembly on 16 December 1966, and in force 23 March 1976.

United Nations (ICERD) (1965) The International Convention on the Elimination of all forms of Racial Discrimination, resolution GA/RES/2106(XX)A-B of the General Assembly on 21 December 1965, in force 4 January 1969.

United Nations (ICMW) (1990) The International Convention on the Protection of the Rights of All Migrant Workers and Members of Their Families, resolution GA/RES/45/158 of the General Assembly on 18 December 1990, in force 1 July 2003.

United Nations (ICRPD) (2006) The International Convention on the Rights of Persons with Disabilities, resolution GA/RES/61/106 of the General Assembly on 13 December 2006, in force 3 May 2008.

United Nations (PJVC) (1985) The Declaration of Basic Principles of Justice for Victims of Crime and Abuse of Power, resolution GA/RES/40/34 of the General Assembly 29 November 1985.

United Nations (RRRVGV) (2005) Basic Principles and Guidelines on the Right to a Remedy and Reparation for Victims of Gross Violations of International Human Rights Law and Serious Violations of International Humanitarian Law, resolution GA/RES/60/147 of the UN General Assembly, 16 December 2005.

United Nations (1992) The Declaration on the Protection of All Persons from Enforced Disappearance, General Assembly, resolution GA/RES/47/133 of the General Assembly on 18 December 1992.

United Nations (2006) International Convention on the Protection of All Persons from Enforced Disappearance, resolution GA/RES/61/177 of the General Assembly on 20 December 2006, in force 23 December 2006.

United Nations Economic and Social Council (UNESC Guideline) (2005) Guidelines on Justice in Matters involving Child Victims and Witnesses of Crime, resolution 2005/20 of the Economic and Social Council on 22 July 2005.

United Nations Transitional Administration in East Timor (UNTAET) (2000a) Regulation No. 2000/11 on the Organization of Courts in East Timor, 6 March 2000.

United Nations Transitional Administration in East Timor (UNTAET) (2000b) Regulation No. 2000/15 on the Establishment of Panels with Exclusive Jurisdiction over Serious Criminal Offences, 6 June 2000.

United Nations Transitional Administration in East Timor (UNTAET) (2000c) Regulation No. 2000/30 on Transitional Rules of Criminal Procedure, 25 September 2000.

Statutes

Bail Act 1976 (UK)
Bail Act 1997 (Ire)
Bail Act 2000 (NZ)
Bail Act 2013 (NSW)
Bail Bill 2015 (Ire)
Canada Evidence Act 1985 (Can) (RSC, 1985, c C-5)
Canadian Criminal Code (RSC 1985 C-46)
Charter of Human Rights and Responsibilities Act 2006 (Vic)
Civil Claims Alien Tort Claims Act (28 USC § 1350)
Code for Criminal Procedure (*Codice di Procedura Penale*) 1988 (Italy)
Code of Criminal Procedure (Act No. 131 of 1948) (Jpn)
Code of Criminal Procedure (Amendment) Act 2008 (Ind)
Code of Criminal Procedure (Código de Processo), Decree-Law No. 3,689 of Oct. 3, 1941
   (Brazil)
Code of Criminal Procedure (France)
Code of Criminal Procedure (Germany)
Code of Criminal Procedure (Jpn)
Code of Criminal Procedure Act 1973 (Ind)
Code of Criminal Procedure of 1838 (The Netherlands)
Code of Criminal Procedure of 1975 (Austria)
Code of Judicial Procedure (Sweden)
Codice di Procedura Penale (Code for Criminal Procedure) (Italy)
Constitution of the Italian Republic
Corrections and Conditional Release Act 1992 (Can)
Courts Legislation (Neighbourhood Justice Centre) Act 2006 (Vic)
Crime Victim Rights Act 2004 (US)
Crime Victims Bill of Rights (Georgia Code) 2010
Crimes (Domestic and Personal Violence) Act 2007 (NSW)
Crimes (High Risk Offenders) Act 2006 (NSW)
Crimes (Sentencing Procedure) Act 1999 (NSW)
*Crimes (Sentencing Procedure) Amendment (Family Member Victim Impact Statement) Act
   2014* (NSW)
Crimes (Sentencing Procedure) Amendment (Victim Impact Statements – Mandatory Consideration) Bill 2014 (NSW)
Crimes Act 1900 (NSW)

Crimes Act 1961 (NZ)
Crimes and Court Act 2013 (UK)
Crimes and Other Legislation Amendment (Assault and Intoxication) Act 2014 (NSW)
Criminal Justice Act 1964 (Ire)
Criminal Justice Act 1967 (UK)
Criminal Justice Act 1984 (Ire)
Criminal Justice Act 1988 (UK)
Criminal Justice Act 1993 (UK)
Criminal Justice Act 2003 (UK)
Criminal Justice Act 2006 (Ire)
Criminal Justice and Public Order Act 1994 (UK)
Criminal Law (Amendment) Act 2013 (Ind)
Criminal Law (Jurisdiction) Act 1976 (Ire)
Criminal Law (Rape) Act 1981 (Ire)
Criminal Law (Sentencing) Act 1988 (SA)
Criminal Law (Sexual Offences) Act 1993 (Ire)
Criminal Law (Sexual Offences) Act 2006 (Ire)
Criminal Law Act 1976 (Ire)
Criminal Law Act 1997 (Ire)
Criminal Law (Consolidation) (Scotland) Act 1995 (Scot)
Criminal Law (Rape) (Amendment) Act 1990 (Ire)
Criminal Procedure Act 1967 (Ire)
Criminal Procedure Act 1977 (SthA)
Criminal Procedure Act 1986 (NSW)
Criminal Procedure Act 2011 (NZ)
Criminal Procedure Code for Kosovo 2012 (Criminal No. 04/L-123)
Criminal Procedure Rules 2010 (UK)
Criminal Procedure (Scotland) Act 1995 (Scot)
Dangerous Prisoners (Sexual Offenders) Act 2003 (Qld)
Domestic Violence, Crime and Victims Act 2004 (UK)
Evidence Act 1872 (Ind)
Evidence Act 2006 (NZ)
Federal Rules of Evidence (28 USC Art. IV)
Gram Nyayalayas Act 2008 (Ind)
Habitual Criminals Act 1957 (NSW)
Human Rights Act 1998 (UK)
Law Enforcement (Powers and Responsibilities) Act 2002 (NSW)
Maintenance and Welfare of Parents and Senior Citizens Act 2007 (Ind)
New Zealand Bill of Rights Act 1990 (NZ)
Non-Fatal Offences Against the Person Act 1997 (Ire)
Offences Against the Person Act 1861 (Ire)
Offences Against the Person Act 1861 (UK)
Offender Rehabilitation Act 2014 (UK)
Penal Code (Código Penal), Decree-Law No. 2,848 of December 7, 1940 (Brazil)
Penal Code (*Keihō*), Law No. 45 of 1907 (Jpn)
Penal Code of 1810 (France)
Penal Code of 1881 (The Netherlands)
Penal Code of 1962 (Sweden)

Penal Code of 1974 (Austria)
Penal Code of the German Empire of 1871
Police and Criminal Evidence Act 1984 (UK)
Powers of Criminal Courts (Sentencing) Act 2000 (UK)
Protection of Women from Domestic Violence Act 2005 (Ind)
Rome Statute (Statute of the ICC) (A/Conf 183/9, 1998)
Sentencing Act 2002 (NZ)
Sex Offences Act 2001 (Ire)
Sexual Offences (Procedure and Evidence) (Scotland) Act 2002 (Scot)
Sexual Offences (Scotland) Act 2009 (Scot)
Statutes Amendment (Victims of Crime) Act 2007 (SA)
Statutes Amendment (Victims of Crime) Act 2009 (SA)
Victims and Witnesses (Scotland) Act 2014 (Scot)
Victims Bill of Rights Act 2015 (Can)
Victims of Crime Act 2001 (SA)
Victims of Crime (Commissioner for Victims' Rights) Amendment Act 2007 (SA)
Victims Rights Act 1996 (NSW)
Victims Rights and Support Act 2013 (NSW)
Vulnerable Witnesses (Scotland) Act 2004 (Scot)
Young Offenders Act 1997 (NSW)
Youth Justice and Criminal Evidence Act 1999 (UK)

Cases

Preface

The rise of victimology and victim rights as central areas of law and policy has been substantially influenced by the emergence of a normative and international framework of victim rights and powers towards the latter part of the twentieth century. The promulgation of victim rights and powers on the domestic level of nation states has been assisted by two key, interrelated movements. These movements have helped centre victim rights and powers as areas of policy development and law reform. Increasingly, this momentum has led to legal change, with the ratification of international and regional victim rights frameworks to reposition the victim as an empowered stakeholder of law and justice.

The first movement recognises the significant and contested position of victims and their right to access justice. This is informed by victimology as a site of contestation that sees the rise of human rights frameworks as an expression of normative rights and power, increasingly utilised by victims following the decline of the welfare state. The recognition of the victim as a person possessed of rights and powers challenged the older conceptualisation that the victim was peripheral and removed from justice for state control. Relevant too is the realisation that victims make up a diverse, heterogeneous group whose harms may be redressed in different and varying ways by justice systems internationally. Increasingly, research in the field has indicated that the justice system itself may contribute to the harm of the victim, with status, standing, and voice being denied by the very systems that ought to bring offenders to justice, while repudiating the experience of the victim as survivor.

The second movement involves the rise of an international and regional human rights framework that encourages development on the local, domestic level of individual states and countries. This has raised suggestions that we are moving towards globalised systems of justice that exhibit degrees of convergence between rights, powers, and processes, for victims, prosecutors, and the courts generally. While degrees of convergence are evident, manifesting in systems of justice such as Japan and Brazil that present hybrid or mixed models, most jurisdictions retain some semblance to an adversarial or inquisitorial system. The functional basis of international and regional human rights frameworks as applied in the context of domestic law and policy is generally constrained by geographic positioning against regional frameworks, constitutional limitations, and the overall organisation of a state's domestic justice system, including its institutions. Important still is the social recognition afforded to victims as institutionally significant agents of justice. Some countries place particular significance on the integration of victims in justice processes, while other states see this as a particular threat to the integrity of the system, which manifests in an intention to remove victims to the periphery out of consideration of a fairly narrow construction of the accused's right to a fair trial.

Victims are therefore positioned differently globally, despite the emergence of fundamental rights and powers providing for greater degrees of procedural consistency and substantive power. These rights and powers include, variably across adversarial, inquisitorial, and hybrid systems: duties to consult with victims during the investigation; the power of victims to inspect the case file; the victim's right to consult with the prosecution regarding key decisions made, including charges brought or plea deals reached; the victim's input into modes of disposal or to proceed to trial with a requirement to present as a witness; to ask for a modified trial process to afford greater protection to victims, especially where they are vulnerable; the proliferation of forms of statement or out-of-court evidence; rules regarding the examination and cross-examination of victims, with limits on personal, insulting or spurious questions; the availability of private counsel to represent the interests of the victim or to protect the victim in court; the availability of intermediaries or support officers to offer assistance to the victim when testifying; the victim's ability to participate as an accessory or subsidiary prosecutor (where available); to make submissions to the court; to tender evidence aside from the state; to address the court or the jury; to present a statement during sentencing on the impact of the crime on the victim; to request an appeal brought by the state; to participate in restorative justice and intervention in appropriate cases; to utilise problem-solving justice and alternative court mechanisms to invite victim participation; to allow victims to make submissions during parole hearings; to seek compensation and reparations during trial or at some other time; and to allow for reparations proceedings for remedies other than, or in addition to, pecuniary compensation and restitution. Select extracts of the international, regional, and domestic rights frameworks informing these developments are consolidated in Chapter 2.

Added to this are the number of ways in which international and regional human rights norms are increasingly informing the development of local rights frameworks. While direct ratification of international or regional convention may be identified as the means of encouraging international convergence, other modes also prevail, particularly where a state is geographically isolated from regional frameworks, such as that of the Council of Europe. For these countries, alternative modes of law reform and policy development may occur through policy transfer and experimental public policy, law reform, inquiries into significant wrongdoing; progression towards recognising the artificiality of traditional boundaries of adversarial versus inquisitorial justice, and a greater recognition of the benefits which may accrue for victims in hybridised or mixed systems.

I have to thank a number of people who have encouraged and supported my writing of this book: Thomas Crofts for his good humour and friendship, Norman Witzleb for his translation of the extracted sections of the Austrian Code of Criminal Procedure, Alison Kirk, my editor, for her belief in this project and for her patience in the delivery of the final manuscript, and my family, and Mario Enio Rodrigues Jr in particular, for their love and support, and for reminding me of what is important in this world.

Tyrone Kirchengast
Sydney 2016

Part I

Victimology and victim rights in comparative contexts

1 Victim issues in international law and context

Introduction

The reform of domestic victim rights frameworks toward regional and international standards may be one of the identifiers of the twenty-first-century movement towards redressing the wrongs occasioned to victims as vulnerable members of society. However, localised attempts to reposition the victim in justice and trial processes are highly variable, and have been met with mixed success. Although international convention seeking a new role for the victim may best afford legal and policy change where a member state or country ratifies the convention consistent with the original instrument, pressure from the international community may see certain reforms emerge, even where states do not ratify convention rights directly. International norms, without direct ratification into law, may also be adopted in local policy. The development of victim interests in law and policy therefore emerge through different mechanisms with regard to different pressures and priorities, according to the legal and political contexts of local jurisdictions. Significant here is the realisation that victims deserve rights and powers that position them as stakeholders of law and justice, and as important to the justice process generally.

Local conditions, or the particular contours of criminal justice as specific to each jurisdiction, remain important determinates in each system of justice. The needs of victims and their desire to participate and to be heard, as well as the normative attitude towards victim participation by justice stakeholders, are important determinants of any system of justice. The extent to which a particular nationalised system allows for the voice of the victim will be largely determined upon pre-existing norms and standards that provide for victims in specific ways. The substantive and procedural requirements that enable participation in each jurisdiction give a strong indication as to the normative positioning of the victim in that particular system. International and regional conventions may influence justice processes, particularly in those countries that provide a limited role for victims. However, local conditions and the needs of individual victims within a particularised justice context will always provide important qualifiers on the actual extent to which we can realise the emergence of an international or regional framework of victim rights and powers on a domestic basis.

While certain justice practices, such as investigation following complaint, followed by arrest and court appearance, and where guilty, conviction and punishment, are common throughout the world, each jurisdiction provides for these in stages of the criminal process in different ways. Where an international instrument is then integrated into the local level, certain practices may be standardised. However, much of the reality of the criminal process for justice professionals may bear little resemblance to these international standards. Added to this is the fact that the recognition and role afforded to the victim of crime may vary considerably within states, let alone across states and countries. The arguments in favour of the internationalisation of victim rights and powers thus need to be read against the reality of the prevailing practices of the local, and the dominance of criminal procedure, as the guiding system of practices that brings context to the substantive arrangements of each justice system. These arrangements also provide for the participation and interaction of victims with justice stakeholders and agencies at the local level.

There is much discussion and evidence of increasing international convergence regarding the integration and support of the victim in both law and policy (see Doak, 2008; Hall, 2009, 2010). Boundaries which were once cited as distinguishing one system of justice from another – adversarial versus inquisitorial, constitutional versus common law, code versus common law – are being slowly dismantled by statutory and policy amendment to afford victims a greater role in government decision-making, in legal proceedings, as community stakeholders, and as individuals with enforceable rights. Convergence between systems of justice has resulted in increased policy transfer between jurisdictions, and a willingness to pilot innovative programs that relocate the victim as a significant stakeholder in criminal law and justice in an international context.

While systems of justice converge, however, assisted by international law and procedure and policy transfer between like jurisdictions, laws and policies that seek to relocate the victim into proceedings are always actioned at the local, domestic level. The actioning of law and policy in local contexts provides for the argument of this book. Despite greater globalisation of victim rights and powers, victim rights are not necessarily universalised according to international standards because of the localised contexts of criminal and administrative law as the main arenas for the integration and provision of victim rights on a domestic basis. The significance of the local may be demonstrated with regard to any of the individual jurisdictions traced in the book. However, where countries are constituted by states that maintain jurisdiction over criminal law and procedure, including the United States of America (USA), Brazil, or Australia, or where criminal law remains the jurisdictional responsibility of individual countries, such as those that make up the United Kingdom (UK), the possibility for jurisdictional divergence is exacerbated, despite adherence to international norms and processes. Thus, the international convergence that allows for a comparative analysis of the jurisdictions covered in this book also recognises and identifies that this convergence must be read within local contexts. This is due to the discrete application of victim rights in a policy context that aims to make sense of and enable individual access to those rights and powers. International law and procedure are therefore interpreted through the lens of local policy to make those processes available to victims in a given jurisdiction. The dynamic of justice relations and nationalised norms of justice in any given jurisdiction therefore vary according to locally determined issues and polemics, including the systemic limitations provided by a state's adherence to adversarial and inquisitorial systems of justice, and the need to enforce regional agreements. The extent to which international norms shape the local also depends on the extent to which each system is victim-focused in the first instance.

Rather than be identified as oppositional, justice systems arguably fit on a continuum from strongly adversarial to inquisitorial. In many instances, insistence of adherence to one or the other system is rhetoric, the result of fervent nationalism and politics of the unknown 'other' (Summers, 2007). Other systems may comprise hybrid systems that may be described as neither adversarial nor inquisitorial. Other factors are also determinative to local processes. These include the extent to which each jurisdiction adheres to international norms, is a signatory to international instruments, ratifies individual instruments, adopts international standards in its local courts, or allows for international courts within its local jurisdiction.

Much will vary between jurisdictions, and this realisation, in the context of assumption of increasing global intervention, necessitates the analysis and evaluation of victim rights on the local level.

The book will provide an international comparative analysis of victim rights frameworks as they have emerged on an international, regional, and domestic basis. The book will also provide comparative materials on victim rights, laws, and policies in England and Wales, Ireland, Scotland, USA, Australia, Canada, New Zealand, India, South Africa, Japan, and Brazil. The continental European approaches will also be considered. In particular, the inquisitorial countries of Germany and France will be compared with the mixed adversarial and inquisitorial systems of Sweden, Austria, and the Netherlands. The instruments of the Parliament of the European Union (EU), or European Parliament, will be considered, as will the jurisprudence of the European Court of Justice, and the European Court of Human Rights (ECtHR) interpreting the European Convention of Human Rights (ECHR), to demonstrate how the existing legal record of member states can be influenced by regional courts and frameworks. International law, specifically the rights of victims before the International Criminal Court (ICC), and before *ad hoc* tribunals exercising international law, including the International Criminal Tribunal for the former Yugoslavia (ICTY) and the International Criminal Tribunal for Rwanda (ICTR), will be considered as forerunners to the development of a victim rights framework to afford substantive participation, as seen with development of the Extraordinary Chambers of the Courts of Cambodia (ECCC), Special Panels of East Timor (Timor Leste) (SPTL), and the Internationalised Panels in Kosovo (IPK), as courts exercising international law in a domestic context.

A multi-jurisdictional approach

The focus on multiple jurisdictions internationally is essential to the remit and argument of this book. The comparison of international frameworks, jurisdictions following a civil European tradition, and common law and other non-European inquisitorial or hybrid-adversarial systems, as well as countries with emerging victim rights records, will indicate the degree of international convergence amongst victim rights and powers while allowing for a focus on the particular detail of local policy practice to demonstrate the actual application of these international norms in a local context. Importantly, this will demonstrate how international norms and practices are often synthesised into domestic law and policy or even alongside local practices sometimes incompatible with international standards, but which continue to exist out of adherence to such practices by local stakeholders, including government and justice professionals.

The limits of this book include the ability to map in specific and direct ways the implementation of actual declarations of victim rights where a jurisdiction is not a signatory to those frameworks. Although most nations are members of the United Nations (UN), a human rights body exercising universal jurisdiction and membership, they may be not be signatories to other international instruments out of choice, or may be precluded on the basis of geography and regional specificity. This does not limit the fact that the law and policy of many jurisdictions are nevertheless influenced by international human rights discourse. Rather than direct ratification, many jurisdictions augment or reform law and policy by making discrete changes at the local level. This characterises international criminal justice through local processes, as between the rights of individuals, potentially depriving it of standing as a mode of global justice (see Mégret, 2014b, 2015, 2016). How this comes about in non-systematised ways or through processes other than direct ratification is covered in Chapter 3. While some jurisdictions make significant changes to their criminal procedure (see Japan, also Italy regarding the 1988 change to a hybrid-adversarial system under the *Codice di Procedura Penale*, Code for Criminal Procedure) in one attempt at reform, others inculcate change in an incremental way, by allowing courts to interpret and utilise international or regional frameworks (see England and Wales), while others principally do this by processes of international treaty, law reform, and policy transfer (see Australia, Canada, New Zealand, and South Africa). However, all jurisdictions will also continue to ratify relevant instruments directly in addition to alternative modes of law and policy reform, where relevant and necessary.

The consequence of focusing on criminal law and justice on the local, jurisdictional level detracts from the larger role of international human rights law as informing a global perspective on gross violations of human rights. This book does not advocate that the proper application of international human rights law is in its localised application to individual criminal justice systems, or indeed to the institution of the criminal trial. Rather, the consequence of the application of international human rights norms to the local level is changing the substantive and participatory rights of victims on the local level. It is doing this because of the application of international criminal processes and standards to the particular injustices faced by individual victims, and as a means of reforming old, resistant justice systems that are otherwise locked into justice traditions that determine the rights and powers of victims by reference to the extent to which they ought to be excluded from that system. The use of international human rights discourses challenges this assumption of the limited uses of victims, and their relationship with other justice stakeholders, to the extent that one cannot reduce international criminal justice to the level of the individual criminal trial. Mégret (2015: 79–80) warns against the reduction of international criminal justice in this way:

> There is little doubt on the face of it that international criminal justice is primarily a form of criminal justice. The application and enforcement of criminal law through criminal trials are, after all, its primary *modus operandi*. This then results in an often single-minded focus on the justice being meted to the accused or possibly the victims, reducing international criminal trials to the *huis-clot* of a confrontation between accuser or accused – what is typically understood as the 'fairness' of international criminal justice. This obscures a more potent question – one increasingly raised at the periphery or 'receiving end' of international criminal justice – about what might be termed the social justice of international criminal justice, that is, the extent to which it can be understood as being socially just in the global community.

The reconsideration of the victim as an agent of justice out of adherence to ideas of international human rights law and jurisprudence arguably challenges the reduction of international criminal law to individual state trials. Instead, the reform of domestic systems based on the availability of international and regional norms that include the victim as an important and valued stakeholder of justice achieves the function of international criminal justice by breaking down normative barriers that would otherwise reduce the prosecution to that of a state trial. The victims, and their desire and need for voice, participation, and reparation, become significant and even paramount factors, and influence the development of localised criminal justice from the normative conceptualisation that criminal justice is 'nothing more than the idea that certain transgressions should be met by particularly strong reactions from the law, including punishment and stigmatization' (Mégret, 2015: 80). The inclusion of the victim changes the system, and the normative arrangement of justice stakeholders, and thus the focus of the trial on purely social transgression in aid of consolidating sovereign, state control, is transcended.

Law and policy/law or policy

The separation of law and policy is essential as far as it denotes the difference between sources of change and innovation from doctrine, as more or less authoritative media through which victims may be integrated. This distinction must be artificial, in that law often plays into policy development and policy, whether local or international, is increasingly cited in court judgements and by parliaments when affecting legal and regulatory change. Increasingly, in the context of international standards that are expected to be ratified on the local level, such policy is to be adopted into local laws and practices. The two sources of law and policy are thus intertwined, and the advent of the development of victim rights and interests is no exception. The distinction between law and policy may also be phrased in the context of the differences between hard and soft law. Over-reliance on hard law, or binding legal instruments, may neglect the significance afforded to soft law, or the quasi-legal or policy instruments that are non-binding in nature. Instruments of international law may be hard or soft law, depending on whether they bind member states. Although the distinction is primarily one of international law and procedure, the distinction is increasingly relevant to domestic states where regulation occurs through non-enforceable rights frameworks. The rise of victim rights on the domestic level thus calls for further consideration of the relevance of soft law as regulating victim interests in a non-enforceable or binding way (see Pemberton, 2014). Alternatively, the consequences of the manifestation of victim rights through sources of policy alone may have unseen consequences for victims, limiting their standing as peripheral to the decision-making processes of criminal justice agencies and the courts.

Criminal justice systems are predicated on an established set of criminal procedures that usually flow from the centrality of the criminal trial, and then put into practice through key justice stakeholders – namely the police, prosecutors, judicial officers, counsel, and government officials aligned with justice infrastructure and institutions. Victims are generally excluded even in those jurisdictions noted as preserving a role for the victim and fostering interplay between victims and state agents. At best, victims are relegated a role aside the state and are expected to subserve those state interests that centralise community concerns, that ultimately advocate the normative positioning of the victim as a peripheral actor. This tends to be argued more stridently at the face of legal practice rather than in the milieu of policy intervention that may seek a greater role for the victim. The reality of the practice of law and procedure and the policies which attempt to normalise an experience for the victim call for the separate consideration of the legal and policy aspects of victimology and victim rights.

Although this book recognises important interconnections between law and policy, and the interplay between the two, the different worlds of law and policy will be interrogated in order to demonstrate how these different sources of victim rights set up and provide for different levels of engagement for victims of crime. How the engagement of the victim is provided for, enabled, or impeded is best discussed through the recognition of the differences between the victim as constituted and regulated in law and policy. For instance, the development of a victim-friendly approach in policy may not be seen to be relevant to the engagement and participation of the victim by the courts. Thus, in many instances, criminal law and procedure may be resistant to an integrative policy approach that affords a greater role for the victim. The focus on law and policy as two separate but related arenas of justice relations will assist the argument that the global policies and approaches that advocate a role for the victim affect the local level in different ways and to different extents. It is on the two levels of executive policy and legal processes that international norms may be received and interpreted differently, with substantially different consequences for victims and their capacity to then access justice.

Victimology and victim rights

The focus on victim rights draws from the increased disciplinary debate over victimology, its development and domain, as a part of criminology and the social sciences more generally. While the focus of this book is on policy and legal frameworks on the international through to the local level, discussion of the integration of internationalised norms on the local level will occur against a background of the recent debates within victimology that recognise the importance of the temporal and spatial dimensions of justice. The relevance of the local as the regulatory milieu and locale where conduct is conducted has been long recognised by the governmentality literature, and victimologists are increasingly recognising how important the local is to the availability of victim rights and powers for the remedying of wrongs for victims. Thus, research on the use of reparations in the ICC is increasingly phrased in the context of what may be done for local communities, rather than be seen as a supranational remedy or sanction, or award of damages, that does little to affect the daily lives of those traumatised by human rights abuses (see Wemmers, 2009, 2010, 2014a, 2014b; Mégret, 2014a).

Work on the cessation of torture, despite international norms and instruments, including the United Nations (1984) Convention against Torture and Other Cruel, Inhuman or Degrading Treatment or Punishment (CAT), resolution GA/RES/39/46 of the General Assembly 10 December 1984, in force 26 June 1987, suggests that local communities must be engaged through victim rights frameworks if victims of torture are to be rehabilitated and resettled. The best approach has long been recognised as one that fuses local or indigenous relationships and modes of conflict resolution with Western dispute resolution techniques (see Nou, 2015). The participation of victims in the proceedings of the Extraordinary Chambers in the Courts of Cambodia may be established as case in point where the consequences of the Khmer Rouge genocide for local populations require specialised services that redress local conditions of low rates of education, employment, and literacy, as well as the poor mental and physical health, poverty, and loss of local custom, consequent of the trauma following the genocide.

The rise of victimology and the development of human rights

Victimology has been characterised as a discipline that responds to the needs of the victim as a discrete agent in the context of the criminal justice system. Modern research into the plight of the victim demonstrates broader concerns, from victims of gross human rights abuses and war, state transformation and the dislocation and resettlement of citizens, to victims of natural disasters (see Dussich, 2013, 2015). The rise of the discipline of victimology was first discussed in the context of the needs of the victim out of the failure of the welfare state. However, the rise of the discipline predates the ability for the state to support the needs of victims as a vulnerable and at-risk group. The first reference to victims as discrete agents of justice occurred in a negative context of acts that may bring about and contribute to the victimised status of persons. While discussion of the way persons contribute to their victimisation continues today in the context of controversial assertions regarding personal responsibility in the context of interpersonal and sexualised violence (for a review of issues, see Koss and Dinero, 1989), the earlier victimologists took a more rudimentary view in that they saw victims directly contributing to or even causing the offending behaviour complained of. Various authors and academics wrote about victims and the causes and consequences of their behaviour (see Beccaria, 1764; Lombroso, 1876; Ferri 1892; Garófalo, 1885; Sutherland, 1924; von Hentig, 1948; Nagel, 1949; Ellenberger, 1955; Wolfgang, 1958; Schafer, 1968); however, the focus on the victim as a discrete object of study and inquiry did not emerge until Benjamin Mendelsohn (1937, 1940, 1956) developed his theory of the 'criminal victim' into the 1940s. The focus on the victim as a relevant site of criminological inquiry saw the genesis of the introduction of the discipline of victimology, necessarily internationally focused with a view to reform on the domestic level. The first, second, third, and fourth phases have developed out of this early recognition and follow successive waves of legal and policy reform that identify the victim as worthy of welfare support following the rise and then decline of the welfare state, the identification of the victim as the subject of human rights, and, more recently, the inclusion of those rights on the institutional and organisational level on an international and domestic basis.

Mendelsohn's theory was developed as a typology that characterised the victim as engaged in a reciprocal relationship with the offender. While the work of Mendelsohn has been generally discredited as blaming victims for the causes of their harm, the notion of the 'criminal victim' gained traction in so far as asserting that victims may be a worthwhile site of criminological inquiry in their own right. The victim therefore came to be identified as a subject of criminology that had otherwise been ignored (see Elias, 1985: 15). While Mendelsohn's theory remains controversial, his contribution to victimology identified the victim as a substantive site of criminological study. Importantly, standing of the victim was identified as separate from the offender. Furthermore, the victim was no longer identified as necessarily secondary to the offender, and an argument could now be made that the victim ought to have individual standing on those institutions of justice that regulate crime and deviance, which were otherwise focused solely on the inclinations of the wrongdoer (Sebba, 1982; Kirchhoff, 2010).

While Mendelsohn's 'criminal victim' enabled discrete focus on the victim in an academic and disciplinary context, regulatory policy continued to focus on the needs of offenders and crime control owed to communities. In the latter part of the 1950s and 1960s, however, regulatory policy shifted to the victim as a person who ought to be owed support from the state. While Mendelsohn's research did not argue for such discrete modes of support, the very focus on the victim as an independent subject of criminal justice helped reserve a place in regulatory policy for the victim as a discrete agent of justice owed certain entitlements not otherwise extended to victims. Western economies shifted to the provision of welfare services for children, families, refugees, and the community. Social services were increasingly provided, identified by a more intrusive state that sought to intervene to eliminate social inequality and disadvantage. The criminal justice system transitioned into one that identified the social needs of offenders and victims as important objects of justice policy. In this shift to the welfare state, victims were identified as in need of resources to assist crime prevention, and where harmed, their recovery as vulnerable and injured subjects. The victim was thus seen to be in need of welfare support and intervention, to be protected and rehabilitated back in to society as a functioning, trusting subject. This shift witnessed the rise of the first phase of victim rights. This era was marked with the rise of criminal injuries compensation, court assistance, and associated social services to rehabilitate the victim after the offence.

This was offered in part out of recognition that crime was a failure of the state, which, now having control of crime, criminalisation, and its prosecution, owed the victim a measure of support and assistance, including financial support, as recompense.

The development of social and legal services for victims of crime came at the expense of the state. The rise of social services and a more active and mobile state seeking to intervene in personal, family, and community life for the sake of redistributing benefits and entitlements was costly. The resort to welfare intervention also came at a personal cost for victims, with the state asserting its right to intervene and take over all matters of interest to it, offering victims those services that were deemed necessary by the state. The voice of the victim, already largely silenced by the rise of the state and its monopolisation of crime control, was further silenced out of a state mandate to offer victims only those services and modes of assistance that were deemed necessary in order to restore the victim. The identification of the victim as a discrete subject of welfare reform removed the victim's individual connection to the offence and offender, and supplanted that connection with costly regulatory mechanisms of the institutions of justice that now stood to direct the victim as removed from the context of the offence. This process further dislocated the victim from the offence and allowed for the characterisation of the victim as removed from criminal justice. The corollary was the consolidation of state power and the further intensification of crime control as an object of state concern alone. This has the undesirable consequence of further removing the victim from the criminal justice system. In the modern policy context, victims contest this characterisation and have asserted the right to be identified as related to criminal offending for the purpose of exercising substantive rights to justice that may include decision-making powers that influence the course of the criminal investigation and prosecution. The second phase of victimology, which Elias (1985; also see van Dijk, 2009; see generally, Friday and Kirchhoff, 2000) identifies as giving rise to a new victimology of human rights, thus involves the decline of welfare services for the realisation that victims are indeed capable of exercising some discretion over their standing as victimised individuals. While the state continues to exercise its control over crime and the criminal process, victims, assisted by the state's lack of willingness to continue to fund the costs associated with intensive state intervention, were able to gain ground over their identification as inherently weak, vulnerable, or fragile.

The third phase of victimology is thus based in the expression of the rights of victims as individuals who are owed rights to natural justice. This period is characterised by the rise of the neoliberal principles that express an ideology of individual self-government and rights to self-determination. The universal declaration of victim rights, the 1985 PJVC, evidences the emergence of a rights framework that identifies the victim as being owed certain fundamental human rights developed out the recognition that victims have certain inalienable natural rights to justice, combined with those support services, such as compensation, that survived the decline of the welfare state. The movement to the articulation of victim rights frameworks identified that certain rights to justice ought to be ratified on the domestic level. Many of these rights form the normative basis of victim rights identified in Chapter 2. However, despite recognition that victims were the subject of human rights, the state continued its monopolisation of crime and justice, granting those victims only those rights which it saw as compatible with or extraneous to the state's existing rights framework. Thus, while many jurisdictions have ratified parts of the 1985 PJVC, the rights now stated into law are generally not enforceable against the accused or state. However, the shift to victim self-realisation and personal government challenged the orthodox characterisation of the victim as essentially silent and passive against the rights and powers of defendants and the state. This second phase of victimology extends today into the twenty-first-century ratification of human rights instruments. With a proliferation of declarative bodies and international and regional organisations, in addition to international and domestic courts exercising international law and procedure, the human rights of the victim are increasingly asserted as making up a normative context of criminal justice relations that includes the victim as a proponent of justice (see Doak, 2008). While victims continue to struggle to see all rights prescribed on the domestic level, jurisdictional variation holds up some countries as forerunners, while others are shown to be lagging. While this variance is to be expected, it does found the basis of the discussion of the differences between the approach and outcomes of domestic ratification, as set out in this book.

The domestic ratification and development of victim rights give rise to the fourth phase of victimology. Administrative arrangements increasingly characterise the institutional and procedural basis for victim participation into the twenty-first century. Although rights frameworks are increasingly prolific on the international, regional, and domestic levels, articulating new and increasingly expansive rights for victims, these instruments in themselves do not afford the victim a rights-based experience. It is the inculcation of these rights and their development into actual processes and procedure of meaning to service providers and victims themselves that are important. It is this process of developing a legal, policy, and procedural response to human rights instruments that characterises the fourth phase. This local development of processes that gives life to human rights frameworks further modifies the existing normative stakeholders of justice that otherwise occupy criminal justice processes. The development of existing offences of criminal justice – the police, prosecutors, the courts, counsel, and corrections – further demonstrates the development of victim rights into the modern era. While this development is again jurisdictionally uneven, while also being uneven across offices within a jurisdiction, most countries have made some intentional progress towards the development of existing and new offices to comprise victim-focused processes to establish a working framework of victim rights.

The fourth phase of victimology is therefore identified by the recognition that human rights instruments have developed existing and new offices albeit in an uneven and differential way, consistent with the disproportionate starting points between jurisdictions and their variable appetite for legal and policy change. The modification of police and prosecution powers by the development of guidelines and codes to implement new rights to inform, support, and consult victims on important developments regarding their matter demonstrates how the ratification of victim rights can augment existing and well-established criminal justice institutions. The development of the office of Commissioner of Victims' Rights as found across various jurisdictions internationally, charged with the responsibility of implementing victim rights instruments on the domestic level, demonstrate the consolidation of universal human rights within a new office, according to local mandate. Other institutions and offices, including the police and prosecution, are implicated in this change. Arguably, those jurisdictions that have a history of excluding the victim will have further to travel to meet the requirement of positive change in support of the victim. Adversarial, common law countries are therefore more likely to need to make more substantial changes than those nations following a European, civil law tradition. However, even continental European countries characterised by inquisitorial or mixed adversarial systems have encountered degrees of change regarding the development of victim rights out of adherence to regional frameworks, such as the directives of the EU and the jurisprudence of the ECtHR (see Ochoa, 2013; see the Netherlands discussed in Chapter 6).

The increased identification of the victim with fundamental human rights of natural justice and others afforded by state process continues to found the development of victim rights frameworks on the local and domestic level. The modern era is characterised by the continued development of these frameworks beyond a mere statement of unenforceable rights, evidenced in the modification of older offices of criminal justice and the development of new authorities to administer those rights frameworks. The fourth phase of victim rights is, however, dependent on the third and second phases in so far as the emergence of substantive and procedural rights to justice has developed out of a history of the critique of state domination and the costs of bureaucratic control, and the need to more than ratify an otherwise unenforceable rights-based instrument on the local level. The institutionalisation of victim rights and powers on the local level therefore characterises the twenty-first-century development of victimology and victim rights (see van Dijk, 1988; Sebba and Berenblum, 2014). This institutionalisation of rights and powers has the consequences of further developing victim rights away from declaratory rights to substantive and enforceable rights, important developments that implicate the modern normative framework of victim rights and powers as stated in Chapter 2 as relevant to the development of victim rights on a differential basis, on the domestic level.

Positivist victimology and the present: the victim's voice, struggles with local suffering, and the positivist agenda

Recent work in victimology indicates the significance of local experiences of persons and the institutional, social, and cultural environment that gives rise to the harms and trauma of individual and collective suffering (see Daly, 2014; McGarry and Walklate, 2015). The present phase of victim rights regards the manifestation of human rights discourse across a set of justice arrangements that afford greater respect and dignity to the voice and participation of victims. Redressing past abuses and trauma through the recognition of the types of suffering experienced through denial of justice and secondary victimisation is also an important characteristic of the movement towards the recognition of individual and collective suffering. Significant to the argument of this book is the provision of this recognition in the context of local commissions and tribunals that seek truth and reconciliation by putting on record the victim's perspective of the abuse suffered and the blame of individuals and institutions, including the inadequacy of past justice responses. Such responses, of which the Royal Commission into Institutional Responses to Child Abuse (RCIRCA) in Australia is one example, demonstrate the need to consider the harm suffered by victims in the particular context of the local dimensions that gave rise to systematic abuse and victimisation (see RCIRCA, 2015). The RCIRCA (2015: 2) recognises the importance of a focus on the local, particularly in terms of listening to individual victims, understanding the dynamic nature of harms suffered, and redressing the needs of individual populations and peoples:

> We also recognise some victim and survivor population groups face additional challenges and barriers to receiving appropriate services or require more tailored or specific approaches. For example, we have heard cultural and healing practices are particularly important for Aboriginal and Torres Strait Islander people. Consequently, we want to better understand the barriers to services and possible solutions for diverse groups such as: Aboriginal and Torres Strait Islander people; those from culturally and linguistically diverse backgrounds; people with a disability; women; care leavers; lesbian, gay, bisexual, transgender, intersex people; and victims and survivors who spent time in correctional facilities.

The focus on the local and the need to consider the rights of victims through local contexts and perspectives can be seen through the Savile inquiry. Following the death of Jimmy Savile, a popular British celebrity with a history of charitable work, allegations of his alleged abuse of young girls began to emerge on a significant scale. This followed complaints made when Savile was alive. The abuse indicated various dimensions of harm and suffering, including the original harms incurred as a result of the assaults, the subsequent not being believed when the offences were initially reported to the police, and poor treatment of victims by the media. The delayed response and not taking the original complaints seriously were also said to inform a level of secondary victimisation that could not be adequately redressed by the law and the courts. This criticism provides focus for a larger criticism of the recourse to law and justice as a means of conceptualising the victim. Positivist victimology, or the conceptualisation and understanding of the victim through prescribed sources of law, may do more to silence the voice of the victim by understanding victims as legal victims only (see Miers, 1989, 1990).

The focus on sexual offending and the number of inquiries which are now addressing these harms creates opportunity to understand the dynamic nature of the offending against victims of crime which, in a context of the normative arrangements of time and place, were neither believed nor investigated at the time of their commissioning.[1] The inquiries which have allowed victims to come forward to tell their stories of victimisation, including the dynamic of secondary and ongoing victimisation resulting from poor institutional responses and a lack of belief in the complainant, indicate how positivist responses that conceptualise the victim though identifiable legal harms may mask many of the harms with which victims identify. The use of law as a vehicle through which to conceptualise and understand the victim may also spawn associated problems of the ideal victim as representing substantial threats to social order (see Christie, 1986). The voice of individual victims may thus be taken up by a larger law-and-order collective to advocate a putative agenda for greater punishments against all offenders (see McGarry and Walklate, 2015: 11). Another consequence of the use of law is its masking of the heterogeneity of victimisation, as dynamic and reflexive, constituted through power and power relations of individuals, institutions, and society.

The assumption, however, that law can understand the victim only in a homogeneous context of the offence must be assessed against the discourses of human rights that international law and procedure may bring to local contexts. The development of domestic laws and policies in light of the trend in international law to allow for the truth and reconciliation of the harms occasioned to the victim is arguably constructive in light of characterisation of positivist victimology as homogenising the experience of the victim. The most reformed legal system will continue to focus on particular prescribed harms in order to meet the requirement that the accused be sentenced following the establishing of facts beyond reasonable doubt; how the victim engages in the process of making the complaint, participates in the investigative and trial process, and is supported as important to that process may be substantially developed out of adherence to international human rights discourses that recognise the importance of the narrative of the individual victim.

Many jurisdictions covered in this book have learnt that victimisation is more dynamic than that prescribed under criminal law. There is a growing international awareness of the need to move away from prescriptive labelling of victims and the harms they have suffered. Although domestic courts presently recognise this dynamism only in a limited way, the use of inquiries of horrific abuse, and increased recognition of secondary harms to victims as a result of poor institutional and societal treatment, has resulted in new responses from justice stakeholders. This includes the police tasked with ways of understanding the plight of historical sex offences victims, their need for recognition and affirmation, and the response of the courts in the provision of new procedures that allow for the tendering of evidence from vulnerable and at-risk victims.[2] The most meaningful outcome from the realisation that victims may be harmed by the legal processes that detect ideal victimisation while denying ongoing, personal, and institutional harm is the reassessment of the power accorded to the normative stakeholders of law and justice. The reconsideration of the power relationship between victims and normative stakeholders attests to the virtues of the reform of law and policy to better recognise victimisation as responding to dynamic individual, collective, and institutional arrangements that may be exacerbated, or ameliorated, by the participants who make up the justice response in the first instance.

Normative stakeholders of law and justice

This book is predicated on a discussion of the way international human rights norms that affect victims are increasingly integrated and actioned on the local level through discrete laws and policies. Significant to this process is the way these international norms and discourses challenge and change the normative stakeholders of justice. The stakeholders of justice that may be identified as normatively positioned within any state system of criminal justice include the police, public prosecutors and investigative magistrates, trial and appellate judges, and legal counsel. Justice officials, court staff, and corrections officers complete the framework of office holders that have some direct relationship over the application and enforcement of laws, the interpretation of laws, or implementation of policies regarding decisions which contribute to the workings of the criminal justice system of each jurisdiction. Absent from this list is the victim of crime. Victims remain peripheral, even in continental European systems of justice that provide a role for the victim in the investigative and trial phase. The ICC model provides for a more encouraging example of victim participation, despite a lack of party status (see Wemmers, 2010, 2014a). Indeed, international criminal tribunals demonstrate how they may serve the ends of international justice, even where questions remain as to the restorative capacity of such tribunals (see Isaacs, 2016). However, in common law, adversarial systems, victims are still largely at the periphery of justice and their fight for recognition continues.

It is the inculcation of international human rights norms through the processes traced in Chapters 2 and 3 that has led to the reconsideration of the placement of the victim within each jurisdiction covered in this book. While the connectedness of each victim to the other stakeholders and the influence the victim may exert on those stakeholders naturally vary by jurisdiction, and by adherence to a particular legal tradition or nationalised system of justice, change is occurring internationally. The normative stakeholders of justice are having to renegotiate their relationship with victims, and this is changing the nature of the normative positioning of justice stakeholders with regard to the exclusivity with which they exercise the responsibilities of their office. The duty to consult victims with regard to charges brought or plea deals reached indicates a shift in the power arrangements during the investigative and prosecution decision-making stages. Other rights have been granted to victims during trial and sentencing and post-conviction that also demonstrate a change in dynamic. These developments are the focus of this book, and demonstrate how the normative stakeholders of justice are faced with new power relations into the twenty-first century as their office becomes one that includes, rather than excludes, the rights and interests of victims.

The Code of Practice for Victims of Crime ('Victims' Code') (England and Wales) sets out the criminal justice agencies which are bound by the Victims' Code in England and Wales.

Although other jurisdictions may have a restricted or expanded list of government agents bound by national standards of service for victims of crime, the Victims' Code does provide an example as to the extension of victim rights to government agents that are expected to modify their standard conduct in order to meet the requirements of the Victims' Code (see Ministry of Justice, 2015):

> Code of Practice for Victims of Crime ('Victims' Code') (England and Wales): Introduction, 8. This Code requires the following organisations to provide services to victims in accordance with this Introduction, and Chapters 1 to 43:
>
> - The Criminal Cases Review Commission
> - The Criminal Injuries Compensation Authority
> - The Crown Prosecution Service (CPS)
> - The First-tier Tribunal (Criminal Injuries Compensation)
> - Her Majesty's Courts and Tribunals Service (HMCTS)
> - Her Majesty's Prison Service
> - National Offender Management Service (NOMS)
> - The Parole Board
> - Police and Crime Commissioners
> - All police forces in England and Wales, the British Transport Police and the Ministry of Defence Police
> - The National Probation Service
> - The UK Supreme Court
> - Witness Care Units
> - Youth Offending Teams.

Although the courts and legal profession are omitted from this list, these stakeholders have a significant relationship to victims of crime, even though that relationship may be at times independent or remote. Although contact with lawyers and judges may be less frequent than service investigators, such as the police or service providers, including witness services or compensation authorities, the roles of counsel and the judiciary are often determinative and victims look to these stakeholders as significant partisans in their justice journey. As such, this book considers judicial officers and legal counsel important stakeholders of justice whose roles may also be implicated by the inculcation of international human rights norms, even where such norms impact the scope of their office indirectly, otherwise than by authoritative instrument.

The continental European approach

Much of the recent development of victim rights and law and policy reform has occurred in those jurisdictions where the victim has been traditionally removed from justice. Although the continental European jurisdictions have a longer history of including the victim on a procedural basis, they too have developed the role of the victim across the phases of the criminal investigative and trial process by implementing the European Union, European Council Framework Decision (2001; 2001/220/JHA, 15 March 2001, Standing of victims in criminal proceedings; CEU FD) and more recently, the European Union, Directive of the European Parliament and of the Council (2012; 2012/29/EU, 25 October 2012, Establishing minimum standards on the rights, support and protection of victims of crime, and replacing council framework decision 2001/220/JHA; CEU DVC). The continental European approach regarding the organisation of victim interests is closely tied to the criminal procedure of each jurisdiction. Although there is jurisdictional variance by adherence to inquisitorial and hybrid, adversarial processes, each continental European country allows the victim to adhere a compensation claim to the criminal trial, and may also allow the victim to participate in decision-making processes regarding the state's decision to prosecute, and to appear alongside the state prosecutor as an accessory or subsidiary prosecutor, or as partie civile. While the frequency of the exercise of the right to appear as subsidiary prosecutor is not high, the power remains an important aspect of the respective criminal procedure of continental European states. This procedure forms part of the criminal procedure of each country (see German Code of Criminal Procedure 1987, amended 2014, extracted in Chapter 2 at 5.7) as developed out of the traditional right for victim participation alongside the state, as a foundational condition of victim rights constitutive of the juridical tradition of civil law states (Safferling, 2011). Even though continental European countries allow common rights of participation as accessory and adhesive prosecutor, each country has developed a distinctive legal tradition of its own, such that it is possible to generalise across continental European states only at the macro level (see Joutsen, 1987; Brienen and Hoegen, 2000).

The specific nature of criminal procedure as it encompasses the rights and powers of victims must be understood in the context of the particular criminal procedure of each continental jurisdiction. While certain continental European jurisdictions have inquisitorial pretrial processes initiated by a prosecutor, only to be then taken over by the investigative magistrate or judge, others have developed a more adversarial pretrial process whereby investigations are conducted by state police, who then present the charges in court before an independent magistrate or pretrial judge. This may be followed by a trial developed as wholly inquisitorial, with the intervening judge soliciting narrative evidence from witnesses as guided or facilitated by counsel, or as a hybrid-adversarial exchange between state and defence. The victim may act through counsel at the pretrial or trial phases in either inquisitorial or adversarial continental European jurisdictions, although the exact powers and role of such counsel are generally prescribed by procedural code (Kury and Kichling, 2011). However, many continental European jurisdictions have developed a modern trial process that is at least partly constituted as an adversarial process that involves the examination of witnesses as adduced by counsel. Such jurisdictions include, but are not limited to, Austria, the Netherlands, and Sweden. Other jurisdictions, including Germany and France, are solely inquisitorial, from the pretrial investigative phase to trial.

Continental European countries provide different levels of resources to assist victim participation in the pretrial and trial process. In certain jurisdictions, this may afford the victim access to information during the investigative phase, or information about the decision not to investigate in the first instance, or continue with a prosecution. Representation at this stage may assist the victim's access to justice by allowing the victim to properly understand and question that state decision to withdraw from the matter (see Roberson and Das, 2016). Victims may have the ability to continue the prosecution privately. Where the victim cannot afford counsel, the state may provide funds or a state-based private lawyer. This is more common for serious interpersonal offences, such as sexual assault and rape, where the victim may be identified as at risk of secondary victimisation through court intrusive processes (Safferling, 2011). Where the victim gains access to private counsel, the victim has an increased capacity to make certain demands of the state investigative and prosecution process. This includes the ability to request that a particular complaint or allegation be investigated by police, to provide access to documents or evidence, to appear in court to question witnesses, to make a claim for compensation or reparation, where permitted to make submissions as to a relevant sentence, and to question outcomes by seeking an appeal where decisions arise adverse to the victim or prosecution case. The right to private prosecution is also preserved in certain jurisdictions, and victims may have the capacity to continue a state-initiated prosecution where it is discontinued or withdrawn. Other parties may also join the prosecution where criminal procedure so allows. France, for example, affords the right of intervenor status to non-government organisations where they have an interest in the outcome of the court (see, generally, Brienen and Hoegen, 2000). In this instance, the intervenors will join as a subsidiary prosecutor or *partie civile*, to the extent that they have a *bona fide* interest in the outcome of the case.

The continental European approach of granting victims access to justice on a substantive and procedural level influences law and policy with regard to the development of victim rights and interests in the greater European context. We therefore see the role of the victim as a participatory agent of justice inform the development of the international law of human rights in so far as aspects of the inquisitorial and hybrid-adversarial traditions of continental Europe have been enacted into the constitutive processes of a number of international tribunals, including the Rome Statute (Statute of the ICC) (A/Conf 183/9, 1998) and the Rules of Procedure and Evidence of the ICC (see Wemmers, 2005, 2010). Although such courts are developed in accordance with general principles of adversarial engagement, and the rules of state inquisition have been departed from in substantial ways, the development of international law and procedure has occurred through an integrative approach that argued for convergence between legal traditions (see Schwikkard, 2008). This has resulted in the development of victim rights on a procedural, participatory, and substantive basis in many of the modern international courts and tribunals, even those on the domestic level. The regional level of the EU and ECtHR is also mindful of the need to support victim's rights and interests on a procedural and substantive basis (see Summers, 2007). This integrative approach, supported by the legal tradition of continental Europe as inclusive of victim rights and powers, has influenced criminal proceedings on an international level towards a participatory model of justice. Importantly, this has allowed for the development of victim rights as human rights, which in turn has influenced the development of common law, adversarial systems around the world through practices of ratification of international convention or otherwise policy transfer.

Although the continental European tradition of civil justice is deemed to be fundamentally different and possibly opposed to the tenets of accusatorial, common law justice (see Summers, 2007; Schwikkard, 2008; Safferling, 2011), important connections exist between the two systems. Chapters 3 through 6 refer to various inquisitorial and mixed adversarial European systems. These chapters demonstrate how the international courts and tribunals and regional frameworks each support processes of law reform and development on the local level. These chapters demonstrate how adversarial or hybrid jurisdictions are progressively reforming their criminal law and procedure and law of evidence to help protect vulnerable and child victims, by introducing court processes that amalgamate aspects of civil law, inquisitorial processes, with an adversarial framework for the tenure and examination of evidence.

Ratification on the domestic level: law, policy, and the victim

International law and policy set out standards and norms that are largely intended to be ratified on the domestic level to bring a measure of standardisation to the human rights interests that ought to prevail across all legal systems. Although international law also sets out standards that are practised in international tribunals, such as the ICC and *ad hoc* courts, or domestic courts exercising an international jurisdiction, victim rights have been substantially advanced on a domestic basis by the setting out of rights and powers across international instruments.

The international, regional, and domestic instruments set out in Chapter 2 have helped establish a normative framework of victim rights and powers that are increasingly changing the rights and powers available to victims on the domestic level, worldwide. These rights and powers remain contested and controversial, but convergence between jurisdictions and alternatives to traditional parliamentary ratification, such as law reform and policy transfer, have enhanced the uptake of victim rights norms in the context of the development of victim rights frameworks at the local level in several key ways.

Several interconnected points arise from the consideration of international human rights discourses as relevant to victims of crime. These discourses establish the normative framework of victim rights that apply to victims internationally, but also characterise the modes of ratification and reform through which these normative rights are enacted on the local level. The duality of the normative scope of rights together with the particular processes of ratification sensitive to local needs and conditions, in particular, the existing legal and policy frameworks of the domestic jurisdiction seeking ratification, presents a number of points relevant to the explanation of the jurisdictional differences covered in Chapters 4 through 6, including discord in the legal and policy context of the inclusion of victim rights in each jurisdiction, as discussed in Chapters 7 and 8:

- the promulgation of international instruments has established a range of human rights norms that specifically regard the standing of the victim in international and domestic systems of criminal justice.
- by affording rights of victim participation in international tribunals that draw from different systems of justice, principally adversarial and inquisitorial frameworks, the international courts have demonstrated that nationalised systems need not adhere to an exclusive view to the development of justice processes. This has led to a wider acceptance of convergence between systems of justice on the domestic basis.
- the introduction of global perspectives on the rights and powers of victims has led to enhanced debate within national systems of justice as to the need to grant victims access to justice with a view to establishing rights in those areas covered in this chapter.
- international norms regarding victim rights and powers have been ratified in different ways according to the legal, constitutional, and policy arrangements of individual nations. This has meant that despite significant development around international victim rights norms, these norms have been ratified into local law and policy in different ways and to different extents, depending on the policy priorities of local jurisdictions.
- certain jurisdictions have been more active in their informing of international victim rights norms by allowing for significant victim participation as part of their nationalised system of justice. These jurisdictions, which mainly draw from continental European countries where victims have long enjoyed rights of actual, substantive participation, continue to ratify international standards, although most European systems would already possess a victim rights framework in excess of the minimum standards set out by international instruments. Finally, and significantly for the argument of this book, the result of the uneven ratification of international norms and standards means that an individual jurisdictional analysis is required in order to fully comprehend how these

international norms and standards of victim rights differ between international sources of law, and how they have been ratified on the local level, or otherwise influence debate and legal and policy reform, where ratified in an indirect way.

The discrete processes that lead to the ratification of victim rights norms on a domestic level must therefore be encountered at the level of the local. The integration of victim rights also bears relevance to existing justice stakeholders. These stakeholders, identified and discussed in this chapter, are relevant to the extent that the rights of victims are often instituted through these existing officeholders. Understanding of how victim rights simultaneously affect and modify these offices and are advanced through them assists the realisation that victim rights are being institutionalised on the local level through adherence to discourses of international human and victim rights.

Reshaping the roles of justice stakeholders

The scope of victim rights and the increasing power of the normative framework of victim rights that carries the force of international human rights law are rapidly changing the relationships between traditional justice stakeholders. For many, the provision of victim rights is a means of enhancing trust in the legal system (see Laxminarayan, 2015), which necessarily occurs in the locale of the criminal wrongdoing. In particular, the ratification of victim rights and powers is occurring on a domestic level of practice and procedure such that the traditional and normatively positioned stakeholders identified in this chapter are being required to accommodate the victim in new ways. This process of adopting and accommodating a new role for the victim as one that is based in human rights and international norms and standards has modified these traditional offices to the extent that the victim is no longer entirely peripheral. The following chapters on consultation rights, access to counsel, and the emergence of substantive and enforceable rights attest to the changes that are being made on an international basis. Chapter 2 covers these changes as they have emerged in a normative context under sources of law and policy, while Chapter 3 examines these issues in a comparative context of current trends, issues, and debates in internationalised systems of justice.

The modification of the traditional roles of justice stakeholders emerges from the increased awareness of the needs of the victim, and the victim's identification as a rights-bearing subject more generally, providing a basis for legal and policy reform. The fourth phase of victimology and victim rights discussed in this chapter takes the rights framework beyond the assumption of the third phase, that victims are owed fundamental human rights, for the need that these rights must be articulated into a framework that makes them compatible with existing laws and processes, on the domestic level (cf. van Dijk, 1988; Sebba, 1996). The movement to ratify victim rights on the local level is realised through a series of processes that operationalise those rights and powers and, importantly, connect them with existing justice processes as they constitute the offices and roles of the stakeholders of justice. It is this process of connecting victim rights to existing powers within the justice context that develops the normative framework of victim rights on the local level. This operationalising connects victims with professional offices, in an institutional locale, such that the rights of the victim develop in an interconnected way. This interconnectedness alters the functions of traditional justice stakeholders within the criminal justice system. Such processes necessarily occur at the level of the particular, evidenced by specific law and policy reforms as relevant to each justice stakeholder and the office they constitute. This does not mean that victims become equal to the other justice stakeholders, who generally retain control over criminal justice processes. Instead, victims become identifiable in law and policy, as relevant to procedural justice and the substantive context of the decisions that other justice stakeholders make on a daily basis (Elias, 1985; van Dijk, 2009).

The development of the normative context of the victim in victimology and victim rights frameworks will be ongoing until victim rights are partly constitutive of the powers exercised by criminal justice agencies in a broad sense. This connection occurs gradually and manifests on the local, domestic level. It may be subject to resistance by the other justice stakeholders and individual legal or policy initiatives may be defeated. However, the rights of the victim and other justice agents converge where victims exercise a substantive agency over decision-making processes within the criminal justice system. By connecting to and modifying the office of the stakeholders of justice, victims are in the process of becoming substantially constitutive of those offices. This is an ongoing and reflexive process such that criminal law and policy are in a state of flux worldwide. Victims are connected to and constitutive of the roles and offices of criminal justice in different ways, and to different extents. The involvement of the victim and the modification of the traditional roles of officeholders in the criminal justice process will continue to change as the normative basis of the rights of victims becomes better recognised and understood, particularly in common law, adversarial jurisdictions where victims continue to struggle for fair recognition. While this process is substantial and has the capacity to change the context of criminal justice relations on an international and domestic basis, it will not establish the victim as the central agent of justice over existing stakeholders. Instead, a power-sharing arrangement will increasingly emerge between stakeholders, with the offender and state remaining primary participants under a due process model of justice. In this model, the victim may take on increasing responsibility to the other stakeholders, with capacity to shape the relationship between justice stakeholders, depending on the number of substantive and enforceable rights granted or ratified on the local level.

The normative repositioning of victim rights has been substantially influenced by the development of international, regional, and domestic instruments, such that the victim cannot be considered peripheral in modern systems of internationalised justice. The victim is now able to make decisions and exercise powers through counsel, or through other justice stakeholders, including the police or prosecution. This development of victim rights at the local level impacts directly on the scope, form, and content of criminal justice processes and changes the way we conceptualise them. The international, regional, and domestic rights frameworks extracted in Chapter 2 demonstrate how modern victim rights are generally more expressive as compared to any point in the recent history of such rights. For this book, it is the trend to ratify the normative context of victim rights on the local level that characterises the fundamental development opportunity for the victim into the twenty-first century. The trend to institutionalise the victim into the mechanisms of the criminal justice systems of various states, as a global trend, draws the international rights of the victim into the local context. In so doing, it inculcates the international norms of victim rights into local process of law and policy reform that develop the role of the victim in the local in specific ways. This institutionalising of victim rights will be the focus of Chapters 4, 5, and 6.

International, regional, and domestic reform: law and policy

The three parts of this book cover the different dimensions of the material presented for discussion. Part 1 of this book covers issues and developments in victimology and victim rights. This part presents the victimology literature that identifies the rise of victim rights as human rights that centres the focus on the development of a normative victim rights framework into the latter part of the twentieth century. This part sets out the sources of law and policy in a normative rights context. This part also examines the comparative issues and forces that allow for a meaningful discussion of victim rights on an international, regional, and domestic basis. Part 1 includes Chapters 1 through 3. Part 2 of this book examines the ratification and development of victim rights on the jurisdictional level. International, regional, and domestic law and practice will be considered in the context of those victim rights frameworks identified in part 1. Part 2 includes Chapters 3 through 6. Part 3 of this book includes discord and debate as to the role of victim rights as a unifying and global discourse for the benefit of victim and justice processes generally. Points of resistance and future directions are considered. Part 3 includes Chapters 7 and 8.

The second chapter of this book sets out the normative framework of victim rights and powers as constituted through selected international, regional, and domestic instruments and policies. This chapter extracts these sources of law and policy to provide ready access to those instruments, to be referred to throughout the chapters of this book. Instruments have been selected based on their influence on law and policy on the international, regional, and domestic level. Domestic instruments have been selected that represent different levels of victim rights, from those which primarily offer levels of service or access to information (see, e.g., the Victims' Code in England and Wales) through to those that provide a comprehensive, substantive rights-based framework (see, e.g., the German Code of Criminal Procedure). The organisation of relevant instruments and the selection of materials are presented to enhance the discussion of those instruments throughout the book.

Chapter 3 sets out the comparative issues that have emerged as trends of legal and policy development on an international basis. These trends and issues are led by the international instruments referred to in Chapter 2, in the context of the emergence of a victimology of the twenty-first century, and the proliferation of victim rights as human rights. The significance of local contexts and the capacity to compare issues of law and policy are set out. The techniques of legal and policy transfer and ratification of international instruments through to policy transfer of local practices will also be covered to demonstrate the differential basis of the ways in which victim rights and powers are being inculcated into the legal systems of states and nations, on an international basis.

Chapter 4 sets out the individual international jurisdictions which have embraced standards of victim rights, encouraging member states, signatories, and relevant parties to develop and promote the normative context of victim rights as human rights. This chapter will demonstrate how international jurisdictions are moving towards the resolution of victim rights frameworks. Chapter 4 will set out the way in which victim rights have been articulated in international law and procedure by considering international declarations and rights frameworks of the UN, including treaty monitoring bodies, in addition to the ICC and *ad hoc* tribunals – specifically, the Nuremberg and Tokyo Tribunals, the ICTY, and the ICTR. The ECCC, the SPTL, and the IPK will be considered as exercising international law and norms domestically.

Chapter 5 considers the development of victim rights and powers on the regional level. Regional frameworks, including those of the EU, the Council of Europe, and the ECtHR, will further demonstrate concern over international standards as set across Europe. This chapter will consider the EU and Council of Europe directives to promote the development of consistent laws and policies that seek to address victim interests and concerns across Europe. Although developed on the local level, the regional level will be considered an important apparatus of institutional development, deploying consistent policy to the member states of the EU in the attempt to standardise victim rights in a normative, regional context.

Chapter 6 examines the ratification of international and regional frameworks for the development of victim rights and powers on the local, domestic level. This chapter will show how states are inculcating victim rights and powers as influenced by the normative context of victim rights as set out in Chapter 2. Although states are acting at different speeds, and with different levels of urgency, local jurisdictions will be examined to demonstrate the ratification and inculcation of normative victim rights frameworks on the domestic level. Inquisitorial systems, specifically Germany and France, will be considered as will the mixed inquisitorial/adversarial systems of Sweden, the Netherlands, and Austria. Adversarial systems will also be considered – specifically, England and Wales, Ireland, Scotland, USA, Australia, Canada, New Zealand, India, South Africa, and mixed or hybrid systems, including Japan and Brazil. While this chapter will not seek to provide comprehensive treatment of all victim rights in each jurisdiction, those tending towards international standards and norms will be set out to demonstrate the argument of how ratification occurs on a local, domestic level.

Chapter 7 takes from the legal issues traced in Chapters 1 through 6 to indicate how victim rights are articulated on a legal and policy basis. Issues regarding recognition, use of laws, enforceability of rights and powers, and the reluctance of engagement on the part of the normative stakeholders of justice will be covered. Points of resistance will also be analysed, as confounded by legal and constitutional constraints, party status regarding international governing bodies and regional frameworks, domestic law and order, the activity and presence of a victim lobby or rights group, and the tenor of domestic politics towards the need to secure the interests of victims as a special needs group. The proliferation of victim rights in a policy context will be discussed in terms of the virtues of policy reform, and the advantages of the provision of rights in a policy, rather than legal, context. Disadvantages and limitation of policy as a medium through which victim rights may be expressed will also be covered. Important points of connection between law and policy will be realised and the interrelationship discussed.

The final chapter discusses the progression towards local victim frameworks in light of the global movement towards international discourses of victim rights as related to the growing global concern of international human rights. This chapter advances the debate that the twenty-first-century movement towards victim rights as human rights is occurring on the level of the local, evidenced by particular instances of law and policy reform, but as connected to broader movement around the debate over the extent to which victim rights are human rights that ought to reshape justice systems, some of which have traditionally excluded or even been hostile towards notions of rights for victims, not least substantive participation in justice decision-making.

Notes

1 See Chapter 2, 'Commissions of Inquiry'.
2 See Chapter 2, 'Protection from the Accused and Others'. The protections afforded to the victim as vulnerable and at risk are discussed throughout this book, with a particular focus on the jurisprudence of the ECtHR and the development of laws and policies on the local level. Also see the individual jurisdictions discussed in Chapter 6.

2 International norms in victimology and victim rights

Introduction

The rights and powers of international, regional, and even select domestic instruments have contributed to the development of a normative framework of rights and powers for victims of crime. However, the normative framework of victim rights and powers established by the international, regional, and domestic instruments and resolutions has had various direct and indirect implications for the development of law and policy on the local level. This chapter moves to consolidate the international, regional, and domestic instruments that have contributed to the setting out of this normative framework to be accessed in discussion throughout this book. As domestic jurisdictions increasingly ratify or otherwise reform laws and policies with regard to these normative rights and powers, the international force of victim rights increases, albeit not in a way that necessarily standardises victims' access to justice through the world. Regional and local differences must be accounted for in the ratification and reform process.

However, increasingly, jurisdictions worldwide are taking account of the international and regional frameworks that set out and encourage the ratification of victim rights and powers. Each jurisdiction will nevertheless move at its own pace, and according to its own constraints, in accordance with local laws and policies and affiliated political arrangements (see Hall, 2010). Systemic issues and the orientation of each justice system towards an identified nationalised system of justice – their openness to international discourses of human rights, and the local attitude of justice stakeholders to the rights of victims in a criminal justice context – are also principal explanatory factors accounting for differences between jurisdictions (see Letschert and Parmentier, 2014). These differences will be discussed in Chapters 3 through 6, with particular emphasis on the domestic level in Chapter 6. This chapter considers the international level of victim rights declarations and frameworks in addition to the statute and rule of the ICC. Regional frameworks are also included, specifically the Counsel of Europe directives and the ECHR. Selected domestic instruments are also included to indicate how these international and regional rights have been represented (or perhaps always were represented) at the state level. England and Wales and New South Wales (NSW), Australia, have been selected as representing common law, adversarial jurisdictions, while the provisions of the German Code of Criminal Procedure have been selected as representing a continental European, or inquisitorial, perspective.

This chapter sets out rights frameworks across the international, regional, and domestic levels relevant to the construction of international norms of victim rights for the analysis of the ratification of those rights on the domestic level. Selective treatment of individual jurisdictions will demonstrate how different international, regional, inquisitorial, and adversarial countries have each articulated victim rights, issues and interests across independent instruments of power. The rights taken from these instruments identify areas of victim rights that have been identified and classified around increasingly dominant themes of victim rights as human rights, as identified in the international literature (see, as a selection, Wemmers, 2005, 2009; Doak, 2008; Hall, 2009, 2010). Although this grouping of rights and powers into normative themes is non-exhaustive, each area should be recognisable as significantly constitutive of areas of legal and policy development for a range of states, globally. This is irrespective of the member status of any jurisdiction, despite members acting with greater degrees of adhesion out of their obligation to the supranational organisation. Various normative rights and powers are therefore identified, including: the need for fair, courteous, and respectful treatment for victims; the need to access information and to be kept informed; access to relevant support services; protection from the accused and others of hostile intention to the victim; procedural and participatory rights – namely in the form of substantive powers to make submissions, for consultation and review; fair trial rights that include proportional rights for victims; access to compensation, restitution, and reparations; restorative intervention and therapeutic justice; domestic ratification of supranational agreements; and provision of these victim rights without prejudicing the offender's right to access justice.

This chapter is intended to be read in conjunction with Chapter 3, which canvasses various comparative issues and perspectives relevant to the international framework of victim rights. Chapter 3 sets out the main modes of ratification of international declaration or resolution, but also covers alternative modes of law reform, policy transfer, and political and institutional change that witness the proliferation of victim rights discourse worldwide. Chapter 2 concludes with a discussion of the ratification of select norms at the regional and domestic level in terms of the positive obligation of the state and the equality of arms requirements of fair trial participation.

International norms of victim rights

A survey of several instruments setting out victim rights and powers identified key victim rights norms that are of key concern to the law reform processes of the countries and states considered in this book. The instruments from which these norms may be generally drawn include:

- UN Declarations and Conventions and UN Treaty Monitoring Bodies;
- international statutes and courts, specifically the Rome Statute (Statute of the ICC) (A/ Conf 183/9, 1998) and ICC;
- regional declarations and courts, including the ECHR and ECtHR, the recommendations of the Council of Europe, the EU Framework Decisions and Directives, the Charter of Fundamental Rights of the European Union (CFREU), the American Declaration of the Rights and Duties of Man 1948 (ADRDM) and the American Convention on Human Rights (ACHR), interpreted by the Inter-American Commission of Human Rights (IACHR) and the Inter-American Court for Human Rights (IACtHR), the African Commission on Human and Peoples' Rights (ACHPR), responsible for implementing the African Charter on Human and Peoples' Rights (ACrHPR), and the African Court on Human and Peoples' Rights (ACtHPR) as merged with the African Human Rights Court (AHRC) to form the African Court of Justice and Human Rights (ACtJHR);

- the *ad hoc* courts, including the Nuremberg and Tokyo Tribunals, the ICTY, and the ICTR;
- the constitutive instruments of international courts and tribunals, even those domestic courts which exercise an international jurisdiction, the Extraordinary Chambers in the Courts of Cambodia, Special Panels of East Timor (Timor Leste), the Internationalised Panels in Kosovo, the Special Court for Sierra Leone, the Special Tribunal for Lebanon (STL), and the Civil Claims Alien Tort Claims Act (28 USC § 1350) as relevant to claims in the USA (see Lai, 2005); and
- the restatements of these rights in local declarations and charters as setting out a generally non-enforceable victim rights framework available on the domestic jurisdictional level. Such declarations may be enacted through statute or be made available in policy as an expectation placed upon government officials, though not ratified into local law. See, for instance, the *Victims Bill of Rights Act 2015* (Can), which enacts the *Canadian Victims Bill of Rights*.

It is beyond this book to set out how each rights instrument and court contribute to the development of a human rights framework through the promulgation of international standards and norms that have shaped victim rights as human rights into the twenty-first century. Others have done this in a dedicated way (see Fernández de Casadevante Romani, 2012; Ochoa, 2013; Moffett, 2014). However, this section will trace those international norms of victim rights that have emerged through the international rights frameworks as identified earlier. Local instruments will also be referred to, to demonstrate how these norms are being ratified on the domestic level. These instruments, declarations, and rights frameworks are discussed through Chapter 3 but are drawn from specifically with regard to internationalised systems of victim rights as set out and discussed jurisdictionally in Chapters 4 through 6.

An assessment of the rights of victims as presently articulated by international, regional and selected domestic human rights instruments include, but may not be limited to:

- the right to fair, courteous, and respectful treatment;
- information and to be kept informed;
- relevant support services;
- protection from the accused and others;
- procedural and participatory rights to make submissions, and for consultation and review of decisions made;
- a fair trial, inclusive of protections for the victim;
- access to compensation, restitution, and reparations;
- restorative intervention and therapeutic justice; and
- adoption of these standards on the domestic level as minimal standards.

Table 2.1 refers to the norms of victim rights as against the international, regional, and domestic instruments that characterise the development of those norms on an international level. While this table is not exhaustive, in that the normative scope of victim rights may be comprehensively informed by a variety of sources of law and policy, including court judgement and precedent, on the local and international level, it does point to the main human rights instruments that help characterise the development of modern victim rights norms as relevant to a range of countries irrespective of legal tradition and notional framework, as found internationally.

Table 2.1 International, regional, and domestic instruments organised by normative rights context

Normative Victim Rights	International Instruments	Regional Instruments	Domestic Instruments
1. Fair, Courteous, and Respectful Treatment	1.1 PJVC (res 4) 1.2 RRRVGV (res 10)	1.3 CEU DVC (pre, cl 9; art 1)	1.4 Canadian Victims Bill of Rights (pre, cl 2); 1.5 Victims' Code (Intro 1); 1.6 2013 Act NSW (s 6, cl 6.1)
2. Information and to Be Kept Informed	2.1 PJVC (res 6(a))	2.2 CEU DVC (pre, cl 31; Pre, cl 32)	2.3 Canadian Victims Bill of Rights (cls 6–8); 2.4 Victims' Code (ch 2, pt A, cl 6.9; ch 5, cl 1.35, ch 5; cl 1.36); 2.5 2013 Act NSW (s 6, cl 6.4, 6.5, 6.15); 2.6 German Code of Criminal Procedure 1987 (ss 406e, 406h)
3. Relevant Support Services	3.1 PJVC (res 6(c), 14, 15, 17) 3.2 RRRVGV (res 10)	3.3 CEU DVC (pre, cl 37; art 9)	3.4 Canadian Victims Bill of Rights (cl 16); 3.5 Victims' Code (ch 1, EE, cl 1.4; ch 1, pt A, VE, cl. 1.2; ch 5, Duties of Other, cl. 1.28; ch 5, Duties of Other, cl. 1.29) 3.6 2013 Act NSW (s 6, cl 6–2, 6.3, 6.17)
4. Protection from the Accused and Others	4.1 PJVC (res 6(d)) 4.2 ICTY Statute (art 22; cf. ICTR Stature art 21)	4.3 CEU DVC (Pre, cl 53)	4.4 Canadian Victims Bill of Rights (cl 9) 4.5 Victims' Code (ch 1, EE, cl 1.9) 4.6 2013 Act NSW (s 6, cl 6.7)
5. Procedural and Participatory Rights: Submissions, Consultation, and Review	5.1 PJVC (res 6(b)) 5.2 RRRVGV (res 8, 9. 12–14) 5.3 Rome Statute (art 68) 5.4 RPE ICC (ch 4, s III, r 90, 91, 93)	5.5 CEU DVC (art 10, 11)	5.6 Canadian Victims Bill of Rights (cl 14, 15) 5.7 Victims' Code (ch 2, pt A, s 1, cl 1.12–1.13; ch 2, pt A, s 2, cl 2.2; ch 2, pt A, s 6, cl 6.27) 5.8 2013 NSW Act (s 6, cl 6.14) 5.9 German Code of Criminal Procedure 1987 (s 395, 397, 406d, 406f, 406g)
6. Fair Trial Rights	6.1 ICCPR (res 14) 6.2 RPE ICC (ch 4, s III, subs 2, r 87, 88) 6.3 ICTY Statute (art 20; cf. ICTR Statute art 19)	6.4 ECHR (art 6, 8, 10) 6.5 Charter of Fundamental Rights of the European Union (ch VI, art 47) 6.6 CEU DVC (pre, cl 54; art 21–24)	6.7 Canadian Victims Bill of Rights cl 12) 6.8 Victims' Code (ch 1, EE, cl 1.13) 6.9 Criminal Procedure Act 1986 NSW (s 306U)

Normative Victim Rights	International Instruments	Regional Instruments	Domestic Instruments
7. Access to Compensation, Restitution, and Reparations	7.1 PJVC (res 8–13) 7.2 RRRVGV (res 11, 15–20) 7.3 RPE ICC (art 75)	7.4 ECHR (art 41) 7.5 CEU DVC (art 16)	7.6 Canadian Victims Bill of Rights (cl 16) 7.7 Victims' Code (ch 2, pt A, VE, s 8, cl 8.1) 7.8 2013 NSW Act (s 6, cl 6.17) 7.9 German Code of Criminal Procedure 1987 (s 403)
8. Restorative Intervention and Therapeutic Justice	8.1 PJVC (res 7)	8.2 CEU DVC (pre, cl 46; art 12)	8.3 Corrections and Conditional Release Act 1992 (Can) (ch 20, s 26.1) 8.4 Victims Code (ch 2, pt A, VE, s 7, cl 7.1–7.4) 8.5 German Code of Criminal Procedure 1987 (s 153a)
9. Domestic Ratification	9.1 PJVC (res 1) 9.2 RRRVGV (res 1)	9.3 CEU DVC (pre 1, cl 3)	
10. Without Prejudice to the Offender	10.1 ICCPR (res 14) 10.2 PJVC (res 2) 10.3 ICTY Statute (art 21; cf. ICTR Stature art 20)	10.4 CEU DVC (pre, cl 12)	

The human rights instruments referred to include those that arguably advance victim rights on an international and regional basis. The domestic instruments referred to are selected from many possible domestic instruments. The instruments selected – namely, from Canada, England and Wales, and New South Wales (NSW), Australia – have been selected because they flow from and were developed in response to the norms contained in those international and regional instruments cited. The criminal procedure of Germany has been selected to offer a comparison of the expression of victim rights of the aggrieved person in a continental European and inquisitorial system.

Victim rights to substantive and participatory justice have been progressively influenced by international human rights law and procedure (see Doak, 2015). Legal and policy change has been increasingly influenced by international norms as the number of international, regional, and local instruments increase which seek to include international human rights norms and processes as foundational and functional aspects of that law and policy. Thus, there is a cumulative effect of increased international convergence (see Hall, 2009, 2010) by a range of international declarations, instruments, *ad hoc* courts, tribunals, and panels, which seek to globalise victim issues relevant to the local level. Norms established by the UN and other governing international bodies and rights organisations investigating gross violations of human rights provide for this framework at the supranational level. State courts and instruments have also formed to redress regional and local human rights abuses and war crimes. Collectively, these have influenced the development of international courts seeking redress for international violations, culminating in the development of the ICC as a model of participatory justice. These processes of the development and ratification of international law and procedure have established a normative framework of human rights relevant to the legal and policy characterisation of the victim of crime. This section sets out the main human rights instruments relevant to victims that constitute and influence the normative context of victim rights as relevant to local law and order.

Articulating the rights of victims on an international, regional, and local level of criminal procedure provides some insight into the law and policy context of victimology and victim rights as it has emerged into the twenty-first century. These rights and powers indicate that victims, from all legal traditions, are able to increasingly access rights of self-determination in proceedings relative to the substantial power exercised by the state and rights of defendants through the general requirements of due process and procedural fairness (see Fernández de Casadevante Romani, 2012; Ochoa, 2013; Moffett, 2014). The ratification of international law on the domestic level has witnessed the growth of localised approaches to victim rights, through both unenforceable and enforceable rights instruments. These rights frameworks speak to local conditions of law and policy in a criminal procedural context, despite being influenced by and developed out of international law and policy. Chapter 6 demonstrates how international human rights discourse has a significant impact on the local level, which even carries over to those states that are not signatories of international instruments by way of law reform and policy transfer (see Dolowitz1 and Marsh, 2002; McFarlane and Canton, 2014).

This section traces the rise of the normative framework of victim rights in international law and domestic human rights discourse. This section will set out the human rights instruments across international, regional, and domestic practice to indicate the language and context through which modern victim rights frameworks are constituted, to be drawn upon throughout Chapters 2 to 6. Chapters 2 and 6 will specifically demonstrate how this discourse has been adapted on the domestic level, in terms of ratification of the rules of criminal procedure and evidence as they characterise legal and policy intervention that repositions the victim and, significantly, other justice stakeholders, with regard to these international norms of victim rights.

Fair, courteous, and respectful treatment

The right to fair, respectful, and courteous treatment is a basic human right in that it is owed to any victim participating in any criminal justice system or proceeding. This right may also be extended to the family members of victims of crime. It is a standard norm of any civilised system of justice that addresses the need to maintain the dignity of the victim as a person in the criminal justice process (see Pemberton, 2014). The right has been set and in various human right instruments and as a basic, universal requirement of justice officials and other stakeholders acting in the justice system, it may preface such instruments – thus:

1.1 United Nations ('PJVC') (1985) The Declaration of Basic Principles of Justice for Victims of Crime and Abuse of Power, resolution GA/RES/40/34 of the General Assembly 29 November 1985:

> **Resolution 4** Victims should be treated with compassion and respect for their dignity. They are entitled to access to the mechanisms of justice and to prompt redress, as provided for by national legislation, for the harm that they have suffered.

1.2 United Nations ('RRRVGV') (2005) Basic Principles and Guidelines on the Right to a Remedy and Reparation for Victims of Gross Violations of International Human Rights Law and Serious Violations of International Humanitarian Law, resolution GA/RES/60/147 of the UN General Assembly, 16 December 2005:

Resolution 10 Victims should be treated with humanity and respect for their dignity and human rights, and appropriate measures should be taken to ensure their safety, physical and psychological well-being and privacy, as well as those of their families. The State should ensure that its domestic laws, to the extent possible, provide that a victim who has suffered violence or trauma should benefit from special consideration and care to avoid his or her re-traumatization in the course of legal and administrative procedures designed to provide justice and reparation.

1.3 *Victims Bill of Rights Act 2015* (Can) enacting the *Canadian Victims Bill of Rights*:

Preamble, Clause 2 Whereas victims of crime and their families deserve to be treated with courtesy, compassion and respect, including respect for their dignity.

1.4 European Union, Directive of the European Parliament and of the Council (2012) 2012/29/EU, 25 October 2012, Establishing minimum standards on the rights, support and protection of victims of crime, and replacing council framework decision 2001/220/JHA:

Recital 9 Crime is a wrong against society as well as a violation of the individual rights of victims. As such, victims of crime should be recognised and treated in a respectful, sensitive and professional manner without discrimination of any kind based on any ground such as race, colour, ethnic or social origin, genetic features, language, religion or belief, political or any other opinion, membership of a national minority, property, birth, disability, age, gender, gender expression, gender identity, sexual orientation, residence status or health. In all contacts with a competent authority operating within the context of criminal proceedings, and any service coming into contact with victims, such as victim support or restorative justice services, the personal situation and immediate needs, age, gender, possible disability and maturity of victims of crime should be taken into account while fully respecting their physical, mental and moral integrity. Victims of crime should be protected from secondary and repeat victimisation, from intimidation and from retaliation, should receive appropriate support to facilitate their recovery and should be provided with sufficient access to justice.

Article 1 The purpose of this Directive is to ensure that victims of crime receive appropriate information, support and protection and are able to participate in criminal proceedings. Member States shall ensure that victims are recognised and treated in a respectful, sensitive, tailored, professional and non-discriminatory manner, in all contacts with victim support or restorative justice services or a competent authority, operating within the context of criminal proceedings. The rights set out in this Directive shall apply to victims in a non-discriminatory manner, including with respect to their residence status.

1.5 Code of Practice for Victims of Crime 2015 ('Victims' Code') (England and Wales):

> **Introduction 1** This Code of Practice for Victims of Crime forms a key part of the wider Government strategy to transform the criminal justice system by putting victims first, making the system more responsive and easier to navigate. Victims of crime should be treated in a respectful, sensitive, tailored and professional manner without discrimination of any kind. They should receive appropriate support to help them, as far as possible, to cope and recover and be protected from re-victimisation. It is important that victims of crime know what information and support is available to them from reporting a crime onwards and who to request help from if they are not getting it.

1.6 *Victims Rights and Support Act 2013* (NSW):

> **Section 6, Clause 6.1** Courtesy, compassion and respect. A victim will be treated with courtesy, compassion, cultural sensitivity and respect for the victim's rights and dignity.

The right to fair and respectful treatment, however, does not raise in itself any enforceable right to treatment, nor to any particular kind of treatment that takes into account particular vulnerabilities or weaknesses. Such vulnerabilities and weaknesses are instead dealt with as a matter of fair trial rights, out of recognition of the equality of arms between participants, and have been the subject of deliberation before the ECtHR and, to a lesser extent, the ICC. As the right to fair, respectful, and courteous treatment is otherwise unenforceable, except by complaint against a government official bound by a declaration or charter, the right is featured across a range of instruments and policy documents. Where a complaint is made, a government official may be required to issue an apology but a lack of fair, respectful, and courteous treatment may otherwise be without remedy.

Information and to be kept informed

The right to information regarding one's matter is an important development, especially in those jurisdictions that have ill afforded the victim any role in proceedings where they would otherwise be kept informed of developments regarding their case. The right to information and to be kept informed of new decisions made and developments in court and regarding the status of the offender is now universalised, despite differences to the content of information and stages of the justice process to which the right to access information relates. Failure to provide the victim with information requested by the victim is generally remedied with the granting of access to the information sought. Most international and domestic instruments contain substantial provisions regarding access to information and extraction of relevant sections is not possible in its entirety. Select norms regarding access to investigative information, court dates, and the status of the offender are set out ahead.

2.1 United Nations ('PJVC') (1985) The Declaration of Basic Principles of Justice for Victims of Crime and Abuse of Power, resolution GA/RES/40/34 of the General Assembly 29 November 1985:

Resolution 6 The responsiveness of judicial and administrative processes to the needs of victims should be facilitated by: (a) Informing victims of their role and the scope, timing and progress of the proceedings and of the disposition of their cases, especially where serious crimes are involved and where they have requested such information . . .

2.2 European Union, Directive of the European Parliament and of the Council (2012) 2012/29/EU, 25 October 2012, Establishing minimum standards on the rights, support and protection of victims of crime, and replacing council framework decision 2001/220/JHA:

Recital 31 The right to information about the time and place of a trial resulting from the complaint with regard to a criminal offence suffered by the victim should also apply to information about the time and place of a hearing related to an appeal of a judgment in the case.

Recital 32 Specific information about the release or the escape of the offender should be given to victims, upon request, at least in cases where there might be a danger or an identified risk of harm to the victims, unless there is an identified risk of harm to the offender which would result from the notification. Where there is an identified risk of harm to the offender which would result from the notification, the competent authority should take into account all other risks when determining an appropriate action. The reference to 'identified risk of harm to the victims' should cover such factors as the nature and severity of the crime and the risk of retaliation. Therefore, it should not be applied to those situations where minor offences were committed and thus where there is only a slight risk of harm to the victim.

2.3 *Victims Bill of Rights Act 2015* (Can) enacting the *Canadian Victims Bill of Rights*:

Clause 6 Every victim has the right, on request, to information about (a) the criminal justice system and the role of victims in it; (b) the services and programs available to them as a victim, including restorative justice programs; and (c) their right to file a complaint for an infringement or denial of any of their rights under this Act.

Clause 7 Every victim has the right, on request, to information about (a) the status and outcome of the investigation into the offence; and (b) the location of proceedings in relation to the offence, when they will take place and their progress and outcome.

Clause 8 Every victim has the right, on request, to information about (a) reviews under the Corrections and Conditional Release Act relating to the offender's conditional release and the timing and conditions of that release; and (b) hearings held for the purpose of making dispositions, as defined in subsection 672.1(1) of the Criminal Code, in relation to the accused, if the accused is found not criminally responsible on account of mental disorder or unfit to stand trial, and the dispositions made at those hearings.

2.4 Code of Practice for Victims of Crime 2015 ('Victims' Code') (England and Wales):

Chapter 2, Adult Victims Part A: Victims' Entitlements, Section 6: Post-Trial, (iii) Victim Contact Scheme, Clause 6.9 If you choose to take part in the VCS you are entitled to: decide whether you want to receive information about key stages of the offender's sentence . . . receive information and make representations to the National Probation Service about victim-related conditions to be included on the offender's release licence or conditions of discharge in the event of release. For example, this could include a condition to prevent the offender from contacting you or your family; be informed by the National Probation Service about any conditions which an offender is subject to on release or discharge which relate to you or your family; be informed of the date on which these conditions will end; be informed about any other information which the National Probation Service considers to be appropriate in the circumstances of the case, including about key stages of the offender's sentence, or treatment in the case of a restricted or unrestricted mental health patient.

Chapter 5, Duties on Other Service Providers, Right to Receive a Decision Not to Investigate or to Cease Investigating, Clause 1.35 The service provider responsible for investigating the offence must, without unnecessary delay, ensure that a victim is notified of their right to receive a decision not to proceed with, or to end, an investigation into that crime. Right to receive information about a prosecution.

Chapter 5, Duties on Other Service Providers, Right to Receive Information about a Prosecution, Clause 1.36 The service provider responsible for prosecuting an offence must, without unnecessary delay, ensure that a victim is notified of their right to receive the following information: a. a decision not to prosecute a suspect; b. the time and place of the trial and the nature of the charges against the suspect.

2.5 *Victims Rights and Support Act 2013* (NSW):

Section 6, Clause 6.4 Information about Investigation of the Crime. A victim will, on request, be informed of the progress of the investigation of the crime, unless the disclosure might jeopardise the investigation. In that case, the victim will be informed accordingly.

Section 6, Clause 6.5 Information about Prosecution of Accused. (1) A victim will be informed in a timely manner of the following: (a) the charges laid against the accused or the reasons for not laying charges, (b) any decision of the prosecution to modify or not to proceed with charges laid against the accused, including any decision to accept a plea of guilty by the accused to a less serious charge in return for a full discharge with respect to the other charges, (c) the date and place of hearing of any charge laid against the accused, (d) the outcome of the criminal proceedings against the accused (including proceedings on appeal) and the sentence (if any) imposed. (2) A victim will be consulted before a decision referred to in paragraph (b) above is taken if the accused has been charged with a serious crime that involves sexual violence or that results in actual bodily harm or psychological or psychiatric harm to the victim, unless: (a) the victim has indicated that he or she does not wish to be so consulted, or (b) the whereabouts of the victim cannot be ascertained after reasonable inquiry.

Section 6, Clause 6.6 Information about trial process and role as witness. A victim who is a witness in the trial for the crime will be informed about the trial process and the role of the victim as a witness in the prosecution of the accused.

Section 6, Clause 6.15 Information about Impending Release, Escape or Eligibility for Absence from Custody. A victim will, on request, be kept informed of the offender's impending release or escape from custody, or of any change in security classification that results in the offender being eligible for unescorted absence from custody.

2.6 German Code of Criminal Procedure 1987, amended 2014:

Section 406e Inspection of Files (1) An attorney may inspect, for the aggrieved person, the files that are available to the court or the files that would be required to be submitted to it if public charges were preferred, and may inspect officially impounded pieces of evidence, if he can show a legitimate interest in this regard. In the cases referred to in Section 395, there shall be no requirement to show a legitimate interest. (2) Inspection of the files shall be refused if overriding interests worthy of protection, either of the accused or of other persons, constitute an obstacle thereto. It may be refused if the purpose of the investigation, also in another criminal proceeding, appears to be jeopardized. It may also be refused if the proceedings could be considerably delayed thereby, unless, in the cases designated in Section 395, the public prosecution office has noted the conclusion of the investigations in the files. (3) Upon application and unless important reasons constitute an obstacle, the attorney may be handed the files, but not the pieces of evidence, to take to his office or private premises. The decision shall not be contestable. (4) The public prosecution office shall decide whether to grant inspection of the files in preparatory proceedings and after final conclusion of the proceedings; in other cases the presiding judge of the court seized of the case shall give this decision. An application may be made for a decision by the court competent pursuant to Section 162, appealing against the decision made by the public prosecution office pursuant to the first sentence. Sections 297 to 300, 302, 306 to 309, 311a and 473a shall apply mutatis mutandis. The court's decision shall be incontestable as long as the investigations have not yet been concluded. These decisions shall not be given with reasons if their disclosure might endanger the purpose of the investigation. (5) Under the conditions in subsection (1) the aggrieved person may be given information and copies from the files; subsections (2) and (4) and Section 478 subsection (1), third and fourth sentences, shall apply mutatis mutandis. (6) Section 477 subsection (5) shall apply mutatis mutandis.

Section 406h Information as to Rights (1) Aggrieved persons shall be informed as early as possible, as a rule in writing, and as far as possible in a language they understand, of their rights following from Sections 406d to 406g and, in particular, shall also be informed of the fact that they may, 1. under the prerequisites of Sections 395 and 396 of this statute or section 80 subsection (3) of the Youth Courts Act, join the public prosecution as private accessory prosecutors and thereby apply, pursuant to Section 397a, to have legal counsel appointed for them or to have legal aid granted for calling in such counsel; 2. in accordance with Sections 403 to 406c of this statute and section 81 of the Youth Courts Act, assert a property claim arising out of the criminal offence in criminal proceedings; 3. in accordance with the Crime Victims Compensation Act, assert a claim for benefits; 4. in accordance with the Act on Civil Law Protection against

Violent Acts and Stalking, apply for the issue of orders against the accused; and
5. obtain support and assistance through victim support institutions, e.g. in the
form of counselling or psychosocial support during the proceedings. Where the
prerequisites for a certain right have obviously not been fulfilled in a particular
case, the information concerned may be dispensed with. There shall be no duty
to inform aggrieved persons who have not specified any address at which documents can be served. The first and third sentences shall also apply to relatives
and heirs of aggrieved persons, insofar as they are entitled to the corresponding
rights.

The scope of relevant information subject to release to victims is ever expanding and now
includes as a standard, albeit allowing for jurisdictional variation, access to information about
victim rights, access to information about the investigation, the decision to prosecute or not,
to court dates and outcomes, the sentence of the offender, change in custodial arrangements
of the offender, including change of correctional location, work arrangements, or escape,
and the parole and release of the offender.

Relevant support services

Services for victims of crime available and actionable at the local level provide necessary support for victims. These services span court support and witness assistance, access to counselling, medical coverage and rehabilitation, and access to affiliated services, including court
participation and compensation, as covered elsewhere. These services seek to enhance the
standing of the victim in the criminal justice system generally, but providing important and
necessary services, that also prevent exclusion from the justice system and secondary victimisation by participation in otherwise aversive court processes. Support services therefore
provide an important means of relief where other rights may not provide substantive access
to justice, or may not be enforceable against the state or accused.

**3.1 United Nations ('PJVC') (1985) The Declaration of Basic Principles of Jus-
tice for Victims of Crime and Abuse of Power, resolution GA/RES/40/34 of the
General Assembly 29 November 1985:**

Resolution 6 The responsiveness of judicial and administrative processes to the
needs of victims should be facilitated by . . . (c) Providing proper assistance to
victims throughout the legal process.

Resolution 14 Victims should receive the necessary material, medical, psychological and social assistance through governmental, voluntary, community-based and
indigenous means.

Resolution 15 Victims should be informed of the availability of health and social
services and other relevant assistance and be readily afforded access to them.

Resolution 16 Police, justice, health, social service and other personnel concerned
should receive training to sensitize them to the needs of victims, and guidelines
to ensure proper and prompt aid.

Resolution 17 In providing services and assistance to victims, attention should be
given to those who have special needs because of the nature of the harm inflicted
or because of factors such as those mentioned in paragraph 3 above.

3.2 United Nations ('RRRVGV') (2005) Basic Principles and Guidelines on the Right to a Remedy and Reparation for Victims of Gross Violations of International Human Rights Law and Serious Violations of International Humanitarian Law, resolution GA/RES/60/147 of the UN General Assembly, 16 December 2005:

See extract 1.2.

3.3 European Union, Directive of the European Parliament and of the Council (2012) 2012/29/EU, 25 October 2012, Establishing minimum standards on the rights, support and protection of victims of crime, and replacing council framework decision 2001/220/JHA:

Recital 37 Support should be available from the moment the competent authorities are aware of the victim and throughout criminal proceedings and for an appropriate time after such proceedings in accordance with the needs of the victim and the rights set out in this Directive. Support should be provided through a variety of means, without excessive formalities and through a sufficient geographical distribution across the Member State to allow all victims the opportunity to access such services. Victims who have suffered considerable harm due to the severity of the crime could require specialist support services.

Article 9 Support from Victim Support Services 1. Victim support services, as referred to in Article 8(1), shall, as a minimum, provide: (a) information, advice and support relevant to the rights of victims including on accessing national compensation schemes for criminal injuries, and on their role in criminal proceedings including preparation for attendance at the trial; (b) information about or direct referral to any relevant specialist support services in place; (c) emotional and, where available, psychological support; (d) advice relating to financial and practical issues arising from the crime; (e) unless otherwise provided by other public or private services, advice relating to the risk and prevention of secondary and repeat victimisation, of intimidation and of retaliation. 2. Member States shall encourage victim support services to pay particular attention to the specific needs of victims who have suffered considerable harm due to the severity of the crime. 3. Unless otherwise provided by other public or private services, specialist support services referred to in Article 8(3), shall, as a minimum, develop and provide: (a) shelters or any other appropriate interim accommodation for victims in need of a safe place due to an imminent risk of secondary and repeat victimisation, of intimidation and of retaliation; (b) targeted and integrated support for victims with specific needs, such as victims of sexual violence, victims of gender-based violence and victims of violence in close relationships, including trauma support and counselling.

Also see extract 6.6.

3.4 *Victims Bill of Rights Act 2015* (Can) enacting the *Canadian Victims Bill of Rights*:

Clause 6 Every victim has the right, on request, to information about . . . (b) the services and programs available to them as a victim, including restorative justice programs . . .

3.5 Code of Practice for Victims of Crime 2015 ('Victims' Code') (England and Wales):

> **Chapter 1, Enhanced Entitlements, Clause 1.4** All victims of a criminal offence are entitled to an assessment by the police to identify any needs or support required, including whether and to what extent they may benefit from Special Measures. The length and content of this assessment depends on the severity of the crime and your individual needs. The assessment will take into account your personal characteristics, the nature and circumstances of the crime, and your views. The more information you are able to provide during the assessment, the more tailored the level of support will be to your individual needs.

> **Chapter 1, Adult Victims Part A: Victims' Entitlements, Section 1: Police Investigation (i) Information, Referral to Victim Support Services and Needs Assessments, Clause 1.2** Victim support services are organisations which offer victims of crime help and support to help them cope and recover after a crime. The police will explain to you that they will automatically pass your details to victim support services within 2 working days of reporting the crime. You are entitled to ask the police not to pass on your details to victim support services. If you are a victim of a sexual offence or domestic violence, or if you are a bereaved close relative, the police will seek your explicit consent before sending your details to victim support services.

> **Chapter 5, Duties on Other Service Providers, Referral to Victim Support Services, Clause 1.28** Where a victim reports a criminal offence to a service provider, the service provider must ask whether the victim wishes to be referred to victim support services. If the victim wishes to be referred, the service provider must facilitate that referral.

> **Chapter 5, Duties on Other Service Providers, Referral to Victim Support Services, Clause 1.29** Where the victim is not present in or has left the territory of England and Wales, whichever country the victim is located in should provide victim support services to that victim.

3.6 *Victims Rights and Support Act 2013* (NSW):

> **Section 6, Clause 6.2** Information about Services and Remedies. A victim will be informed at the earliest practical opportunity, by relevant agencies and officials, of the services and remedies available to the victim.

> **Section 6, Clause 6.3** Access to Services. A victim will have access where necessary to available welfare, health, counselling and legal assistance responsive to the victim's needs.

> **Section 6, Clause 6.17** Financial Assistance for Victims of Personal Violence. A victim of a crime involving sexual or other serious personal violence is entitled to make a claim under the Victims Support Scheme.

Protection from the accused and others

The participation of the victim in criminal justice processes ought to be conditional on the basis that that participation not exacerbate existing harm or injuries, or cause further trauma by putting the welfare of the victim at risk. This relates most acutely to the accused's access to the victim in court or elsewhere. However, it may also relate to the victim's need for protection from the family or friends of the accused, or from hostile justice stakeholders, including defence counsel, that may traumatise the victim in court. Thus, the right to protection is connected to the procedural and participatory rights of the victim as set out ahead in so far as they seek to limit secondary victimisation in court by exposing vulnerable and child victims, or others at risk of reprisal, from potentially damaging processes. This is particularly important where the victim must appear as witness to testify for the prosecution and where no alternative evidence may replace that testimony.

4.1 United Nations ('PJVC') (1985) The Declaration of Basic Principles of Justice for Victims of Crime and Abuse of Power, resolution GA/RES/40/34 of the General Assembly 29 November 1985:

> **Resolution 6** The responsiveness of judicial and administrative processes to the needs of victims should be facilitated by . . . (d) Taking measures to minimize inconvenience to victims, protect their privacy, when necessary, and ensure their safety, as well as that of their families and witnesses on their behalf, from intimidation and retaliation.

4.2 Statute of the International Criminal Tribunal for the former Yugoslavia:

> **Article 22** Protection of victims and witnesses The International Tribunal shall provide in its rules of procedure and evidence for the protection of victims and witnesses. Such protection measures shall include, but shall not be limited to, the conduct of in camera proceedings and the protection of the victim's identity.

4.3 European Union, Directive of the European Parliament and of the Council (2012) 2012/29/EU, 25 October 2012, Establishing minimum standards on the rights, support and protection of victims of crime, and replacing council framework decision 2001/220/JHA:

> **Recital 53** The risk of secondary and repeat victimisation, of intimidation and of retaliation by the offender or as a result of participation in criminal proceedings should be limited by carrying out proceedings in a coordinated and respectful manner, enabling victims to establish trust in authorities. Interaction with competent authorities should be as easy as possible whilst limiting the number of unnecessary interactions the victim has with them through, for example, video recording of interviews and allowing its use in court proceedings. As wide a range of measures as possible should be made available to practitioners to prevent distress to the victim during court proceedings in particular as a result of visual contact with the offender, his or her family, associates or members of the public. To that end, Member States should be encouraged to introduce, especially in relation to court buildings and police stations, feasible and practical measures enabling the facilities to include amenities such as separate entrances and waiting areas for victims. In addition, Member States should, to the extent possible, plan the criminal proceedings so that contacts between victims and their family members and offenders are avoided, such as by summoning victims and offenders to hearings at different times.

4.4 *Victims Bill of Rights Act 2015* (Can) enacting the *Canadian Victims Bill of Rights*:

Clause 9 Every victim has the right to have their security considered by the appropriate authorities in the criminal justice system.

Clause 10 Every victim has the right to have reasonable and necessary measures taken by the appropriate authorities in the criminal justice system to protect the victim from intimidation and retaliation.

Clause 11 Every victim has the right to have their privacy considered by the appropriate authorities in the criminal justice system.

Clause 12 Every victim has the right to request that their identity be protected if they are a complainant to the offence or a witness in proceedings relating to the offence.

4.5 Code of Practice for Victims of Crime 2015 ('Victims' Code') (England and Wales):

Chapter 1, Enhanced Entitlements, Persistently Targeted Victims, Clause 1.9 You are eligible for enhanced entitlements under this Code as a persistently targeted victim if you have been targeted repeatedly as a direct victim of crime over a period of time, particularly if you have been deliberately targeted or you are a victim of a sustained campaign of harassment or stalking.

4.6 *Victims Rights and Support Act 2013* (NSW):

Section 6, Clause 6.7 Protection from Contact with Accused A victim will be protected from unnecessary contact with the accused and defence witnesses during the course of court proceedings.

Section 6, Clause 6.8 Protection of identity of victim. A victim's residential address and telephone number will not be disclosed unless a court otherwise directs.

Participatory, procedural, and substantive rights

Different courts and jurisdictions provide victims with varying levels of access to justice. The international framework of victim rights, however, draws from various legal traditions which have a history of granting the victim direct access to the pretrial and trial phases, including direct participation through counsel. The ICC provides a clear case study of the rights of victims to participate in hearings, having been instituted through the Victims and Witnesses Unit and the Office of Public Counsel for Victims. While these developments in international law and procedure feature as significant developments against models of justice that afford only minor opportunities for participation, the normative context of the right to counsel and for participation (though not party status) is connected to and flows from other international instruments and frameworks, including rules of court of international tribunals and forums where victims are provided counsel. Collectively, these instruments demonstrate a movement towards rights of a substantive character, which may be enforced against the state or the accused. They provide the victim the capacity to be heard, to make submissions, and, importantly, to be listened to and taken seriously, where a decision-making authority is seeking to arrive at a decision that regards the interests of the victim.

These international instruments and frameworks may not provide direct access to representation as is presented in a model of organised access to counsel in the ICC. However, the rights of victims to make submissions, to participate, and to enforce their entitlements against the state or accused provide evidence of the emerging normative context of participatory, procedural, and substantive rights of victims to access justice internationally. Groenhuijsen and Pemberton (2009) argue, however, that framework decisions such as those of the Council of Europe will not necessarily bring about legal and policy change because such instruments generally lack a means of enforcement, and do not contain mechanisms against member states. This is the advantage of a directive over a decision (see Ezendam and Wheldon, 2014), where directives come with the expectation of ratification by member states:

5.1 United Nations ('PJVC') (1985) The Declaration of Basic Principles of Justice for Victims of Crime and Abuse of Power, resolution GA/RES/40/34 of the General Assembly 29 November 1985:

> **Resolution 6** The responsiveness of judicial and administrative processes to the needs of victims should be facilitated by . . . (b) Allowing the views and concerns of victims to be presented and considered at appropriate stages of the proceedings where their personal interests are affected, without prejudice to the accused and consistent with the relevant national criminal justice system.

5.2 United Nations ('RRRVGV') (2005) Basic Principles and Guidelines on the Right to a Remedy and Reparation for Victims of Gross Violations of International Human Rights Law and Serious Violations of International Humanitarian Law, resolution GA/RES/60/147 of the UN General Assembly, 16 December 2005:

> **Resolution 8** For purposes of the present document, victims are persons who individually or collectively suffered harm, including physical or mental injury, emotional suffering, economic loss or substantial impairment of their fundamental rights, through acts or omissions that constitute gross violations of international human rights law, or serious violations of international humanitarian law. Where appropriate, and in accordance with domestic law, the term 'victim' also includes the immediate family or dependants of the direct victim and persons who have suffered harm in intervening to assist victims in distress or to prevent victimization.
>
> **Resolution 9** A person shall be considered a victim regardless of whether the perpetrator of the violation is identified, apprehended, prosecuted, or convicted and regardless of the familial relationship between the perpetrator and the victim.
>
> **Resolution 12** A victim of a gross violation of international human rights law or of a serious violation of international humanitarian law shall have equal access to an effective judicial remedy as provided for under international law. Other remedies available to the victim include access to administrative and other bodies, as well as mechanisms, modalities and proceedings conducted in accordance with domestic law. Obligations arising under international law to secure the right to access justice and fair and impartial proceedings shall be reflected in domestic laws. To that end, States should: (a) Disseminate, through public and private mechanisms, information about all available remedies for gross violations of international human rights law and serious violations of international humanitarian law; (b) Take measures to minimize the inconvenience to victims and their representatives, protect against unlawful interference with their privacy as appropriate and ensure their safety

from intimidation and retaliation, as well as that of their families and witnesses, before, during and after judicial, administrative, or other proceedings that affect the interests of victims; (c) Provide proper assistance to victims seeking access to justice; (d) Make available all appropriate legal, diplomatic and consular means to ensure that victims can exercise their rights to remedy for gross violations of international human rights law or serious violations of international humanitarian law.

Resolution 13 In addition to individual access to justice, States should endeavour to develop procedures to allow groups of victims to present claims for reparation and to receive reparation, as appropriate.

Resolution 14 An adequate, effective and prompt remedy for gross violations of international human rights law or serious violations of international humanitarian law should include all available and appropriate international processes in which a person may have legal standing and should be without prejudice to any other domestic remedies.

5.3 Rome Statute (Statute of the ICC) (A/Conf 183/9, 1998):

Article 68 Protection of the Victims and Witnesses and Their Participation in the Proceedings. 1. The Court shall take appropriate measures to protect the safety, physical and psychological well-being, dignity and privacy of victims and witnesses. In so doing, the Court shall have regard to all relevant factors, including age, gender as defined in article 7, paragraph 3, and health, and the nature of the crime, in particular, but not limited to, where the crime involves sexual or gender violence or violence against children. The Prosecutor shall take such measures particularly during the investigation and prosecution of such crimes. These measures shall not be prejudicial to or inconsistent with the rights of the accused and a fair and impartial trial. 2. As an exception to the principle of public hearings provided for in article 67, the Chambers of the Court may, to protect victims and witnesses or an accused, conduct any part of the proceedings in camera or allow the presentation of evidence by electronic or other special means. In particular, such measures shall be implemented in the case of a victim of sexual violence or a child who is a victim or a witness, unless otherwise ordered by the Court, having regard to all the circumstances, particularly the views of the victim or witness. 3. Where the personal interests of the victims are affected, the Court shall permit their views and concerns to be presented and considered at stages of the proceedings determined to be appropriate by the Court and in a manner which is not prejudicial to or inconsistent with the rights of the accused and a fair and impartial trial. Such views and concerns may be presented by the legal representatives of the victims where the Court considers it appropriate, in accordance with the Rules of Procedure and Evidence. 4. The Victims and Witnesses Unit may advise the Prosecutor and the Court on appropriate protective measures, security arrangements, counselling and assistance as referred to in article 43, paragraph 6. 5. Where the disclosure of evidence or information pursuant to this Statute may lead to the grave endangerment of the security of a witness or his or her family, the Prosecutor may, for the purposes of any proceedings conducted prior to the commencement of the trial, withhold such evidence or information and instead submit a summary thereof. Such measures shall be exercised in a manner which is not prejudicial to or inconsistent with the rights of the accused and a fair and impartial trial. 6. A State may make an application for necessary measures to be taken in respect of the protection of its servants or agents and the protection of confidential or sensitive information.

5.4 Rules of Procedure and Evidence (ICC):

Chapter 4, Provisions Relating to Various Stages of the Proceedings, Section III, Rule 90 Legal Representatives of Victims. 1. A victim shall be free to choose a legal representative. 2. Where there are a number of victims, the Chamber may, for the purposes of ensuring the effectiveness of the proceedings, request the victims or particular groups of victims, if necessary with the assistance of the Registry, to choose a common legal representative or representatives. In facilitating the coordination of victim representation, the Registry may provide assistance, inter alia, by referring the victims to a list of counsel, maintained by the Registry, or suggesting one or more common legal representatives. 3. If the victims are unable to choose a common legal representative or representatives within a time limit that the Chamber may decide, the Chamber may request the Registrar to choose one or more common legal representatives. 4. The Chamber and the Registry shall take all reasonable steps to ensure that in the selection of common legal representatives, the distinct interests of the victims, particularly as provided in article 68, paragraph 1, are represented and that any conflict of interest is avoided. 5. A victim or group of victims who lack the necessary means to pay for a common legal representative chosen by the Court may receive assistance from the Registry, including, as appropriate, financial assistance. 6. A legal representative of a victim or victims shall have the qualifications set forth in rule 22, sub-rule 1.

Chapter 4, Provisions Relating to Various Stages of the Proceedings, Section III, Rule 91 Participation of Legal Representatives in the Proceedings. 1. A Chamber may modify a previous ruling under rule 89. 2. A legal representative of a victim shall be entitled to attend and participate in the proceedings in accordance with the terms of the ruling of the Chamber and any modification thereof given under rules 89 and 90. This shall include participation in hearings unless, in the circumstances of the case, the Chamber concerned is of the view that the representative's intervention should be confined to written observations or submissions. The Prosecutor and the defence shall be allowed to reply to any oral or written observation by the legal representative for victims. 3. (a) When a legal representative attends and participates in accordance with this rule, and wishes to question a witness, including questioning under rules 67 and 68, an expert or the accused, the legal representative must make application to the Chamber. The Chamber may require the legal representative to provide a written note of the questions and in that case the questions shall be communicated to the Prosecutor and, if appropriate, the defence, who shall be allowed to make observations within a time limit set by the Chamber. (b) The Chamber shall then issue a ruling on the request, taking into account the stage of the proceedings, the rights of the accused, the interests of witnesses, the need for a fair, impartial and expeditious trial and in order to give effect to article 68, paragraph 3. The ruling may include directions on the manner and order of the questions and the production of documents in accordance with the powers of the Chamber under article 64. The Chamber may, if it considers it appropriate, put the question to the witness, expert or accused on behalf of the victim's legal representative. 4. For a hearing limited to reparations under article 75, the restrictions on questioning by the legal representative set forth in sub-rule 2 shall not apply. In that case, the legal representative may, with the permission of the Chamber concerned, question witnesses, experts and the person concerned.

Chapter 4, Provisions Relating to Various Stages of the Proceedings, Section III, Rule 93 Views of Victims or Their Legal Representatives. A Chamber may seek the views of victims or their legal representatives participating pursuant to rules 89 to 91 on any issue, inter alia, in relation to issues referred to in rules 107, 109, 125, 128, 136, 139 and 191. In addition, a Chamber may seek the views of other victims, as appropriate.

5.5 European Union, Directive of the European Parliament and of the Council (2012) 2012/29/EU, 25 October 2012, Establishing minimum standards on the rights, support and protection of victims of crime, and replacing council framework decision 2001/220/JHA:

Article 10 Right to be Heard. 1. Member States shall ensure that victims may be heard during criminal proceedings and may provide evidence. Where a child victim is to be heard, due account shall be taken of the child's age and maturity. 2. The procedural rules under which victims may be heard during criminal proceedings and may provide evidence shall be determined by national law.

Article 11 Rights in the Event of a Decision Not to Prosecute. 1. Member States shall ensure that victims, in accordance with their role in the relevant criminal justice system, have the right to a review of a decision not to prosecute. The procedural rules for such a review shall be determined by national law. 2. Where, in accordance with national law, the role of the victim in the relevant criminal justice system will be established only after a decision to prosecute the offender has been taken, Member States shall ensure that at least the victims of serious crimes have the right to a review of a decision not to prosecute. The procedural rules for such a review shall be determined by national law. 3. Member States shall ensure that victims are notified without unnecessary delay of their right to receive, and that they receive sufficient information to decide whether to request a review of any decision not to prosecute upon request. 4. Where the decision not to prosecute is taken by the highest prosecuting authority against whose decision no review may be carried out under national law, the review may be carried out by the same authority. 5. Paragraphs 1, 3 and 4 shall not apply to a decision of the prosecutor not to prosecute, if such a decision results in an out-of-court settlement, in so far as national law makes such provision.

5.6 *Victims Bill of Rights Act 2015* (Can) enacting the *Canadian Victims Bill of Rights*:

Clause 14 Every victim has the right to convey their views about decisions to be made by appropriate authorities in the criminal justice system that affect the victim's rights under this Act and to have those views considered.

Clause 15 Every victim has the right to present a victim impact statement to the appropriate authorities in the criminal justice system and to have it considered.

5.7 Code of Practice for Victims of Crime 2015 ('Victims' Code') (England and Wales):

Chapter 2, Adult Victims Part A: Victims' Entitlements, Section 1: Police Investigation, (ii) Victim Personal Statement, Clause 1.12 A Victim Personal Statement (VPS) gives you an opportunity to explain in your own words how a crime has affected you, whether physically, emotionally, financially or in any other way. This is different from a witness statement about what happened at the time, such as what you saw or heard. The VPS gives you a voice in the criminal justice process. However you may not express your opinion on the sentence or punishment the suspect should receive as this is for the court to decide.

Chapter 2, Adult Victims Part A: Victims' Entitlements, Section 1: Police Investigation, (ii) Victim Personal Statement, Clause 1.13 You are entitled to be offered the opportunity to make a VPS at the same time as giving a witness statement about what happened to the police about a crime. When making your VPS, you are entitled to say whether or not you would like to have your VPS read aloud or played (where recorded), in court if a suspect is found guilty. You are also entitled to say whether you would like to read your VPS aloud yourself or to have it read aloud by someone else (for example, a family member or the CPS advocate). The decision as to who reads out the VPS is ultimately for the court, but it will always take into account your preferences, and follow them unless there is good reason not to do so.

Chapter 2, Adult Victims Part A: Victims' Entitlements, Section 2, Pre-Trial – Charge and Bail, (i) Charge and Bail, Clause 2.2 Following a police or CPS decision not to prosecute you are entitled to be notified of the reasons why this decision was made, how you can access further information about the decision and how you can seek a review of the decision if you are dissatisfied with it, in accordance with their 'Victims' Right to Review' Schemes.

Chapter 2, Adult Victims Part A: Victims' Entitlements, Section 6: Post Trial, (vii) The Parole Board and Victim Personal Statements, Clause 6.27 The VPS gives you the opportunity to explain in your own words how a crime has affected you and your family, whether physically, emotionally, financially or in any other way. You may have already made a VPS closer to the time of the offence or prior to the trial. At this stage, you will have the chance to make a new VPS for use by the Parole Board to reflect your current views or feelings. The VPS will be taken by your VLO. The Parole Board will always read your VPS when they are considering an offender's release or move to open conditions.

5.8 *Victims Rights and Support Act 2013* (NSW):

Section 6, Clause 6.14 Victim Impact Statement. A relevant victim will have access to information and assistance for the preparation of any victim impact statement authorised by law to ensure that the full effect of the crime on the victim is placed before the court;

Section 6, Clause 6.16 Submissions on parole and eligibility for absence from custody of serious offenders. A victim will, on request, be provided with the opportunity to make submissions concerning the granting of parole to a serious offender or any change in security classification that would result in a serious offender being eligible for unescorted absence from custody.

5.9 German Code of Criminal Procedure 1987, amended 2014:

Section 395 Right to Join as a Private Accessory Prosecutor (1) Whoever is aggrieved by an unlawful act pursuant to 1. sections 174 to 182 of the Criminal Code, 2. sections 211 and 212 of the Criminal Code, that was attempted, 3. sections 221, 223 to 226a and 340 of the Criminal Code, 4. sections 232 to 238, section 239 subsection (3), sections 239a and 239b, and section 240 subsection (4) of the Criminal Code, 5. section 4 of the Act on Civil Law Protection against Violent Acts and Stalking, 6. section 142 of the Patent Act, section 25 of the Utility Models Act, section 10 of the Semi-Conductor Protection Act, section 39 of the Plant Variety Protection Act, sections 143 to 144 of the Trade Mark Act, sections 51 and 65 of the Designs Act, sections 106 to 108b of the Copyright and Related Rights Act, section 33 of the Act on the Copyright of Works of Fine Art and Photography, and sections 16 to 19 of the Act against Unfair Competition may join a public prosecution or an application in proceedings for preventive detention as private accessory prosecutor. (2) The same right shall vest in persons 1. whose children, parents, siblings, spouse or civil partner were killed through an unlawful act, or 2. who, through an application for a court decision (Section 172), have initiated the preferment of public charges. (3) Whoever is aggrieved by another unlawful act, in particular pursuant to sections 185 to 189, section 229, section 244 subsection (1), number 3, sections 249 to 255 and section 316a of the Criminal Code, may join the public prosecution as private accessory prosecutor if, for particular reasons, especially because of the serious consequences of the act, this appears to be necessary to safeguard his interests. (4) Joinder shall be admissible at any stage of the proceedings. It may also be effected for the purpose of seeking an appellate remedy after judgment has been given. (5) If prosecution is limited pursuant to Section 154a, this shall not affect the right to join the public prosecution as private accessory prosecutor. If the private accessory prosecutor is admitted to the proceedings, a limitation pursuant to Section 154a subsection (1) or (2) shall not apply insofar as it concerns the private accessory prosecution.

Section 397 Rights of the Private Accessory Prosecutor (1) The private accessory prosecutor shall be entitled to be present at the main hearing even if he is to be examined as a witness. He shall be summoned to the main hearing; Section 145a subsection (2), first sentence, and Section 217 subsections (1) and (3) shall apply mutatis mutandis. The private accessory prosecutor shall also be entitled to challenge a judge (Sections 24 and 31) or an expert (Section 74), to ask questions (Section 240 subsection (2)), to object to orders by the presiding judge (Section 238 subsection (2)) and to object to questions (Section 242), to apply for evidence to be taken (Section 244 subsections (3) to (6)), and to make statements (Sections 257 and 258). Unless otherwise provided by law, he shall be called in and heard to the same extent as the public prosecution office. Decisions which are notified to the public prosecution office shall also be notified to the private accessory prosecutor; Section 145a subsections (1) and (3) shall apply mutatis mutandis. (2) The private accessory prosecutor may avail himself of the assistance of an attorney or be represented by such attorney. The attorney shall be entitled to be present at the main hearing. He shall be notified of the date set down for the main hearing if his selection has been notified to the court or if he has been appointed as counsel.

Section 400 Private Accessory Prosecutor's Right to Appellate Remedy (1) The private accessory prosecutor may not contest the judgment with the objective of another legal consequence of the offence being imposed, or of the defendant being sentenced for a violation of the law which does not justify joinder by the private accessory prosecutor. (2) The private accessory prosecutor shall have the right to lodge an immediate complaint against the order refusing to open the main proceedings or terminating the proceedings pursuant to Sections 206a and 206b, insofar as the order concerns the offence on the basis of which the private accessory prosecutor is entitled to joinder. In other respects the decision by which the proceedings are terminated cannot be contested by the private accessory prosecutor.

Section 406d Notification of the Aggrieved Person (1) The aggrieved person shall, upon application, be notified of the termination of the proceedings and of the outcome of the court proceedings to the extent that they relate to him. (2) Upon application, the aggrieved person shall be notified as to whether 1. the convicted person has been ordered to refrain from contacting or consorting with the aggrieved person; 2. custodial measures have been ordered or terminated in respect of the accused or the convicted person, or whether for the first time a relaxation of the conditions of detention or leave has been granted, if he can show a legitimate interest and if there is no overriding interest meriting protection of the person concerned in excluding the notification; in the cases referred to in Section 395 subsection (1), numbers 1 to 5, as well as in the cases referred to in Section 395 subsection (3), in which the aggrieved person was admitted as private accessory prosecutor, there shall be no requirement to show a legitimate interest; 3. the convicted person is again granted a relaxation of the conditions of detention or leave if a legitimate interest can be shown or is evident and if there is no overriding interest meriting protection of the convicted person in excluding the notification. (3) Notification need not be furnished if delivery is not possible at the address which the aggrieved person indicated. If the aggrieved person has selected an attorney as counsel, if counsel has been assigned to him or if he is legally represented by such counsel, Section 145a shall apply mutatis mutandis.

Section 406f Assistance and Representation of the Aggrieved Person (1) Aggrieved persons may avail themselves of the assistance of an attorney or be represented by such attorney. Legal counsel appearing at the aggrieved person's examination shall be permitted to be present. (2) At the examination of aggrieved persons, a person whom they trust who has appeared at the examination shall, at their request, be permitted to be present, except where this could endanger the purpose of the investigation. The person conducting the examination shall decide; the decision shall not be contestable. The reasons for denying the request shall be documented on the files.

Section 406g Assistance for an Aggrieved Person Entitled to Private Accessory Prosecution (1) Persons who are entitled to join the proceedings as a private accessory prosecutor pursuant to Section 395 may also avail themselves of the assistance of an attorney or be represented by such attorney, prior to preferment of public charges and without declaration of joinder. They shall be entitled to be present at the main hearing, even if they are to be examined as witnesses. If it is in doubt whether a person is entitled to private accessory prosecution, the court shall decide upon hearing the person and the public prosecution office whether the person is entitled to be present; the decision shall be incontestable. Persons entitled to private accessory prosecution shall be notified of the date set down for the main hearing if they have so requested. (2) The attorney of the person entitled to private accessory prosecution shall be entitled to be present at the main hearing; subsection (1), third sentence, shall apply mutatis mutandis. He shall be notified of the date set down for the main hearing if his selection has been notified to the court or if he has been appointed as counsel. The first and second sentences shall apply mutatis mutandis at judicial examinations and judicial inspections, unless the presence or notification of the attorney would jeopardize the purpose of the investigation. (3) Section 397a shall apply mutatis mutandis to 1. the appointment of an attorney and 2. the granting of legal aid for calling in an attorney. In preparatory proceedings the court which would be competent pursuant to Section 162 shall decide. (4) Upon application by the person entitled to join the proceedings as a private accessory prosecutor an attorney may, in the cases referred to in Section 397a subsection (2), be appointed as counsel provisionally if 1. this is imperative for special reasons, 2. the assistance of counsel is urgently required and 3. the granting of legal aid appears to be possible, but a decision cannot be expected on it in time. Section 142 subsection (1) and Section 162 shall apply mutatis mutandis to the appointment. The appointment shall end unless an application for granting legal aid is filed within a time limit to be set by the judge, or if the granting of legal aid is refused.

Fair trial rights

For a criminal trial to proceed fairly the rights of the accused must be asserted against those of the powerful state. However, the ECtHR and limited jurisprudence from the ICC indicate that the needs of the victim are a factor in the consideration of the equality of arms requirement of trial participants – specifically, that the interests of the victim are relevant to the balance between the accused and state. This means that in relevant proceedings, victims will be entitled to be protected as vulnerable or at-risk participants, availing victims of a modified court process to enhance the security needs of the victim and to prevent secondary victimisation (see Bassiouni, 1999; Jackson, 2009; Johnson, 2009; Englebrecht, 2011; McAsey, 2011). The jurisprudence is developed in the ECtHR (see Wąsek-Wiaderek, 2000). The jurisprudence of the ECtHR indicates how member states ought to ratify the ECHR on a domestic and procedural basis, taking local practice into account in the application of the judgement of the court. This provides some guidance as to how international law and procedure ought to influence the local, with particular reference to the rights of the victim as they ought to be integrated into the adversarial trial, where victim rights may not otherwise be prescribed by local instrument (also see *Barton v The Queen* (1980) 147 CLR 75).

Following the emergence of these international, regional, and domestic frameworks, jurisdictions internationally are increasingly willing to support victims' access to justice by providing protective mechanisms adaptable to the criminal trial so that vulnerable and at-risk victims and witnesses are able to provide supported evidence at trial. This section sets out the law and procedure regarding victim participation in criminal trials as it flows from international instruments through to the domestic level.

6.1 United Nations ('ICCPR') (1966) International Covenant on Economic, Social and Cultural Rights, International Covenant on Civil and Political Rights

and Optional Protocol to the International Covenant on Civil and Political Rights, resolution GA/RES/2200(XXI) A-C of the General Assembly on 16 December 1966, and in force 23 March 1976: Fair trial rights:

See extract 10.1.

6.2 Rules of Procedure and Evidence (ICC):

Chapter 4, Provisions Relating to Various Stages of the Proceedings, Section III. Victims and Witnesses, Subsection 2. Protection of Victims and Witnesses: Rule 87 Protective Measures 1. Upon the motion of the Prosecutor or the defence or upon the request of a witness or a victim or his or her legal representative, if any, or on its own motion, and after having consulted with the Victims and Witnesses Unit, as appropriate, a Chamber may order measures to protect a victim, a witness or another person at risk on account of testimony given by a witness pursuant to article 68, paragraphs 1 and 2. The Chamber shall seek to obtain, whenever possible, the consent of the person in respect of whom the protective measure is sought prior to ordering the protective measure. 2. A motion or request under sub-rule 1 shall be governed by rule 134, provided that: (a) Such a motion or request shall not be submitted ex parte; (b) A request by a witness or by a victim or his or her legal representative, if any, shall be served on both the Prosecutor and the defence, each of whom shall have the opportunity to respond; (c) A motion or request affecting a particular witness or a particular victim shall be served on that witness or victim or his or her legal representative, if any, in addition to the other party, each of whom shall have the opportunity to respond; (d) When the Chamber proceeds on its own motion, notice and opportunity to respond shall be given to the Prosecutor and the defence, and to any witness or any victim or his or her legal representative, if any, who would be affected by such protective measure; and (e) A motion or request may be filed under seal, and, if so filed, shall remain sealed until otherwise ordered by a Chamber. Responses to motions or requests filed under seal shall also be filed under seal. 3. A Chamber may, on a motion or request under sub-rule 1, hold a hearing, which shall be conducted in camera, to determine whether to order measures to prevent the release to the public or press and information agencies, of the identity or the location of a victim, a witness or other person at risk on account of testimony given by a witness by ordering, inter alia: (a) That the name of the victim, witness or other person at risk on account of testimony given by a witness or any information which could lead to his or her identification, be expunged from the public records of the Chamber; (b) That the Prosecutor, the defence or any other participant in the proceedings be prohibited from disclosing such information to a third party; (c) That testimony be presented by electronic or other special means, including the use of technical means enabling the alteration of pictures or voice, the use of audio-visual technology, in particular videoconferencing and closedcircuit television, and the exclusive use of the sound media; (d) That a pseudonym be used for a victim, a witness or other person at risk on account of testimony given by a witness; or (e) That a Chamber conducts part of its proceedings in camera.

Chapter 4, Provisions Relating to Various Stages of the Proceedings, Section III. Victims and Witnesses, Subsection 2. Protection of Victims and

Witnesses: Rule 88 Special Measures 1. Upon the motion of the Prosecutor or the defence, or upon the request of a witness or a victim or his or her legal representative, if any, or on its own motion, and after having consulted with the Victims and Witnesses Unit, as appropriate, a Chamber may, taking into account the views of the victim or witness, order special measures such as, but not limited to, measures to facilitate the testimony of a traumatized victim or witness, a child, an elderly person or a victim of sexual violence, pursuant to article 68, paragraphs 1 and 2. The Chamber shall seek to obtain, whenever possible, the consent of the person in respect of whom the special measure is sought prior to ordering that measure. 2. A Chamber may hold a hearing on a motion or a request under sub-rule 1, if necessary in camera or ex parte, to determine whether to order any such special measure, including but not limited to an order that a counsel, a legal representative, a psychologist or a family member be permitted to attend during the testimony of the victim or the witness. 3. For inter partes motions or requests filed under this rule, the provisions of rule 87, sub-rules 2 (b) to (d), shall apply mutatis mutandis. 4. A motion or request filed under this rule may be filed under seal, and if so filed shall remain sealed until otherwise ordered by a Chamber. Any responses to inter partes motions or requests filed under seal shall also be filed under seal. 5. Taking into consideration that violations of the privacy of a witness or victim may create risk to his or her security, a Chamber shall be vigilant in controlling the manner of questioning a witness or victim so as to avoid any harassment or intimidation, paying particular attention to attacks on victims of crimes of sexual violence.

6.3 Statute of the International Criminal Tribunal for the former Yugoslavia:

Article 20 Commencement and conduct of trial proceedings. 1. The Trial Chambers shall ensure that a trial is fair and expeditious and that proceedings are conducted in accordance with the rules of procedure and evidence, with full respect for the rights of the accused and due regard for the protection of victims and witnesses.

6.4 European Convention of Human Rights (ECHR):

Article 6 Right to a Fair Trial. 1. In the determination of his civil rights and obligations or of any criminal charge against him, everyone is entitled to a fair and public hearing within a reasonable time by an independent and impartial tribunal established by law. Judgment shall be pronounced publicly but the press and public may be excluded from all or part of the trial in the interests of morals, public order or national security in a democratic society, where the interests of juveniles or the protection of the private life of the parties so require, or to the extent strictly necessary in the opinion of the court in special circumstances where publicity would prejudice the interests of justice. 2. Everyone charged with a criminal offence shall be presumed innocent until proved guilty according to law. 3. Everyone charged with a criminal offence has the following minimum rights: (a) to be informed promptly, in a language which he understands and in detail, of the nature and cause of the accusation against him; (b) to have adequate time and facilities for the preparation of his defence; (c) to defend himself in person or through legal assistance of his own choosing or, if he has not sufficient means to pay for legal assistance, to be given it free when the interests of justice so require; (d) to examine or have examined witnesses against him and to obtain the attendance and examination of witnesses on his behalf under the·same conditions as witnesses against him; (e) to have the free assistance of an interpreter if he cannot understand or speak the language used in court.

Article 8 Right to Respect for Private and Family Life. 1. Everyone has the right to respect for his private and family life, his home and his correspondence. 2. There shall be no interference by a public authority with the exercise of this right except such as is in accordance with the law and is necessary in a democratic society in the interests of national security, public safety or the economic wellbeing of the country, for the prevention of disorder or crime, for the protection of health or morals, or for the protection of the rights and freedoms of others.

Article 10 Freedom of Expression. 1. Everyone has the right to freedom of expression. This right shall include freedom to hold opinions and to receive and impart information and ideas without interference by public authority and regardless of frontiers. This Article shall not prevent States from requiring the licensing of broadcasting, television or cinema enterprises. 2. The exercise of these freedoms, since it carries with it duties and responsibilities, may be subject to such formalities, conditions, restrictions or penalties as are prescribed by law and are necessary in a democratic society, in the interests of national security, territorial integrity or public safety, for the prevention of disorder or crime, for the protection of health or morals, for the protection of the reputation or rights of others, for preventing the disclosure of information received in confidence, or for maintaining the authority and impartiality of the judiciary.

6.5 Charter of Fundamental Rights of the European Union:

Chapter VI, Justice, Article 47 Right to an Effective Remedy and to a Fair Trial Everyone whose rights and freedoms guaranteed by the law of the Union are violated has the right to an effective remedy before a tribunal in compliance with the conditions laid down in this Article. Everyone is entitled to a fair and public hearing within a reasonable time by an independent and impartial tribunal previously established by law. Everyone shall have the possibility of being advised, defended and represented. Legal aid shall be made available to those who lack sufficient resources in so far as such aid is necessary to ensure effective access to justice.

6.6 European Union, Directive of the European Parliament and of the Council (2012) 2012/29/EU, 25 October 2012, Establishing minimum standards on the rights, support and protection of victims of crime, and replacing council framework decision 2001/220/JHA:

Recital 54 Protecting the privacy of the victim can be an important means of preventing secondary and repeat victimisation, intimidation and retaliation and can be achieved through a range of measures including non-disclosure or limitations on the disclosure of information concerning the identity and whereabouts of the victim. Such protection is particularly important for child victims, and includes non-disclosure of the name of the child. However, there might be cases where, exceptionally, the child can benefit from the disclosure or even widespread publication of information, for example where a child has been abducted. Measures to protect the privacy and images of victims and of their family members should always be consistent with the right to a fair trial and freedom of expression, as recognised in Articles 6 and 10, respectively, of the European Convention for the Protection of Human Rights and Fundamental Freedoms.

Article 21 Right to Protection of Privacy. 1. Member States shall ensure that competent authorities may take during the criminal proceedings appropriate measures to protect the privacy, including personal characteristics of the victim taken into account in the individual assessment provided for under Article 22, and images of victims and of their family members. Furthermore, Member States shall ensure that competent authorities may take all lawful measures to prevent public dissemination of any information that could lead to the identification of a child victim. 2. In order to protect the privacy, personal integrity and personal data of victims, Member States shall, with respect for freedom of expression and information and freedom and pluralism of the media, encourage the media to take self-regulatory measures.

Article 22 Individual Assessment of Victims to Identify Specific Protection Needs. 1. Member States shall ensure that victims receive a timely and individual assessment, in accordance with national procedures, to identify specific protection needs and to determine whether and to what extent they would benefit from special measures in the course of criminal proceedings, as provided for under Articles 23 and 24, due to their particular vulnerability to secondary and repeat victimisation, to intimidation and to retaliation. 2. The individual assessment shall, in particular, take into account: (a) the personal characteristics of the victim; (b) the type or nature of the crime; and (c) the circumstances of the crime. 3. In the context of the individual assessment, particular attention shall be paid to victims who have suffered considerable harm due to the severity of the crime; victims who have suffered a crime committed with a bias or discriminatory motive which could, in particular, be related to their personal characteristics; victims whose relationship to and dependence on the offender make them particularly vulnerable. In this regard, victims of terrorism, organised crime, human trafficking, gender-based violence, violence in a close relationship, sexual violence, exploitation or hate crime, and victims with disabilities shall be duly considered. 4. For the purposes of this Directive, child victims shall be presumed to have specific protection needs due to their vulnerability to secondary and repeat victimisation, to intimidation and to retaliation. To determine whether and to what extent they would benefit from special measures as provided for under Articles 23 and 24, child victims shall be subject to an individual assessment as provided for in paragraph 1 of this Article. 5. The extent of the individual assessment may be adapted according to the severity of the crime and the degree of apparent harm suffered by the victim. 6. Individual assessments shall be carried out with the close involvement of the victim and shall take into account their wishes including where they do not wish to benefit from special measures as provided for in Articles 23 and 24. 7. If the elements that form the basis of the individual assessment have changed significantly, Member States shall ensure that it is updated throughout the criminal proceedings.

Article 23 Right to Protection of Victims with Specific Protection Needs during Criminal Proceedings. 1. Without prejudice to the rights of the defence and in accordance with rules of judicial discretion, Member States shall ensure that victims with specific protection needs who benefit from special measures identified as a result of an individual assessment provided for in Article 22(1) may benefit from the measures provided for in paragraphs 2 and 3 of this Article. A special measure envisaged following the individual assessment shall not be made available if operational or practical constraints make this impossible, or where there is a [sic] an urgent need to interview the victim and failure to do so could harm the victim or another person or could prejudice the course of the proceedings. 2. The following measures shall be available during criminal investigations to victims with specific protection needs identified in accordance with Article 22(1): (a) interviews with the victim being carried out in premises designed or adapted for that purpose; (b) interviews with the victim being carried out by or through professionals trained for that purpose; (c) all interviews with the victim being conducted by the same persons unless this is contrary to the good administration of justice; (d) all interviews with victims of sexual violence, gender-based violence or violence in close relationships, unless conducted by a prosecutor or a judge, being conducted by a person of the same sex as the victim, if the victim so wishes, provided that the course of the criminal proceedings will not be prejudiced. 3. The following measures shall be available for victims with specific protection needs identified in accordance with Article 22(1) during court proceedings: (a) measures to avoid visual contact between victims and offenders including during the giving of evidence, by appropriate means including the use of communication technology; (b) measures to ensure that the victim may be heard in the courtroom without being present, in particular through the use of appropriate communication technology; (c) measures to avoid unnecessary questioning concerning the victim's private life not related to the criminal offence; and (d) measures allowing a hearing to take place without the presence of the public.

Article 24 Right to Protection of Child Victims during Criminal Proceedings. 1. In addition to the measures provided for in Article 23, Member States shall ensure that where the victim is a child: (a) in criminal investigations, all interviews with the child victim may be audiovisually recorded and such recorded interviews may be used as evidence in criminal proceedings; (b) in criminal investigations and proceedings, in accordance with the role of victims in the relevant criminal justice system, competent authorities appoint a special representative for child victims where, according to national law, the holders of parental responsibility are precluded from representing the child victim as a result of a conflict of interest between them and the child victim, or where the child victim is unaccompanied or separated from the family; (c) where the child victim has the right to a lawyer, he or she has the right to legal advice and representation, in his or her own name, in proceedings where there is, or there could be, a conflict of interest between the child victim and the holders of parental responsibility. The procedural rules for the audiovisual recordings referred to in point (a) of the first subparagraph and the use thereof shall be determined by national law. 2. Where the age of a victim is uncertain and there are reasons to believe that the victim is a child, the victim shall, for the purposes of this Directive, be presumed to be a child.

6.7 *Victims Bill of Rights Act 2015* (Can) enacting the *Canadian Victims Bill of Rights*:

Clause 12 Every victim has the right to request that their identity be protected if they are a complainant to the offence or a witness in proceedings relating to the offence.

Clause 13 Every victim has the right to request testimonial aids when appearing as a witness in proceedings relating to the offence.

6.8 Code of Practice for Victims of Crime 2015 ('Victims' Code') (England and Wales):

Chapter 1, Enhanced Entitlements, Clause 1.13 If you give evidence at court you will do so as a witness. Special Measures is the term used to describe the measures a court can order to assist vulnerable or intimidated witnesses to give their best evidence in court. Special Measures are mentioned in Chapters 2, 3 and 5 of the Code. When your needs are assessed by a relevant service provider and you are identified as being eligible for Special Measures, the relevant service provider will discuss the measures available with you and record what you think will best help you to give evidence. You are entitled to ask the relevant service provider, which could be the police or your Witness Care Unit, for Special Measures to be used during the trial to help to give your best evidence. The CPS will take your views into account when deciding whether to make an application. In cases where the CPS do make an application for Special Measures, you are entitled to be informed of the outcome of this application. It is the court that decides whether Special Measures should be ordered. Once the court orders Special Measures, you are entitled to receive them. If you are a vulnerable or intimidated victim (in accordance with paragraphs 1.10–1.12 above) the following Special Measures may be available: screens/curtains in the courtroom, so the witness does not have to see the defendant, and, in some cases, the public gallery; a live video link allowing a witness to give evidence away from the courtroom. This could be from a separate room within the court, or from a dedicated live-link site outside the court building; evidence in private – the public gallery can be cleared in cases involving a sexual offence, human trafficking, or where the court is satisfied that someone other than the accused may seek to intimidate the witness; removal of wigs and gowns by judges, defence and prosecution advocates; video-recorded statements – these allow a witness to use a prerecorded video statement as their main prosecution evidence.

6.9 *Criminal Procedure Act 1986* (NSW):

Section 306U Vulnerable person entitled to give evidence in chief in form of recording (1) A vulnerable person is entitled to give, and may give, evidence in chief of a previous representation to which this Division applies made by the person wholly or partly in the form of a recording made by an investigating official of the interview in the course of which the previous representation was made and that is viewed or heard, or both, by the court. The vulnerable person must not, unless the person otherwise chooses, be present in the court, or be visible or audible to the court by closed-circuit television or by means of any similar technology, while it is viewing or hearing the recording. (2) Subject to section 306Y, a person is entitled to give, and may give (no matter what age the person is when the evidence is given), evidence as referred to in subsection (1) in the form of a recording of a previous representation to which this Division applies made by the person when the person was less than 16 years of age. Note: Under section 306Y, a court may order that a vulnerable person not give evidence in the form of a recording if it is satisfied that it is not in the interests of justice for the evidence to be given by a recording. (3) If a vulnerable person who gives evidence as referred to in subsection (1) is not the accused person in the proceeding, the vulnerable person must subsequently be available for cross-examination and re-examination: (a) orally in the courtroom, or (b) if the evidence is given in any proceeding to which Division 4 applies – in accordance with alternative arrangements made under section 306W.

Access to compensation, restitution, and reparations

Access to compensation, restitution, and reparations is increasingly common amongst international instruments, international law and procedure, and the rules of procedure and evidence that constitute that procedure. While these processes may be accessed through adjunctive relief, in an administrative context, or as annexed to sentencing proceedings but in the civil jurisdiction of the court, other courts have moved to include reference to compensation and reparations as part of the broader remit of criminal proceedings. This is particularly common in those international courts and tribunals seeking to remedy gross violations and harm. While such tribunals may not always award compensation or have sought alternative means of reputation where restitution from the offender is unlikely or impossible, local courts on the domestic level are increasingly awarding restitution to be then compensated or converted by the offender following sentence.

7.1 United Nations ('PJVC') (1985) The Declaration of Basic Principles of Justice for Victims of Crime and Abuse of Power, resolution GA/RES/40/34 of the General Assembly 29 November 1985:

> **Resolution 8** Offenders or third parties responsible for their behaviour should, where appropriate, make fair restitution to victims, their families or dependants. Such restitution should include the return of property or payment for the harm or loss suffered, reimbursement of expenses incurred as a result of the victimization, the provision of services and the restoration of rights.
>
> **Resolution 9** Governments should review their practices, regulations and laws to consider restitution as an available sentencing option in criminal cases, in addition to other criminal sanctions.
>
> **Resolution 10** In cases of substantial harm to the environment, restitution, if ordered, should include, as far as possible, restoration of the environment, reconstruction of the infrastructure, replacement of community facilities and reimbursement of the expenses of relocation, whenever such harm results in the dislocation of a community.
>
> **Resolution 11** Where public officials or other agents acting in an official or quasi-official capacity have violated national criminal laws, the victims should receive restitution from the State whose officials or agents were responsible for the harm

inflicted. In cases where the Government under whose authority the victimizing act or omission occurred is no longer in existence, the State or Government successor in title should provide restitution to the victims.

Resolution 12 When compensation is not fully available from the offender or other sources, States should endeavour to provide financial compensation to: (a) Victims who have sustained significant bodily injury or impairment of physical or mental health as a result of serious crimes; (b) The family, in particular dependants of persons who have died or become physically or mentally incapacitated as a result of such victimization.

Resolution 13 The establishment, strengthening and expansion of national funds for compensation to victims should be encouraged. Where appropriate, other funds may also be established for this purpose, including those cases where the State of which the victim is a national is not in a position to compensate the victim for the harm.

7.2 United Nations ('RRRVGV') (2005) Basic Principles and Guidelines on the Right to a Remedy and Reparation for Victims of Gross Violations of International Human Rights Law and Serious Violations of International Humanitarian Law, resolution GA/RES/60/147 of the UN General Assembly, 16 December 2005:

Resolution 11 Remedies for gross violations of international human rights law and serious violations of international humanitarian law include the victim's right to the following as provided for under international law: (a) Equal and effective access to justice; (b) Adequate, effective and prompt reparation for harm suffered; (c) Access to relevant information concerning violations and reparation mechanisms.

Resolution 15 Adequate, effective and prompt reparation is intended to promote justice by redressing gross violations of international human rights law or serious violations of international humanitarian law. Reparation should be proportional to the gravity of the violations and the harm suffered. In accordance with its domestic laws and international legal obligations, a State shall provide reparation to victims for acts or omissions which can be attributed to the State and constitute gross violations of international human rights law or serious violations of international humanitarian law. In cases where a person, a legal person, or other entity is found liable for reparation to a victim, such party should provide reparation to the victim or compensate the State if the State has already provided reparation to the victim.

Resolution 16 States should endeavour to establish national programmes for reparation and other assistance to victims in the event that the parties liable for the harm suffered are unable or unwilling to meet their obligations.

Resolution 17 States shall, with respect to claims by victims, enforce domestic judgements for reparation against individuals or entities liable for the harm suffered and endeavour to enforce valid foreign legal judgements for reparation in accordance with domestic law and international legal obligations. To that end, States should provide under their domestic laws effective mechanisms for the enforcement of reparation judgements.

Resolution 18 In accordance with domestic law and international law, and taking account of individual circumstances, victims of gross violations of international human rights law and serious violations of international humanitarian law should, as appropriate and proportional to the gravity of the violation and the circumstances of each case, be provided with full and effective reparation, as laid out in principles 19 to 23, which include the following forms: restitution, compensation, rehabilitation, satisfaction and guarantees of non-repetition.

Resolution 19 Restitution should, whenever possible, restore the victim to the original situation before the gross violations of international human rights law or serious violations of international humanitarian law occurred. Restitution includes, as appropriate: restoration of liberty, enjoyment of human rights, identity, family life and citizenship, return to one's place of residence, restoration of employment and return of property.

Resolution 20 Compensation should be provided for any economically assessable damage, as appropriate and proportional to the gravity of the violation and the circumstances of each case, resulting from gross violations of international human rights law and serious violations of international humanitarian law, such as: (a) Physical or mental harm; (b) Lost opportunities, including employment, education and social benefits; (c) Material damages and loss of earnings, including loss of earning potential; (d) Moral damage; (e) Costs required for legal or expert assistance, medicine and medical services, and psychological and social services.

7.3 Rules of Procedure and Evidence (ICC):

Article 75 Reparations to Victims. 1. The Court shall establish principles relating to reparations to, or in respect of, victims, including restitution, compensation and rehabilitation. On this basis, in its decision the Court may, either upon request or on its own motion in exceptional circumstances, determine the scope and extent of any damage, loss and injury to, or in respect of, victims and will state the principles on which it is acting. 2. The Court may make an order directly against a convicted person specifying appropriate reparations to, or in respect of, victims, including restitution, compensation and rehabilitation. Where appropriate, the Court may order that the award for reparations be made through the Trust Fund provided for in article 79. 3. Before making an order under this article, the Court may invite and shall take account of representations from or on behalf of the convicted person, victims, other interested persons or interested States. 4. In exercising its power under this article, the Court may, after a person is convicted of a crime within the jurisdiction of the Court, determine whether, in order to give effect to an order which it may make under this article, it is necessary to seek measures under article 93, paragraph 1. 5. A State Party shall give effect to a decision under this article as if the provisions of article 109 were applicable to this article.

7.4 European Convention of Human Rights (ECHR):

Article 41 Just satisfaction: If the Court finds that there has been a violation of the Convention or the Protocols thereto, and if the internal law of the High Contracting Party concerned allows only partial reparation to be made, the Court shall, if necessary, afford just satisfaction to the injured party.

7.5 European Union, Directive of the European Parliament and of the Council (2012) 2012/29/EU, 25 October 2012, Establishing minimum standards on the rights, support and protection of victims of crime, and replacing council framework decision 2001/220/JHA:

> **Article 16** Right to decision on compensation from the offender in the course of criminal proceedings. 1. Member States shall ensure that, in the course of criminal proceedings, victims are entitled to obtain a decision on compensation by the offender, within a reasonable time, except where national law provides for such a decision to be made in other legal proceedings. 2. Member States shall promote measures to encourage offenders to provide adequate compensation to victims.

7.6 *Victims Bill of Rights Act 2015* (Can) enacting the *Canadian Victims Bill of Rights*:

> **Clause 16** Every victim has the right to have the court consider making a restitution order against the offender.
>
> **Clause 17** Every victim in whose favour a restitution order is made has the right, if they are not paid, to have the order entered as a civil court judgment that is enforceable against the offender.

7.7 Code of Practice for Victims of Crime 2015 ('Victims' Code') (England and Wales):

> **Chapter 2, Adult Victims Part A: Victims' Entitlements, Section 8: Applying for Compensation, (i) Making an Application, Clause 8.1** The Criminal Injuries Compensation Authority (CICA) processes all applications made under the Criminal Injuries Compensation Scheme. The Scheme is funded by the Government to compensate blameless victims of crime and intended to be one of last resort. CICA expects you to try to claim compensation from the person, or persons, who caused your injury or loss. However, if you do not know who injured you, or your assailant does not have the means to pay you compensation, you can make a claim under the Scheme.

7.8 *Victims Rights and Support Act 2013* (NSW):

> **Section 6, Clause 6.17** Financial assistance for victims of personal violence. A victim of a crime involving sexual or other serious personal violence is entitled to make a claim under the Victims Support Scheme.

7.9 German Code of Criminal Procedure 1987, amended 2014:

> **Section 403** Conditions. The aggrieved person or his heir may, in criminal proceedings, bring a property claim against the accused arising out of the criminal offence if the claim falls under the jurisdiction of the ordinary courts and is not yet pending before another court, in proceedings before the Local Court irrespective of the value of the matter in dispute.
>
> **Section 405** Dispensing with a Decision: (1) Upon application by the aggrieved person or his heir, and of the accused, the court shall include, in the court record,

a settlement in respect of the claims arising out of the criminal offence. Upon unanimous application by the persons named in the first sentence, the court shall make a proposal for a settlement.

Restorative intervention and therapeutic justice

Victims' access to justice that encourages a therapeutic intervention between victims and normative trial stakeholders is increasingly imputed from criminal procedural instruments internationally. While the victim may not be afforded a restorative intervention across all processes out of the state's need to apprehend and prosecute crime, international instruments are referring to restorative intervention as a policy priority. On the international level, courts such as the ICC have developed restorative processes as part of their trial procedure, to afford the victim a measure of inclusive justice by allowing trial participation. Restorative practices that allow for a therapeutic intervention are increasingly making their way into domestic law and policy such that courts are increasingly sentencing offenders to restorative exercises involving the victim. These take a range of forms, and may include sentencing offenders before indigenous circles inclusive of the victim, to a punishment that incorporates making amends to the victim or community, to apologise to the victim, or otherwise restore the victim as part of the sentencing process. Increasingly, domestic courts are including restorative processes in the pretrial phase, including intervention as a condition of bail.

8.1 United Nations ('PJVC') (1985) The Declaration of Basic Principles of Justice for Victims of Crime and Abuse of Power, resolution GA/RES/40/34 of the General Assembly 29 November 1985:

> **Resolution 7** Informal mechanisms for the resolution of disputes, including mediation, arbitration and customary justice or indigenous practices, should be utilized where appropriate to facilitate conciliation and redress for victims.

8.2 European Union, Directive of the European Parliament and of the Council (2012) 2012/29/EU, 25 October 2012, Establishing minimum standards on the rights, support and protection of victims of crime, and replacing council framework decision 2001/220/JHA:

> **Recital 46** Restorative justice services, including for example victim-offender mediation, family group conferencing and sentencing circles, can be of great benefit to the victim, but require safeguards to prevent secondary and repeat victimisation, intimidation and retaliation. Such services should therefore have as a primary consideration the interests and needs of the victim, repairing the harm done to the victim and avoiding further harm. Factors such as the nature and severity of the crime, the ensuing degree of trauma, the repeat violation of a victim's physical, sexual, or psychological integrity, power imbalances, and the age, maturity or intellectual capacity of the victim, which could limit or reduce the victim's ability to make an informed choice or could prejudice a positive outcome for the victim, should be taken into consideration in referring a case to the restorative justice services and in conducting a restorative justice process. Restorative justice processes should, in principle, be confidential, unless agreed otherwise by the parties, or as required by national law due to an overriding public interest. Factors such

as threats made or any forms of violence committed during the process may be considered as requiring disclosure in the public interest.

Article 12 Right to safeguards in the context of restorative justice services. 1. Member States shall take measures to safeguard the victim from secondary and repeat victimisation, from intimidation and from retaliation, to be applied when providing any restorative justice services. Such measures shall ensure that victims who choose to participate in restorative justice processes have access to safe and competent restorative justice services, subject to at least the following conditions: (a) the restorative justice services are used only if they are in the interest of the victim, subject to any safety considerations, and are based on the victim's free and informed consent, which may be withdrawn at any time; (b) before agreeing to participate in the restorative justice process, the victim is provided with full and unbiased information about that process and the potential outcomes as well as information about the procedures for supervising the implementation of any agreement; (c) the offender has acknowledged the basic facts of the case; (d) any agreement is arrived at voluntarily and may be taken into account in any further criminal proceedings; (e) discussions in restorative justice processes that are not conducted in public are confidential and are not subsequently disclosed, except with the agreement of the parties or as required by national law due to an overriding public interest. 2. Member States shall facilitate the referral of cases, as appropriate to restorative justice services, including through the establishment of procedures or guidelines on the conditions for such referral.

8.3 *Corrections and Conditional Release Act 1992* (Can):

Chapter 20, Section 26.1 The Service shall provide every victim, and every person referred to in subsection 26(3), who has registered themselves with the Service for the purposes of this section with information about its restorative justice programs and its victim–offender mediation services, and, on the victim's or other person's request, may take measures to provide those services.

8.4 Code of Practice for Victims of Crime 2015 ('Victims' Code') (England and Wales):

Chapter 2, Adult Victims Part A: Victims' Entitlements, Section 7: Restorative Justice, Clause 7.1 Restorative Justice is the process of bringing together victims with those responsible for the harm, to find a positive way forward.

Chapter 2, Adult Victims Part A: Victims' Entitlements, Section 7: Restorative Justice, Clause 7.2 Restorative Justice offers you an opportunity to be heard and sometimes to have a say in the resolution of offences. This can include agreeing activities for the offender to do as part of taking responsibility for their actions and to repair the harm that they have done. Restorative Justice can provide a means of closure and enable you to move on, while providing an opportunity for offenders to face the consequences of their actions and to understand the impact that it has had upon other people.

Chapter 2, Adult Victims Part A: Victims' Entitlements, Section 7: Restorative Justice, Clause 7.3 Restorative Justice can take place while criminal proceedings are ongoing, as part of a sentence after criminal proceedings have finished or as part of an out of court disposal. Any Restorative Justice will be led by a trained facilitator who will take your needs into consideration and deliver services in line with recognised quality standards.

Chapter 2, Adult Victims Part A: Victims' Entitlements, Section 7: Restorative Justice, Clause 7.4 Restorative Justice is voluntary – you do not have to take part, and both you and the offender must agree to it before it can happen. You can ask to participate in Restorative Justice at a time that is right for you or you may be asked to take part because the offender has requested Restorative Justice. Even if both parties want to take part, it might not be appropriate and the facilitator will make an assessment of this.

8.5 German Code of Criminal Procedure 1987, amended 2014:

Section 153a Provisional Dispensing with Court Action; Provisional Termination of Proceedings (1) In a case involving a misdemeanour, the public prosecution office may, with the consent of the accused and of the court competent to order the opening of the main proceedings, dispense with preferment of public charges and concurrently impose conditions and instructions upon the accused if these are of such a nature as to eliminate the public interest in criminal prosecution and if the degree of guilt does not present an obstacle. In particular, the following conditions and instructions may be applied: 1. to perform a specified service in order to make reparations for damage caused by the offence; 2. to pay a sum of money to a non-profit-making institution or to the Treasury; 3. to perform some other service of a non-profit-making nature; 4. to comply with duties to pay a specified amount in maintenance; 5. to make a serious attempt to reach a mediated agreement with the aggrieved person (perpetrator–victim mediation) thereby trying to make reparation for his offence, in full or to a predominant extent, or to strive therefor; 6. to participate in a social skills training course; or 7. to participate in a course pursuant to section 2b subsection (2), second sentence, or a driver's competence course pursuant to section 4a of the Road Traffic Act.

Domestic ratification

The premise of international human right instruments is to influence law and policy at various levels. However, where an international or regional organisation is constituted by member states, the object of domestic ratification is important, in order to put into local practice those international principles of justice that might otherwise remain lofty statements of principle with little or no connection to domestic life. Although the international literature well acknowledges alternatives to parliamentary ratification (see, generally, McFarlane and Canton, 2014), criticisms remain as to the voluntary enactment of decisions from supranational organisations designed to standardise practice throughout a region. The framework decisions of the EU and Council of Europe have been criticised in this regard (Hall, 2009; Groenhuijsen, 2014; as for criticisms regarding non-enforceable frameworks, see, generally, Beloof, 2005). However, increasingly, international and regional instruments contain explicit provisions indicating the desirability of local ratification. Despite this, local ratification may occur through a variety of legal and policy channels, and may occur to different extents between jurisdictions, in accordance with the needs of the local justice context. What can be agreed upon is the desirability of ratification where a domestic legal system is substantially inconsistent with international norms, that the local system be reformed to meet those international standards.

9.1 United Nations ('PJVC') (1985) The Declaration of Basic Principles of Justice for Victims of Crime and Abuse of Power, resolution GA/RES/40/34 of the General Assembly 29 November 1985:

> **Resolution 1** Affirms the necessity of adopting national and international measures in order to secure the universal and effective recognition of, and respect for, the rights of victims of crime and of abuse of power.

9.2 United Nations ('RRRVGV') (2005) Basic Principles and Guidelines on the Right to a Remedy and Reparation for Victims of Gross Violations of International Human Rights Law and Serious Violations of International Humanitarian Law, resolution GA/RES/60/147 of the UN General Assembly, 16 December 2005:

> **Resolution 1** The obligation to respect, ensure respect for and implement international human rights law and international humanitarian law as provided for under the respective bodies of law emanates from: (a) Treaties to which a State is a party; (b) Customary international law; (c) The domestic law of each State. 2. If they have not already done so, States shall, as required under international law, ensure that their domestic law is consistent with their international legal obligations by: (a) Incorporating norms of international human rights law and international humanitarian law into their domestic law, or otherwise implementing them in their domestic legal system; (b) Adopting appropriate and effective legislative and administrative procedures and other appropriate measures that provide fair, effective and prompt access to justice; (c) Making available adequate, effective, prompt and appropriate remedies, including reparation, as defined below; (d) Ensuring that their domestic law provides at least the same level of protection for victims as that required by their international obligations.

9.3 European Union, Directive of the European Parliament and of the Council (2012) 2012/29/EU, 25 October 2012, Establishing minimum standards on the rights, support and protection of victims of crime, and replacing council framework decision 2001/220/JHA:

> **Recital 3** Article 82(2) of the Treaty on the Functioning of the European Union (TFEU) provides for the establishment of minimum rules applicable in the Member States to facilitate mutual recognition of judgments and judicial decisions and police and judicial cooperation in criminal matters having a cross-border dimension, in particular with regard to the rights of victims of crime; (11) This Directive lays down minimum rules. Member States may extend the rights set out in this Directive in order to provide a higher level of protection.

9.4 *Victims Bill of Rights Act 2015* (Can) enacting the *Canadian Victims Bill of Rights*:

> **Clause 25(3)** Every federal department, agency or body that is involved in the criminal justice system must have a complaints mechanism that provides for (a)

a review of complaints involving alleged infringements or denials of rights under this Act; (b) the power to make recommendations to remedy such infringements and denials; and (c) the obligation to notify victims of the result of those reviews and of the recommendations, if any were made.

Without prejudice to the offender

The equality of arms requirement of the ECHR as interpreted by the ECtHR indicates an acute awareness that the rights of victims should not trump the requirement that the accused receive a fair trial. However, what this means in terms of article 4 of the ECHR requires some examination.[1] Other international declarations and instruments also refer to the requirement that victim rights be read against the accused's need to receive a fair trial, and without prejudicing the presumption of innocence to be afforded to the accused. These instruments are set out ahead. The ECtHR has a developed jurisprudence regarding the equality of arms arguments in favour of the accused's access to fair trial rights, notwithstanding those protections to be afforded to the victim.

10.1 United Nations ('ICCPR') (1966) International Covenant on Economic, Social and Cultural Rights, International Covenant on Civil and Political Rights and Optional Protocol to the International Covenant on Civil and Political Rights, resolution GA/RES/2200(XXI) A-C of the General Assembly on 16 December 1966, and in force 23 March 1976:

> **Resolution 14** 1. All persons shall be equal before the courts and tribunals. In the determination of any criminal charge against him, or of his rights and obligations in a suit at law, everyone shall be entitled to a fair and public hearing by a competent, independent and impartial tribunal established by law. The press and the public may be excluded from all or part of a trial for reasons of morals, public order (ordre public) or national security in a democratic society, or when the interest of the private lives of the parties so requires, or to the extent strictly necessary in the opinion of the court in special circumstances where publicity would prejudice the interests of justice; but any judgement rendered in a criminal case or in a suit at law shall be made public except where the interest of juvenile persons otherwise requires or the proceedings concern matrimonial disputes or the guardianship of children. 2. Everyone charged with a criminal offence shall have the right to be presumed innocent until proved guilty according to law. 3. In the determination of any criminal charge against him, everyone shall be entitled to the following minimum guarantees, in full equality: (a) To be informed promptly and in detail in a language which he understands of the nature and cause of the charge against him; (b) To have adequate time and facilities for the preparation of his defence and to communicate with counsel of his own choosing; (c) To be tried without undue delay; (d) To be tried in his presence, and to defend himself in person or through legal assistance of his own choosing; to be informed, if he does not have legal assistance, of this right; and to have legal assistance assigned to him, in any case where the interests of justice so require, and without payment by him in any such case if he does not have sufficient means to pay for it; (e) To examine, or have examined, the witnesses against him and to obtain the attendance and examination of witnesses on his behalf under the same conditions as witnesses against him; (f) To have the free assistance of an interpreter if he cannot

understand or speak the language used in court; (g) Not to be compelled to testify against himself or to confess guilt.

10.2 United Nations ('PJVC') (1985) The Declaration of Basic Principles of Justice for Victims of Crime and Abuse of Power, resolution GA/RES/40/34 of the General Assembly 29 November 1985:

> **Resolution 2** Stresses the need to promote progress by all States in their efforts to that end, without prejudice to the rights of suspects or offenders.

10.3 Statute of the International Criminal Tribunal for the former Yugoslavia:

> **Article 21** Rights of the accused. 1. All persons shall be equal before the International Tribunal. 2. In the determination of charges against him, the accused shall be entitled to a fair and public hearing, subject to article 22 of the Statute. 3. The accused shall be presumed innocent until proved guilty according to the provisions of the present Statute. 4. In the determination of any charge against the accused pursuant to the present Statute, the accused shall be entitled to the following minimum guarantees, in full equality: (a) to be informed promptly and in detail in a language which he understands of the nature and cause of the charge against him; (b) to have adequate time and facilities for the preparation of his defence and to communicate with counsel of his own choosing; (c) to be tried without undue delay; (d) to be tried in his presence, and to defend himself in person or through legal assistance of his own choosing; to be informed, if he does not have legal assistance, of this right; and to have legal assistance assigned to him, in any case where the interests of justice so require, and without payment by him in any such case if he does not have sufficient means to pay for it; (e) to examine, or have examined, the witnesses against him and to obtain the attendance and examination of witnesses on his behalf under the same conditions as witnesses against him; (f) to have the free assistance of an interpreter if he cannot understand or speak the language used in the International Tribunal; (g) not to be compelled to testify against himself or to confess guilt.

10.4 European Union, Directive of the European Parliament and of the Council (2012) 2012/29/EU, 25 October 2012, Establishing minimum standards on the rights, support and protection of victims of crime, and replacing council framework decision 2001/220/JHA:

> **Recital 12** The rights set out in this Directive are without prejudice to the rights of the offender. The term 'offender' refers to a person who has been convicted of a crime. However, for the purposes of this Directive, it also refers to a suspected or accused person before any acknowledgement of guilt or conviction, and it is without prejudice to the presumption of innocence.

Normative victim rights in context: positive state obligations and fair trial rights in international law and policy

The normative framework established by the international, regional, and domestic instruments draws from a broader human rights framework and discourse that are transferable between jurisdictions worldwide. While discussion of individual jurisdictions is necessary in order to identify how these discourses have been included on the local level, law and policy reform at the regional level provides a case study of the ways in which victim rights are expressed with a view to domestic change between member states. Although this tends to occur at the level of fair trial rights in the context of the jurisprudence of the ECtHR, other norms give context to the policy framework through which these fair trial rights emerge. The rules and practices of the ICC have also sought to protect vulnerable victims. The framework decisions and directives of the EU provide important points of comparison in this regard. These instruments also indicate the broader policy framework through which decisions of the European Court of Justice and ECtHR may be understood and actioned.

This section begins with a discussion of the centrality of the victim under international law by considering a series of cases that focus the state's consideration of the positive obligations owed to victims in a normative rights context. The focus on the positive obligations placed on the state indicates how victim rights have emerged in a normative context as central to the operations of the state's control of crime, and specifically the responsibility to investigate accusations from victims, as discussed in terms of the jurisprudence of the ECtHR. The equality of arms requirements of international courts provides a case analysis of the contested status of the expression of victim rights through the fair trial requirements under the ICTY and ECHR, and statutes and practice requirements of the ICC, and as against the directives of 2001 CEU FD and 2012 CEU DVC. This section places the fair trial requirements that may allow for a degree of victim participation and protection in the context of other normative concerns, particularly those owed to the offender in the context of the fair trial process. This section further connects to the discussion of individual jurisdictions in Chapters 4 through 6.

Realising the centrality of the victim: positive obligations to protect victim rights

In terms of the protective measures that have emerged through the decisions of ECtHR as relevant to the normative context of victim rights, the matter of *McCann and Ors v United Kingdom* (1995) 21 EHRR 97 asserts the requirement that the state is under a positive obligation to protect all human life (also see *O'Keeffe v Ireland* (2014) ECHR 35810/09). This necessarily extends certain obligations to the victim. Article 2 of the ECHR protects against the taking of life.[2] However, states are further obliged to guard against threats made by third parties. *Osman v United Kingdom* (1998) 29 EHRR 245 is a relevant case example. Osman's widow sought protection from the police after Osman complained of threats from a teacher. The English courts applied *Hill v Chief Constable of West Yorkshire Police* [1999] AC 53, which held that the police were not under a specific responsibility to prevent crime. The court held that the police were immune from allegations of negligence where they failed to account for evidence that could have stopped or minimised further offending. The matter proceeded to the ECtHR, which did not go as far as to extend a positive obligation on the police, albeit highlighting several measures that may relate to the standing of victim in a normative procedural context, at pars [115]–[116]:

> The Court notes that the first sentence of Article 2 § 1 enjoins the State not only to refrain from the intentional and unlawful taking of life, but also to take appropriate steps to safeguard the lives of those within its jurisdiction (see the L.C.B. v the United Kingdom judgment of 9 June 1998, Reports of Judgments and Decisions 1998-III,

p. 1403, § 36). It is common ground that the State's obligation in this respect extends beyond its primary duty to secure the right to life by putting in place effective criminal-law provisions to deter the commission of offences against the person backed up by law-enforcement machinery for the prevention, suppression and sanctioning of breaches of such provisions. It is thus accepted by those appearing before the Court that Article 2 of the Convention may also imply in certain well-defined circumstances a positive obligation on the authorities to take preventive operational measures to protect an individual whose life is at risk from the criminal acts of another individual. The scope of this obligation is a matter of dispute between the parties.

For the Court, and bearing in mind the difficulties involved in policing modern societies, the unpredictability of human conduct and the operational choices which must be made in terms of priorities and resources, such an obligation must be interpreted in a way which does not impose an impossible or disproportionate burden on the authorities. Accordingly, not every claimed risk to life can entail for the authorities a Convention requirement to take operational measures to prevent that risk from materialising. Another relevant consideration is the need to ensure that the police exercise their powers to control and prevent crime in a manner which fully respects the due process and other guarantees which legitimately place restraints on the scope of their action to investigate crime and bring offenders to justice, including the guarantees contained in Articles 5 and 8 of the Convention.

In the opinion of the Court where there is an allegation that the authorities have violated their positive obligation to protect the right to life in the context of their above-mentioned duty to prevent and suppress offences against the person (see paragraph 115 above), it must be established to its satisfaction that the authorities knew or ought to have known at the time of the existence of a real and immediate risk to the life of an identified individual or individuals from the criminal acts of a third party and that they failed to take measures within the scope of their powers which, judged reasonably, might have been expected to avoid that risk.

The positive obligations placed on the state do not give rise to victim rights that may provide a substantive basis for participation. They do, however, place the rights of victims as factors relevant to state decisions to investigate and control crime. *Osman* therefore raised the standing of victims relevant to the interpretation of the ECHR, and provided for a basis that, in certain circumstances, victims possess substantive rights against the state. *Razzakov v Russia* (2015) ECHR 57519/09 demonstrates the requirement that the state investigate the complaints of the victim under Article 3 where a complaint against torture is made. In this instance, the victim was awarded compensation by the civil courts. However, the criminal complaint was not properly investigated. The ECtHR ruled that the victim was entitled to relief. The accusation in this case was that the accused had been unlawfully deprived of his liberty when held in custody in order to induce a confession. It was alleged that no effective investigation was undertaken following the complaint. The ECtHR held that the victim was tortured under Article 3 of the ECHR,[3] and further held at par. [64]:

The Court finds that the significant delay in opening the criminal case and commencing a full criminal investigation into the applicant's credible assertions of serious ill-treatment at the hands of the police disclosing elements of a criminal offence, as well as the way the investigation was conducted thereafter, show that the authorities did not take all reasonable steps available to them to secure the evidence and did not make a serious attempt to find out what had happened (see, among other authorities, *Labita v Italy [GC]*, no. 26772/95, § 131, ECHR 2000-IV, and *Assenov and Others v Bulgaria*, 28 October 1998, §§ 103 et seq., Reports of Judgments and Decisions 1998-VIII). They thus failed in their obligation to conduct an effective investigation into the applicant's ill-treatment in police custody.

Opuz v Turkey (2009) ECHR 33401/02 further argues for the recognition of positive state obligations to victims as a normative rights expressed under the ECHR. In this matter, HO made continuous serious threats to the complainant and was initially convicted but released due to time served. Upon release, further threats were made. In this instance, the ECtHR determined that Turkey's laws provided insufficient protection to victims because they did not have an adequate deterrent effect on the accused, and were generally insufficient because other victims may not be protected, which contravened the rights owed to them pursuant to Articles 2 and 3 of the ECHR.[4]

In *Y v Slovenia* (2015) ECHR 41107/10, the ECtHR noted that the Council of Europe adopted the Convention on Preventing and Combating Violence against Women and Domestic Violence, Treaty No. 210, which entered into force on 1 August 2014, providing sex offences victims discrete rights to timely investigation of a sexual complaint, at par. [96]:

> As regards the Convention requirements relating to the effectiveness of an investigation, the Court has held that it should in principle be capable of leading to the establishment of the facts of the case and to the identification and punishment of those responsible. This is not an obligation of result, but one of means. The authorities must have taken the reasonable steps available to them to secure the evidence concerning the incident, such as witness testimony and forensic evidence, and a requirement of promptness and reasonable expedition is implicit in this context (see *Denis Vasilyev v Russia*, no. 32704/04, § 100, 17 December 2009, with further references). The promptness of the authorities' reaction to the complaints is an important factor (see *Labita v Italy* [GC], no. 26772/95, §§ 133 et seq., ECHR 2000-IV). Consideration has been given in the Court's judgments to matters such as the opening of investigations, delays in identifying witnesses or taking statements (see *Mătăsaru and Savițchi v Moldova*, no. 38281/08, §§ 88 and 93, 2 November 2010), the length of time taken for the initial investigation (see *Indelicato v Italy*, no. 31143/96, § 37, 18 October 2001), and unjustified protraction of the criminal proceedings resulting in the expiry of the statute of limitations (see *Angelova and Iliev v Bulgaria*, no. 55523/00, §§ 101–103, 26 July 2007). Moreover, notwithstanding its subsidiary role in assessing evidence, the Court reiterates that where allegations are made under Article 3 of the Convention the Court must apply a particularly thorough scrutiny, even if certain domestic proceedings and investigations have already taken place (see *Cobzaru v Romania*, no. 48254/99, § 65, 26 July 2007).

In this matter, the ECtHR found that the investigation into the applicant's complaint of sexual abuse infringed the victim's Article 3 right because proceedings were marked by a number of periods of complete inactivity, such that:

> more than seven years elapsed from the time the applicant lodged her complaint until the first-instance judgment was rendered. While it is not possible to speculate whether

these delays, for which no justification has been put forward by the Government, prejudiced the outcome of the proceedings in any way, in the Court's opinion they cannot be reconciled with the procedural requirement of promptness. (par. 99)

Fair trial rights in context: equality of arms in international law

The rights of the victim during the criminal trial generally flow from the law of evidence in so far as the victim is often required to testify as witness for the prosecution. The modern trial in common law, adversarial jurisdictions generally provides few participatory rights for victims with the exception that victims may be required to appear as a witness for the prosecution. However, unless required, the prosecution will not call the victim to testify at trial. Rather, the prosecution will assert their theory of the case by relying on physical or forensic evidence, or by requiring the testimony of other secondary witnesses. Historically, the law of evidence, which provides a substantive framework that regulates the admissibility of evidence, failed to take into account the personal or protective needs of the victim during the criminal trial. This left many victims exposed to harsh practices of cross-examination, and many victims, especially more vulnerable sex offences, cognitively impaired, and child victims, were further traumatised by the experience of testifying in their own trial.[5] Although variable dependent on whether the trial is counsel-led, civil law jurisdictions usually require the victim to appear more frequently out of adherence to a model of narrative evidence that allows the victim to tell his or her version of events without an overly prescribed law of evidence eliminating those aspects not relevant to the elements of the offence or defence. The need for protective measures, however, is as important in civil law as it is in common law jurisdictions. However, towards the end of the twentieth century, many jurisdictions began to recognise the discrete needs of victims called to testify and most began to provide a criminal procedure to accommodate the needs of victims during the trial process.

The law of evidence and trial process has developed more radically in common law, adversarial jurisdictions out of recognition of the harsh practices adopted by counsel, and the independence of the judge, who is not in a position to specifically protect the victim, during proceedings. Specific provisions now protect the victim, to enable participation as protected witness in proceedings. Changes include protective mechanisms that limit unfair or prejudicial questioning, or allow meaningful participation facilitated by technology or an intermediary. Victims may be able to testify by non-traditional means, by giving evidence out of court, by CCTV delivered to the courtroom composed of the judge, the accused, counsel, and the jury, or by alternative means, such as a statement. The treatment of victims in the civil law tradition where intervening counsel and the judiciary offer a mode of protection for the victim, in addition to private counsel who may appear solely to offer the victim support and protect his or her rights while giving evidence, has increasingly influenced the domestic laws of common law, adversarial states. Alternatives to the adversarial criminal trial may increase victim participation and satisfaction; however, such reform remains controversial, and potentially comes at the cost of compromising the defendant's right to face his or her accuser and examine the victim in open court. Certain types of offences have been disproportionately targeted as the subject of reform, out of recognition of the specific needs of victims in that area. For sex offences, for instance, the prior practice of examining the victim regarding his or her sexual reputation and history rendered the prospects of giving evidence particularly difficult, and proved to inhibit the reporting of such offences in the first instance. For all courts and jurisdictions, moreover, it is noted that the quality of evidence from at-risk and vulnerable victims will be enhanced if they are offered court support. Alternative modes of testifying, including procedures that allow for evidence by statement, or oral out-of-court evidence, may also provide such support. The risk of not developing a local criminal procedure to account for the needs of at-risk and vulnerable victims means that charges may not proceed to trial, out of a fear that the victim may be harshly examined in open court, may need to testify multiple times across pretrial and trial phases, or proceed to a new trial should a conviction be quashed and a retrial ordered (see, generally, Ellison, 2002; Bowden, Henning and Plater, 2014; Hoyano, 2015).

Support to victims in order to provide testimony at trial is thus increasingly regulated and protected. These protections are contentious in that they modify the accused's access to the victim, to cross-examine the victim on his or her accusation, and to build a defence case based upon the unfair blaming of the victim. However, courts continue to operate under the presumption that the accused be provided access to justice. This access resides in the general requirements of a 'fair trial', which takes the form of due process rights to challenge the prosecution case, responding with evidence of their own to challenge that case. While the reform of criminal procedure to better protect the victim's trial interests is a clear area of legal and policy concern, and jurisdictions are correct to ratify international and regional conventions that afford victims greater protection, the accused always maintains the right to challenge evidence, and insists upon some contact with the victim in order to operationalise their due process and procedural fairness rights at trial. The victim as a trial participant is therefore heavily contested and the normative rights of victims are not necessarily readily accepted by normative trial stakeholders, who may argue that increased protective rights unfairly alter or limit the equality of arms obligations on courts. The right to access and assess the prosecution case is captured by the equality of arms requirement under the jurisprudence of the ICTY and ECtHR, and to a modified extent by the ICC, out of the possibility of direct victim participation, discussed in this section.

Victim participation presents a more significant challenge where a court is required to provide for an adversarial exchange between the prosecution and defence. For certain international courts, including the ICTY and the ICC, this participation extends beyond the passive role of witness to include representational rights and access to private counsel, which allows the victim to test the evidence of other witnesses and to make submissions to the court. For instance, the Appeal Chamber of the ICTY in *The Prosecutor v Dario Kordić and Mario Čerkez* (IT-95-14/2-A) Appeals Chamber, 17 December 2004, *Decision on Application by Mario Čerkez for Extension of Time to File His Respondent's Brief*, the chamber rules that the principle of equality of arms captured the broader concept of a fair trial – thus at par. [6]:

> In *Brandstetter v Austria*, the Court emphasised that both the prosecution and the accused must be given equal opportunities in relation to the evidence tendered by the other. *In Dombo Beheer BV v The Netherlands*, when referring to the Court's case law concerning the requirements of a fair trial, described the requirement of equality of arms as providing a 'fair balance' between the parties and as implying that each party must be afforded a reasonable opportunity to present his case – including his evidence – under conditions that do not place him at a substantial disadvantage vis-à-vis his opponent.

The Appeals Chamber of the ICTY stated in *The Prosecutor v Du [Ko Tadi]* (IT-94-1-A) Appeals Chamber, 15 July 1999, following the case of *The Prosecutor v Duško Tadic*

(IT-94–1-T) Trial Chamber, 7 May 1997, that the principle of equality of arms between prosecution and accused goes to the point of a fair trial 'guarantee', at par. [44]:

> The parties do not dispute that the right to a fair trial guaranteed by the Statute covers the principle of equality of arms. This interpretation accords with findings of the Human Rights Committee ('HRC') under the ICCPR. The HRC stated in *Morael v France* that a fair hearing under Article 14(1) of the ICCPR must at a minimum include, inter alia, equality of arms. Similarly, in *Robinson v Jamaica* and *Wolf v Panama* the HRC found that there was inequality of arms in violation of the right to a fair trial under Article 14(1) of the ICCPR. Likewise, the case law under the ECHR cited by the Defence accepts that the principle is implicit in the fundamental right of the accused to a fair trial. The principle of equality of arms between the prosecutor and accused in a criminal trial goes to the heart of the fair trial guarantee. The Appeals Chamber finds that there is no reason to distinguish the notion of fair trial under Article 20(1) of the Statute from its equivalent in the ECHR and ICCPR, as interpreted by the relevant judicial and supervisory treaty bodies under those instruments. Consequently, the Chamber holds that the principle of equality of arms falls within the fair trial guarantee under the Statute.

The chamber in *The Prosecutor v Duško Tadic* understood the concept of equality of arms as involving *inter alia* procedural equality provided to the parties before the chamber, as enforced by the court. Note that victims are not able to participate in hearings of the ICTY directly or through counsel, and thus the judgement of the ICTY must be read in the context that the tribunal does not need to deal with the issue of victim participation in a direct way (see, generally, Fernandez de Gurmendi, 2001; Ambos, 2003; Abass, 2006). Despite lacking party status before the ICC, victims may participate in proceeding directly. The Rome Statute does not mention the principle of equality of arms directly, however, and recourse must turn to the principle as it has emerged through the jurisprudence of the court. In *The Prosecutor v Thomas Lubanga Dyilo*, Trial Chamber I (ICC-01/04–01/06, 14 December, 2007), the chamber addressed equality of arms requirements pursuant to Article 67 of the Rome Statute, at par. [18]:

> Article 67 of the Statute states the entitlement of the accused to 'a public hearing, having regard to the provisions of the Statute, to a fair hearing conducted impartially, and to [certain] minimum guarantees, in full equality'. The Chamber considers this article encompasses the principle of 'equality of arms'. This provision (and in particular the phrase 'in full equality') suggests that the minimum guarantees must be generously interpreted, so as to ensure the defence is placed insofar as possible on an equal footing with the prosecution, in order to protect fully the right of the accused to a fair trial.

The rights of the victim before the ICC are enhanced by the victim's capacity to participate with the assistance of counsel, who may utilise the rules of court to call evidence and test witnesses to establish the requirement that the truth of the matter be told. This emerges as an equality of arms issue as there is a need to maintain an adversarial exchange between parties and the bench (see Johnson, 2009). Where victims elect to call evidence, they must submit their request in writing, explaining how it will arrive at the truth of issues before the court. However, although victims can utilise the powers of the court to call witnesses, there is no requirement to disclose evidence to the defence. In *The Prosecutor v Katanga and Chui*

(ICC-01/04–01/07 OA 11, 16 July 2010, Judgment on the Appeal of Mr Katanga against the Decision of Trial Chamber II of 22 January 2010 Entitled 'Decision on the Modalities of Victim Participation at Trial'), the appeals chamber held that the victim has no disclosure obligation to the defence, which continues to rest with the prosecution. The court held the following at par. [81]:

> In this context, the Appeals Chamber recalls that under article 54 (1) (a) of the Statute, the Prosecutor has a duty to investigate exonerating and incriminating circumstances equally. Under article 54 (3) (b) of the Statute, the Prosecutor may, with respect to his investigations '[r]equest the presence of and question persons being investigated, victims and witnesses'. The Appeals Chambers therefore considers that it is reasonable that, in particular where the submissions in the victims' applications for participation indicate that victims may possess potentially exculpatory information, the Prosecutor's investigation should extend to discovering any such information in the victims' possession. Such information would then be disclosed to the accused pursuant to article 67 (2) of the Statute and rule 77 of the Rules of Procedure and Evidence.

The rulings of the ICC and the court's position toward victim participation is discussed in detail in Chapter 4. The Rome Statute together with the rules of procedure and evidence of the ICC grants the victim the ability to participate in proceedings before the ICC, which modifies the ICC's approach to equality of arms arrangements. Although participatory rights do not extend to standing rights, the process requires a consideration of the extent to which normative bipartite processes are affected. The ECtHR's jurisprudence on the rights of the victim to protective measures under the criminal procedure of member states, which takes into account the policy directive that the accused needs to receive a fair trial in the context of the need to support at-risk and vulnerable victims, is instructive here. The jurisprudence of the ECtHR is directed at addressing disputes of the domestic courts of member states. Different member states retain an inquisitorial trial process; however, many states have introduced procedures in support of an adversarial criminal trial. The jurisprudence of the ECtHR is generally construed as facilitating an adversarial exchange between participants to proceedings.[6] As such, judgements of the ECtHR support a developed discourse on the rights of vulnerable witnesses and victims, as trial participants in an adversarial trial framework. The framework decisions and directives of the EU have also directed member states to develop a criminal procedure to protect the needs of victims in this context.

In 2001, the Council of the EU adopted the CEU FD setting out a framework for the ratification of the rights of victims in the laws relating to the domestic criminal proceedings of member states of the EU. In *Criminal Proceedings against Pupino* [2005] EUECJ C-105/03, the European Court of Justice determined that the 2001 CEU FD provided the following, at par. [61]:

> the answer to the question must be that Articles 2, 3 and 8(4) of the Framework Decision must be interpreted as meaning that the national court must be able to authorise young children, who, as in this case, claim to have been victims of maltreatment, to give their testimony in accordance with arrangements allowing those children to be guaranteed an appropriate level of protection, for example outside the trial and before it takes place. The national court is required to take into consideration all the rules of national law and to interpret them, so far as possible, in the light of the wording and purpose of the Framework Decision.

The general failure to ratify the 2001 CEU FD throughout Europe encouraged the Council of the EU to pass the 2012 CEU DVC. This instrument repeals and re-enacts certain provisions of the 2001 CEU FD, extending on the framework of victim rights to be encouraged in legal and policy reform. The 2012 instrument is also designed to bind member states. Paragraph 9 of the preamble of 2012 CEU DVC provides the normative context that was not fully realised by the 2001 instrument:

> Crime is a wrong against society as well as a violation of the individual rights of victims. As such, victims of crime should be recognised and treated in a respectful, sensitive and professional manner . . . victims of crime should be protected from secondary and repeat victimisation, from intimidation and from retaliation, should receive appropriate support to facilitate their recovery and should be provided with sufficient access to justice.

The 2012 CEU DVC sets out minimum standards that require member states grant victims the capacity to access information, support provisions, modes of protection, and procedural rights in criminal proceedings.[7] In terms of criminal trial rights, these generally include the right to: be heard during criminal proceedings and to provide evidence; to be protected from secondary victimisation; and a right to the individual assessment of protective requirements.

Notes

1 Also see Chapter 2, International Norms of Victim Rights, extracted in Chapter 2 at 6.6.
2 Article 2 of the ECHR provides '1. Everyone's right to life shall be protected by law. No one shall be deprived of his life intentionally save in the execution of a sentence of a court following his conviction of a crime for which this penalty is provided by law. 2. Deprivation of life shall not be regarded as inflicted in contravention of this article when it results from the use of force which is no more than absolutely necessary: a. in defence of any person from unlawful violence; b. in order to effect a lawful arrest or to prevent the escape of a person lawfully detained; c. in action lawfully taken for the purpose of quelling a riot or insurrection.'
3 Article 3 of the ECHR provides 'No one shall be subjected to torture or to inhuman or degrading treatment or punishment.'
4 Also see Chapter 5, The European Court of Human Rights. See discussion of *Y v Slovenia* (2015) ECHR 41107/10.
5 Sex offences generally require the cooperation and participation of the victim as a witness during the trial phase. Unlike other offences, which may be able to be established on physical or forensic evidence alone, sexual offences often require the victim's testimony as to lack of consent or acknowledgement of the numerous acts of sexual touching that found the counts on the indictment. For sex offences, it is not uncommon for there to be multiple counts between acts of indecent or sexual assault, or rape.
6 See *Berger v France* (2002) ECHR 48221/99. This case is discussed in Chapter 5, The European Court of Human Rights.
7 The position in England and Wales regarding the implementation of 2012 CEU DVC and the requirement that member states adopt the framework directive in national or domestic law is now modified by *Assange v The Swedish Prosecution Authority* (2012) UKSC 22. The Supreme Court of the United Kingdom ruled that, while the ruling will not affect the outcome of *Pupino*, the UK parliament may continue to legislate as though *Pupino* has been applied, and was thus not bound to adopt the framework directive. Lord Phillips at par. [10] states, 'I have read with admiration Lord Mance's analysis of the effect of the decision in *Pupino* and I accept, for the reasons that he gives, that it does not bind this Court to interpret Part 1 of the 2003 Act, in so far as this is possible, in a manner that accords with the Framework Decision. I consider none the less that it is plain that the Court should do so. This is not merely because of the presumption that our domestic law will accord with our international obligations.' *Assange*

thus modified the general position regarding the ratification of laws that correspond to EU framework directives, pursuant to *Dabas v High Court of Justice in Madrid, Spain* (2007) 2 AC 31. Lord Bingham stated at par. [5] that 'By article 34(2)(b) of the Treaty on European Union, reflecting the law on directives in article 249 of the EC Treaty, framework decisions are binding on member states as to the result to be achieved but leave to national authorities the choice of form and methods. In its choice of form and methods a national authority may not seek to frustrate or impede achievement of the purpose of the decision, for that would impede the general duty of cooperation binding on member states under article 10 of the EC Treaty. Thus while a national court may not interpret a national law *contra legem*, it must "do so as far as possible in the light of the wording and purpose of the framework decision in order to attain the result which it pursues and thus comply with article 34(2)(b) EU" (Criminal Proceedings against Pupino (Case C – 105/03) [2005] QB 83, [2005] EUECJ C-105/03, paras 43, 47).'

3 Comparative issues and perspectives

Introduction

The comparison of victim rights frameworks between like, hybrid, and distinct jurisdictions draws out the degree to which each jurisdiction is converging towards international norms as identified in Chapter 2. Although this book is concerned with convergence, it is the degree of convergence in the context of the local which seeks to establish the argument regarding the importance of local context for the integration of international human rights norms for victims of crime. As such, the comparison of the countries, states, and jurisdictions set out in this book will be considered in terms of several interrelated trends in legal and policy change, as relevant and dominant characteristics of the twenty-first-century repositioning of the victim as an agent of justice.

While the comparative issues considered in this chapter are not exhaustive, this chapter does set out the major driving forces for legal and policy change on an international and local level. Certain jurisdictions will be influenced by all factors considered, while others may be driven to change by certain factors over others. However, this chapter assists the argument of this book by demonstrating how the ratification of international human rights discourses occurs in varied and at times indirect ways. This may include alternative ways of ratifying international instruments other than by executive act, such as court judgement or processes of law reform, and also identifies main policy concerns regarding victim rights and participation as have emerged across jurisdictions internationally (see Roberson and Das, 2016). Such concerns include representation for victims of crime, the rise of substantive rights frameworks for victims, the importance of reparations, and the growth of restorative and therapeutic justice. The driving factors of each jurisdiction are, however, individual, and this focuses our attention back to the development of international norms on the local level.

Inculcating international standards in law and policy

International law and procedure significantly influence local practice. However, the way international law and practice influence the practices of individual jurisdictions varies depending on how that jurisdiction adopts the discourses of human rights relevant to their justice system. Although ratification by executive act may appear to be the main way through which international human rights instruments augment change on the jurisdictional level, many jurisdictions affect change by other means and methods. This section will set out the main institutional arrangements through which international instruments come to be ratified in law and policy on the local level.

The influence of international law and procedure is ably demonstrated where member states grant domestic courts the power to utilise human rights instruments, or otherwise as ratified locally, in court decisions. The influence of international law and procedure is generally more difficult to trace where a state or country is not a signatory to a particular human rights instrument, but nonetheless develops local responses in law and policy consistent to the normative framework that emerges from such instruments. Such reform may be more appropriately identified as influenced by local practices of parliamentary intervention, law reform, or policy transfer.

Ratification of international declarations and instruments

The main means by which international human rights norms and standards are made available and developed on the local jurisdictional level is through the parliamentary ratification of the instrument as developed by the governing body or human rights organisation. Most notably, this occurs where the UN passes a universal declaration to which the member country or state is signatory. Although there is nothing to stop a jurisdiction for partial adoption of the universal declaration or standard, most countries that are signatories to the instrument will adopt the instrument or declaration in full in order to demonstrate their support for the objects of the instrument. Where local rights and processes conflict with the specific requirements of the international instrument modification or part adoption may be required. Otherwise, a jurisdiction may amend the international standard to local conditions where there is political or popular pressure to do so, or where Parliament reaches an impasse that cannot guarantee majority numbers for the Bill as proposed. Thus, most jurisdictions will need to amend the original instrument in order to pass it into law.

The UN understands that universal adoption of declarations and conventions may not be possible where local conditions and standards forebode unaltered ratification. This may be ably seen through the widely supported and at least partly ratified universal declaration, the United Nations (PJVC) (1985) The Declaration of Basic Principles of Justice for Victims of Crime and Abuse of Power, resolution GA/RES/40/34 of the General Assembly 29 November 1985. Although met with widespread praise, and supported by jurisdictions internationally as bringing into greater prominence the rights of crime victims that may otherwise have fallen to the periphery of justice, the PJVC was not ratified universally by signatories and member states. This was because the criminal justice processes of certain states did not afford a role for the victim of crime to any extent. Thus, automatic adoption through parliamentary process was not an option for many states. Rather, states ratified those rights that were feasible at the time. Victim compensation programmes, which were already part of the administrative processes of many states, were taken as early evidence of adoption. However, some jurisdictions took decades to ratify declarations or charters of victim rights that set out basic and minimal rights for victims of crime and the justice stakeholders that engage with them through their journey in the criminal justice system. Some states are yet to ratify such declarations of rights by parliamentary process, with some resorting to a statement of such rights in policy rather than law.

The directives of the EU Parliament – for instance, the European Union, Directive of the European Parliament and of the Council (2012) 2012/29/EU, 25 October 2012, Establishing minimum standards on the rights, support and protection of victims of crime, and replacing council framework decision 2001/220/JHA (CEU DVC) – recognise that individual member states will seek to adapt the broader procedural reforms to local standards out of recognition of the difference between the adherence of each member state to adversarial, mixed, or inquisitorial criminal justice processes. Thus the EU directives provide only a framework of processes that, ideally, member states should strive towards, and incomplete or modified ratification into law is expected and foreseen by the EU.

Policy transfer of international standards

Where ratification is not possible by virtue of an impeded parliamentary process or divisional interests, victim interests may be supported or encouraged through direct policy reform at the executive level. This is a less formal and transparent process by which governments seek to take lessons from policies or laws implemented in other jurisdictions, and implement similar processes in their home jurisdiction (see Wemmers, 2005). This process may occur in two distinct but interrelated ways. Firstly, where parliamentary ratification is not possible or achievable, a government may extract rights from the international instrument directly by developing the individual clauses of the instrument into policy that may be enforced through local, departmental directives. Secondly, governments may seek to take lessons from like states or jurisdictions usually of a similar nationalised system of justice. Similarities often lie along lines of a state's adherence to the normative framework and assumptions of justice arrangements as found in adversarial, common law, inquisitorial, mixed, or hybrid systems. Mixed or hybrid systems necessarily depart from a standard approach to the organisation of justice processes which more readily avails them of policy transfer processes, least without the need for substantial modification to meet the requirements of their nationalised system.[1] This, however, would not stop hybrid countries with recognised hybrid systems from making changes to suit their specific needs (see Das and Unterlerchner, 2014; Lomax, 2014).

Policy transfer is common where law reform bodies seek to investigate the successes of programmes piloted in other like jurisdictions, making recommendations as to their suitability in the home jurisdiction.[2] Note that where law reform or government bodies consider the rights of victims elsewhere the home jurisdiction may be more open to policy transfer from states following different or apparently conflicting legal traditions where the victim is displaced or peripheral in the home jurisdiction. This is because there may be a lack of an existing legal framework accommodating victims' rights and needs. Thus, it is open to the home jurisdiction to transfer in policies which otherwise may not have developed organically in the home state, assisted by the possibility of relocating the victim in an administrative context that does not impact on the functions of conventional stakeholders of law and justice (see Dolowitz1 and Marsh, 2002; McFarlane and Canton, 2014).

There are, however, limitations to feasible policy transfer between jurisdictions. Policy in conflict with law, superior rights, or constitutional instruments will be invalid, providing some restriction on an untrammelled transfer of policy across jurisdictions internationally. Such policy transfers are still possible within existing legal arrangements because most jurisdictions do not contain constitutional or legal restrictions on the development of victim policy, save where such policy detracts from rights otherwise guaranteed to the defendant or state. However, the setting out of rights to fair treatment, information, and consultation, now advocated under the PJVC and CEU DVC, has made its way into policy across numerous jurisdictions internationally because such rights do not necessarily take away from the rights of other justice stakeholders and are thus beyond direct challenge.

Dismantling adversarial/inquisitorial boundaries

The twenty-first century is witness to the dismantling of legal boundaries that once separated and isolated jurisdictions, internationally. Concepts of adversarial and inquisitorial are still meaningful in so far as they denote a jurisdiction's identification with certain processes that afford the defendant, state, and victim certain roles and protections. Each system may also be embraced on the national and cultural level, such that certain jurisdictions identify as fervently adversarial, with a general reluctance to give up or modify the rites of common law processes, such as access to trial by jury. Similarly, continental European jurisdictions may embrace the role of the investigating magistrate and prosecutor, with a capacity to make early decisions or rulings that may limit unnecessary or unsupported prosecutions into otherwise unworthy suspects.

A closer look into most jurisdictions reveals, however, some movement away from a fixed adversarial or inquisitorial position. Most European states are a hybrid of adversarial and inquisitorial processes, as are many jurisdictions outside of Europe, including Japan and Brazil. Even where a jurisdiction identifies as adversarial, this may relate only to the popular conceptualisation of the criminal process of trial by jury. Often, investigative and pretrial phases are a hybrid of adversarial and inquisitorial processes, as are sentencing, appeal, and parole processes. Each of the USA, England and Wales, Scotland, Ireland, Australia, Canada, New Zealand, South Africa, and India departs from strict requirements of adversarial, common law processes, with regard to the phases of the criminal trial.

The advent of the work and influence of the UN and EU Parliament and their increasing influence on the development of legal system internationally means that many countries once separated from the world are encouraged to develop their legal systems in accordance with global practices and standards. This inherently develops each system away from a fixed or nationalised system and opens up opportunities for convergence between adversarial and inquisitorial processes. The laws of England and Wales, which traditionally identify as consolidated around an adversarial process that resonates with their national identity as a common law country, have subtly moved away from the requirements of such processes being signatories to the European Convention of Human Rights (ECHR). Decisions of the ECtHR may be drawn upon in domestic courts under the *Human Rights Act 1998* (UK), thus opening up opportunities to develop English law away from the strict requirements of adversarial justice that ordinarily see the exclusion of victims from criminal processes. *R v Camberwell Green Youth Court* [2005] 1 All ER 999 provides a case study of consideration of victim rights of vulnerable and intimidated witnesses as required by the *Youth Justice and Criminal Evidence Act 1999* (UK) and the rights to a fair trial as provided under the ECHR.

Hybrid systems: criminal law, criminal justice, and mixed systems of administration

Certain nationalised systems of criminal justice may be classified as hybrid systems, no longer specifically identifying with nor adhering to a particular legal tradition (see, generally, Dickinson, 2003). These jurisdictions identify, directly or indirectly, as hybrid and arrive at this position in a number of ways. Jurisdictions may develop out of a mixed or inherited legal tradition that, through processes of colonisation, saw the arrival of different possibly competing systems of justice. Such nations may also retain distinct indigenous systems that have since been formally recognised as part of that country's legal system. South Africa and India are examples of states where colonisation introduced systems that have been made compatible with local conditions.[3] The decline of colonisation and the assertion of local customary law and practice, combined with the influence of international organisations, including the UN, further developed such nations away from any one distinct legal tradition through the normative frameworks provided under international law. Other countries may seek to abandon or reform their legal system in an attempt to develop a set of different legal principles. Italy provides an example of a deliberate reform to invoke a new criminal procedure with the introduction of a hybrid process in 1988 under the Code for Criminal Procedure (*Codice di Procedura Penale*) 1988 (Italy), as permitted by the Constitution of the Italian Republic. Japan provides another case in point, where deliberate reform of the criminal process was made with the introduction of the Fundamental Plan in 2005 and amendments to the Code of Criminal Procedure (Act No. 131 of 1948) (Jpn), through introduction of the Act to Amend Parts of the Code of Criminal Procedure and Others in Order to Protect Rights and Interests of Victims of Crime (*Hanzaihigaishatō no kenririeki no hogo wo hakarutame no keijisoshōhōtō no ichibu wo kaisesuru hōritsu*), Law No. 95 of 2007 (Jpn), allowing greater victim participation in criminal trials and to remove other restrictions for victims. These reforms significantly modified the dynamic of the criminal trial and built upon associated changes to the jury trial by introducing lay panels that may convict and sentence the accused. These reforms are now contained in the Code of Criminal Procedure (Jpn), as amended by the Act concerning Participation of Lay Assessors in Criminal Trials (*Saiban'in no sanka suru keiji saiban ni kansuru hōritsu*), Law No. 63 of 2004 (Jpn). These changes were deemed necessary because past criminal trials excluded and marginalised the victim, who otherwise had little say in the prosecution process. Chapter 6 provides a focused analysis of the victim in Japan's criminal justice system. Brazil is also presented as a case study of a hybrid system following both inquisitorial and adversarial traditions.

Despite identifying as a hybrid system, it is important to consider the individual jurisdictions or areas of law and practice within each hybrid jurisdiction. Countries such as South Africa and India, despite identifying as hybrid generally, may nonetheless identify as common law in so far as criminal law and procedure continue to draw substantially from statute and judgement as based on precedent. However, further analysis indicates that even where a particular area of law and practice is identified as common law, changes abound such that distinctions may continue to be drawn that distinguish one system from other similar, common law systems. For instance, the absence of the jury trial in India modified to a significant extent the ability to classify the Indian criminal justice process as adversarial, as based on the traditional procedural availability of adversarial exchange before independent judge and jury. While India may still identify as utilising the common law method in terms of sources of law which set out its system of criminal justice, it is a modified system that departs from the classical understanding of common law process that developed to embrace the requirements of adversarial exchange from the seventeenth century. Hybrid systems are therefore open to a variety of sources of reform such that general identification of criminal law and procedure as common law or even adversarial may not preclude substantive and procedural changes that may continue its identification as a hybrid system.

Hybrid systems that otherwise include the victim may originate within jurisdictions that otherwise strongly identify with a particular legal tradition. These are systems that may seek to utilise administrative law as an alternative milieu for the regulation of victim interests, effectively removing the victim from the law for administrative or executive processes alone. This is common where claims for victim compensation or assistance are managed outside the criminal courts, by executive authority, or by providers in agency agreement with the state (see, generally, Miers, 2014a, 2014b).

Law reform processes

The use of law reform bodies to systematically review the law and procedure in a given area is a hallmark of a developed justice system intent on improving access to justice through well-deliberated and thought-through recommendations. Other than processes of ratification that may see international instruments enacted into law through usual parliamentary processes, law reform bodies may also seek to draw from international instruments and standards in order to further develop responses to questions posed to them by government. For victims of crime, this is a key means by which victim interests and issues may be developed into a domestic legal system where Parliament or the courts are otherwise unable or reluctant to change the law to include victims into legal processes, and where such states are not signatories to human rights frameworks that may allow for alternative pathways of reform. References to law reform bodies may also be required where the intended reforms are complex and where outcomes and consequences of existing legal arrangements may be uncertain. In such cases, public exposure and consultation to the thinking informing the proposed changes become vital.

A case study of the inclusion of international standards by processes of law reform rather than direct ratification may be found in the 2014 reference of the attorney general of Victoria asking the Victorian Law Reform Commission (VLRC) to review and report on the role of victims in the criminal trial process. This law reform reference covers the various phases of the criminal trial and is original because it invites recommendations for the development of Victorian law, based on relevant civil and international law practice. The terms of reference request that the VLRC review and report on the common law origins of the criminal trial, comparative processes in civil law jurisdictions, recent innovations that affect victim participation in the trial process, the role of victims in the trial and sentencing process, compensation and restitution, and the need for victim support in relation to the criminal trial process (see VLRC, 2015a). The final report of the VLRC is due in September 2016.

Commissions of inquiry

Where no alternative mode of reform is made available or where the scope of injustice is such that it cannot be dealt with by a conventional court or parliamentary inquiry, executive commissions of inquiry, or royal commissions as known in the UK, Canada, Australia, and New Zealand, may provide a degree of access to justice for victims. Executive commissions of inquiry act under letters patent, act of parliament, or presidential order, granting the commission the power to compel witnesses and production of evidence in order to ventilate issues, resolve disputes, or uncover corruption or otherwise hidden offences which may be beyond the scope of normal police operations. Recommendations from such commissions may lead to prosecutions of offenders and may provoke systemic change leading to the adaptation or development of standards and norms implemented elsewhere, including international human rights norms and standards.

In Ireland, the Commission to Inquire into Child Abuse (CICA) began in 1999 and concluded in 2009 with a remit of investigating all types of child abuse in Irish institutions for children, with most allegations referring to reformatory and industrial schools operated by the Catholic Church. This remit included the ability to inquire into different forms of child abuse, including physical, sexual, and emotional abuse, and neglect. The final report, *CICA Investigation Committee Report Vols. I–V*, otherwise known as the Ryan Report (2009), made several recommendations, including the erection of a memorial for victims, increased services for victims, review policies, and the need to develop a formal approach to deal with breaches and to manage organisational inaction, pursuant to recommendation 7.10:

> The failures that occurred in all the schools cannot be explained by the absence of rules or any difficulty in interpreting what they meant. The problem lay in the implementation of the regulatory framework. The rules were ignored and treated as though they set some aspirational and unachievable standard that had no application to the particular circumstances of running the institution. Not only did the individual carers disregard the rules and precepts about punishment, but their superiors did not enforce the rules or impose any disciplinary measures for breaches. Neither did the Department of Education. (Ryan Report, 2009: 462–463)

The Ryan Report recommended that the policy document *Children First: National Guidance for the Protection and Welfare of Children* (DCYA, 2011) be implemented throughout Ireland.

From 1996, several inquiries were established across the states of Australia examining institutional child abuse within their state. The most recent of these was established in Victoria in 2011, known as the Protecting Victoria's Vulnerable Children Inquiry (VVCI). The inquiry was completed in 2012. Various recommendations emerged, seeking to develop a new policy framework to protect vulnerable children by systematising protective measure around the needs of children by identifying how programmes and policies interact to help established a protective network for those most vulnerable:

> The Inquiry's approach articulates and develops recommendations around a system for protecting vulnerable children that is focused on a child's needs . . . A systems approach examines all the factors that impact on the incidence of child abuse and neglect and issues arising from these. It then considers the context of how the service response of Victoria's policies and programs come together, interact with one another and function as a whole to protect vulnerable children and young people. (VVCI, Vol. 2: 110)

The Gillard government announced a royal commission into similar matters in Australia in 2012. This commission sought to cover the whole of Australia and is due to give its final report by 2017, unless further extended. The remit of the RCIRCA is to 'inquire into institutional responses to allegations and incidents of child sexual abuse and related matters' as provided by letters patent, 11 January 2013.[4]

Emerging international reforms in law and policy

Inculcating international norms relating to victim rights and powers in local legislative, legal, and policy frameworks tends to occur through emerging issues and trends. These issues and trends may be informed by international debate and policy reform, or by local issues that have emerged regarding a perceived injustice or need. While some connection with local issues is required for international debate to resonate on the local level, international trends regarding the empowerment of victims and the relocation of victims within systems of justice have a way of connecting with victims generally, by providing hope of better personal empowerment and working relations with justice stakeholders. Otherwise, a poor outcome in a particular case or matter may drive public debate and political engagement, and the perceived need for law reform bringing local standards in line with international ones.

The issues and trends traced in this section seek to present the array of victim interests that are topical and current, affecting the development of victim rights frameworks in law and policy on local levels. While this list is not exhaustive, with jurisdictions covered being selected for purpose, the issues presented flow from the previous sections setting out the international norms of victim rights and the modes through which reforms may be actioned into law and policy at the local level. The reforms analysed in this section draw from a broader normative framework of victim rights as discussed earlier in Chapter 2. They demonstrate the ratification of those norms in particular legislative and policy contexts. These issues are organised jurisdictionally in Chapters 4 through 6.

Trial participation and the right to be consulted

There is increased international concern over the role of the victim throughout the phases of the criminal justice process. This includes a concern over the role and participation of the victim in the investigation, the trial, from pretrial through to sentencing and appeal procedures, and the post-conviction phase, including punishment of the offender and parole. While victims have always been concerned with the entire process as relevant to their particular matter, much of the criminal trial has remained hidden from the public gaze of what constitutes the trial process, which has tended to focus on the hearing or jury trial phase alone. Thus, greater concern for the rights and powers of victims across the whole of the criminal trial, writ large, is bringing attention to those parts of the trial that were once identified as of little relevance to the victim.

An example of the need to expose the whole of the criminal trial as relevant to the victim is the recent move to increase victim rights to consultation during the investigative and pretrial phase. This is a period of the criminal trial that was once squarely focused on state decisions, from which the victim's views and expectations were generally excluded. While this phase is still currently organised around the need to apprehend and prosecute crime in the public interest, inroads have been made regarding victims' access to information and desire for consultation regarding decisions made. The development towards the duty to consult has founded modern reforms to allow victims access to other normative stakeholders, who may now be placed under an expectation to speak to the victim regarding decisions made.

For instance, the *Victims Bill of Rights Act 2015* (Can) enacts the *Canadian Victims Bill of Rights*, also amending other Canadian Acts, such as the Canadian Criminal Code, in terms of various victim rights and powers. This Act also places obligations on government departments that are owed to victims generally. The *Canadian Victims Bill of Rights* provides rights that are presently available to victims across Canada. Various rights regard victims' access to information and, importantly, to communicate their views where their rights are considered by a relevant authority. Section 2 of the 2015 Act sets out the *Canadian Victims Bill of Rights*. Clauses 7 and 14 prescribe rights regarding the victim's right to be informed and consulted during the investigation phase:

Clause 7 Every victim has the right, on request, to information about (a) the status and outcome of the investigation into the offence; and (b) the location of proceedings in relation to the offence, when they will take place and their progress and outcome.

Clause 14 Every victim has the right to convey their views about decisions to be made by appropriate authorities in the criminal justice system that affect the victim's rights under this Act and to have those views considered.

While these rights do not necessarily modify the power of the police to charge, or the state to prosecute, they do establish rights through which a complaint may be made and resolved, should a victim be denied rights under the *Canadian Victims Bill of Rights*. Clause 25 requires that dispute resolution ought to be provided by the criminal justice agency required to provide that right to the victim.

In NSW, police are not required to consult with victims when investigating an offence, nor do they need to discuss charge options with victims, despite having the discretion to do so. The *Victims Rights and Support Act 2013* (NSW) provides the Charter of Rights of Victims of Crime in NSW under section 6 of the Act. Clause 6.4 sets out the victim's right to information in such an instance:

> **Section 6, Clause 6.4** Information about investigation of the crime. A victim will, on request, be informed of the progress of the investigation of the crime, unless the disclosure might jeopardise the investigation. In that case, the victim will be informed accordingly.

England and Wales set out consultative rights for victims pursuant to section 37 of the *Police and Criminal Evidence Act 1984* (UK). Under the 1984 Act, section 37A requires that guidance may be issued by the director of public prosecutions under section 37(7), granting the police various options regarding changing decisions. This follows the determination of the evidence against the suspect.[5] The *Directors Guidance on Charging* provides the various standards against which evidence may be assessed to determine if a suspect should be charged, including the conditions of the charge, such as out-of-court disposal (CPS, 2013a, 2013b, 2013c; also see CPS, 2014). The *Directors Guidance on Charging* provides that the decision to charge is that of the police or Crown Prosecution Service (CPS), although the victim does possess some rights relevant to the process (CPS, 2013c).

With respect to the rights of the victim to be informed and to consult, section 2 of the *Code of Practice for Victims of Crime* or Victims' Code requires the following, however:

> **Chapter 2, Adult Victims Part B: Duties on Service Providers, Section 2: Pre-trial, Clause 2.1** The police must inform victims of all decisions to prosecute or to give the suspect an out of court disposal, including all police cautions.

> **Chapter 2, Adult Victims Part B: Duties on Service Providers, Section 2: Pre-trial, Clause 2.2** The police must inform victims of all police decisions not to prosecute a suspect and they must give reasons for the decision to the victim.

> **Chapter 2, Adult Victims Part B: Duties on Service Providers, Section 2: Pre-trial, Clause 2.3** Where the CPS decides not to prosecute during a charging consultation, the police must inform the victim of the decision, the reason for the decision (insufficient evidence or on public interest grounds), how they can access further information about the decision from the CPS and how they can seek a review of the decision if they are dissatisfied with it.

> **Chapter 2, Adult Victims Part B: Duties on Service Providers, Section 2: Pre-trial, Clause 2.4** Victims of the most serious crime, persistently targeted victims and vulnerable or intimidated victims must be provided with the information in paragraphs 2.1–2.3 above within 1 working day of the suspect being charged, being told that no charges will be brought, or being informed that they will be given an out of court disposal. All other victims must be provided with this information within 5 working days.

In England and Wales, the director of public prosecutions also provides guidance as to the consultative requirements relevant to the Victims' Code. The *Code of Practice for Victims of Crime: CPS Legal Guidance* requires that the victim be kept informed, referring to the Victims' Right to Review Scheme where the victim is not informed and therefore not satisfied with a charging decision made:

> Duties on both the police and CPS in respect of charging are outlined in section 2, Chapter 2, Part B of the revised Victims' Code, which does not create any additional responsibilities for either the police or CPS.
>
> Paragraph 2.1 – the police will continue to inform victims of all decisions to prosecute or to give the suspect an out of court disposal, including police cautions.
>
> Paragraph 2.3 – where the CPS decides not to prosecute during a charging consultation (this includes face-to-face meetings, Area consultations, telephone and digital consultations held in accordance with the DPP's guidance), the police must inform the victim of the decision, how they can access further information about the decision from the CPS and how they can seek a review of the decision if they are dissatisfied with it under the Victims' Right to Review (VRR) scheme.

The international norms that are established through various instruments set out in Chapter 2 have been substantially ratified into local law and policy in direct and indirect ways. These norms regarding the victim's right to be kept informed and to consult with charging authorities have been drafted in the context of the need to make charging decisions in the public interest. Where a decision averse to the interests of the victim is made, the victim may possess a right to review, as a corollary right that allows the victim greater input into the decision-making process. Such connected rights, discussed in detail ahead, flow from Article 11 of the 2012 CEU DVC providing the victim enhanced substantive and procedural rights to question decisions of the state.

Counsel for victims of crime

The international courts and tribunals are increasingly permitting victim participation and even party status by enabling victims to present through counsel at trial. The tendency to allow victim participation follows the ICC model whereby victims have participatory but not party status, in that they cannot appear with equal standing to the prosecution or defence. The victim's right to private counsel is gaining momentum in domestic, common law jurisdictions, which have a limited record of allowing victims access to private counsel in the pretrial process. The capacity to appoint counsel is better established in the continental European tradition, discussed in Chapter 1 and as set out across numerous jurisdictions in Chapter 6.

The appointment of private counsel to act against the accused or state is increasingly provided as a victim's right in international and domestic courts. Many states are providing access to counsel across different phases of the criminal trial, supported by a general right to counsel recognised under the criminal procedure of the jurisdiction, or as provided by the ratification of a charter or declaration of rights that grant victims substantive rights which may be enforced against the accused or state. The victim's right to counsel is variable across jurisdictions and courts. At the international trial level, counsel may intervene to inform the court of a submission the victim wishes to make regarding evidence before the court, or as relevant to a submission raised by the prosecution or defence. In certain international tribunals, such as the ECCC, the victim may prosecute, consistent with rights of the victim in certain civil law states. Under the ICC model, victims have access to counsel who are able to participate in the different phases of the trial, although only in so far as the victim is able to make relevant submissions on matters already before the court. The ICC has expressed concerns, however, regarding the victim's capacity to participate on the assumption that the victim may be seen to have similar rights to those assigned to the prosecution and defence. Although the victim does not attain party status, the victim may call a witness by exercising the ICC's power to call evidence required to establish the truth of the matter. The victim may then make submissions on that evidence as it is before the court (see Rome Statute, Article 69[3]).

In *The Prosecutor v Lubanga* (ICC-01/04–01/06–1432, 11 July 2008, Judgment on the Appeals of the Prosecutor and the Defence against Trial Chamber I's Decision on Victims' Participation of 18 January 2008), the appeals chamber considered the victim's capacity to utilise the rules of court to call evidence. Despite the need to establish the truth of the matter before the court, proving the guilt of the accused remained the prosecution's main duty at pars [93]–[95]:

> Presumptively, it is the Prosecutor's function to lead evidence of the guilt of the accused. In addition, the regime for disclosure contained in rules 76 to 84 of the Rules which sets out the specific obligations of the parties in this regard is a further indicator that the scheme is directed towards the parties and not victims.
>
> However, the Appeals Chamber does not consider these provisions to preclude the possibility for victims to lead evidence pertaining to the guilt or innocence of the accused and to challenge the admissibility or relevance of evidence during the trial proceedings.
>
> While mindful that the Prosecutor bears the onus of proving the guilt of the accused, it is nevertheless clear that 'the Court has the authority to request the submission of all evidence that it considers necessary for the determination of the truth' (article 69 (3) of the Statute). The fact that the onus lies on the Prosecutor cannot be read to exclude the statutory powers of the court, as it is the court that 'must be convinced of the guilt of the accused beyond reasonable doubt' (article 66 (3) of the Statute).

The Prosecutor v Lubanga and *Prosecutor v Katanga and Chui* (see earlier) establish the rights of the victim in a procedural context of trial processes before the ICC. The granting of participatory rights with the support of counsel suggests that the ICC's jurisdiction is best characterised as a hybrid system of justice with points of convergence between adversarial and inquisitorial systems, although the court identifies principally as one that utilises an adversarial approach (Johnson, 2009). The assemblage of processes from different legal traditions leaves the ICC open to the criticism that it is seeking to integrate different system of justice that ill afford the accused the procedural protections which they would receive under a nationalised system (Johnson, 2009; Pena and Carayon, 2013).

Despite a criminal process that identifies more readily with known adversarial techniques, the ICC departs from the normative adversarial model established by common law process so that victims may call evidence to assist the mission of the court, by ventilating all issues to establish the truth of the matter being prosecuted. Victim participation also supports the restorative remit of the ICC. However, a matter remains under the control of the court, with the prosecution still bringing a matter to trial, even where victim participation is permitted at trial. The jurisdiction of the ICC differs from domestic courts in that it investigates and prosecutes war crimes and gross violations of human rights. As such, the court addresses and remedies mass victimisation, such that the rights that pass to a victim cannot be instantly compared to a domestic trial court. However, the procedural rights granted to victims before the ICC have influenced the development and further ratification of victim rights elsewhere, including greater access to counsel, where domestic courts otherwise have a limited record of granting victims access to counsel (see VLRC, 2015b).

Domestic law provides some access to counsel during the criminal trial. This is better established and embraced across continental European jurisdictions; however, counsel may also be available in the pretrial phase in certain common law countries. In common law, adversarial countries, therefore, rights to counsel are generally provided in accordance with the discrete needs of the victim. The power of the police and prosecution to make charging decisions, including plea deals, generally precludes victim participation (see Verdun-Jones and Yijerino, 2002), with the exception of those decisions made contrary to executive rules of guidance, or where permitted by statute.[6] However, victims do have a general power to challenge pretrial decisions where the accused seeks to subpoena information regarding the victim that is likely to be of limited probative value to the court. Confidential medical information or counselling notes may be subject to challenge and constitutes one scenario where a victim may oppose discovery by appointing private counsel. For example, section 299A of the *Criminal Procedure Act 1986* (NSW) makes standing provisions for victims of sexual offences in criminal proceedings. A protected confider is defined as a victim or alleged victim of a sexual assault offence by, to, or about whom a protected confidence is made. A protected confidence refers to a counselling communication that is made by, to, or about a victim or alleged victim of a sexual assault offence. Section 299A provides the following:

> A protected confider who is not a party may appear in criminal proceedings or preliminary criminal proceedings if a document is sought to be produced or evidence is sought to be adduced that may disclose a protected confidence made by, to or about the protected confider.

The matter of *KS v Veitch (No. 2)* [2012] NSWCCA 266 involved the appointment of private counsel to contest subpoenaed counselling notes that should otherwise have been protected. Such cases demonstrate the inclusion of private counsel as third parties.[7] In this case, the director of public prosecutions watched the brief and the attorney general intervened, but otherwise did not participate in proceedings. Basten JA suggests the victim's right to counsel in such cases:

> The person being counselled, if the victim of the alleged offence, is referred to as the 'principal protected confider' and, though not a party to the criminal proceedings, may appear in those proceedings 'if a document is sought to be produced or evidence is sought to be adduced that may disclose a protected confidence made by, to or about the protected confider': s 299A. (*KS v Veitch* (No 2) [2012] NSWCCA 266, [22])

The United States Code (USC), Federal Rules of Evidence 28 USC Article IV § 412(c), provides rights to counsel in sex offences matters:

> Rule 412. Sex-Offense Cases: The Victim's Sexual Behaviour or Predisposition
>   (c) Procedure to Determine Admissibility.
>   (1) Motion. If a party intends to offer evidence under Rule 412(b), the party must:

(A) file a motion that specifically describes the evidence and states the purpose for which it is to be offered;

(B) do so at least 14 days before trial unless the court, for good cause, sets a different time;

(C) serve the motion on all parties; and

(D) notify the victim or, when appropriate, the victim's guardian or representative.

(2) Hearing. Before admitting evidence under this rule, the court must conduct an in camera hearing and give the victim and parties a right to attend and be heard. Unless the court orders otherwise, the motion, related materials, and the record of the hearing must be and remain sealed.

In the case of *United States v Stamper* (1991) 766 F Supp 1396 (WDNC 1991), the district court determined during a pretrial evidentiary hearing that counsel for 'all three parties' has a capacity to examine witnesses, which would ordinarily include the victim (also see *In re: One Female Juvenile Victim and United States of America v Stamper* (1992) 959 F 2d 231).

In Ireland, the *Sex Offences Act 2001* (Ire) provides that a sex offences victim may retain counsel to question the admission of evidence to establish the victim's sexual history. Changes to the law of evidence in Scotland, however, go beyond the right to contest the victim's sexual history for rules to protect victims who may be required to be cross-examined on character or sexual history, pursuant to the *Sexual Offences (Procedure and Evidence) (Scotland) Act 2002* (Scot) and the *Vulnerable Witnesses (Scotland) Act* 2004 (Scot). These Acts recognise the at-risk status of sex offences victims and limit counsel's ability to cross-examine such victims. These rules allow counsel to represent victims in the pretrial phase where an application is made for pretrial discovery (Raitt, 2010, 2013). The *Victims and Witnesses (Scotland) Act 2014* (Scot) expands these protections to child and vulnerable victims during the trial phase. This reform expands the availability of private counsel beyond the pretrial phase, to afford vulnerable victims and witnesses support during the main trial phase (also see Hoyano, 2015: 119).

Braun (2014) analyses points of convergence between adversarial and inquisitorial systems and notes that while differences exist in terms of party standing and equality of arms arrangements, counsel for sexual assault victims need not necessarily compromise the accused's right to a fair trial. Rather than allying the prosecution, counsel for victims in interlocutory matters may enhance victim participation regarding directions that involve rights to maintain one's dignity and privacy. However, Braun (2014) notes that while similarities exist between the German system of affording vulnerable victims enhanced representation under the German Code of Criminal Procedure 1987, these similarities are limited to the support of victims with discrete needs in the trial process. The use of state-funded legal representation in the German system may thus demonstrate a degree of convergence, although there is less of a case to argue for the development of rights to accessory prosecution within adversarial systems of justice. However, Braun (2014: 825) notes a degree of conflation may be feasible given the benefits of legal representation during the trial proper:

Affording sexual assault victims the right to be legally represented could therefore increase their confidence in criminal trials and contribute to reducing anxiety over their treatment in the criminal process. This could potentially increase the low reporting rates and reduce the high attrition rates in sexual assault cases.

Moreover, affording victims the right to legal representation could help to increase the low conviction rates in sexual assault cases. The cross-examination of legally represented sexual assault victims could be faster and the content of a victim's testimony more accurate. As previously noted, sexual assault victims can find testifying in court to be a traumatising and stressful experience.

The German Code of Criminal Procedure 1987, amended 2014, provides pursuant to section 395 the right to join as a private accessory prosecutor, and section 397 the rights of the private accessory prosecutor. The relevant provisions are extracted in Chapter 2 at 5.8 and allow the victim to retain counsel to appear at trial in order to challenge a judge or an expert, to ask questions, to object to orders by the presiding judge, to object to questions, to apply for evidence to be taken, and to make statements. Unless otherwise provided by law, the accessory prosecutor shall be called in and heard to the same extent as the public prosecutor.

Substantive and enforceable rights for victims of crime

There have been broader movements aside from those regarding the emergence of protective measures in the law of evidence and criminal procedure, and the victim's access to private counsel. The emergence of substantive and enforceable victim rights brings together the first two areas traced in this section but does so in the context of the domestic ratification of international and regional standards that seek to grant victims a rights-based framework that provides accessible rights to substantive justice. This is in contrast to those rights that grant the victim levels of promised treatment, or perhaps access to information, but are otherwise rights that are non-enforceable in character. The emergence of participatory rights in the ICC and the integration of victim interests in the jurisprudence of the ECtHR provide background to the increased momentum towards providing victims with an enforceable rights framework against the accused and state. Such frameworks are particularly novel in common law jurisdictions, where victims are otherwise afforded few substantive rights. This section indicates how international law and procedure may influence the rights-based frameworks of domestic jurisdictions, where international rules and standards may encourage the offering of rights consistent with their mixed or hybrid context of convergence between adversarial and inquisitorial, or civil law traditions, where victims may already possess rights to challenge key defence and prosecution decisions.

The jurisprudence of the ECtHR has influenced the development of laws and procedures which cater to the vulnerable status of the victim, and these rules are increasingly finding their way into domestic laws and policies to better protect the victim. Increasingly, these processes are of right to the victim, such that they may give rise to rights which may be enforced against the accused where they are owed to the victim in court. The framework decisions and directives of the EU have also directed member states to ratify rights to procedural safeguards in the criminal trial process. The CEU DVC 2012, extracted in Chapter 2 at 5.4, indicates the rights framework that encourages the ratification of certain enforceable rights for victims. This extract sets out Articles 10 and 11 of the 2012 directive of the EU Parliament and Council, which provides for participation and the tenure of evidence, as well the victim's power to seek review of the decision not to proceed with a prosecution.

The ability to tender evidence is presently supported in a range of ways, with significant variance between jurisdictions. Continental European states may allow the victim to make submissions and to examine witnesses through modes of accessory prosecution. Common law countries will take a more restrictive approach. However, most allow the victim to make relevant submissions regarding discrete aspects of the pretrial and sentencing process. The use of counsel to challenge confidential communication subpoenas as noted earlier provides one demonstration of this. The other involves the use of victim impact statements (VIS) and community impact statements (CIS) as evidence available throughout proceedings. In England and Wales, for example, the *Criminal Justice Act 1967* (UK), section 9, and *Criminal Procedure Rules 2010* (UK), Part 27, allow statements to be tendered and accepted as evidence. Community impact evidence may be drafted in this fashion, submitted to the court by whoever is able to do so by law or statute. Often this will be an office holder who is appointed to represent the perspective of the community. This may be a police officer, as in England and Wales, or other public official, such as a local mayor, or in Canada, under the *Victims Bill of Rights Act 2015* (Can), the lieutenant governor in council, or executive, of the province in which the court exercises jurisdiction. For VIS, this will be the victim of crime.

The case of *R v Killick* [2011] EWCA Crim 1608 provides a case study of the ratification of the directive of the EU that victims are able to seek review of the decision not to prosecute. This case, in which the Court of Appeal of England and Wales considered the 2011 CEU DD (now finalised as the 2012 CEU DVC), sets out a rule for the development of a rights framework that allows victims to seek review of the CPS decision not to prosecute or to continue with a matter. *R v Killick* indicates that the consideration of human rights instruments in domestic court decisions provides a feasible means by which victims may be granted enforceable rights on a domestic level. This is particularly important where the content of such rights is otherwise unknown to the legal system seeking ratification. In *R v Killick*, the CPS made the decision not to prosecute, bringing complaints from the victims about that decision. An internal review was provided under the existing CPS complaints procedure. The review supported the original decision. Another 'third-tier' review by the CPS found that the accused could be prosecuted. The accused requested that the proceedings be stayed as an abuse of process, but the court rejected this submission, and the accused was put on trial and convicted.

Examining the draft provisions of the 2011 CEU DD, the Court of Appeal of England and Wales (Criminal Division) ruled that the 'decision not to prosecute is in reality a final decision for a victim, there must be a right to seek a review of such a decision, particularly as the police have such a right under the charging guidance' (par. 48). The Crown argued that victims had no right to request a review because the CPS has an existing complaints procedure.[8] The submission essentially sought to preserve the right to review as that of the CPS and not the victim. The directive of the EU envisages that this would be a victim-led process. However, given the obligation to consider and then ratify instruments of the EU, the court of appeal held that:

> [w]e can discern no reason why what these complainants were doing was other than exercising their right to seek a review about the prosecutor's decision. That right under the law and procedure of England and Wales is in essence the same as the right expressed in Article 10 of the Draft European Union Directive on establishing minimum standards on the rights, support and protection of victims of crime dated 18 May 2011 which

provides: 'Member States shall ensure that victims have the right to have any decision not to prosecute reviewed.' (*R v Killick* [2011] EWCA Crim, 1608, par. 49)

Following this judgement, the director of public prosecutions for England and Wales issued the *Victims Right to Review Guidance* in July 2014 (CPS, 2014; Director of Public Prosecutions for England and Wales, 2014). This guidance sets out the circumstances and procedures through which victims may seek to review a decision not to prosecute. The CPS guidance (CPS, 2014: 3; also see City of London Police, 2015) makes clear those circumstances that may give rise to the review mechanisms:

The right to request a review arises where the CPS:

(i) makes the decision not to bring proceedings (i.e. at the pre-charge stage); or

(ii) decides to discontinue (or withdraw in the Magistrates' Court) all charges involving the victim, thereby entirely ending all proceedings relating to them;

(iii) offers no evidence in all proceedings relating to the victim; or

(iv) decides to leave all charges in the proceedings to 'lie on file'.

Where the CPS decides not to proceed, the victim will be informed of its decision to do so. The CPS will indicate whether the decision is a qualifying decision, which if so, gives rise to the review mechanisms. The ratification of the victim's right to review through alternative means of court judgement and its articulation through the policies of the director of public prosecutions establish case in point the validity of alternative means to inculcate international and regional instruments on the local level.

Restorative justice

The emergence of restorative justice and alternative pathways to justice, particularly for offences in the lower domestic courts, has assisted the relocation of the victim into the criminal justice system. Courts are now empowered to consider restorative options for offenders that may connect them to victims through processes that encourage an apology, making amends, conferencing, or mediation. These options are increasingly recognised as sentencing options but may also be available in pretrial processes, and may be set as a condition of bail. However, restorative practices not only have evolved at the local level of domestic court practice but also are identified as part of the constitutive principles of trial participation in the international human rights courts and tribunals. The modes of participation across such tribunals, in particular the focus on establishing the truth regarding human rights violations or atrocities, may encourage reconciliation and restoration through such processes. Therefore, restorative justice occurs through court processes as much as it does through specifically tailored opportunities to connect the victim and the offender in meaningful, beneficial ways. The next section considers therapeutic intervention as a discrete area of development for victims of crime; however, the focus on restorative justice through the strategic design of court processes evidences how restorative justice and therapeutic justice are interconnected concepts.

The ICC is considered a model for the offering of powers that afforded the victim opportunities for participation that may assist in the restoration. Opportunities to participate potentially span the pretrial, trial, and appeal phases in the ICC, and victims are able to make submissions, call evidence, and even examine witnesses, through counsel. This significantly develops the rules of procedure and evidence of the ICTY and the ICTR which do not grant victims standing or a participatory role. Pena and Carayon (2013: 521) have argued that the ICC develops its restorative context by drawing from other international truth commissions, such as the ICTR and ICTY, which seek to establish the truth of the violations being prosecuted:

> In this victim-centered or victim-oriented movement, the victim goes from the position of 'object' to that of 'subject.' It is generally agreed that restorative justice comprises a series of principles and values that include not only reparation but also the participation of victims in redress processes, respect for victims' dignity and recognition of the victim and the harm suffered as a result of a crime. In that regard, parallels can be drawn between trials and other transitional justice measures, particularly truth commissions.

The level of victim participation before the ICC has been controversial (see Zappala, 2010). However, modes of victim participation are permitted that encourage a therapeutic intervention by allowing victims to make submissions that may be taken into account in the substantive outcomes of the court.

Wemmers (2009, 2010) has argued that the ICC integrates the principles of restorative justice in a procedural model which makes court processes available to victims. The ICC model can therefore be characterised as an integrative one; however, Wemmers (2009: 416) has been critical of the lack of party status afforded to victims. Despite being granted participatory rights with leave of the court, the dichotomy between state and defence is maintained, and victims do not have equal standing, such that 'we need to begin to recognize that crime affects victims as well as society and that victims belong in the criminal justice system.' The preamble of the Rome Statute reminds us of the place of victims in the daily work of the court: 'Mindful that during this century millions of children, women and men have been victims of unimaginable atrocities that deeply shock the conscience of humanity'. Despite the limitations and lack of party status, the ICC model presents a criminal trial that includes the principles of restorative justice and does this in a way that overcomes the usual practices of removing the victim from adversarial processes which limit victim participation to witness alone. The restorative benefits of the ICC model arguably derive from the fact that the victim may participate throughout proceedings, with the assistance of counsel, rather than proceed through discrete trial processes that limit victim participation to particular statements, such as a VIS, or to particular programmes, such as mediation, conducted outside court. However, a substantial focus on the role of the victim may detract from the work of the court such that it may become more difficult to effectively determine if an offence has been actually committed (see Damaška, 2009).

On the domestic level, restorative programmes generally include those that divert young offenders from the court system altogether, including youth justice conferencing, or those that involve alternative sentencing processes, such as forum and circle sentencing. Intervention programmes may also be available as a final sentencing option, requiring offender participation in a community justice programme that connects the victim with the offender. Courts usually have several options from which to choose, depending on the type of intervention appropriate to the offender and the availability of the victim. Programmes may include making amends-type programmes, where the offender meets the victim, such as graffiti control, serious traffic offenders, those combating drug addiction, community work, or work for the victim, or meeting with the victim to offer of an apology in a controlled, facilitated setting. Although not all modes of court-based restorative justice connect offender and victim, most seek to involve the victim out of recognition that the interaction between offender and victim in a voluntary and consensual context may assist the recovery of the victim and the restoration of the offender (Morris, 2002, Van Ness, 2003). The German Code of Criminal Procedure 1987, amended 2014, section 153a, Provisional Dispensing with Court Action, Provisional Termination of Proceedings, provides access to restorative process in the case of misdemeanours dealt with by a criminal court. The public prosecutor may, with the consent of the accused and court, dispense with criminal charges and impose conditions upon the accused as extracted in Chapter 2 at 8.7.

Restorative programmes as alternative or adjunctive court processes may encourage restorative outcomes because they provide for the direct participation of the victim (see Van Camp and Wemmers, 2013; van Dijk, 2013; Restorative Justice Council, 2014). The direct modes of participation, similar to the ICC model of participatory justice, allow victims to affect the outcome of intervention proceedings as relevant to an offender. The outcome of the programme may be particularly important to an offender out of a personal, private need to display contrition or seek forgiveness, or because the outcome is to be factored into the final sentence of the court. Several intervention and restorative justice programmes invite participation from the victim personally. Forum and circle sentencing in NSW courts provides a direct role for the victim in the sentencing process, by allowing the victim to contribute to the 'circle' by making statements and offering opinions on the offence and relevant sentencing options that would otherwise not be permitted in court. Youth justice conferencing diverts young offenders from court proceedings altogether, where offenders may meet the victim, under the supervision of a conference facilitator.

International and regional protocols increasingly call for the development of restorative justice principles into criminal justice mechanisms of member states. While this has occurred where members are signatories, or may be part of existing procedural arrangements as found across civil law jurisdictions, policy transfer between jurisdictions has also realised the potential of restorative processes and programmes. Many jurisdictions now offer modes of pre- and post-sentence intervention as important opportunities for intervention.[9] As such restorative justice processes are increasingly seen as the main arena for the offering of justice solutions relevant to offenders, replacing the criminal trial or hearing altogether (see Braithwaite, 2003). The engagement of various participants – contrition from the offender, the understanding from the victim, and a willingness to take responsibility and offer an apology or remedy to the victim – means that restorative practices are increasingly embraced as principles of justice on the international level. Although restorative processes will not always bring about a desired outcome, such practices increasingly supplement normative trial process. Furthermore, restorative justice brings the victim into the justice process as an engaged, direct participant of justice.

Therapeutic justice

The usefulness of legal processes as modes of delivering therapy to the victims has deservedly received critical attention and analysis. While some herald the use of court processes as enhancing the victim's ability to heal following a crime, others have criticised the capacity of the justice system to deliver meaningful therapeutic intervention to any extent. Creating new court processes for victims on the basis that they supposedly add to the therapeutic experience of the victim but which contribute little or nothing to the substantive outcome to be decided upon is particularly dubious, as these processes lull victims into a false sense that their participation actually matters, when it does not (see Erez, 2004; Cassell and Erez, 2011). Debate remains as to the potential benefits and detriments of identifying court processes as therapeutic intervention for victims. The common ground between these positions may identify that where existing processes can be reformed to enhance a potential therapeutic outcome for victims then a jurisdiction is morally obliged to change the process to assist victims, even if it means that the process is only slightly more pleasant or protective than before. The evolution of VIS in the sentencing phase in common law jurisdictions provides a case study of the justification of court processes that are partly justified out of the therapeutic intervention they provide for victims (Cassell, 2009), albeit some victims may experience degrees of secondary victimisation where they present emotionally to the court. This may occur for less serious offences, because the victim statement may be taken to be less creditable when compared to more serious offences (Lens, van Doorn, Lahlah, Pemberton, and Bogaerts, 2016).

It is well recognised that processes may lead to therapeutic outcomes for victims where they include the victim in a direct and meaningful may. Care must be taken to avoid secondary victimisation and trauma (Cassell and Erez, 2011: 171). Not all invitation to be included in court or justice system processes will be met enthusiastically by victims, who may seek to minimise their contact with the system. However, where possible, court and other justice authorities ought to design their processes to accommodate the needs of victims, to minimise trauma to the victim, and to enhance beneficial outcomes, including restoration and rehabilitation. Research conducted in the ICC demonstrates that substantive participation that brings the victim within the system of court operations, including the investigation, prosecutorial decisions, the offering of evidence, and decisions of the court, encourages therapeutic outcomes for victims (see Wemmers, 2009; Pena and Carayon, 2013). Being taken seriously is essential (see Erez, 2004). The offering of processes to merely contain the victim in a court process with a view to therapeutic intervention which does not lead to a substantive outcome may confound the trauma to the victim.

In common law, adversarial jurisdictions, substantive participation was initially offered to victims in the form of VIS in the sentencing process. Such initiatives sought to provide victims with an opportunity to tell of the impact of the crime in their own words. Schemes were widely introduced in legislation in the 1990s. The availability of VIS for most offences, and now CIS for community perspectives on the harm caused, demonstrates the movement of victim rights from procedural justice to substantive rights, in an adversarial context that was always hostile to victim participation beyond that of witness for prosecution. Originally, the VIS was tolerated as a process that granted the victim a degree of personal and therapeutic intervention, not otherwise relevant to court processes. However, courts have increasingly come to see the merit of such statements as potentially relevant to the sentencing process. This is particularly so for sex offences where the trauma to the victim is ongoing. This has arguably increased their potential as relevant to the sentencing process, which maximises their use as therapeutic aids for victims. As courts and normative justice stakeholders accept that the VIS is an important source of information in the sentencing process, victims are increasingly being taken seriously and not excluded as prejudicial to the ends of justice. This is an outcome that brings victims in common law, adversarial jurisdictions slightly closer to victims in civil law countries, where counsel is able to make submissions across all phases of the trial, including sentencing for the punishment and preventive detention of the accused.

A focus on reparations

The international human rights instruments that bear relevance to the declaration of victim rights provide a focus on the nuances of reparations as relevant to the remedies available to the international court. Reparations may be characterised separately from compensation and restitution because reparations can be constituted through on-pecuniary orders that do not involve awards of damages or the return or repair of property. Rather, reparations may be defined as making amends for a wrong that has been done. As such, reparations may be constituted through acts of restorative justice, and may even include an apology. Reparations may be defined more broadly, however, to include restitution from the offender or compensation from a fund or trust, or from the state. Increasingly, international and regional instruments include reference to the provision of reparations, in addition to mechanisms for restitution and compensation, which may even be of benefit to the development of local approaches in common law jurisdictions (Doak, 2015).

The international level of the ICC makes specific provisions for reparations proceedings. In the reparations decision in *The Prosecutor v Thomas Lubanga Dyilo* (ICC-01/04–01/06–2904, 7 August 2012, Decision Establishing the Principles and Procedures to be Applied to Reparations), Trial Chamber I provided various general principles for the determination of reparations. In doing so, the chamber did not attempt to limit the scope of reparations in accordance with its definition as a principle of general application, nor did the chamber restrict the award of reparations to specific persons, nor detail how they should be specifically supplied. Instead, the chamber ruled that principal responsibility for reparations lay with the Trust Fund for Victims. The chamber determined that a collective approach to the reparation of victims was best where gross violations meant that numerous victims would be seeking compensation or restitution, although the chamber also acknowledged that individual reparations might be warranted. In the particular matter of *The Prosecutor v Lubanga*, the ICC determined that funds ought to be allocated from the Trust Fund for Victims as at the time of trial accused was indigent.

The ICC ruled that the primary function of reparations was as follows, at par. [179]:

> Reparations fulfil two main purposes that are enshrined in the Statute: they oblige those responsible for serious crimes to repair the harm they caused to the victims and they enable the Chamber to ensure that offenders account for their acts. Furthermore, reparations can be directed at particular individuals, as well as contributing more broadly to the communities that were affected. Reparations in the present case must – to the extent achievable – relieve the suffering caused by these offences; afford justice to the victims by alleviating the consequences of the wrongful acts; deter future violations; and contribute to the effective reintegration of former child soldiers. Reparations can assist in promoting reconciliation between the convicted person, the victims of the crimes and the affected communities (without making Mr Lubanga's participation in this process mandatory).

The chamber also considered alternative modes of reparations, including the role of apology, despite indicating a reluctance to issue such a request as part of a reparations order, at par. [269]:

> The convicted person has been declared indigent and no assets or property have been identified that can be used for the purposes of reparations. The Chamber is, therefore,

of the view that Mr Lubanga is only able to contribute to non-monetary reparations. Any participation on his part in symbolic reparations, such as a public or private apology to the victims, is only appropriate with his agreement. Accordingly, these measures will not form part of any Court order.

The ICC indicates that the welfare of victims is an important consideration in the context of restoring community and personal life, and 'should guarantee the development of the victims' personalities, talents and abilities to the fullest possible extent and, more broadly, they should ensure the development of respect for human rights and fundamental freedoms', at par. [213]. The limits of reparations for the ICC lie in its inability to monitor extended programmes of restoration. However, the ICC may rule that an award ought to cover an extended programme of rehabilitation that could be administered by the Trust Fund for Victims. The ICC Registry and Office of Public Counsel for Victims and other partner organisations may be able to assist through non-pecuniary measures for victims, as part of the ongoing functions of each office and the overall responsibilities of the court. The institutional capacity of the ICC may therefore help overcome any specific limitation regarding reparation because the multiple offices that make up the ICC have a particular duty to victims and their forward restoration (see Mégret, 2014a).

Compensation and restitution

While the international courts have moved towards reparation that includes non-pecuniary awards to support and rehabilitate local populations devastated by war or other atrocities, domestic courts continue to focus on restitution and compensation. Increasingly, however, courts are moving to restitution from the offender directly in order to communicate the policy directive that offenders take responsibility for the trauma and harm they have caused. Domestic courts increasingly order offenders to compensate the victim directly for the loss that the victim has incurred as a result of the offence. Although domestic courts have been able to order compensation for restitution for some time, usually commensurate with the rise of victims' compensation in the 1960s and 1970s, the tendency has been to utilise state funds to compensate victims and to have this allocated by government authority or tribunal outside of court (Miers, 2014a, 2014b; Ministry of Justice, 2012a; see *R (JC) v First-tier Tribunal Criminal Injuries Compensation: Reasons* [2010] UKUT 396 (AAC); *CICA v First-tier Tribunal and CP (CIC)* [2013] UKUT 0638). England and Wales and South Australia (SA), however, now have the power to issue a restitution order as part of the sentence of the accused (see *Powers of Criminal Courts (Sentencing) Act 2000* (UK) sections 130, 148–149; *Criminal Injuries Compensation Act 1995* (UK); *Criminal Law (Sentencing) Act, 1988* (SA) section 53). These Acts grant the courts the ability to order repayment of a loss caused to a victim, and to factor this into the proportionate sentence of the accused. The *Powers of Criminal Courts (Sentencing) Act 2000* (UK), sections 149–149, also allows for restitution of property such that stolen goods be restored to the victim or to any person entitled to them, where the accused has continuing possession of the goods in question. This order may be made by the victim or by others entitled to the goods. Where an accused has otherwise sold or profited from the transfer of the stolen goods, the victim is entitled to recover the proceeds of that transfer, or order that the victim or another person be paid an equivalent amount.

Restitution and the recovery of stolen property are thus a key initiative empowering victims in the sentencing process in England and Wales. The holding of the accused to account by requiring that the offender repay victims is outlined as a policy directive in England and Wales by the UK government in *Breaking the Cycle: Government Response* (Ministry of Justice, 2011b: 5): 'We will make offenders pay back to victims and society for the harm they have caused – both directly and indirectly.' Conflating payment of compensation, restitution, and punishment offers new means of restoring the victim in the justice process. Victims have the power to seek a civil claim in the context of the continental European criminal trial by adhesive proceedings that may involve participation through counsel, or by seeking such an order as part of the sentencing process. This process may be referred to as an adhesive prosecution, where the civil claim is adhered to the state prosecution claim, to be determined in connection with the offender's liability to punishment. The court hearing the primary charge against the accused will therefore specify the award of compensation to be paid by the accused. The German Code of Criminal Procedure 1987, amended 2014, section 403, provides that the aggrieved person or his or her heir may bring a property claim against the accused as connected to the criminal offence. Section 405 allows the court to award a settlement in respect of the claim arising from the criminal offence (extracted in Chapter 2 at 7.9).

Notes

1 See, for example, the discussion of the Japanese legal system as an example of a mixed or hybrid system in Chapter 6.
2 See discussion of law reform processes in this section.
3 As to the continued relevance of local customary law, see the Panchayat system of informal justice founded in village rule in India, discussed in Chapter 6.
4 Letters Patent, *Royal Commission into Institutional Responses to Child Sexual Abuse*, 11 January 2013. Terms of reference include: 'NOW THEREFORE We do, by these Our Letters Patent issued in Our name by Our Governor-General of the Commonwealth of Australia on the advice of the Federal Executive Council and under the Constitution of the Commonwealth of Australia, the Royal Commissions Act 1902 and every other enabling power, appoint you to be a Commission of inquiry, and require and authorise you, to inquire into institutional responses to allegations and incidents of child sexual abuse and related matters, and in particular, without limiting the scope of your inquiry, the following matters: a. what institutions and governments should do to better protect children against child sexual abuse and related matters in institutional contexts in the future; b. what institutions and governments should do to achieve best practice in encouraging the reporting of, and responding to reports or information about, allegations, incidents or risks of child sexual abuse and related matters in institutional contexts; c. what should be done to eliminate or reduce impediments that currently exist for responding appropriately to child sexual abuse and related matters in institutional contexts, including addressing failures in, and impediments to, reporting, investigating and responding to allegations and incidents of abuse; d. what institutions and governments should do to address, or alleviate the impact of, past and future child sexual abuse and related matters in institutional contexts, including, in particular, in ensuring justice for victims through the provision of redress by institutions, processes for referral for investigation and prosecution and support services. AND We direct you to make any recommendations arising out of your inquiry that you consider appropriate, including recommendations about any policy, legislative, administrative or structural reforms. AND, without limiting the scope of your inquiry or the scope of any recommendations arising out of your inquiry that you may consider appropriate, We direct you, for the purposes of your inquiry and recommendations, to have regard to the following matters: e. the experience of people directly or indirectly affected by child sexual abuse and related matters in institutional contexts, and the provision of opportunities for them to share their experiences in appropriate ways while recognising that many of them will be severely traumatised or will have special support needs; f. the need to focus your inquiry and recommendations on systemic issues, recognising nevertheless that you will be informed by individual cases and may need to make referrals to appropriate authorities in individual cases;

g. the adequacy and appropriateness of the responses by institutions, and their officials, to reports and information about allegations, incidents or risks of child sexual abuse and related matters in institutional contexts; h. changes to laws, policies, practices and systems that have improved over time the ability of institutions and governments to better protect against and respond to child sexual abuse and related matters in institutional contexts.'

5 A 'victims' right to review scheme' at police level was implemented as of 1 April 2015 'for all National Recording Standard Offences'. City of London Police, Victims' Right to Review Scheme.

6 See *R v DPP, Ex parte C* (1995) 1 Cr App R 136; *Maxwell v The Queen* (1996) 184 CLR 501; also see section 35A, *Crimes (Sentencing Procedure) Act 1999* (NSW), as to consultative rights between police and victims where further charges are taken into account upon sentencing.

7 Cf. Canadian Criminal Code, RSC 1985 C-46, sections 278.1–278.91; Federal Rules of Evidence 28 USC Art. IV § 412(a)–(c).

8 Although characterised as a complaints procedure, the CPS process is not initiated out of dissatisfaction with any particular prosecutor, but may be invoked where a questionable decision has been reached.

9 See the recent changed in England and Wales, where the *Crimes and Court Act 2013* (UK) cements restorative intervention in the pre-sentencing process by amending the *Powers of Criminal Courts (Sentencing) Act 2000* (UK) to allow for the court to defer sentencing to enable an offender to participate in a restorative justice activity. Post-sentence, the *Offender Rehabilitation Act 2014* (UK) amends the *Criminal Justice Act 2003* (UK) to offer a rehabilitation activity requirement as part of sentence. Extracted in Chapter 2 at 8.2 as to the requirements of the 2012 CEU DVC regarding the ratification of restorative justice principles on the domestic level.

Part II

The victim in internationalised systems of criminal justice

4 Victims in international law and policy

Introduction

The international level of human rights and the constitutive bodies, courts, and tribunals which exercise a jurisdiction under international law have proven to be a significant source of inspiration for the development of victim rights into the twenty-first century. While rights frameworks continue to develop on the international and regional level, the ratification of these frameworks on the local, domestic level of individual jurisdictions establishes the argument of this book that international and regional human rights discourses are developed in the particular context of local jurisdictional concerns (see Beigbeder, 2011).

This chapter will set out the international level of victim rights that offer various rights frameworks and court processes that establish the victim is a substantive agent of justice into the twenty-first century. The declarations and conventions of the UN and the role of treaty monitoring bodies and the international courts, specifically the *ad hoc* tribunals, including the Nuremberg and Tokyo Tribunals, the ICTY, and the ICTR, will be discussed as preceding the establishment of the ICC. Despite the lack of clear process to enable the direct participation of victims other than as witnesses, the *ad hoc* tribunals made a significant contribution to internationalised justice by focusing on victim interests in new ways, but seeking to establish the truth of war crimes and human rights atrocities, in a way that distinguishes these courts from tasks of the domestic, local criminal courts. The establishing of the ICC, however controversially, provided a greater role for victims despite a lack of party standing.

This chapter will also set out the role of the domestic courts that exercise an international jurisdiction, or alternatively, a local jurisdiction under international law. The ECCC, SPTL, and IPK will be discussed as continuing to support the rights of the victims to participate in international trials, with the ECCC providing an example as to how such trials may operate with respect to victims as a standing party to proceedings.

Supranational bodies

The supranational level of human rights organisations provides international, intergovernmental governance and intervention where human rights issues and abuses go beyond the capacity or control of any one national government. Alternatively, the supranational level is also required where the conduct of any one state falls below standards that are required under international law. Where a country is already a signatory to the governing body, and to particular treaties or resolutions, bringing that country into the framework of international rights may be expected, though complete ratification is not always certain. Where a country falls outside the jurisdiction of the supranational organisation, pressure may be applied through international channels and diplomacy to bring that country within international standards. Almost all countries of the world are member states of the UN, founded in 1945, which is now well positioned to advocate a normative praxis of victim rights and interests to traverse regional and local politics and justice traditions, to express rights and powers of fundamental concern to victims globally.

United Nations declarations

The development of victim rights at the UN level supports the internationalisation of victim rights norms and principles that ought to be of universal application worldwide. Through a process of ratification, many states have enacted the declarations and conventions, either partially or completely, in local law and policies for the security and protection of specific victims, or for the enactment of a fair process that ought to be afforded to victims. Most importantly, however, the UN is well positioned to influence the normative context of victim rights and the instruments of the UN continue to identify areas of risk and reform for victims and other stakeholders related to the exercise and expression of victim rights. As member states draw from various legal traditions, the instruments of the UN encourage convergence between jurisdictions by recognising victim rights and powers that draw from inquisitorial and adversarial contexts (see van Boven, 1999; Alston and Mégret, 2013).

The UN International Covenant on Economic, Social and Cultural Rights, International Covenant on Civil and Political Rights and Optional Protocol to the International Covenant on Civil and Political Rights, resolution GA/RES/2200(XXI) A-C of the General Assembly on 16 December 1966, and in force 23 March 1976 (ICCPR), established an early substantive, international framework for victims regarding access to justice by establishing certain fundamental rights to civil and political freedom, including the right to life, freedom of religion, freedom of speech, freedom of assembly, electoral rights, and rights to due process and a fair trial. Although the ICCPR sought to centre defendant rights, it did so by emphasising fair trial rights and access to justice for all. The ICCPR has been ratified to different extents across signatory states. New Zealand, for example, chose to incorporate various measures contained in the ICCPR into local law under the *New Zealand Bill of Rights Act 1990* (NZ).[1] The core provisions, including the right to liberty and security of the person, have led many jurisdictions to enact laws that seek to protect groups and populations specifically at risk of vilification. Section 20 of the 1990 New Zealand Act provides, for example, protection for individuals on the basis of their identification as ethnic, religious, and linguistic minorities.

In 1985, the PJVC provided the first major declaration for the benefit of crime victims and those subject to abuses of power that led to the integration and development of new approaches to victim rights on an international, regional, and local level. Domestic rights frameworks covered in Chapter 6 also continue to draw from the substantive provisions of the declaration (extracted in Chapter 2 at 1.1, 2.1, 3.1, 4.1, 5.1, 7.1, 8.1, 9.1, 10.2). Many conventions first enumerated in the 1985 PJVC have been ratified into rights for fair treatment, for provision of information relevant to the victim, to facilitate access to justice, and to compensate victims and provide for restitution. Many jurisdictions have since extended these local declarations or charters, and some are now progressing towards substantive and enforceable rights frameworks.[2] The UN has continued to pursue a normative basis for victim rights by developing rights-based frameworks with regard to particular threats to the dignity of particular groups or classes of victims. This includes remedial options not otherwise covered by the PJVC, which identifies remedies in the context of local, domestic systems. The Basic Principles and Guidelines on the Right to a Remedy and Reparation for Victims of Gross Violations of International Human Rights Law and Serious Violations of International Humanitarian Law by the UN Commission on Human Rights and by the UN General Assembly in 2005 (RRRVGV) were developed out of recognition of the particular needs of victims of gross violations of human rights, where the reparation of such harms was beyond the remit of a localised or domestic framework. The 1985 PJVC and 2005 RRRVGV declarations constitute a concerted framework for the expression of the right of victims in the administration of criminal justice at the international and domestic level, with the 2005 RRRVGV consolidating an international approach around the victim's right to reparations and the duty of the state to ensure sufficient funds and other support services are available to assist victims. The 1985 PJVC was the first major international instrument to provide victims access to justice in addition to a range of other rights to compensation and reparations, and access to justice generally. This instrument placed expectations of ratification on signatories that sought new relationships and levels of respect between victims and traditional justice stakeholders, and the domestic ratification process was intended to develop normative principles of victim rights on the domestic level, thereby modifying the justice system of ratifying states to include the victim in new and substantive ways. The 2005 RRRVGV enumerated the duties of the state to investigate gross violations of human rights under international law and procedure, to bring perpetrators to justice, and to further develop a system of remedies and reparation for victims, in aid of establishing the 'truth' of the violation.

Combined, the PJVC and the RRRVGV are major instruments guiding the normative context of international victim rights law and policy, and their influence continues today, even where not directly ratified by states, by setting out a broader policy framework which amplifies victim rights as important, substantive rights that are of a fundamental character. The instruments encourage member states to ratify a coherent range of victim rights by considering the need to access different levels and forms of justice, and by transforming domestic law to be one that accounts for the role of the victim as a substantive participant of justice. While the PJVC focuses on the reform of domestic systems in light of international norms and standards, the RRRVGV focuses on reparations as a remedy more appropriate for mass victimisation. These declarations, however, act to provide a framework that identifies the different participatory needs of victim as stakeholders of justice, and as relevant to the administration of justice, by setting out fundamental rights to justice, redress for wrongdoing, and access to compensation. The specific rights are extracted in Chapter 2 but a useful summary includes the following:

- Extract 1.1 **Resolution 4** victims ought to be treated with compassion and respect for their dignity;
- Extract 2.1 **Resolution 6(a)** informing victims of their role and the scope, timing and progress of the proceedings and of the disposition of their cases;
- Extract 3.1 **Resolution 6(c)** the responsiveness of judicial and administrative processes to the needs of victims should be facilitated by providing proper assistance to victims throughout the legal process; **Resolution 14** victims should receive the necessary material, medical, psychological and social assistance through governmental, voluntary, community-based and indigenous means;
- **Resolution 15** victims should be informed of the availability of health and social services and other relevant assistance and be readily afforded access to them; **Resolution 16** police, justice, health, social service and other personnel concerned should receive

training to sensitize them to the needs of victims, and guidelines to ensure proper and prompt aid; **Resolution 17** in providing services and assistance to victims, attention should be given to those who have special needs because of the nature of the harm inflicted . . .;

- Extract 4.1 **Resolution 6(d)** taking measures to minimize inconvenience to victims, protect their privacy, when necessary, and ensure their safety, as well as that of their families and witnesses on their behalf, from intimidation and retaliation;
- Extract 5.1 **Resolution 6(b)** allowing the views and concerns of victims to be presented and considered at appropriate stages of the proceedings where their personal interests are affected, without prejudice to the accused and consistent with the relevant national criminal justice system . . .;
- Extract 7.1 **Resolution 8** offenders or third parties responsible for their behaviour should, where appropriate, make fair restitution to victims, their families or dependants; **Resolution 9** governments should review their practices, regulations and laws to consider restitution as an available sentencing option in criminal cases, in addition to other criminal sanctions; **Resolution 10** in cases of substantial harm to the environment, restitution . . . should include restoration of the environment, reconstruction of the infrastructure, replacement of community facilities and reimbursement of the expenses of relocation, whenever such harm results in the dislocation of a community; **Resolution 11** where public officials or other agents acting in an official or quasi-official capacity have violated national criminal laws, the victims should receive restitution from the State whose officials or agents were responsible for the harm inflicted . . . **Resolution 12** when compensation is not fully available from the offender or other sources, States should endeavour to provide financial compensation to . . . victims and their families . . . **Resolution 13** national funds for compensation to victims should be encouraged . . .;
- Extract 8.1 **Resolution 7** mediation, arbitration and customary justice or indigenous practices, should be utilized where appropriate to facilitate conciliation and redress for victims;
- Extract 9.1 **Resolution 1** necessity of adopting national and international measures in order to secure the universal and effective recognition of, and respect for, the rights of victims of crime and of abuse of power . . .; and
- Extract 10.2 **Resolution 2** the need to promote progress by all States in their efforts to that end, without prejudice to the rights of suspects or offenders.

The 2005 RRRVGV builds upon this framework with respect to foundational victim rights to access justice, but also includes specific reference to reparations as interconnected in international law and procedure and, as already ratified in the ICC, as noted in the preamble of the RRRVGV:

> *Reaffirming* the principles enunciated in the Declaration of Basic Principles of Justice for Victims of Crime and Abuse of Power, including that victims should be treated with compassion and respect for their dignity, have their right to access to justice and redress mechanisms fully respected, and that the establishment, strengthening and expansion of national funds for compensation to victims should be encouraged, together with the expeditious development of appropriate rights and remedies for victims.
>
> *Noting* that the Rome Statute of the International Criminal Court requires the establishment of 'principles relating to reparations to, or in respect of, victims, including

restitution, compensation and rehabilitation', requires the Assembly of States Parties to establish a trust fund for the benefit of victims of crimes within the jurisdiction of the Court, and of the families of such victims, and mandates the Court 'to protect the safety, physical and psychological well-being, dignity and privacy of victims' and to permit the participation of victims at all 'stages of the proceedings determined to be appropriate by the Court'.

Affirming that the Basic Principles and Guidelines contained herein are directed at gross violations of international human rights law and serious violations of international humanitarian law which, by their very grave nature, constitute an affront to human dignity.

The specific rights are extracted in Chapter 2 but a useful summary includes the following:

- Extracts 1.2 and 3.2 **Resolution 10** victims should be treated with humanity and respect for their dignity and human rights, and appropriate measures should be taken to ensure their safety, physical and psychological well-being and privacy . . . The State should ensure that its domestic laws, to the extent possible, provide that a victim who has suffered violence or trauma should benefit from special consideration and care to avoid his or her re-traumatization in the course of legal and administrative procedures designed to provide justice and reparation;
- Extract 5.2 **Resolution 8** victims are persons who individually or collectively suffered harm, including physical or mental injury, emotional suffering, economic loss or substantial impairment of their fundamental rights, through acts or omissions that constitute gross violations of international human rights law, or serious violations of international humanitarian law; **Resolution 9** a person shall be considered a victim regardless of whether the perpetrator of the violation is identified, apprehended, prosecuted, or convicted and regardless of the familial relationship between the perpetrator and the victim; **Resolution 12** a victim of a gross violation of international human rights law or of a serious violation of international humanitarian law shall have equal access to an effective judicial remedy as provided for under international law . . . . States should: (a) Disseminate, through public and private mechanisms, information about all available remedies for gross violations of international human rights law and serious violations of international humanitarian law; (b) Take measures to minimize the inconvenience to victims and their representatives, protect against unlawful interference with their privacy as appropriate and ensure their safety from intimidation and retaliation, as well as that of their families and witnesses, before, during and after judicial, administrative, or other proceedings that affect the interests of victims; (c) Provide proper assistance to victims seeking access to justice; (d) Make available all appropriate legal, diplomatic and consular means to ensure that victims can exercise their rights to remedy for gross violations of international human rights law or serious violations of international humanitarian law; **Resolution 13** States should endeavour to develop procedures to allow groups of victims to present claims for reparation and to receive reparation, as appropriate; **Resolution 14** an adequate, effective and prompt remedy for gross violations of international human rights law or serious violations of international humanitarian law should include all available and appropriate international processes in which a person may have legal standing and should be without prejudice to any other domestic remedies;
- Extract 7.2 **Resolution 11** remedies for gross violations of international human rights law and serious violations of international humanitarian law include the victim's

right to the following as provided for under international law: (a) Equal and effective access to justice; (b) Adequate, effective and prompt reparation for harm suffered; (c) Access to relevant information concerning violations and reparation mechanisms; **Resolution 15** prompt reparation is intended to promote justice by redressing gross violations of international human rights law or serious violations of international humanitarian law. Reparation should be proportional to the gravity of the violations and the harm suffered . . . In cases where a person, a legal person, or other entity is found liable for reparation to a victim, such party should provide reparation to the victim or compensate the State if the State has already provided reparation to the victim; **Resolution 16** States should endeavour to establish national programmes for reparation and other assistance to victims . . .; **Resolution 17** States shall, with respect to claims by victims, enforce domestic judgements for reparation against individuals or entities liable for the harm suffered and endeavour to enforce valid foreign legal judgements for reparation . . .; **Resolution 18** victims of gross violations of international human rights law and serious violations of international humanitarian law should, as appropriate and proportional to the gravity of the violation and the circumstances of each case . . .; **Resolution 19** Restitution should, whenever possible, restore the victim to the original situation before the gross violations of international human rights law . . . Restitution includes, as appropriate: restoration of liberty, enjoyment of human rights, identity, family life and citizenship, return to one's place of residence, restoration of employment and return of property; **Resolution 20** Compensation should be provided for any economically assessable damage, as appropriate and proportional to the gravity of the violation and the circumstances of each case; and

- Extract 9.2 **Resolution 1** if they have not already done so, States shall, as required under international law, ensure that their domestic law is consistent with their international legal obligations by: (a) Incorporating norms of international human rights law and international humanitarian law into their domestic law, or otherwise implementing them in their domestic legal system; (b) Adopting appropriate and effective legislative and administrative procedures and other appropriate measures that provide fair, effective and prompt access to justice; (c) Making available adequate, effective, prompt and appropriate remedies, including reparation, as defined below; (d) Ensuring that their domestic law provides at least the same level of protection for victims as that required by their international obligations.

The 1985 PJVC and 2005 RRRVGV declarations have significantly influenced domestic law and policy by encouraging states to provide victim rights that set out substantive, enforceable rights to justice. This policy directive distinguishes the past practice of providing victims non-enforceable rights that encourage a level of fair or courteous treatment, with perhaps some recourse to compensation or limited reparations, but do not allow for substantive participation in decision-making processes. This trend towards substantive, enforceable rights has been continued in direct ways under the European frameworks developed by the EU and ECtHR. The development of local charters or declarations of rights encourages administrators of justice, the police, prosecutions, and affiliated non-government organisations (NGOs) to treat victims in a professional way, by respecting the victim. The Victim's Code is an example of such a framework, developed out of respective human rights instruments, including the PJVC and RRRVGV, in so far as it applied to domestic law and order. The genesis of a rights framework at the level of the UN therefore continued to influence the development of local approaches, and latter amendments have included the right to access information and be kept informed. However, recent changes to domestic frameworks include the movement towards declarations of enforceable rights, such as providing victims consultative rights with the public prosecutor or state attorney, specifically regarding charge decision-making and plea deals.[3] The significance of the 1985 PJVC and 2005 RRRVGV declarations, therefore, is that they have repositioned the victim as an international agent of justice down to the local level. By focusing on international human rights across legal traditions and nationalised systems of law and policy, the 1985 PJVC and 2005 RRRVGV have made victim rights relevant to local policies and debates about the place of the victim in localised systems of criminal justice. This has encouraged the development of a rights framework that provides a hierarchy of rights from levels of basic treatment and respect to rights enforceable against the state, including justice stakeholders normatively positioned to control justice operations by exercising a key discretion to charge and prosecute. The 1985 PJVC and 2005 RRRVGV declarations thus establish a policy framework to be expanded upon on the domestic level, permitting increased internationalisation of victim rights by transcending regional and national boundaries, by making certain rights normative. This policy framework has been further developed by the UN though resolutions regarding child victims and other disadvantaged groups.

The Guidelines on Justice in Matters involving Child Victims and Witnesses of Crime, for example, established by the UN Economic and Social Council in 2005 ('UNESC Guidelines'), provide for the protection of child victims, including children who have witnessed crime. The 2005 UNESC Guidelines protect the dignity of child victims, encouraging the development of policies which treat such victims with compassion, and without discrimination. Child victims are to be granted the rights of adult victims, which specifically involve such rights as the capacity to access information on judicial processes relating to the victim, for the child victim to be heard, and to express his or her views and concerns on justice processes, and rights for effective assistance in order to prepare for court. The UNESC Guidelines also provide rights to privacy, safety, and reparation.

Other declarations that form a framework of victim rights and powers as adopted by the UN General Assembly oblige states to implement the universal jurisdiction granted to enforce specific victim rights. The Convention against Torture and Other Cruel, Inhuman or Degrading Treatment or Punishment of the UN General Assembly in 1984 (CAT) established base-level treatment and constitutes an offence of acts of torture within a domestic jurisdiction in accordance with Article 4. If the state does not extradite a suspect of torture, then it should submit the case for prosecution in the home jurisdiction. Articles 5 and 14 of the CAT provide the following:

> **Article 5** 1. Each State Party shall take such measures as may be necessary to establish its jurisdiction over the offences referred to in article 4 in the following cases: (a) When the offences are committed in any territory under its jurisdiction or on board a ship or aircraft registered in that State; (b) When the alleged offender is a national of that State; (c) When the victim is a national of that State if that State considers it appropriate. 2. Each State Party shall likewise take such measures as may be necessary to establish its jurisdiction over such offences in cases where the alleged offender is present in any territory under its jurisdiction and it does not extradite him pursuant to article 8 to any of the States mentioned in paragraph I of this article. 3. This Convention does not exclude any criminal jurisdiction exercised in accordance with internal law.
> **Article 14** 1. Each State Party shall ensure in its legal system that the victim of an act of torture obtains redress and has an enforceable right to fair and adequate compensation,

including the means for as full rehabilitation as possible. In the event of the death of the victim as a result of an act of torture, his dependants shall be entitled to compensation. 2. Nothing in this article shall affect any right of the victim or other persons to compensation which may exist under national law.

The Declaration on the Protection of All Persons from Enforced Disappearance by the UN General Assembly in 1992, and later the International Convention on the Protection of All Persons from Enforced Disappearance by the UN General Assembly in 2006, provides a universal jurisdiction that recognises the disappeared persons before the law, provides for the security of the person, provides that the person not be subject to torture, and provides the right to identity, reparation, and the truth of the matter. The preamble of the 1992 Declaration provides that enforced disappearance transpires when:

> [P]ersons are arrested, detained or abducted against their will or otherwise deprived of their liberty by officials of different branches or levels of Government, or by organized groups or private individuals acting on behalf of, or with the support, direct or indirect, consent or acquiescence of the Government, followed by a refusal to disclose the fate or whereabouts of the persons concerned or a refusal to acknowledge the deprivation of their liberty, which places such persons outside the protection of the law.

The four Geneva Conventions 1864–1949 and amending protocols and the final tribunal of the United Nations Security Council (UNSC) oblige states to search for persons or alleged offenders who are suspected as committing breaches of the Conventions, and to extradite offenders where a case for prosecution is made out.

Treaty monitoring bodies

The treaty monitoring bodies of the UN determine state fulfilment of international human rights frameworks and conventions. The treaty monitoring bodies are panels of experts that assess state compliance with the core conventions. States submit regular reports to the committees that make up the monitoring bodies, who may then provide recommendations back to the state for implementation. In limited circumstances, the treaty monitoring bodies may take a complaint from a victim personally, but would otherwise monitor compliance to prevent abuse of human rights in member states in the first instance.

The committees include: the Human Rights Committee, which oversees the implementation of the 1976 ICCPR; the Committee on the Elimination of Racial Discrimination, which monitors the implementation of the International Convention on the Elimination of all forms of Racial Discrimination (ICERD); the Committee against Torture, which monitors the implementation of the 1984 UN CAT; the Committee on the Elimination of All Forms of Discrimination against Women, which monitors the implementation of the Convention on the Elimination of All Forms of Discrimination against Women (CEDAW); the Committee on the Protection of the Rights of All Migrant Workers and Members of Their Families, which monitors the implementation of the International Convention on the Protection of the Rights of All Migrant Workers and Members of Their Families (ICMW); and the Committee on the Rights of Persons with Disabilities, which monitors the implementation of the International Convention on the Rights of Persons with Disabilities (ICRPD).

International courts and tribunals

The international courts comprise those courts on the international level that deal with cases involving human rights abuses the world over, or within a particular region or territory. These may include *ad hoc* international courts. Domestic courts may also operate under international law, or are otherwise convened under international law and procedure, despite dealing with cases within a domestic or home jurisdiction. The Nuremberg and Tokyo Tribunals, the ICTY, and the ICTR, together with the ICC, make up the international tribunals, with the ICC being the permanent tribunal or court. The domestic tribunals that are convened under international law include the ECCC, SPTL, and the IPK. International courts and tribunals are generally established by UN protocol or by agreement of the UN and domestic government (see Bellelli, 2010; Isaacs, 2016).

Ad hoc *tribunals: the Nuremberg and Tokyo Tribunals, the International Criminal Tribunal for the Former Yugoslavia, and the International Criminal Tribunal for Rwanda*

The significance of the *ad hoc* tribunals lies in their focus on truth and reconciliation, and not in any particular role afforded to the victim other than that of a witness before each tribunal. The *ad hoc* tribunals are therefore not known for progressive modes of victim participation as we may see with the ICC; however, the focus on establishing a true account of the criminal atrocities and human rights abuses of victims provides renewed focus on the rights of victims as stakeholders of justice (see, generally, Bellelli, 2010: 12–14). Thus, even though victims were not granted party status nor rights of participation to be involved in or make submissions seeking to influence decision-making processes, the first tribunals did establish a modern international system of laws and procedures for the determination and remedying of gross violations of human rights. This focus on gross violations of human rights was nonetheless victim-focused, despite a paucity of rights and powers identifiable to individual victim rights as we see them emerge today. However, these *ad hoc* tribunals did lead to the extension of international laws and practices regarding discrete victim rights over time. The development of *ad hoc* tribunals helped established a recognisable set of international laws and procedures that function to maintain access to human rights, and the trial mechanism established by the first tribunals saw this body of law develop to the point of the establishing of permanent courts and tribunals where victims have been granted individual powers and processes. Further, the *ad hoc* tribunals have developed the customary range of human rights including principles of post-conflict resolution, by standardising the rules that apply to post-conflict zones and encouraging the local adoption of international standards and processes. International human rights law as implemented and developed through the *ad hoc* tribunals has also sought to end impunity by developing an international criminal law and justice system. Such laws have required states to ratify legislation against impunity for international crimes and gross violations of human rights, encouraging the internationalisation of individual state responsibility for war crimes and crimes against humanity (see Beigbeder, 2011: 20–48).

The Nuremberg and Tokyo Tribunals were established following the Second World War. The four major allied powers of France, the Soviet Union, the UK, and the USA established the International Military Tribunal (IMT) in Nuremberg, Germany, to prosecute and punish war criminals. The IMT, known as the Nuremburg Tribunal, tried senior Nazi political and military figures. The International Military Tribunal for the Far East (IMTFE), known as the Tokyo Tribunal, tried the leaders of the Empire of Japan for their war crimes. The Nuremberg and Tokyo Tribunals were heard separately according to different arrangements and jurisdiction. The St James Declaration of 1942 sought to prosecute senior German political and military leaders; however, this was followed by the 1945 London Agreement, which formalised processes by establishing the IMT, creating the Charter of the International Military Tribunal, which set out the tribunal's functions and jurisdiction. The Nuremberg Tribunal was constituted by a single judge and prosecuting team from the separate allied powers. Article 6 of the Charter of the International Military Tribunal – Annex to the Agreement for the Prosecution and Punishment of the Major War Criminals of the European Axis ('Nuremberg Charter') sets out the war crimes that could be prosecuted:

(a) Crimes against Peace: namely, planning, preparation, initiation or waging of a war of aggression, or a war in violation of international treaties, agreements or assurances, or participation in a Common Plan or Conspiracy for the accomplishment of any of the foregoing;

(b) War Crimes: namely, violations of the laws or customs of war. Such violations shall include, but not be limited to, murder, ill-treatment or deportation to slave labor or for any other purpose of civilian population of or in occupied territory, murder or ill-treatment of prisoners of war or persons on the seas, killing of hostages, plunder of public or private property, wanton destruction of cities, towns, or villages, or devastation not justified by military necessity;

(c) Crimes against Humanity: namely, murder, extermination, enslavement, deportation, and other inhumane acts committed against any civilian population, before or during the war, or persecutions on political, racial, or religious grounds in execution of or in connection with any crime within the jurisdiction of the Tribunal, whether or not in violation of domestic law of the country where perpetrated.

The Nuremberg and Tokyo Tribunals sought to prosecute and punish only major war crimes figures. Following the Tribunals, other war criminals were prosecuted by domestic courts or tribunals. The Nuremberg and Tokyo Tribunals did not afford a substantial role for victims of war crimes. However, each contributed to a developing international criminal law. Prior to the war crimes tribunals of the 1990s, the Nuremberg and Tokyo Tribunals provided the main examples of an international war crimes tribunal. As such, these tribunals were seen as a precedent for new international criminal tribunals, as found in the ICTY and ICTR.

The ICTY and ICTR represent *ad hoc* tribunals established by the UN with a duty to hear prosecutions to determine and punish gross violations of human rights (see Bassiouni, 2006: 209–210). Although not providing a role for the victim, the tribunal gave renewed focus on the plight of the victim by seeking to establish the 'truth' of the atrocities of each location, thereby engaging the voice of the victim in the fact-finding process.

The ICTY was established by the UN in order to redress the mass atrocities in Croatia and Bosnia and Herzegovina. The crimes included the killing of thousands of civilians, as well as the torture and sexual assault of persons held in detention camps. Many thousands of citizens were dislocated. The ICTY was the first war crimes tribunal since the Nuremberg and Tokyo Tribunals and was established by the UN Security Council under chapter 7 of the UN Charter. The ICTY's main objective was to prosecute persons most responsible for murder, torture, rape, enslavement, and the destruction of property prescribed under the

ICTY's statute. The statute of the ICTY prescribes various rights for victim protection and support. Although these do not grant the victim standing or rights of actual participation beyond the role of witness, the ICTY does centre victims in the context of allowing victims to present their version of evidence in order to establish the facts and truth of the matter. The statute of the ICTY provides the following:

> **Article 20** Commencement and conduct of trial proceedings 1. The Trial Chambers shall ensure that a trial is fair and expeditious and that proceedings are conducted in accordance with the rules of procedure and evidence, with full respect for the rights of the accused and due regard for the protection of victims and witnesses.
> **Article 22** Protection of victims and witnesses. The International Tribunal shall provide in its rules of procedure and evidence for the protection of victims and witnesses. Such protection measures shall include, but shall not be limited to, the conduct of in camera proceedings and the protection of the victim's identity.

The Rules of Procedure and Evidence of the ICTY further provide:

> **Rule 69** Protection of Victims and Witnesses (A) In exceptional circumstances, the Prosecutor may apply to a Judge or Trial Chamber to order the non-disclosure of the identity of a victim or witness who may be in danger or at risk until such person is brought under the protection of the Tribunal. (B) In the determination of protective measures for victims and witnesses, the Judge or Trial Chamber may consult the Victims and Witnesses Section. (C) Subject to Rule 75, the identity of the victim or witness shall be disclosed in sufficient time prior to the trial to allow adequate time for preparation of the defence.

The case of *The Prosecutor v Dragomir Milošević* (IT-98–29/1-A) Appeals Chamber, 12 November 2009, sets out the scope of relevant victims or victim populations that may be heard under the ICTY statute. The court rules at par. [58]:

> Concerning the status of victims of crimes under Article 5 of the Statute, the Appeals Chamber recalls that 'there is nothing in the text of Article 5 of the Statute, or previous authorities of the Appeals Chamber, that requires that individual victims of crimes against humanity be civilians'. Nonetheless, it notes that the civilian status of the victims remains relevant for the purpose of the *chapeau* requirement of Article 5 of the Statute as one of the factors to be assessed in determining whether the civilian population was the primary target of an attack. Furthermore, 'the fact that a population, under the *chapeau* of Article 5 of the Statute, must be "civilian" does not imply that such population shall only be comprised of civilians. Accordingly, the civilian status of the victims and the proportion of civilians within a population are factors relevant to satisfy the *chapeau* requirement that an attack was directed against a "civilian population", yet it is not an element of the crimes against humanity that individual victims of the underlying crimes be civilians'.

The matter of *The Prosecutor v Zdravko Tolimir* (IT-05–88/2-A) Appeals Chamber, 8 April 2015, further clarifies the requisite test for the identification of victims relevant to Article 5 of the ICTY statute, at par. [141]:

> With respect to Tolimir's argument that the Trial Chamber erred in law in applying an incorrect standard to establish the mens rea of extermination by not requiring that

the civilian population was the intended target of mass murder, the Appeals Chamber recalls that, as noted by the Trial Chamber, it is well-established that with regard to the victims of the underlying acts of crimes against humanity, '[t]here is nothing in the text of Article 5 of the Statute, or previous authorities of the Appeals Chamber that requires that individual victims of crimes against humanity be civilians'. The Appeals Chamber has more specifically clarified that:

> whereas the civilian status of the victims, the number of civilians, and the propor-tion of civilians within a civilian population are factors relevant to the determination of whether the *chapeau* requirement of Article 5 of the Statute that an attack be directed against a 'civilian population' is fulfilled, there is no requirement nor is it an element of crimes against humanity that the victims of the underlying crimes be 'civilians'.

The case law therefore broadly interprets the identification of victims that gives rise to the jurisdiction of the ICTY. The statute does not restrict the identification of victims to the extermination of civilian populations. It is therefore sufficient that the prosecution offers evidence of the intent to kill on a mass scale. This evidence may support an intent to effect a widespread or systematic attack directed against a civilian population.

The ICTR is identified as a sister tribunal to the ICTY and was similarly established by UN Security Council under Resolution 955 to hold to account those persons responsible for the Rwandan genocide. The operations of the ICTR were expanded several times, with a requirement that the work of the ICTR be completed by 2012. The jurisdiction of the ICTR covers genocide, crimes against humanity, and other war crimes, defined as violations of Common Article Three and Additional Protocol II of the Geneva Conventions. The statute of the ICTR identifies several protections for victims consistent with those available in the ICTY. The ICTR statute provides the following:

> **Article 19** Commencement and conduct of trial proceedings. 1. The Trial Chambers shall ensure that a trial is fair and expeditious and that proceedings are conducted in accordance with the rules of procedure and evidence, with full respect for the rights of the accused with due regard for the protection of victims and witnesses.
> **Article 21** Protection of victims and witnesses. The International Tribunal for Rwanda shall provide in its rules of procedure and evidence for the protection of victims and wit-nesses. Such protection measures shall include, but shall not be limited to, the conduct of in camera proceedings and the protection of the victim's identity.

In the case of *Theoneste Bagorora and Anatole Nsengiyumva v The Prosecutor* (ICTR-98–41-A) Appeals Chamber, 14 December 2011, the court ruled that the protections that ought to be afforded to victims pursuant to the Rules of Procedure and Evidence (see rule 69 extracted earlier for the ICTY) were not insurmountable and required observance of the procedural fairness requirements of justice, at pars [82]–[84]:

> Although the disclosure requirements under Rule 66 of the Rules are subject to Rule 69, the Appeals Chamber recalls that while a Trial Chamber may order the non-disclosure of the identity of a victim or witness who may be in danger or at risk pur-suant to Rule 69(A) of the Rules, it must first establish the existence of exceptional circumstances . . .

. . . the Appeals Chamber does not consider that, as stated by the Trial Chamber, such disregard for the explicit provision of the Rules was necessary for the protection of witnesses. It notes that in the previous witness protection decision in the I case prior to the joinder, the Trial Chamber had ordered the temporary redaction of identifying information until witnesses were brought under the protection of the Tribunal, but had nonetheless required that the Defence be provided with unredacted witnesses statements 'within sufficient time prior to the trial in order to allow the Defence a sufficient amount of time to prepare itself'. At no point did the Trial Chamber indicate that any problems had arisen from this previous arrangement justifying a more restrictive disclosure schedule.

The term 'victim' is defined under the Rules of Procedure and Evidence of both tribunals to include 'a person against whom a crime over which the Tribunal has jurisdiction has allegedly been committed'. The term 'against' restricts the interpretation of harms and injuries that give rise to the jurisdiction of each tribunal to those persons suffering a direct harm as the result of an act or genocide or one of the other enumerated war crimes. This meant that certain victims were excluded, although the tribunals did seek to expand the application of victims to whom the offences related pursuant to *The Prosecutor v Zdravko Tolimir*, discussed earlier. It is, however, the broader framing of each tribunal that provides their foundation in international law and procedure with respect to the development of victim rights norms. Despite a lack of participatory rights and jurisprudence that would otherwise characterise the rights of victims before each tribunal, the Rules of Procedure and Evidence did allow for victim and witness support, and provided measures for victim protection, particularly where there were reasonable concerns for reprisal or retaliation (see Knoops, 2014). Greater focus was placed upon the offering of services to victims, particularly psychological and physical rehabilitation for victims of rape and sexual assault. The ICTY and ICTR are, however, credited as substantially developing international human rights law and procedure, which developed the need for a permanent international court to deal with criminal matters.

The International Criminal Court

The ICC developed out of the successes and limitations of the *ad hoc* tribunals and the recognised need to establish a permanent court with jurisdiction over international causes and crimes. The statute of the ICC (A/Conf 183/9) was ratified in Rome on 17 July 1998. It came into effect on 1 July 2002. The ICC is constituted through a pretrial chamber, a trial chamber, and an appeals chamber. The development of the Rome Statute and ICC is derived from the standards and practices of international law and of the various international courts with concern over gross violations of human rights (Bassiouni, 1999). The jurisprudence regarding the participation of victims in the ICC flows largely from remarks made in the matter from the Democratic Republic of Congo, brought by the International Federation for Human Rights. In the matter, the *Decision on the Applications for Participation in the Proceedings of VPRS 1–6*, Pre-Trial Chamber I (ICC 01/04, 17 January 2006), the ICC held the following with regard to the participation of victims in hearings before the ICC, at par. [51]:

In the Chamber's opinion, the Statute grants victims an independent voice and role in proceedings before the Court. It should be possible to exercise this independence, in particular, vis-à-vis the Prosecutor of the International Criminal Court so that victims can present their interests. As the European Court has affirmed on several occasions, victims participating in criminal proceedings cannot be regarded as 'either the opponent – or for that matter necessarily the ally – of the prosecution, their roles and objectives being clearly different'. (Citations omitted)

Victims may participate personally, or with the assistance of counsel, pursuant to Article 68(3) of the Rome Statute:

> Where the personal interests of the victims are affected, the Court shall permit their views and concerns to be presented and considered at stages of the proceedings determined to be appropriate by the Court and in a manner which is not prejudicial to or inconsistent with the rights of the accused and a fair and impartial trial. Such views and concerns may be presented by the legal representatives of the victims where the Court considers it appropriate, in accordance with the Rules of Procedure and Evidence.

The Rome Statute provides for the enactment of the Rules of Procedure and Evidence of the ICC. The Rules of Procedure and Evidence provide a framework through which victims participate in proceedings.[4] Where victims are seeking to participate in proceedings, they make an application to the court. The requisite pretrial chamber determines the status of individual applicants as actual victims before the court, to determine if their injuries and trauma are within the jurisdictional responsibilities of the court. Once established as actual victims before the ICC, the pretrial chamber determines their mode of participation, and specifically whether they will proceed through counsel. The registrar will usually require that victims proceed through common counsel where many victims present to the court. Victims may choose their own representative or may allow the court to allocate counsel, particularly where multiple victims present.

Under the ICC model, the Rules of Procedure and Evidence provide the participatory rights of the victim consistent with those of the partie civile, acting alongside the state and accused. The participation of the victim has been referred to as partie civile; however, the role of the victim in the ICC merges with the role of the victim in civil law, so that the victim as participant before the ICC takes on a role similar to the accessory and adhesive prosecutor in the continental European tradition. Victims as partie civile before the ICC may even be characterised as an intervener or amicus curiae, as they lack party status and present in order to make submissions and produce evidence necessary for the establishing of the 'truth' of the accusation. The Rules of Procedure and Evidence identify relevant provisions for victims under chapter 4, section 3, which provides rules regarding the participation of victims and witnesses. These rules allow for protective and special measures, for victim participation before the different chambers of the ICC, and for participation through counsel, as well as victim input into the determination of reparations (see Wyngaert, 2011; Mégret, 2014a; Moffett, 2014; Wemmers, 2014b). Counsel is able to be nominated by victims to allow for formal participating in hearings. Counsel acting for victims may examine witnesses already before the court, make submissions on fact or law, address the court during opening and closing addresses, and submit new evidence, with leave of the court. As victims lack party standing before the ICC, victims must apply to participate during the pretrial phase. Counsel acting for victims must observe the general requirements of the equality of arms between prosecution and defence, as required by the court (Jackson, 2009; Johnson, 2009). Rule 91(3)(b) provides the following:

> The Chamber shall then issue a ruling on the request, taking into account the stage of the proceedings, the rights of the accused, the interests of witnesses, the need for a fair, impartial and expeditious trial and in order to give effect to article 68, paragraph 3. The ruling may include directions on the manner and order of the questions and the production of documents in accordance with the powers of the Chamber under article 64. The Chamber may, if it considers it appropriate, put the question to the witness, expert or accused on behalf of the victim's legal representative.

In the case of *The Prosecutor v Katanga and Chui*, Appeals Chamber (ICC- 01/04–01/07, 22 January 2010, Judgement Entitled 'Decision on the Modalities of Victim Participation at Trial'), the ICC ruled the following, at par. [52]:

> . . . article 68(3) does not preclude the Legal Representatives of the Victims from being permitted to request the Chamber to order the submission of certain evidence. The Chamber would point out that this is not a right, but a mere possibility granted to the victims, under certain conditions, in order to give full effect to the provisions of article 68(3) of the Statute, after having duly balanced their interests with those of the accused.

The Rome Statute lacks a specific provision setting out an equality of arms between the prosecution and defence. However, the ICC nonetheless requires a degree of fairness between trial participants. Where hearings depart from the required adversarial exchange between prosecution and defence for the inclusion of the victim, the court requires that the submissions and questions of counsel representing victims adhere to the standing of the prosecution and their role as bringing the case to answer, and the fairness requirements of the accused, that allow the court to reject unfair or prejudicial evidence. Thus the ICC allows victim participation where the views of the victim may be relevant to the establishing of a fact relevant to the court, but will otherwise limit participation where the rights of the prosecution and defence to progress the case or to test or challenge relevant evidence ought to prevail. Some have argued that this participation evidences a shift from a retributive model of justice to one that is restorative, based on the capacity for victim participation and their intervening in proceedings that otherwise, under an adversarial-hybrid model, ought to limit or to preclude non-party participation (see War Crimes Research Office, 2009; Ochoa, 2013: 36; also see War Crimes Research Office, 2007). Counsel representing victims has participated in pretrial hearings to bring to the court's attention any evidence that may otherwise be relevant in the trial phase.[5] As such, participation during the trial phase is not as frequent, where the concerns of victims may be better addressed through the evidence on record before the court than through victim-led submissions and calls for new evidence. The court is also necessarily guarded out of the requirement of maintaining fairness to the prosecution and defendant.

The role and functions of the ICC as an international tribunal that determines liability for abuse of human rights limit the extent to which the court may be directly comparable to domestic trial courts. Although adopting a model of adversarial exchange between parties and the bench, the role of the victim and the focus on the international practice of establishing the 'truth' of the matter mean that the court has been characterised as adversarial, with some qualities found in an inquisitorial model of justice. Johnson (2009: 491) argues that the ICC is still to be regarded as adversarial, against other approaches to justice:

> The ICC is more adversarial than inquisitorial in its structure. The ICC prosecutor presents his case to the court as an adversary; we do not have a recognizable civil law system at the ICC where an investigating magistrate collects and presents evidence in a more complete format in an attempt to find the truth. Instead, the parties litigate the inclusion and exclusion of evidence before the court.

The Prosecutor v Lubanga and *Prosecutor v Katanga and Chui*, discussed in Chapter 2 in the context of fair trial rights and equality of arms requirements in international justice, indicate that victims enjoy foundational powers before the ICC, distinguishing the court from other international courts that lack specific powers for victim participation. The court is further distinguished from local, domestic adversarial courts in common law states. The inclusion of the victim in the Rome Statute and in the Rules of Procedure and Evidence focuses the court's jurisdiction around a set of arrangements that, despite acknowledging limitations on victim participation in accordance with equality of arms requirements, nonetheless establishes the court's jurisdiction as a hybrid system that develops principally as an adversarial court but with substantive victim rights that characterise the court as at least of mixed tradition. The development of the ICC out of different legal traditions supports the argument that the ICC model represents one of convergence between legal traditions (see Schwikkard, 2008). However, the merging of traditions has left the ICC open to criticism that the compromised due process requirements afforded to accused persons undermine the integrity of the court as a tribunal that deals with major international crimes (Johnson, 2009). The ICC generally is regarded as more adversarial than inquisitorial, where the role of the victim is regulated as an additional participant that must work in accordance with the requirement that parties that constitute the court are those with recognised standing before the court. Pena and Carayon (2013: 534) argue that the role of victims is regulated in accordance with the assumption that they are not part of the prosecution and that their role is limited to that of intervenor:

> One of the aspects of participation regarding which victims have expressed dissatisfaction is their inability to influence the charges brought against the accused. According to the Court's jurisprudence, a link must be established between the harm suffered by the victim and the charges brought against the accused and the incidents for which s/he will be tried. Given that the ICC prosecutor has adopted a policy of 'focused investigations and prosecutions,' this requirement poses significant challenges, in practice leaving many victims out of the scope of the cases. Although the prosecutor has pledged to ensure that investigations and prosecutions are representative of the whole scope of criminality and the main forms of victimization practice has demonstrated that this is not always the case.

The ICC maintains an adversarial character by reference to the requirement that the court determine the course of the investigation and the prosecution determine relevant charges from the outset. Although both investigation and prosecution seek to represent the interests of the victim, they do not answer to them, and must ensure that the evidence is established independently of the concerns of particular victims and individuals affected by the alleged crimes. Although this presents as antithetical to the interests of victims, the work of the ICC proceeds on the basis that victims are essential to the mission of the court, and that victims will alert investigators to evidence that established the facts of each allegation and the overall truth of the case that is prosecuted. Significantly, however, the case before the ICC is never taken over by the victim or his or her individual interests, despite providing a specific role for victims in court.

The ICC is also empowered to hear and determine reparations orders under Article 75 of the Rome Statute. The ICC may consider an order for reparations against an offender or state following a guilty plea or a conviction in the trial phase. The ICC will consider reparations where victims participate before the court or where particular orders are sought against a particular accused. The ICC may grant a reparations order against individual offenders, which may include a pecuniary component. The Trust Fund for Victims, established under Article 79 of the Rome Statute, will also serve to meet the costs of a reparation (or compensation or restitution) order where an accused is indigent. The Trust Fund for Victims may also be drawn upon as an alternative to proceedings (Keller, 2007; McCarthy, 2012).

The capacity to grant an order of reparations is provided pursuant to Article 75(2) of the Rome Statute:

> The Court may make an order directly against a convicted person specifying appropriate reparations to, or in respect of, victims, including restitution, compensation and rehabilitation.
>
> Where appropriate, the Court may order that the award for reparations be made through the Trust Fund provided for in article 79.

Victims apply to the Victims Participation and Reparations Section of the ICC Registry where reparations orders are sought. The determination of reparations may include an award of compensation or restitution. Reparations are ordinarily determined at the end of the trial phase, after liability for the substantive offences and crimes is established. Where guilt is determined, the court will consider applications for reparations, which may require a greater degree of participation from the victim. The reparations phase may require that new evidence be presented. This may mean that witnesses are called to testify to the terms of the orders sought. As reparations orders draw from the evidence presented at trial, reparations may become part of the trial process in so far as they may be included in the trial process as an expedient means of putting relevant questions to witnesses and victims testifying at trial. This may overcome the burden of multiple appearances. Difficulty arises, however, where questions that relate to reparations are put to witnesses because those questions may assume the guilt of the accused, denying the accused of their due process rights during trial (Keller, 2007; McCarthy, 2012).

The ICC recognises the valuable role of reparations in the fulfilment of the remit of the court's role to restore victims to their pre-victimised position. The matter of *The Prosecutor v Lubanga* (ICC-01/04–01/06–2904, 7 August 2012, Decision Establishing the Principles and Procedures to be Applied to Reparations) provided the ICC's guidelines for reparations orders. The court sought to provide a broad approach to the determination of reparations. In particular, the court refused to limit the range of reparations orders that could be made and the people to which such orders may apply. The court identified the Trust Fund for Victims as the principal authority for reparations, as the administrative authority for the management of reparations orders. Where the court is confronted with mass victimisation out of gross violations of human rights, a collective award may best meet the needs of the many victims who cannot be easily identified on an individual basis, and non-pecuniary orders may be relevant in such circumstances. However, individual reparations may continue to be awarded. In *The Prosecutor v Lubanga*, the ICC determined that an award should be made from the Trust Fund for Victims because the accused is destitute.

The ICC indicates the main rationale of reparations at par. [179]:

> Reparations fulfil two main purposes that are enshrined in the Statute: they oblige those responsible for serious crimes to repair the harm they caused to the victims and they enable the Chamber to ensure that offenders account for their acts. Furthermore, reparations can be directed at particular individuals, as well as contributing more broadly to the communities that were affected. Reparations in the present case must – to the extent achievable – relieve the suffering caused by these offences; afford justice to the victims by alleviating the consequences of the wrongful acts; deter future violations; and contribute to the effective reintegration of former child soldiers. Reparations can assist in promoting reconciliation between the convicted person, the victims of the crimes and the affected communities (without making Mr Lubanga's participation in this process mandatory).

The ICC further provides context for the other orders which may restore the victim. The court considered the relevance of restitution, compensation, and rehabilitation, before focusing on pecuniary compensation, at par. [269]:

> The convicted person has been declared indigent and no assets or property have been identified that can be used for the purposes of reparations. The Chamber is, therefore, of the view that Mr Lubanga is only able to contribute to non-monetary reparations. Any participation on his part in symbolic reparations, such as a public or private apology to the victims, is only appropriate with his agreement. Accordingly, these measures will not form part of any Court order.

Reparations before the ICC go beyond pecuniary compensation and extend to improving the welfare of victims. This satisfied the remit of the ICC as to the need to restore victims and communities following gross violations of human rights. The case of *The Prosecutor v Lubanga* makes this clear by emphasising that the award of reparations 'should guarantee the development of the victims' personalities, talents and abilities to the fullest possible extent and, more broadly, they should ensure the development of respect for human rights and fundamental freedoms' at par. [213]. Although the court is unable to supervise any extended order that seeks to restore a community over time, which may be essential to particularly vulnerable or traumatised groups of victims, the court is able to utilise the institutional capacity of the ICC and the Trust Fund for Victims in particular, to offer ongoing support to damaged communities. The Registry and Office of Public Counsel for Victims together with partner organisations may be able to assist the Trust Fund for Victims where further restorative measures are needed. The court thus endorses a collective approach to the meting out of reparation, which may be desirable given the ongoing needs of most victims, and the ICC's institutional capacity to manage reparations across its several departments. Distinct from most court awards for compensation, which focuses on a monetary settlement, the ICC may utilise its own expanded administrative framework to the benefit of victims and communities.

Domestic courts under international law

Several courts within a domestic court structure are organised around the principles of international law and procedure. These courts, which comprise the ECCC, SPTL, and IPK, each provide a role for the victim that goes beyond the *ad hoc* framework of allowing the victim to present as witness. In particular, the victim may participate with standing and present as a partie civile in order to bring a prosecution, participate alongside the state as a subsidiary prosecutor, or seek reparations in the capacity as an adhesive prosecutor. The extent to which these rights are available to the victim varies between courts, and is constrained by the rules and procedures that compose them. Collectively, however, they present a substantial departure from domestic courts in common law countries, with key points of connection to the continental European approach and that of the ICC in international law and procedure.

Extraordinary Chambers of the Courts of Cambodia

The ECCC operates under the law and procedure of international law. The ECCC is a domestic court charged with the duty to prosecute senior members of the Khmer Rouge responsible for gross violations of human rights in Kampuchea between 1975 and 1979. The ECCC was constituted through consultation between the UN and the government of Cambodia. The articles of the court were enacted into domestic law, such that the ECCC is part of the domestic court system of Cambodia. The ECCC therefore operates in accordance with Cambodian law and procedure, and it is not otherwise administered by the UN. The ECCC was constituted in 2006 and has received international attention because it presents a court model that provides the victim of crime substantial rights in addition to those normative rights under international law. The instruments establishing the ECCC granted victims substantial powers under Cambodian law. Victim rights include the normative rights of victims to testify as witnesses, but also include novel powers not otherwise seen in the international tribunals, including the ability to act as complainant or partie civile. Cambodian criminal procedure would otherwise enable the victim only to make a complaint, but would not allow the victim to become the complainant, which is a nominal function of the police and prosecution. The use of the tribunal system to address gross violations of human rights has allowed the Cambodian government to expand the role of the victim in addition to adapting standards of criminal procedure found in continental European law and practice. The role of partie civile as adapted to the ECCC model now permits victims to initiate proceedings. This includes circumstances where the state prosecutor decides not to bring proceedings. Victims may also decide to act as a subsidiary prosecutor, alongside the state prosecutor (see Beigbeder, 2011: 145–169; Hinton, 2014; Killean, 2015; Palmer, 2016).

Victims before the ECCC therefore have the capacity to participate in proceedings as a victim might before the ICC. However, they also have standing before the ECCC in their capacity to act as partie civile. Victims therefore have a series of rights and powers that extend beyond other international tribunals. Victims are able to access the case file and evidence collected, and may require that an allegation be investigated where the state prosecutor has not been willing to do so.

The Internal Rules (revised 16 January 2015) set out the requisite victim rights and powers relevant to the role of the victim as partie civile. Rule 23(3) provides the following:

> At the pre-trial stage, Civil Parties participate individually. Civil Parties at the trial stage and beyond shall comprise a single, consolidated group, whose interests are

represented by the Civil Party Lead Co-Lawyers as described in IR 12 *ter*. The Civil Party Lead Co-Lawyers are supported by the Civil Party Lawyers described in IR 12 *ter* (3). Civil Party Lead Co-Lawyers shall file a single claim for collective and moral reparations.

The Internal Rules provide the procedural basis for standing as partie civile. The Internal Rules, rule 23 *bis*. (1), provides the following:

> In order for Civil Party action to be admissible, the Civil Party applicant shall:
>
> a)   be clearly identified; and
> b)   demonstrate as a direct consequence of at least one of the crimes alleged against the Charged Person, that he or she has in fact suffered physical, material or psychological injury upon which a claim of collective and moral reparation might be based.

Victims have the ability to present individually during the investigative phase. However, once the case proceeds to trial, victims are required to be represented by counsel. This is particularly important where the victims present as a group, and representation is required in order allow for the expedient functioning of the court. Victims also possess the capacity to appeal decisions of the trial chamber. Rights of appeal are prescribed under Internal Rules, rule 105(1)(c): 'The Civil Parties may appeal the decision on reparations. Where the Co-Prosecutors have appealed, the Civil Parties may appeal the verdict. They may not appeal the sentence.' The Internal Rules also constitute a Victim Support Section which is required to coordinate services to assist victims seeking to make a partie civile claim. Internal Rules, rule 12 *bis*. (1), prescribes the following:

> The Victims Support Section shall:
>
> a)   Under the supervision of the Co-Prosecutors, assist Victims in lodging complaints;
> b)   Under the supervision of the Co-Investigating Judges, assist victims in submitting Civil Party applications;
> c)   Maintain a list of foreign and national lawyers registered with the BAKC who wish to represent Victims or Victims' Associations before the ECCC;
> d)   Receive, verify and translate applications by foreign lawyers to represent Civil Parties before the ECCC and forward completed applications to BAKC for registration in accordance with the procedure determined by BAKC after consultation with the Victims Support Section;
> e)   Administer applications for admission to the list of Victims' Associations approved to act on behalf of Civil Parties before the ECCC, pursuant to the criteria set out in Rule 23 *quater*, and maintain a list of Victims' Associations so approved;
> f)   Provide general information to victims, especially Civil Parties;
> g)   Under the supervision of the Co-Investigating Judges or the Pre-Trial Chamber, as appropriate, present the above mentioned lists of, and information on, lawyers and Victims Associations to Victims or Civil Parties and facilitate legal representation as described in Rule 23;

h)   Assist and support Civil Party and complainants' attendance in court proceedings;
i)   In consultation with the Civil Party Lead Co-Lawyers and the Public Affairs Section, where appropriate, undertake outreach activities related to Victims, especially Civil Parties; and
j)   Adopt such administrative regulations as required to give effect to this Rule.

The rights of the victim before the ECCC therefore go beyond legislative rights of participation and party status. The ECCC also maintains substantial support mechanisms for the partie civile. This is provided from investigation to appeal. Levels of support are comparable to that offered in the ICC, but are otherwise unparalleled on a domestic basis. The ECCC relies on existing mechanisms for reparations as available under Cambodian law and as are able to be awarded by the court by utilising the existing legal framework. Victims may seek a reparations order from the state where the accused is indigent or otherwise where the state has confiscated proceeds which may now be made available to support victims.

Special Panels of East Timor (Timor Leste)

The Special Panels of East Timor (Timor Leste) were introduced by the UN Transitional Administration in East Timor (UNTAET) to bring to justice those responsible for crimes regarding the referendum of independence in 1999 (see Reiger and Wierda, 2006; Beigbeder, 2011: 125–144; Ochoa, 2013: 216). The special panels are part of the domestic court structure of the District Court of Dili. The special panels exercise their jurisdiction as domestic courts operating under international human rights law. International lawyers and staff investigate matters and proceeds before the special panels. These special panels and the international legal framework that constitutes practice before them are enacted under UNTAET Regulation No. 2000/11 on the Organization of Courts in East Timor (6 March 2000), UNTAET Regulation No. 2000/15 on the Establishment of Panels with Exclusive Jurisdiction over Serious Criminal Offences (6 June 2000), and UNTAET Regulation No. 2000/30 on Transitional Rules of Criminal Procedure (25 September 2000) (see UNTAET, 2000a, 2000b, 2000c):

> **UNTAET Regulation No. 2000/30 on Transitional Rules of Criminal Procedure (25 September 2000) Section 12** The Victim. 12.1 A victim shall be accorded those rights provided in the present regulation, in addition to any other rights provided by law or other UNTAET regulations. 12.2 The status of a person, organization or institution as a victim is not related to whether the perpetrator is identified, apprehended, prosecuted or convicted, and is independent of any familial relationship with the perpetrator. 12.3 Any victim has the right to be heard at a review hearing before the Investigating Judge, and at any hearing on an application for conditional release pursuant to Section 43 of the present regulation. In the exercise of this right, the victim may be represented in court by a legal representative. An individual victim has the right to be notified by the prosecutor, or by the police in proceedings pursuant to Section 44 of the present regulation, in advance of the time and place of review hearings referred to in Sections 20, 29.5 and 43 of the present regulation, provided that the victim has previously indicated in a reasonable manner to the court, prosecutor or investigating officer a desire to be so notified. 12.4 It is not required that the notification of a victim be written or that it be in strict accord with Section 2.4 of the present regulation; provided, however, that the

notice is of a nature which is reasonable under the circumstances and is likely to convey actual notice of the proceedings in sufficient time to permit the exercise of the victim's rights. Defects in the notification of a victim at any stage shall not deprive the Court of jurisdiction to proceed. 12.5 A victim may request to the court to be heard at stages of the criminal proceedings other than review hearings. 12.6 The victim has the right to request the public prosecutor to conduct specific investigations or to take specific measures in order to prove the guilt of the suspect. The public prosecutor may accept or reject the request. 12.7 The Investigating Judge or a court may direct that several victims will be represented in the same case through a single representative. 12.8 The Prosecutor shall take reasonable steps to keep the victims informed of the progress of the case.

UNTAET Regulation No. 2000/11 on the Organization of Courts in East Timor (6 March 2000) Section 27 Legal Representation at Hearings. 27.1 A party to a proceeding before a court in East Timor has the right to a legal representative of its own choosing. 27.2 UNTAET shall ensure that efficient procedures and responsive mechanisms for effective and equal access to lawyers are provided for all persons within the territory of East Timor, without any discrimination based on sex, race, color, language, religion, political or 10 other opinion, national, ethnic or social origin, association with a national minority, property, birth or any other status.

UNTAET Regulation No. 2000/15 on the Establishment of Panels with Exclusive Jurisdiction over Serious Criminal Offences (6 June 2000), Section 24 Witness Protection. 24.1 The panels shall take appropriate measures to protect the safety, physical and psychological well-being, dignity and privacy of victims and witnesses. In so doing, the panels shall have regard to all relevant factors, including age, gender, health and the nature of the crime, in particular, but not limited to, where the crime involves sexual or gender violence or violence against children.

UNTAET Regulation No. 2000/15 on the Establishment of Panels with Exclusive Jurisdiction over Serious Criminal Offences (6 June 2000) Section 25 Trust Fund. 25.1 A Trust Fund may be established by decision of the Transitional Administrator in consultation with the National Consultative Council for the benefit of victims of crimes within the jurisdiction of the panels, and of the families of such victims. 25.2 The panels may order money and other property collected through fines, forfeiture, foreign donors or other means to be transferred to the Trust Fund.

The special panels comprise one national and two international judges. The rules of the special panels were created by reference to those of the ICC. As such, victims possessed enhanced rights powers that grant them standing before the panels pursuant to section 12 of UNTAET Regulation No. 2000/30 and section 27 of UNTAET Regulation No. 2000/11. Victims also enjoy protective measures under UNTAET Regulation No. 2000/15. Victims may request investigations (see UNTAET Regulation No. 2000/30 section 12.6), to be heard during a hearing (see UNTAET Regulation No. 2000/30 sections 12.5, 12.7, 12.8), and to be kept informed throughout proceedings (see UNTAET Regulation No. 2000/30 section 12.8).

Early analysis of the functioning of the special panels raised some concerns as to the integration of the panels in the domestic court structure. This raises the issue of the extent to which the special panels are able to positively influence the development of local laws and policies in an effort to challenge the normative culture of the court towards offenders and offences:

It is also unclear whether the Special Panels have been able to add to the development of law at the national level, particularly given the limited interaction between the Special Panels and judges of the ordinary national courts. It remains to be seen how the ordinary courts will deal with serious crimes cases, but indications are that suspects simply will be processed under domestic criminal law. Although the heavy reliance on international standards and practices had the potential to introduce such concepts at a national level, such standards are predicated on the existence of fully functioning justice systems and assume a certain skill level within the legal profession. (Reiger and Wierda, 2006: 25)

The special panels provide evidence of an integrated criminal procedure that includes standing for victims in the investigative and prosecution process. Although victims are unable to take over a prosecution, they have access to the prosecutor and courts through counsel and are able to seek that specific allegation be investigated by the prosecution. This provides victims before the special panels a degree of substantive and enforceable rights and powers that draw from distinct legal traditions, including those available to the accessory prosecutor in the European context and the victim before the ICC.

Internationalised Panels in Kosovo

Following the bombing of Kosovo by the North Atlantic Treaty Organisation (NATO) in 1999, the IPK were established to hear and determine allegations of ethnic war crimes committed principally by Serb forces against the ethnic Albanians in Kosovo. The IPK were established under UNSC Resolution 1244, providing for a UN mission and administration of Kosovo. The suggestion of a specialist court for ethnic war crimes was abandoned for a specialty court within Kosovo's domestic judicial system (Dickinson, 2003; Hehir, 2010). Although provided for within Kosovo's domestic system, the internationalised panels were formed *ad hoc* by a decision of the special representative of the UN secretary general. The special representative of the UN secretary general appointed an international judge and prosecutor to work within the domestic courts in order to address concerns that the judiciary of Kosovo may not be impartial (see Dickinson, 2003: 1066). However, the UN extended this to appointment of special panels of two international judges, and a domestic judge, with an international prosecutor appointed to guarantee independence and impartiality.

Victims are understood to have broad powers before the IPK, characterised as a hybrid court within the domestic system. The Criminal Procedure Code for Kosovo, 2012 (Criminal No. 04/L-123) establishes the rights and powers granting victim participation and standing. Ochoa (2013: 214) notes:

These articles of the Provisional Criminal Procedure Code of Kosovo support the proposition that the legitimate interests of victims in the criminal proceedings for serious human rights violations include seeking the clarification of the facts, and the identification and prosecution of those responsible. Additionally, victims are entitled to submit a compensation claim before courts in Kosovo.

Article 79(1) of the Code establishes the capacity of the victim to inform of an offence: 'Any person is entitled to report a criminal offence which is prosecuted ex officio and shall have a duty to do so when the failure to report a criminal offence constitutes a criminal offence.' The process across all trial phases allows the individual victim, or the victim advocate should the injured party not appoint a representative, to examine witnesses and evidence before the Panels: Article 9(3) of the Code provides the following:

> The injured party has the right and shall be allowed to make a statement on all the facts and evidence that affects his or her rights, and to make a statement on all the facts and evidence. He or she has the right to examine witnesses, cross-examine witness and to request the state prosecutor to summon witnesses.

Article 214(1) of the Code affords access to the evidence and case file to allow the victim to assess material relevant before the panel:

> The injured party, his or her legal representative or authorized representative, or victim advocate shall be entitled to inspect, copy or photograph records and physical evidence available to the court or to the state prosecutor if he or she has a legitimate interest.

The victim or the victim's advocate is also allowed rights of appeal pursuant to Article 217(4) of the Code:

> If the state prosecutor rejects the application to collect evidence, he or she shall render a decision supported by reasoning and notify the injured party, the injured party's authorized representative, or victim advocate. The injured party, the injured party's authorized representative, or victim advocate may appeal such decision to the pre-trial judge.

Dickinson (2003: 1068–1069) identifies that the internationalised panels as a modified or hybrid tribunal may offer greater levels of legitimacy to war-affected populations and states, where people are traumatised and displaced, and infrastructure destroyed. Such tribunals may add vital capacity where the judiciary and court system have been interrupted by war. This 'capacity building' not only may provide local infrastructure that allows justice to be done, but also engages local actors to improve the integrity of justice:

> Hybrid tribunals, as suggested by their use in Kosovo, can offer at least partial solutions to both these legitimacy and capacity problems. The sharing of responsibilities among international and local actors in the administration of justice, particularly with respect to accountability for serious human rights crimes, helps to establish the legitimacy of the process as well as strengthen the capacity of local actors.

The provision of rights to victims that allow for trial participation in a reconfigured judiciary under international law and procedure has the capacity to provide legitimacy and help restore victims of crime within local systems of justice.

Notes

1 See the discussion of the laws of New Zealand discussed in chapter 6.
2 See, for example, the extracts from the Victims' Charter in England and Wales in Chapter 2 (at 1.5, 2.4, 3.5, 4.5, 6.8, 8.4). Also see the discussion of the transformation of victim charters and declarations in the USA and Australia in Chapter 2. The USA provides a key case study of the repeal of unenforceable rights for the re-enactment of an enforceable rights framework under the *Crime Victims Rights Act 2004* (US).

3 See the legal framework in Australia, the USA, England, and Wales as relevant examples of jurisdictions which have moved towards local declarations of rights that embrace substantive and enforceable rights.

4 See Rule 16 of the Rules of Procedure and Evidence ICC: 'In relation to victims, the Registrar shall be responsible for the performance of the following functions in accordance with the Statute and these Rules: (a) Providing notice or notification to victims or their legal representatives; (b) Assisting them in obtaining legal advice and organizing their legal representation, and providing their legal representatives with adequate support, assistance and information, including such facilities as may be necessary for the direct performance of their duty, for the purpose of protecting their rights during all stages of the proceedings in accordance with rules 89 to 91; (c) Assisting them in participating in the different phases of the proceedings in accordance with rules 89 to 91; (d) Taking gender-sensitive measures to facilitate the participation of victims of sexual violence at all stages of the proceedings.'

5 See discussion of the limitations placed on counsel for victims in the ICC in Chapter 1. Also see *The Prosecutor v Thomas Lubanga Dyilo*, Trial Chamber I (ICC-01/04–01/06, 14 December 2007); *The Prosecutor v Katanga and Chui* (ICC-01/04–01/07 OA 11, 16 July 2010, Judgment on the Appeal of Mr Katanga against the Decision of Trial Chamber II of 22 January 2010 Entitled 'Decision on the Modalities of Victim Participation at Trial').

5 Victims in regional law and policy

Introduction

Various human rights frameworks relevant to the setting of victim rights and powers exist on the regional level. The Council of Europe and the European Union are discussed in this context, although other regional frameworks not covered in detail in this book also provide for human rights on this level.[1] The ECtHR also contributes to the development of a regional human rights discourse by giving interpretation to the ECHR in the context of international and regional laws and procedures. Significantly, this brings together various legal traditions, including those of the continental European approach, together with those that apply to common law, adversarial jurisdictions.

The framework decisions and directives of the Council of Europe provide regional guidance and instruction in an attempt to standardise the criminal procedures of member states. The repeal of the 2001 CEU FD through assent of the CEU DVC in 2012 provided greater instruction to standardise by the promulgation of a directive (extracted in Chapter 2 at 9.3 regarding domestic ratification of the CEU DVC). In terms of the ECHR and the influence of European law and policy on standardised norms of human rights, the jurisprudence of the ECtHR is available to domestic courts through ratification of those decisions in domestic proceedings (see Greer and Williams, 2009; McBride, 2009; Stivachtisa and Habeggera, 2011). Therefore, the regional level discussed here is significantly integrative on the domestic level and has proven to be a unifying force with regard to the domestic development of victim rights. As the next section will demonstrate, however, the national framework adopted by each member state continues to provide a measure of independence and, the regional influence notwithstanding, individual states continue to integrate regional decisions in accordance with local procedural requirements.

Council of Europe, the European Commission, and the European Union

The Council of Ministers of the Council of Europe recommended in 1985 that the needs of victims be taken into account in the development of criminal procedure on the domestic level of member states. The recommendation sought to encourage legal and policy reforms amongst European states, emphasising the need to develop and ratify criminal procedure that provides victim rights to information, to seek to continue a prosecution or to contest the withdrawal of a charge where a decision has been reached not to proceed, to allow for a general right of private prosecution, and to grant victims universal rights to crimes compensation. The Council of the European Union adopted the CEU FD in 2001 in the attempt to encourage the development of rights frameworks by member states to allow greater recognition of rights for victims in local systems of criminal justice. The CEU FD sought to grant victims better assistance in the investigative and trial phases, including the post-sentencing phase, by developing rights in criminal procedure that granted victims a degree of substantive participation. The 2001 CEU FD was later superseded by the CEU DVC in 2012, after the development and exposure of a draft directive, the CEU DD in 2011. On 5 May 2011, the Council of Europe also adopted the Convention on Preventing and Combating Violence against Women and Domestic Violence, Treaty No. 210, which entered into force on 1 August 2014. This convention is covered in the context of the jurisprudence of the ECtHR in the next section.

The Council of Europe has issued numerous other regulations, decisions, and directives that seek to protect victims in discrete circumstances and against specific threats to safety. These include a range of related decisions and council directives that relate to the transposition of the CEU FD of 2001 and implementation of the CEU DVC of 2012. Other instruments seek to grant rights to victims of human trafficking and afford greater rights to information for accused persons (relevant here in so far as such information may affect the victim); to protect particular victims, such as child sex offences victims; to provide protection orders for child victims; and to provide rights and standards for refugees and asylum seekers, who may be subject to victimisation as a result of mass diaspora:

- DG Justice Guidance Document of December 2013 related to the transposition and implementation of Directive 2012/29/EU of the European Parliament and of the Council of 25 October 2012 establishing minimum standards on the rights, support and protection of victims of crime, and replacing Council Framework Decision 2001/220/JHA (see discussion of extracts in this section);
- Council Directive 2004/81/EC of 29 April 2004 on the residence permit issued to third-country nationals who are victims of trafficking in human beings or who have been the subject of an action to facilitate illegal immigration, who cooperate with the competent authorities;
- Directive 2011/36/EU of the European Parliament and of the Council of 5 April 2011 on preventing and combating trafficking in human beings and protecting its victims;
- Directive 2011/93/EU on combating the sexual abuse and sexual exploitation of children and child pornography;
- Directive 2011/99/EU of the European Parliament and of the Council of 13 December 2011 on the European protection order;
- Directive 2012/13/EU of the European Parliament and of the Council of 22 May 2012 on the right to information in criminal proceedings;
- Council Directive 2003/9/EC of 27 January 2003 laying down minimum standards for the reception of asylum seekers;
- Directive 2013/33/EU of the European Parliament and of the Council of 26 June 2013 laying down standards for the reception of applicants for international protection;
- Council Directive 2005/85/EC of 1 December 2005 on minimum standards on procedures in member states for granting and withdrawing refugee status; and
- Council Decision (EU) 2015/1523 of 14 September 2015 establishing provisional measures in the area of international protection for the benefit of Italy and of Greece and Council Decision (EU) 2015/1601 of 22 September 2015 establishing provisional measures in the area of international protection for the benefit of Italy and Greece.

The CEU DVC establishes a revised framework for the development of a criminal procedure with a view to standardising victim rights across member states on a procedural basis. The EU member states were given the deadline to implement the provisions of the CEU DVC into state law by 16 November 2015. The CEU DVC prescribes a range of rights consistent with the CEU FD of 2001. However, the 2012 instrument extends the rights framework provided in 2001, stressing the need for rights to protect against offences committed because of the victim's gender or gender identity, while also emphasising the need to develop responses to crimes against women, and domestic and partner violence. Other developments are emphasised, including the mutual recognition of protected measures by member states, as well as a renewed focus on the problems of mass victimisation and terrorism. Characteristics of a modern criminal justice system are also presented, including the minimum standards for service provision, such as reporting to the police, access to information and victim assistance, and rights of redress, remedy, or reparation. Restorative justice as an alternative pathway in criminal justice and the need to restore victims are also considered (see Wieczorek, 2012).

The Guidance Document issued by the European Commission assists with the ratification of the provisions of the CEU DVC into local criminal procedure. The intent is to render the provision of victim rights as substantive and enforceable rights against the accused or state in appropriate circumstances. The Guidance Document (European Commission, 2013: 3) provides the following:

> Improving the rights, support, protection and participation of victims in criminal proceedings is a Commission priority. Thus, the Directive forms an essential part of a horizontal package of measures, launched by the European Commission in May 2011. This aims to strengthen the rights of victims of crime so that any victim can rely on the same basic level of rights, whatever their nationality and wherever in the EU the crime takes place. In addition to this horizontal Directive on rights, support and protection of all victims of crime, other Directives, such as Directive on Trafficking in Human Beings and Directive on Child Sexual Exploitation, were previously adopted by the EU in order to address specific situation of victims of these crimes.

Recital 20 of the CEU DVC of 2012 sets out the requisite procedural dimensions of the ratification of the directive, to ensure a measure of consistency between victim rights as expressed across European states irrespective of the legal tradition from which the state jurisdiction emerges:

> The role of victims in the criminal justice system and whether they can participate actively in criminal proceedings vary across Member States, depending on the national system, and is determined by one or more of the following criteria: whether the national system provides for a legal status as a party to criminal proceedings; whether the victim is under a legal requirement or is requested to participate actively in criminal proceedings, for example as a witness; and/or whether the victim has a legal entitlement under national law to participate actively in criminal proceedings and is seeking to do so, where the national system does not provide that victims have the legal status of a party to the criminal proceedings. Member States should determine which of those criteria apply to determine the scope of rights set out in this Directive where there are references to the role of the victim in the relevant criminal justice system. (Recital 20, CEU DVC 2012)

The framework decisions of the EU have been criticised as lacking an enforcement mechanism. Groenhuijsen and Pemberton (2009) have indicated that directives including those of the EU may not lead to legal and policy reform because member states retain the discretion to implement them in accordance with local need. Further, developing the directives of the EU into 'hard law' may constrict the capacity of local authorities to assist victims by increasing the administrative burden on states.[2] The ratification of such instruments would, however, allow for the enforcement of the principles and rules developed out of the instrument on the local level. The issue with the resort to 'soft law', or a framework of victim rights that emerges solely through policy initiative, is the lack of accountability of government and other official and justice stakeholders more generally (see, generally, Thornhill, 2012; Sithole, 2013; Manco, 2015). For this reason, the twenty-first-century movement to victim rights frameworks has necessarily developed through a combination of law and policy that allows for levels of enforcement in a procedural and administrative context.

The European Commission (2013: 5) has stressed the need to accede to the requirement of the CEU DVC in the context of local laws and policies. It is thus left to individual member states to best ratify the requirements of the CEU DVC into law and policy:

> To meet the high demands for a modern coherent legal framework on victims' rights set out in the Directive, Member States may consider *a priori* as suitable for national transposition of the Directive the following options: (a) to adopt an all-embracing criminal law Victims' Codex (Statute) or (b) to divide the transposition between the Criminal Code of Procedure and (creating) an all-embracing criminal law Victims' Statute depending on the categories of Articles.

- The choice of the overall transposition technique may assess the best option between:
    - Amending the existing general Criminal Code of Procedure;
    - Creating a single criminal law Victims' Statute;
    - Divide the transposition between Criminal Code of Procedure, an administrative law instrument and/or (creating) a single criminal law Victims' Statute.

- As for practical assistance to victims, Member States will have to decide:
    - How to ensure the proper functioning of general and specialist victims' support services, which form a significant and prominent part of the requirements of the Directive, at the national level;
    - What existing national action plans aimed at combating some specific crimes, such as all or certain forms of violence against women, are to be amended;
    - What technical modalities on legislation in this sphere already exist (would any be created);
    - How the system of financing and mutual coordination among national authorities and the private and non-governmental sector would be governed.

However, every Member State – each with different criminal justice systems – must assess each article of the directive to determine the most suitable instrument of transposition for the different objectives set in the directive.

The requirement that the CEU DVC be adapted to local requirements is thus consistent with the practical reality of the operation of criminal justice as a state concern (cf. Mégret, 2015), and the need to maintain the functions of the criminal justice system as a response to local law and order. The tendency of the ratification of the CEU DVC has been to modify the criminal procedural codes of member states rather than provide for victim rights in a consolidated codex or statute.

The United Kingdom's decision to leave the European Union in the poll of June 2016 will affect future initiatives to provide for degrees of local ratification of regional instruments of the EU; however, this will not preclude the continued development of English law and policy through alternative mechanisms and rights frameworks. The significance of the UK's decision to leave the EU may, however, have further ramifications for other member states of the EU, and its ability to encourage and provide coherent legal and policy development for victims and criminal justice more generally. At worst, removal from the EU may see a reassertion of the common law, adversarial processes, and rationales that exclude victim participation, with a disinclination to continue to modify English law and policy to allow greater participation consistent with continental models of justice.

The European Court of Justice

The European Court of Justice has helped position victims in the context of the criminal procedural framework of individual member states. The European Court of Justice is the highest court in the EU regarding the interpretation of EU law. Importantly, the European Court of Justice does not determine matters of national or state law, and individual judgements of member states cannot be appealed to the European Court of Justice. Rather, decisions of the European Court of Justice consider the application of EU law across the whole of the EU, and it is for member states to consider the decisions of the European Court of Justice and apply them to state law. The European Court of Justice sits as part of the Court of Justice of the European Union. The European Court of Justice was established in 1952.

The relevant jurisprudence of the European Court of Justice has centred on the interpretation of the rights stated under the CEU FD of 2001. The leading case is *Criminal Proceedings against Pupino* [2005] EUECJ C-105/03. This matter, discussed in chapter 2, determined that national courts must be able to allow juvenile witnesses or victims, being the subject of maltreatment, to testify in a way that affords them a suitable level of protection. This includes protection prior to the trial occurring. This case goes towards the standing of victims in criminal proceedings, and the protections to be granted to vulnerable persons in court. Courts of member states must consider their domestic laws and policies when ratifying the framework decision, by introducing laws consistent with the intent of the CEU FD, and the criminal procedures of their domestic system. Thus, the European Court of Justice rules at par. [36] that:

> [It] follows from Article 34(2)(b) EU and from the principle of loyalty to the Union that every framework decision obliges national courts to bring their interpretation of national laws as far as possible into conformity with the wording and purpose of the framework decision, regardless of whether those laws were adopted before or after the framework decision, so as to achieve the result envisaged by the framework decision.

The case of *György Katz v István Roland Sós* [2008] EUECJ C-404/07 provides further support to victims by defining their substantive rights in an ancillary prosecution. Articles 2 and 3 of CEU FD of 2001 provide that the victim should not be able to testify in criminal proceedings where such proceedings are instituted by way of a substitute private prosecution. The victim may be required to testify, however, where his or her evidence is required in proceedings as necessary to the establishing of the charges raised. The European Court of Justice set out the initial issue for the *Fővárosi Bíróság*, the Hungarian court exercising original jurisdiction, in pars [21]–[22]:

> In his oral submissions to the referring court, Mr Katz claimed that, by refusing to hear the victim, who is also prosecutor, as a witness, the referring court infringed the principles concerning the right to a fair trial and equality of arms enshrined in the Convention for the Protection of Human Rights and Fundamental Freedoms signed at Rome on 4 November 1950 ('the ECHR'). He also maintained that he had already suffered harm during the investigation by reason of the fact that the investigating authority did not comply with its obligation to establish the facts, whereas the legal mechanism of the substitute private prosecution precisely enables that situation to be remedied so that, thanks to the testimony of the victim appearing in person, the truth can be ascertained and the latter can obtain reparation for the harm suffered. According to Mr Katz, the victim would otherwise be placed at a disadvantage compared to the person being prosecuted.
>
> At a subsequent hearing before that court, held on 6 July 2007, the court reopened the criminal investigation. It pointed out that, while Paragraph 236 of Law No XIX of 1998 derogates from the prohibition on a substitute private prosecutor acting in the capacity of the public prosecutor, there is no provision in that Law derogating from the prohibition contained in Paragraph 31(1), under which a witness may not act in the capacity of public prosecutor. The Fővárosi Bíróság inferred from this that a substitute private prosecutor may not be heard as a witness in such criminal proceedings. With regard to a private prosecution, the Law in question contains an express provision under which the private prosecutor may be heard as a witness. Even though private prosecutions and substitute private prosecutions are undoubtedly similar, the same rules cannot, in the absence of any cross-reference between them, be applied to those two distinct types of proceedings.

The issue for the court was whether the substitutive prosecutor derives the same powers as the private prosecutor as provided under criminal procedure. Where a victim acts as a private prosecutor, he or she has the ability to make out the prosecution case while also being able to testify as a witness in that prosecution. However, where the victim acts as a substitutive prosecutor, the *Fővárosi Bíróság* inferred that the victim may not present as a witness. The European Court of Justice rules at par. [50] that:

> the answer to the question referred must be that Articles 2 and 3 of the Framework Decision are to be interpreted as not obliging a national court to permit the victim to be heard as a witness in criminal proceedings instituted by a substitute private prosecution such as that in issue in the main proceedings. However, in the absence of such a possibility, it must be possible for the victim to be permitted to give testimony which can be taken into account as evidence.

The matter of *Criminal Proceedings against Magatte Gueye and Valentín Salmerón Sánchez* [2011] EUECJ C-483/09 and C-1/10, Articles 2, 3, and 8 of CEU FD of 2001, develops the notion of the standing of the victim further by allowing for an injunction against persons accused of family violence as an ancillary penalty issued under the criminal law of member states. An injunction taken out against a violent family member may therefore preclude the offender from contacting other family members, requiring them to stay away from family victims for a minimum period. Such an injunction may be issued even where the victim of crime opposes the application of such injunctive restrictions. Further, Article 10(1) can be interpreted as permitting member states to exclude access to mediation in all criminal proceedings regarding such offences, therefore minimising contact between offender and victim.

In *Criminal Proceedings against Maurizio Giovanardi and Others* [2012] EUECJ C-79/11, with regard to the victim's ability to access compensation, where liability to compensation arises in main proceedings, Article 9 of the CEU FD of 2001 enables the victim to seek compensation where the alleged act committed may be more appropriately classified as an administrative offence. In the case of *Giovanni Dell'Orto* [2007] EUECJ C-467/05–395 (also see *Criminal Proceedings against Giovanni Dell'Orto* [2007] EUECJ C-467/05–152), the court determined that the return of property in criminal proceedings must depend on whether the seized property is determined to be within the ownership of the victim at trial. Where this is established the property must be returned to the victim; otherwise conversion is a matter for the civil courts at pars [95–96]:

> the victim cannot claim the return of disputed property where the criminal proceedings did not produce such findings. In this respect the Member States are free to leave the dispute over the property for the civil courts to decide. The question possibly arises as to the extent to which Framework Decision 2001/220 requires the court to make appropriate findings where these are not absolutely necessary for the conclusion of the criminal proceedings.
>
> It must therefore be stated that seized property must be returned to the victim immediately pursuant to Article 9(3) of Framework Decision 2001/220 if the victim's ownership of the property is undisputed or has been established with legally binding effect in criminal proceedings.

The case of *James Wood v Fonds de Garantie des Victimes des Actes de Terrorisme et d'autres Infractions* [2007] EUECJ C-164/07 determined that community law could not be interpreted as precluding laws of a member state where foreign nationals who live in the state seek compensation regarding offences to their person, on the sole ground of the claimant's foreign nationality. The European Court of Justice ruled, at par. [17], that:

> Community law precludes legislation of a Member State which excludes nationals of other Member States who live and work in its territory from the grant of compensation intended to make good losses resulting from offences against the person where the crime in question was not committed in the territory of that State, on the sole ground that they do not have the nationality of that State.

The European Court of Human Rights

The Council of Europe developed and adopted the ECHR in 1950, which took effect in 1953. The ECtHR developed out of the European Commission of Human Rights, which merged with the ECtHR in 1998. Victims both direct and indirect, as well as NGOs and states, have the ability to refer complaints under the ECHR to the ECtHR for determination. Individual victims personally harmed or injured or family members of kin affected by the crime have the ability to exercise rights under the ECHR. The ECtHR will generally require that claimants seek redress in their home state prior to approaching the ECtHR for resolution. Where all avenues for appeal have been considered, the victim may approach the ECtHR for relief. The remedies of the court are limited to the extent to which they are recognised by the member state, despite most states having mechanisms in place to give effect to the jurisprudence of the ECtHR. For victims exposed to unfair processes in the criminal justice system or otherwise denied rights to natural justice, this may not lead to any particular outcome or remedy in the home state, although future processes may develop in respect to the precedent set by the case. Victims may continue to be awarded compensation or reparations by the ECtHR or their home state. The decisions of the ECtHR will bind the Council of Europe, which is charged with a duty to stop present or future violations of the ECHR. Where the ECtHR makes findings relevant to the regional level, further investigations may be initiated by the Council of Europe to uncover proof of new allegations, such as evidence of atrocities, war crimes, or gross violations of human rights (Goss, 2014).

The case of *Berger v France* (2002) ECHR 48221/99 develops the principle of equality of arms before the ECtHR. This case specifically regards the extent to which the victim, participating as partie civile, affects the degree of fairness and due process owed to the state and defendant in court proceedings. Proceedings in the ECtHR are conducted through adversarial exchange between the state and accused, victim and state, or victim and accused, depending on the arrangement of the litigants. The ordinary process of dual litigants engaged in adversarial argument may be modified where the court allows a victim, acting as partie civile, to make submissions and express rights alongside the state and defendant. The ECtHR will generally reflect upon trial participation in the trial courts of member states under the assumption that proceedings are constituted through an adversarial exchange between the parties, which in criminal matters will be the accused and the state.

In *Berger v France* (2002) ECHR 48221/99 the court determined that where victims present at trial, they present in their own capacity and not as attached to the state, at par. [38]:

> Having regard to the role accorded to civil actions within criminal trials and to the complementary interests of civil parties and the prosecution, the Court cannot accept that the equality-of-arms principle has been infringed in the instant case. In that connection the Court agrees with the Government that a civil party cannot be regarded as either the opponent – or for that matter necessarily the ally – of the prosecution, their roles and objectives being clearly different.

The ECtHR recognises that victims ought to be granted rights of participation more consistent with that of the ICC than common law, adversarial courts. Arguably, however, *Berger v France* recognises that the participation of the victim as partie civile is compatible with common law processes.[3] For instance, the ECtHR allows victims access to evidence relevant to their case in the ECtHR's registry, and counsel acting for a victim is able to address the court and make submissions during hearings.

Article 6 of the ECHR provides the right to a fair trial. The ECtHR has addressed victim rights in the context of fair trial rights. These rights are seen to provide substantive rights to participation, and may be enforced against the state or accused where otherwise denied in proceedings. Fair trial rights have been interpreted in the context of the additional right to privacy under Article 8 of the ECHR. These rights have been identified as combining to support the victims' right to apply for protective modes of trial participation. The right to a fair trial is provided under Article 6 of the ECHR, interpreted as the accused's right to fairness in a proportional context of the protective and support needs of other trial participants, including those of the victim. Article 8 provides the right to secure the privacy needs of individuals.[4] Most cases considering the substantive rights of the victim in the trial process have been brought under Articles 6 and 8 of the ECHR, in terms of the protections that ought to be made available to victim when giving evidence at trial, particularly where the victim is faced with a hostile accused, or legitimately fear their reprisal. Victim issues have also been raised under Article 2 of the ECHR, which raises the right to life.[5] Article 3 of the ECHR provides a prohibition on torture or degrading treatment or punishment.[6] Together, these rights have been raised in the context of a denial of fundamental rights by police during the investigative or pretrial process. The cases of *Osman v United Kingdom* (1998) 29 EHRR 245 and *Razzakov v Russia* (2015) ECHR 57519/09 (also see *Gutsanovi v Bulgaria* [2013] ECHR 34529/10) raise rights under Articles 2 and 3 of the ECHR respectively. While these cases pertain to rights other than those of the fair trial, they raise issues regarding the treatment and standing of victims that give context to the procedural rights of victims expected under Articles 6 and 8 of the ECHR.

The standard arrangement of the examination of victims in open court has been reviewed under Articles 6 and 8 of the ECHR. This has raised the plight of vulnerable and other at-risk victims and witnesses and led to the consideration of the provision of evidence in alternative ways. As such, the ECtHR has been instrumental in the offering of substantive rights to victims by modifying the normative scope of the criminal trial process to better accommodate the needs of vulnerable victims called to give evidence. This is particularly true of sex offences and child victims, each of whom has recognised special needs of security and privacy when giving evidence (see Ellison, 2002: 78–79; Starmer, 2014). Where it is necessary that a witness give personally distressing evidence, Article 6 the ECHR has been interpreted as requiring proportionality between the accused's right to a fair trial and the needs of the victim. Article 8 of the ECHR provides a right to privacy that in the case of victims has been interpreted as requiring that certain protections be afforded to victims in the trial process. Where victims are called to give personally distressing evidence, the ECtHR has demonstrated a willingness to extend human rights discourse to processes that require victims to testify under distressing circumstances in order to offset the rights of the accused to critically examine the victim. The proportionality requirement requires that the protections afforded to the victim be counterweighted by processes that allow defendants to continue to test the prosecution case, to ensure they receive a fair trial.

The requirement of a fair trial and the availability of modified trial processes to accommodate vulnerable victims was affirmed in *Y v Slovenia* (2015) ECHR 41107/10. The court took the opportunity to affirm the centrality of the proportionality requirement, consistent with requirements iterated by the Council of Europe in its Convention on Preventing and Combating Violence against Women and Domestic Violence, Treaty No. 210, which entered into force on 1 August 2014,[7] which provided that, at par. [105]–[106]:

> As regards the manner in which the applicant's rights were protected in the criminal proceedings in issue, the Court observes, firstly, that her testimony at the trial provided the only direct evidence in the case. In addition, other evidence presented was conflicting, the psychologist's report confirming sexual abuse being countervailed by the orthopaedics report. In this light, it must be reiterated that the interests of a fair trial

required the defence to be given the opportunity to cross-examine the applicant, who by that time was no longer a minor. Nevertheless, it needs to be determined whether the manner in which the applicant was questioned struck a fair balance between her personal integrity and X's defence rights.

In this connection the Court reiterates that, as a rule, the defendant's rights under Article 6 §§ 1 and 3 (d) require that he be given an adequate and proper opportunity to challenge and question a witness against him either when he makes his statements or at a later stage of the proceedings (see *Saïdi v France*, 20 September 1993, § 43, Series A no. 261-C, and *A.M. v Italy*, no. 37019/97, § 25, ECHR 1999-IX). Furthermore, the Court must be cautious in making its own assessment of a specific line of questioning, considering that it is primarily the role of the competent national authorities to decide upon the admissibility and relevance of evidence (see *Schenk v Switzerland*, 12 July 1988, § 46, Series A no. 140, and *Engel and Others v the Netherlands*, 8 June 1976, § 91, Series A no. 22). This being said, the Court has also already held that a person's right to defend himself does not provide for an unlimited right to use any defence arguments (see, mutatis mutandis, *Brandstetter v Austria*, 28 August 1991, § 52, Series A no. 211). Thus, since a direct confrontation between the defendants charged with criminal offences of sexual violence and their alleged victims involves a risk of further traumatisation on the latter's part, in the Court's opinion personal cross-examination by defendants should be subject to most careful assessment by the national courts, the more so the more intimate the questions are.

Dooson v The Netherlands (1996) ECHR 20524/92 sets out the line of authority that identifies the needs of the defendant and victim as regards the proportionality requirement of fairness. This case assesses the compatibility of the process allowing the witness to remain anonymous out of a fear of reprisal against the need for the accused to identify and confront their victim in court. The ECtHR determined that a trial might proceed where the victim or witness remains anonymous so long as countermeasures were provided to allow the accused access to the testimony of the witness with a view to still being able to examine the content of that testimony, albeit through alternative means. The court held that states are required to offer an alternative process to accommodate the needs of such vulnerable witnesses. Article 8 of the ECHR therefore permits the consideration of effective measures to preserve witness safety as long as the defence retains access to the content of the testimony with a capacity to test its veracity in a legitimate way.

In the case of *Baegen v The Netherlands* (1994) ECHR 16696/90, the victim was able to testify anonymously after receiving threats of reprisal. The defendant sought to cross-examine the victim, who chose to have her identity concealed. The ECtHR ruled that Article 6 required a degree of proportionality between the parties such that where reprisals had been threatened, victims ought to be able to rely on protective measures to grant them a degree of fairness in proceedings. However, the accused should be able to utilise alternative measures to ensure their procedural fairness requirements are met. Thus, it was appropriate that, in certain circumstances, questions were put to the victim at trial and on appeal. The court ruled that the victim has a right to anonymity, secured by Article 8. The Article is identified as providing a positive right, obliging the court to offer protection to vulnerable victims and witnesses, but only if alternative processes are available to allow the accused to exercise their right to test the prosecution case by putting questions to the victim. Additionally, if the victim testifies anonymously or presents by statement, corroborative evidence should be offered to support the testimony of the victim, especially where the victim is unable to be cross-examined as to the content of his or her testimony. The ECtHR determined the following at pars [78]–[79]:

> The Commission observes that, during the preliminary judicial investigation, the applicant failed to avail himself of the offer of the investigating judge to put written questions to Ms. X., that in the proceedings before the Regional Court he did not request an examination of Ms. X. either before this court or the investigating judge, and that the applicant did not request the prosecution authorities to summon her as a witness for the hearing of 6 September 1988 before the Court of Appeal. It was only in the course of that last hearing that he requested the court to order an examination of Ms. X.
>
> The Commission further observes that the applicant's conviction did not rest solely on the statements of Ms. X. The Court of Appeal also used in evidence statements of police officers, the statement of Ms. X.'s mother, and the statement of K. All those statements, more or less, corroborated the version of events Ms. X. had given. They were not, however, consistent with the applicant's statements on a number of points. In the course of the proceedings before the trial courts, the applicant never requested an examination of these persons.

The uses of anonymous measures to support the victim's need for security are important complements to the fair trial process in aid of victim rights. In the case of *Bocos-Cuesta v The Netherlands* (2005) ECHR 54789/00, which relies upon *Finkensieper v The Netherlands* (1995) ECHR 19525/92, the adequacy of countermeasures to maintain the accused's capacity to test the veracity of the evidence of the victim is central to the determination as to whether the proportionality requirement has been maintained. The applicant in *Bocos-Cuesta* submitted that he did not receive a fair trial under Article 6(1),(3)(d) of the ECHR. At trial, the victims, all minors, presented their testimony by statement. The accused was not denied the opportunity to test the statements presented by the children. The ECtHR ruled the following at pars [7.1]–[7.2]:

> The remaining question is whether the statements of the four children can be used in evidence although the suspect has not had the opportunity to question them himself. The court's first consideration is the fact that Article 6 [of the Convention], particularly in the light of some recent [Strasbourg] decisions given on applications brought against the Netherlands, does not unconditionally oppose the use in evidence of statements given by witnesses whom a suspect has not been able to question. There is room for the balancing of interests. In its judgment of 26 March 1996 in the case of *Doorson v the Netherlands*, the European Court [of Human Rights] considered in this respect that the principles of a fair trial also require that, in appropriate cases, the interests of the suspect in questioning [witnesses] are to be balanced against the interests of witnesses and victims in the adequate protection of their rights guaranteed by Article 8 [of the Convention]. In the opinion of the European Court, briefly summarised, in balancing these interests much weight must be given to the question whether the handicaps under which the defence labours on account of the inability to questioning a witness in an indirect manner are compensated, and whether a conviction is based either solely or to a decisive extent on the statement of this witness. In its report of 17 May 1995 [in the case of *Finkensieper v the Netherlands*, no. 19525/92], the European Commission [of Human Rights] adopted an essentially similar opinion.

In the light of these decisions, the following can be said. As already found by the court, the interests of the four children in not being exposed to reliving a possibly traumatic experience weigh heavily. With that, as also already found by the court, stands the fact that the confrontations of these four witnesses with the suspect have been carried out with the required care, and that the results thereof, as already found earlier, are particularly reliable. As regards the acts themselves of which the suspect stands accused, the court finds it established that the four children have all been questioned by (or assisted by) investigation officers of the Amsterdam Juvenile and Vice Police Bureau with extensive experience in questioning very young persons. It has become plausible from the records drawn up by them and from the oral evidence given in court by these civil servants that the four children have been questioned in an open, careful and non-suggestive manner.

The ECtHR has therefore developed substantial case law in favour of supporting victims where they present as a vulnerable witness. Carefully designed and executed countermeasures are required, however, for any departure from the standards of the fair trial. In this instance, fairness ordinarily requires the testing of evidence in open court. In the matter of *Kostovski v The Netherlands* (1989) 12 EHRR 434, for instance, a magistrate introduced hearsay evidence into proceedings. The ECtHR determined that this departed substantially from the standard expected because hearsay evidence could not be sufficiently tested by the accused. The ECtHR determined that such evidence needed to be adduced before the accused because satisfaction of the proportionality requirement went towards the sufficiency of the accused's ability to test the evidence against them within the limits of the need to protect the vulnerable victim. Written records or statements obtained from witnesses or victims during the investigation or pretrial process were tenable only where the accused had sufficient access to the person making the statement to test the content of the statement. The ECtHR ruled the following (at 4477–4448):

> In principle, all the evidence must be produced in the presence of the accused at a public hearing with a view to adversarial argument. This does not mean, however, that in order to be used as evidence statements of witnesses should always be made at a public hearing in court: to use as evidence such statements obtained at the pre-trial stage is not in itself inconsistent with paragraphs (3)(d) and (1) of Article 6, provided the rights of the defence have been respected.
>
> As a rule, these rights require that an accused should be given an adequate and proper opportunity to challenge and question a witness against him, either at the time the witness was making his statement or at some later stage of the proceedings.

The case of *Kostovski v The Netherlands* (1989) 12 EHRR 434 sets out the appreciable limits of departing from fair trial requirements. The case of *Van Mechelen v Netherlands* (1997) 25 EHRR 647 demonstrates this as a case in point. In this matter, the applicants were convicted after anonymous statements were tendered by police. The investigating judge allowed the evidence as defence counsel would be able to examine the police by audio link. The ECtHR determined that Article 6 of the ECHR has been denied, as the accused could not observe the police giving their evidence, and was not able to adequately test the veracity of the evidence.[8] *Kostovski v The Netherlands* and *Van Mechelen v Netherlands* therefore establish the precedent that the fairness of the trial must be assessed from the trial as a whole (see Doak, 2008: 74). Starmer (2014) notes that there is a difference between establishing victim rights or privileges in the trial, and the modification of the law of criminal procedure and evidence that focuses on the rights of the accused to a fair trial process. Modification of the latter is more likely to result in a balance of principles that continue to support the fairness requirements of the trial over the overt privileging of the victim.

The European Union and victim rights in focus

The CEU FD of 2001 and now CEU DVC of 2012 the Counsel of Europe regarding the procedures available to victims of crime in the criminal process demonstrate the convergence of international victim rights within the context of the criminal procedural codes of each member state. While cognate decisions and directives of the Council also support and develop the framework of victim rights and powers across Europe, it is the 2001 and 2012 instruments that have afforded victims greater substantive and enforceable powers and rights at law. Although the 2001 instrument manifests as a decision of the Council, the 2012 instrument is expected to be implemented by each member state. Klip (2015) argues that the rights of the accused to a fair trial are manifest in the 2012 instrument, which affords victims greater rights of participation and protection, but in particular circumstances and without displacing the state prerogative to prosecute or the accused's right to access justice. Despite this, the CEU DVC of 2012, Klip (2015: 185) reminds us that:

> Directive 2012/29 refers to the general setting in which the rights of the victim must be placed and its relation with the fairness of the proceedings. Whilst it does recognize the relationship between the rights of the defence and the rights of the victim, it leaves quite some ambiguity as to which rights in the end prevail.

With regard to the particular aspects of a fair trial, Klip (2015: 183) recites the clauses of the directive, specifically:

> Whereas it may often be inevitable that the victim will be interrogated, Article 18 provides that the manner in which this is done must protect the dignity of the victim. Interviews of victims must be conducted without undue delay (Article 20, paragraph 1), the number of interviews not exceed what is really necessary (paragraph 2), victims may be accompanied by a legal representative (paragraph 3) and medical examinations must be kept to a minimum (paragraph 4).

However, the conditions required to provide victims with access to justice are dependent on the extent to which member states are able to successfully integrate and organise the CEU DVC of 2012 within their existing criminal procedural codes. This brings us to one of the central arguments explored throughout this book, that international and regional norms of victim rights will need to be interpreted and made relevant to the local legal and policy context.

The significance of the local, despite attempts to unify European criminal procedure with regard to the provision of victim rights, will therefore remain important and determinant regarding the extent to which victims are afforded access to justice across Europe, into the twenty-first century. While most member states already possess procedures that meet or exceed the CEU DVC of 2012, there is some alarm regarding the extent to which victim rights may be served by criminal procedures and within the context of the criminal trial in particular. Although this should be an issue only for common law, adversarial states – specifically, England and Wales, Ireland, and Scotland – other European states following a civil law tradition, and where partially modified to accommodate adversarial trial practices (see Sweden, the Netherlands, and Austria, discussed in Chapter 6), concern seems to have been raised for all member states:

> Directive 2012/29 has created the conditions for rather chaotic and blurring situations in criminal proceedings in which it is predictable that expectations of victims and other participants will be heavily disappointed. The increasing role of the victim in criminal proceedings raises some more existential question as to what its purpose is and whether that purpose could be served within the scope of a criminal trial without affecting the rights of an accused still presumed innocent. Only if that becomes clear, it will be possible to respect all interests involved. (Klip, 2015: 189)

As is the case with Austria, which retains aspects of adversarial practice within its criminal procedure, the extent to which the CEU DVC of 2012 ought to sound alarm amongst member states of the EU may be dependent on the extent to which their individual, domestic system is already hostile to victims in the first instance. It will also be dependent on the extent to which the normatively positioned stakeholders express concerns about the participation of victims as an affront to justice. Given that most member states have a long procedural history of granting the victim rights to justice, the CEU DVC of 2012 should not be taken as limiting the capacity of criminal courts to grant a fair trial to the accused, given the discrete ways in which victims are provided rights at the local level. Rather than universal access to justice, which arguably is what the accused enjoys by way of broadly framed rights to procedural fairness and due process, victim empowerment tends to occur at the level of micro reforms to procedural law. The cases traced in this chapter indicate that the jurisprudence of the European Court of Justice and the ECtHR is firmly directed towards particular instances of unfairness or the denial of rights of victims. This means that it is unlikely that the reform of European criminal procedure will afford victims plenary rights of substantive participation. Rather, victims are granted privileges and protections where it has been shown that present practices manifest unfairly on victims, or otherwise cause them real damage or harm, including secondary harms in trial processes.

Notes

1 See chapter 2, 'International Norms of Victim Rights'.
2 See, for example, the processes of ratification through court judgement permitted under the *Human Rights Act 1998* (UK).
3 Also see *Perez v France* (2004) ECHR 47287/99, at par. [68].
4 Extracted in Chapter 2 at 6.4.
5 See Chapter 1, n. 2.
6 See Chapter 1, n. 3.
7 On 5 May 2011, the Council of Europe adopted the Convention on Preventing and Combating Violence against Women and Domestic Violence, Treaty No. 210, which entered into force on 1 August 2014: 'Article 49 General Obligations: 1. Parties shall take the necessary legislative or other measures to ensure that investigations and judicial proceedings in relation to all forms of violence covered by the scope of this Convention are carried out without undue delay while taking into consideration the rights of the victim during all stages of the criminal proceedings. 2. Parties shall take the necessary legislative or other measures, in conformity with the fundamental principles of human rights and having regard to the gendered understanding of violence, to ensure the effective investigation and prosecution of offences established in

accordance with this Convention.' 'Article 54 Investigations and Evidence: Parties shall take the necessary legislative or other measures to ensure that, in any civil or criminal proceedings, evidence relating to the sexual history and conduct of the victim shall be permitted only when it is relevant and necessary.' 'Article 56 Measures of Protection: 1. Parties shall take the necessary legislative or other measures to protect the rights and interests of victims, including their special needs as witnesses, at all stages of investigations and judicial proceedings, in particular by: (a) providing for their protection, as well as that of their families and witnesses, from intimidation, retaliation and repeat victimisation; (b) ensuring that victims are informed, at least in cases where the victims and the family might be in danger, when the perpetrator escapes or is released temporarily or definitively; (c) informing them, under the conditions provided for by internal law, of their rights and the services at their disposal and the follow-up given to their complaint, the charges, the general progress of the investigation or proceedings, and their role therein, as well as the outcome of their case; (d) enabling victims, in a manner consistent with the procedural rules of internal law, to be heard, to supply evidence and have their views, needs and concerns presented, directly or through an intermediary, and considered; (e) providing victims with appropriate support services so that their rights and interests are duly presented and taken into account; (f) ensuring that measures may be adopted to protect the privacy and the image of the victim; (g) ensuring that contact between victims and perpetrators within court and law enforcement agency premises is avoided where possible; (h) providing victims with independent and competent interpreters when victims are parties to proceedings or when they are supplying evidence; (i) enabling victims to testify, according to the rules provided by their internal law, in the courtroom without being present or at least without the presence of the alleged perpetrator, notably through the use of appropriate communication technologies, where available. 2. A child victim and child witness of violence against women and domestic violence shall be afforded, where appropriate, special protection measures taking into account the best interests of the child.'

8 Also see *Doorson v The Netherlands* (1996) 22 EHRR 330.

6 Victims in domestic law and policy

Introduction

The local level of state or national jurisdictions provides the domestic context in which supranational and regional human rights frameworks are ratified into law and policy. This is the level of the greatest diversity because the international norms that seek to standardise victim rights and powers are interpreted in accordance with existing laws and policies that necessarily modify or alter the principles of the norm to make sense of local contexts. Alternatively, nations or states may decline to ratify a particular right or process, and may fail to do so due to many, varied reasons. These may include a lack of member or signatory status, local politics, the disinclination of Parliament towards the norm or right to be ratified, or the lack of compatibility with local processes. Further still, local jurisdictions may not ratify a particular instrument because local law and policy already meet or exceed the standard. This may be the case for continental European jurisdictions regarding the right of the victim to prosecute privately, to review the decisions of the prosecutor, and to make submissions throughout the trial pursuant to the recommendations of the Council of Europe.[1] As international instruments regarding the rights and powers of victims are often drawn from leading jurisdictions that already provide the victim with access to justice, only those nations that currently fall below international standards will be under pressure to reform law and policy and to ratify a rights framework.

The domestic level covered in this text comprises the inquisitorial systems of Germany and France, and mixed systems of Sweden, Austria, and the Netherlands. Common law and developing systems will include England and Wales, Ireland, Scotland, USA, Australia, Canada, New Zealand, India, South Africa, Japan, and Brazil. These countries have been selected because they demonstrate an adherence to alternative inquisitorial, adversarial, mixed, or hybrid legal traditions. Adherence to a notional tradition of system will modify the approach taken to the expression of victim rights, as will a country's motivation and capacity for change. Minor law reform would be expected in any jurisdiction; however, in the case of certain countries, such as Japan, new mixed systems of justice have been constituted to address particular concerns over the lack of victim involvement in past systems. The developing countries are also considered to evaluate how a victim rights framework can be articulated out of a concern for human rights and the observance of international standards. Local conditions and context particular to each jurisdiction will also be evaluated.

While this chapter will trace the development of victimology and victim rights in terms of the ratification of international and regional instruments, the focus will be on the local to the extent that it will set out the distinct arrangement of human rights records and the focus on the provision of victim rights in the domestic context. While substantial debate has emerged over the extent to which victim rights are globalised (see Doak, 2008; Hall, 2009, 2010) out of the identification of victim rights as human rights and the increasing influence of supranational agreements and the ability of the courts to take account of international instruments in individual decisions, the development of victim rights still responds to local laws and policies. This focus on the global in the context of the local means that while we can talk of trends between jurisdictions, some of which have emerged as normative between or across nations or regions, victim rights as an accessible framework continued to manifest on the local level. This is the face of victim rights that makes those rights accessible to individuals in each jurisdiction. Arguably, it is this local level which provides the greatest indications as to the degree of internationalisation of victim rights, including the rights which are identified as necessary, irrevocable, or natural rights constitutive of the role of the victim as an agent of justice in the justice traditions of the jurisdiction.

This chapter will present the selective treatment of rights and powers relevant to the victim of crime. It is not intended to be a comprehensive reference to all rights in each jurisdiction. However, to the extent possible, this chapter will set out the pretrial, trial, sentencing, and appellate rights of victims in the context of their local framework. On the international level, the declarations and conventions of the UN not already extracted in Chapter 2 together will be added to by reference to local instruments that attest to the ratification or reform of normative issues on the local level. The individual domestic jurisdictions will also contain brief reference to the sources of criminal law and the organisation of the criminal court to facilitate a better understanding of the differences between the domestic jurisdictions covered.

Inquisitorial systems

The continental European system is broadly characterised as inquisitorial and quasi-adversarial. Some prefer the term non-adversarial, to indicate that the offices of public prosecution may be included in the court structure, which perform a quasi-judicial role in the earlier part of the investigative process. While neither of these ways of categorising the systems of justice in a country or state tells us about the specific modes of victim participation and support offered, they do offer a broader understanding of the rights that may constitute the victim in the justice system. In particular, adherence to an inquisitorial and quasi-adversarial tradition informs us about the relationship between justice stakeholders, and between victims and the police, prosecution, court, and judiciary, in particular. Inquisitorial systems are characterised by a wholly interventionist system of justice, composed of an investigative prosecutor or magistrate at the pretrial level, through to an interventionist judge at trial. Counsel serve the court in so far as they seek to arrive at the truth of the matter, and witnesses tend to give narrative evidence rather than evidence led by examination and cross-examination around the particular elements of the case of the offence. This does not mean that counsel never question witnesses, but rather are led by the judge, who will intervene in proceedings to determine their course. The partie civile system of participation is found across numerous European jurisdictions and incorporates the office of the accessory or auxiliary prosecutor and the adhesive prosecutor. This essentially allows the victim to participate in proceedings with standing before the court, usually with the assistance of counsel. Although powers exist to allow the victim standing before the criminal courts, privately led prosecutions or participation as an auxiliary prosecutor is nonetheless relatively infrequent. These rights, however, provide important substantive rights that support the role of the victim as a stakeholder and participant of justice, albeit exercised infrequently.

Germany

The criminal justice system of Germany is constituted under federal law. The German Criminal Code, the *Strafgesetzbuch*, dates to the Penal Code of the German Empire of 1871. The current German Criminal Code was promulgated in 1998, and amended as of 2013. The German Code of Criminal Procedure 1987, amended as of 2014, provides substantive and procedural rights for trial participants. The rights and powers available to victims are set out throughout the German Code of Criminal Procedure. The criminal law of Germany is set out in the 1998 code, which was initially developed out of the *Reichsstrafgesetzbuch*, or code of the German Empire, otherwise known as imperial criminal law. The Penal Code sets out the criminal law of Germany, while supplementary laws and the German Code of Criminal Procedure set out the processes relevant to the prosecution, the accused, counsel, courts, and victims. German public prosecutors gained the power to start prosecuting war crimes and genocide under international law pursuant to the *Völkerstrafgesetzbuch*, or Code of Crimes against International Law.

The criminal courts of Germany consist of the local, regional, and higher regional courts, all of which exercise first instance jurisdiction over criminal matters. Appeals also go to the higher regional court from the local and regional court, and to the federal court of justice from regional and higher regional on points of law. Appeals on fact are limited to those made to the regional court from the local court; otherwise the accused will need to demonstrate an error of law. The police will refer relevant cases to the public prosecutor's office. The initiating court will determine the sufficiency of the charge. Should a case exist, the local court or *Amtsgericht* is the court of first instance for most cases, where the matter will be heard and determined by a single judge where the sentence carries less than two years' imprisonment. Where the matter carries a sentence of between two and four years, or carries a mandatory minimum of a year's imprisonment, the matter will be heard before a judge and two lay assistants, the *Schöffengericht*. The regional court, or *Landgericht*, will hear more serious matters, with the small criminal chamber of the regional court, or *Strafkammer*, determining all matters that carry a sentence of over four years' imprisonment. The *Strafkammer* will also hear applications to commit an individual to a psychiatric hospital, or where post-imprisonment preventive detention is sought. Matters that are particularly serious or those involving death will be heard before three professional and two lay judges, in the grand criminal chamber, known as the *Schwurgericht*. The higher regional court or *Oberlandesgericht*, constituted by three to five professional judges, may hear criminal matters in exceptional circumstances, such as serious political crimes or crimes against the state.

The victim enjoys the rights of the accessory or auxiliary prosecutor under the German Criminal Code. The powers of the accessory prosecutor are extracted in Chapter 2 (extracted in Chapter 2 at 5.9; also see Braun, 2014). The right to join a prosecution as a private accessory prosecutor is organised in terms of the offence charged, but otherwise the victim is free to join at any stage of proceedings, including on appeal. Section 395 of the German Criminal Code 1987 provides that the children, parents, siblings, spouse, or civil partner may join as accessory prosecutor where the primary victim was killed through an unlawful act. The rights of the private accessory prosecutor extend to those functions enumerated under section 397 of the German Criminal Code:

- being present at the main hearing, even if they are to be examined as a witness;
- being entitled to challenge a judge or an expert, to ask questions, to object to orders by the presiding judge and to object to questions, to apply for evidence to be taken, and to make statements;

- being called in and heard to the same extent as the public prosecution office, unless excepted by law;
- decisions which are notified to the public prosecution office shall also be notified to the private accessory prosecutor; and
- the private accessory prosecutor may avail himself of the assistance of an attorney or be represented by such attorney. The attorney shall be entitled to be present at the main hearing, and shall be notified of the date set down for the main hearing if his selection has been notified to the court or if he has been appointed as counsel.

The victim is also entitled to subsidiary rights consistent with his or her party standing in court. These include that the victim, pursuant to section 406d of the German Criminal Code:

- be notified of the termination of the proceedings and of the outcome of the court proceedings to the extent that they relate to him; and
- be notified as to whether the convicted person has been ordered to refrain from contacting or consorting with the aggrieved person, or if custodial measures have been ordered or terminated in respect of the accused or the convicted person, or whether for the first time a relaxation of the conditions of detention or leave has been granted, so long as the victim can show a legitimate interest and if there is no overriding interest meriting protection of the person concerned in excluding the notification (however, if the victim was granted standing as an accessory prosecutor under section 395 there shall be no requirement to show a legitimate interest).

Where victims seek assistance because of their aggrieved status, they may be entitled to the following, pursuant to sections 397a and 406g of the German Criminal Code:

- avail themselves of the assistance of an attorney or be represented by such attorney, prior to preferment of public charges and without declaration of joinder. They shall be entitled to be present at the main hearing, even if they are to be examined as witnesses. If it is in doubt whether a person is entitled to private accessory prosecution, the court shall decide upon hearing the person and the public prosecution office whether the person is entitled to be present; the decision shall be incontestable. Persons entitled to private accessory prosecution shall be notified of the date set down for the main hearing if they have so requested;
- be present at the main hearing;
- the victim shall be notified of the date set down for the main hearing if his selection has been notified to the court or if he has been appointed as counsel. This shall apply at judicial examinations and judicial inspections, unless the presence or notification of the attorney would jeopardize the purpose of the investigation;
- once the charges have been made out, the victim may appoint an attorney and/or seek legal aid for calling in an attorney;
- upon application by the person entitled to join the proceedings as a private accessory prosecutor an attorney may be appointed as counsel provisionally if there is imperative for special reasons, or if the assistance of counsel is urgently required and the granting of legal aid appears to be possible, but a decision cannot be expected in time;[2]
- the appointment shall end unless an application for granting legal aid is filed within a time limit to be set by the judge, or if the granting of legal aid is refused.

The rights of the victim to make a claim for compensation and restitution as adhesive prosecutor are provided for under section 403 of the German Criminal Code. The aggrieved person or his heir may bring a property claim against the accused as connected to the offence should the court have jurisdiction over the offence. The court may make an order where there is no claim pending elsewhere, irrespective of the value of the matter in dispute. Where agreement is reached between the victim and accused, the court will record a settlement in respect of the claims arising out of the criminal offence, and the court will order the settlement where agreed to by the person named in the sentence.

The German Criminal Code also provides for alternative dispute resolution and mediation under section 153a. This section allows for the dispensation of usual court proceedings where a case involves a misdemeanour, and where the public prosecution office, together with the consent of the accused and the court able to open main proceedings, seeks to dispose of those proceedings for alternative proceedings. This will result in the preferment of public charges, such that the court will concurrently impose conditions and instructions upon the accused, so long as public interest in proceeding with a criminal prosecution is not thwarted, and if the degree of guilt of the accused allows. The court may impose conditions on the accused, including that they: perform a specified service in order to make reparations for damage caused by the offence; pay a sum of money to a non-profit-making institution or to the Treasury; perform some other service of a non-profit-making nature; comply with duties to pay a specified amount in maintenance; make a serious attempt to reach a mediated agreement with the aggrieved person (also known as perpetrator–victim mediation), thereby trying to make reparation for their offence, in full or to a significant extent, or to participate in a social skills training course; or to participate in a course pursuant to section 2b subsection (2), second sentence, or a driver's competence course pursuant to section 4a of the Road Traffic Act. Section 155a provides for perpetrator–victim mediation, such that:

> At every stage of the proceedings the public prosecution office and the court are to examine whether it is possible to reach a mediated agreement between the accused and the aggrieved person. In appropriate cases they are to work towards such mediation. An agreement may not be accepted against the express will of the aggrieved person.

France

The rights of victim in the French criminal process were strengthened in the 1980s with policies to relocate victims in the criminal prosecution and court process. The basic criminal law of France is contained in the Penal Code of 1810, or *Code Pénal*, and the Code of Criminal Procedure of 1808, or *Code de Procédure Pénale* (see Guinchard and Buisson, 2011). Both codes have been revised continuously since original assent. The victim or injured party, otherwise partie civile combining the role of auxiliary and adhesive prosecutor, is enshrined in the Code of Criminal Procedure, Preliminary Article, II, which provides that 'The judicial authority ensures that victims are informed and that their rights are respected throughout any criminal process.' The right of the victim to present at trial and to initiate a private prosecution is also recognised under the Code of Criminal Procedure:

> **Article 1** Public prosecution for the imposition of penalties is initiated and exercised by the judges, prosecutors or civil servants to whom it has been entrusted by law. This prosecution may also be initiated by the injured party under the conditions determined by the present Code.

Article 528–2 The provisions of the present chapter do not preclude the right of the injured party to have the offender directly summoned before the police court under the conditions provided for by the present Code. Where the summons is served after a criminal order has been made for the same offence, the police court rules: on the public prosecution and on any civil claim if the criminal order has been challenged by an application to set aside within the time limits provided for in article 527 and at the latest at the opening of the hearing; on the civil claim only if no application to set aside has been filed or if the defendant has expressly stated, at the opening of the hearing at the latest, that he has waived his application to set aside or his right to file such an application. The same applies if it is established that the criminal order has been voluntarily paid.

The Code of Criminal Procedure also prescribes the right to attach a claim for compensation or reparation:

Article 2 Civil action aimed at the reparation of the damage suffered because of a felony, a misdemeanour or a petty offence is open to all those who have personally suffered damage directly caused by the offence. The waiver of a civil action will not interrupt or suspend the exercise of the public prosecution, subject to the cases set out under the third paragraph of article 6.

Article 40–1 Where the victim wishes to exercise the rights of the civil party and requests that an advocate be appointed after being informed of this right pursuant to 3 of articles 53–1 and 75, the district prosecutor, informed by the judicial police officer or agent, where he has decided to initiate a prosecution, notifies the president of the Bar of this. If he does not, he informs the victim, when telling him that his case has been dropped, that he make a request directly to the president of the Bar if he still intends to seek compensation for the harm he has suffered.

The criminal courts of France build upon the administrative courts that may deal with claims against the government. The criminal courts include the police tribunal, or tribunal de police, which disposes of minor contraventions; the criminal court or correctional court, or tribunal correctionnel, for more serious offences, such as délits, the less serious felonies, and misdemeanours; the assize court, or *cour d'assises*, for the more serious felonies; the appeal court, or *cours d'appel*, which hears appeals; and the supreme appeals court, the court of cassation or *cour de cassation*, for final appeals on questions of law.

For the more serious offences, French criminal procedure includes a pretrial system of specialty judges, known as investigating judges or *juges d'instruction*. The investigative judges will be instructed by a public prosecutor, or victim seeking to bring a civil claim for damages during a criminal proceeding. The investigative judge will collect inculpatory or exculpatory evidence against an accused person, although he or she will fall short of reaching a verdict on the accused. The investigative judge may conduct interviews, seek assistance from the police, issue warrants, take statements from suspects or from persons seeking damages, seek further evidence by search and seizure, make orders for telephone intercepts, and appoint expert advisors. Bail will be ordered by a judge for freedom and detention, or *juge des libertés et de la détention*. At the conclusion of the investigation, the investigating judge may commit the accused to one of the higher-level courts for trial, including the *cour d'assises* for trial. If there is insufficient evidence the investigative judge may discharge the accused. More complex offences may be investigated by *pôles de l'instruction* (or multiple *juges d'instruction*).

The Code of Criminal Procedure also sets out the right of victims to have their complaint actioned by the police:

> **Article 15–3** The judicial police are obliged to receive complaints filed by victims of offences committed against the criminal law and to transmit them, should the occasion arise, to the service or group of judicial police competent for the area in question.
>
> **Article 53–1** (cf. A 75) Judicial police officers and agents inform victims, using any means of communication, of their right: 1 to obtain compensation for the harm suffered; 2 to exercise the rights of the civil party if the public prosecution has been instigated by the public prosecutor or by directly citing the perpetrator to appear before the competent court or by lodging an official complaint before the investigating judge; 3 if they wish to exercise the civil party's right to be assisted by an advocate of their choice or, at their request, by one nominated by the president of the bar attached to the competent court, the costs are to be borne by the victims, unless they are eligible for legal aid, or are covered by legal protection insurance; 4 to be assisted by a service pertaining to one or more local authorities or an approved victim support association; 5 to transfer the case, where appropriate, to the committee for the compensation of victims of offences, where the offence falls under the remit of articles 706–3 and 706–14.

Victims have the right to be assisted during proceedings with the help of an advocate. This is similar to an intermediary offered to victims and witnesses in England and Wales and in certain states in Australia; however, the advocate representing the assisted witness has extensive powers to make submissions for the witness not available in the intermediary system:

> **Article 113–2** Any person mentioned by name in a complaint or implicated by the victim may be heard as an assisted witness. Where he appears before the investigating judge, he is compulsorily heard in this capacity if he requests this. Any person implicated by a witness or against whom there is evidence making it seem probable that he could have participated, as the perpetrator or accomplice, in committing the offence of which the investigating judge is seised, may be heard as an assisted witness.
>
> **Article 113–3** The assisted witness benefits from the right to be assisted by an advocate, who is informed prior to the hearings and who has access to the case file, in accordance with the provisions of articles 114 and 114–1. He may also ask the investigating judge to be confronted with the person or persons who have implicated him, in accordance with the provisions of article 82–1. This advocate is chosen by the assisted witness or appointed ex officio by the president of the bar association if the person concerned requests this.

Hearings in camera for the benefit of the vulnerable victim are available when so requested. Should the accused be a juvenile offender, proceedings may also proceed in camera unless qualifying conditions are met and the partie civile agrees that proceedings are held in camera:

> **Article 306** (cf. 706–47–1; 706–48; 706–49; 706–52; 706–53) The hearing is public unless publicity would be dangerous for order or morality. In such a case, the court so declares by a ruling made in open court. The presiding judge may nevertheless prohibit access to the courtroom for minors, or for certain minors. In the case of a prosecution for the offences of rape or torture and acts of barbarity accompanied by sexual

aggression, a hearing in camera is granted as of right where the civil party victim or one of the victims so requires; in the other cases a hearing in camera may only be ordered where the civil party victim or one of the civil party victims does not oppose it. Where a hearing in camera has been ordered, this applies to the reading of any judgments that may be made in respect of any procedural objections considered under article 316. The judgment on the merits must always be read in open court. If the accused, who was a minor when the charges were brought against him, reaches his majority by the first day of proceedings, the provisions of the present article are applicable before the juvenile assize court if he requests it, unless there is another defendant who is still a minor, or was a minor when the charges were brought and has reached his majority by the first day of proceedings, and who opposes this request.

Although the victim has the capacity to seek standing before the court as partie civile from start of the trial, the victim is limited to presenting evidence on oath once granted that status. If the victim is required to testify at trial he or she must do so on oath, so in that event the usual process is for the victim to seek partie civile status early on in the trial. However, if the victim is not required to give evidence he or she may seek partie civile standing after the close of the state prosecution, allowing the victim to participate other than on oath during the trial. This allows the victim to make submissions and present additional evidence without the need to take an oath, which may otherwise restrict participation (Brienen and Hoegen, 2000: 323). As a party with standing before the court, the partie civile is able to seek information about the case not otherwise available to a witness. This includes being informed of key developments on the issues before the court, being able to question and challenge court decisions, and being able to present supplementary evidence to the court in their own right, without support from either the state prosecutor or defendant.

Where the matter does proceed to trial, the state prosecutor may dispose of the matter by referring the offender to a mode of restorative diversion from court. A formalised mediation process is available for misdemeanours.[3] If intervention is also likely to restore the victim and provide for his or her reparation, the prosecutor may make several directions to divert the offender and restore the victim, for less serious offences:

> **Article 41–1** Where it appears that such a measure is likely to secure reparation for the damage suffered by the victim, or to put an end to the disturbance resulting from the offence or contribute to the reintegration of the offender, the district prosecutor may, directly or by delegation; 1 bring to the attention of the offender the duties imposed by law; 2 direct the offender towards a public health, social or professional organisation. In cases where the offence was committed while driving a motor vehicle, this measure may consist of requiring the offender to take a road safety awareness course at his own expense; 3 require the offender to regularise his situation under any law or regulation; 4 require the offender to make good the damage caused by the offence; 5 put in train, with the consent of the parties, mediation between the offender and the victim.

French criminal procedure permits victims to tender a statement in court proving particulars of the losses and injuries suffered by them that relate to the proceedings before the court (Brienen and Hoegen, 2000: 319). The process for claiming civil damages follows the trial process, such that the civil claim is heard after the evidence is presented to the judges and lay jury. Victims may therefore wait until the close of the main prosecution to attach their civil claim to the trial process. The process generally allows victims to make their submissions and claim for compensation following the close of the state prosecution and the reply from the defence. At this point, counsel acting for the victim may address the court on matters important to the victim, followed by a response from the state prosecution and defence (see Guinchard and Buisson, 2011). The judges and lay jury ascertain the guilt of the accused in terms of the charges before the court; however, the civil claim is determined by the judges alone. The court also has the power to award reparations.

Claims for compensation may be made at the outset of proceedings where there is a decision not to proceed with the trial. If the *juge d'instruction* investigates the complaint and determines that the matter should not proceed to trial, the victim may apply for compensation directly from the state. Compensation or restitution may be sought from the offender personally, or through the state fund, the *fonds de garantie*. This fund is available to victims of especially violent offences – in particular, gross trespass to the person, including homicide, serious interpersonal harm, and sexual assault, and harms related to acts of terrorism. There are no limits for the more serious harms caused by interpersonal violence or terrorism. However, compensation for minor offences is limited to treatment and associated costs. The victim may also claim compensation from the Crime Victim Compensation Commission, or the *Commission d'Indemnisation des Victimes d'Infractions*. Here, a commissioner will examine different forms of damage occasioned to the victim, such as psychological injuries, emotional trauma, and future economic losses.

Mixed inquisitorial/adversarial systems

The continental European approach to criminal justice grants victims substantial access to justice by granting the victim rights to accessory and auxiliary prosecution, while allowing the victim to adhere a compensation claim to be determined at trial. While victims do not act as the auxiliary prosecutor often, the power to do so has been long recognised in the European civil law tradition (see Safferling, 2011). Although different continental European jurisdictions grant comparable rights in respect of victim participation, each country has developed legal tradition, moving away from the inquisitorial approach for a mixed or hybrid system of adversarial justice. The framework decisions of the Council of Europe and the jurisprudence of the ECtHR have encouraged the development of the adversarial approach across Europe, with some jurisdictions now retaining an inquisitorial pretrial process initiated by a prosecutor or investigative magistrate or judge, with an adversarial trial characterised by an adversarial exchange between the prosecuting state and defence. Where the victim presents during trial, usually through counsel, the equality of arms may require a greater shift towards adversarial processes in order to clearly demarcate the main interests of the state and accused over those of the victim. Such a quasi-adversarial trial will usually be convened around a judge who is more independent than the investigative judge or magistrate of the pretrial phase. Most continental European jurisdictions now possess a criminal procedure which articulates a trial process constituted by identifiable adversarial procedures. These involve a movement away from narrative evidence for examination of witnesses by counsel. Such jurisdictions include Sweden, the Netherlands, and Austria. Other jurisdictions, such as Germany and France, are wholly inquisitorial, although there have been attempts of limited success to move different phases of the trial in these countries to a more adversarial process (see Guinchard and Buisson, 2011; Kury and Kichling, 2011).

Sweden

The Swedish criminal process may be identified across distinct phases, the investigative phase or preliminary investigation or förundersökning, and the trial phase, or rättegång, where the accused is subject to indictment, or åtals väckande. The criminal law of Sweden flows from the Swedish Penal Code of 1962 and court processes, including those relevant to victim standing before the court, are contained in the Code of Judicial Procedure of 1942, or *Rättegångsbalk*. The Code of Judicial Procedure contains both civil and criminal provisions.

There are various criminal courts in Sweden. These include the general courts, which comprise district courts or *tingsrätt*, the courts of appeal or *hovrätt*, and the Supreme Court or *Högsta Domstolen*. When the victim or aggrieved person alleges a crime has occurred, the police will investigate the matter and launch a preliminary investigation where sufficient evidence presents. The preliminary investigation will be led by the police or a state prosecutor, and is usually conducted privately. Upon completion, the police or prosecutor conducting the preliminary investigation may discharge the accused and discontinue the investigation. Where the preliminary investigation garners sufficient evidence against an accused, the prosecutor will commit the accused for trial at the district court. For less serious offences, the prosecutor may dispose of the matter by summary penalty so long as the accused agrees to enter a guilty plea.

The Code of Judicial Procedure provides for the cross-examination of witnesses by counsel. The hybrid status of the justice system is, however, developed out of the use of public or lay judges in the trial phase. Victims are granted the right to private counsel, who may accompany the public prosecutor as an auxiliary or adhesive prosecutor in court (Joutsen, 1987; Brienen and Hoegen, 2000: 890; Zila, 2006). The pretrial phase is an integrated quasi-adversarial model as victims may appoint counsel to present alongside the public prosecutor. The pretrial investigative process is otherwise constituted by the accused and state prosecution, although the judge is more impartial than inquisitorial. The Code of Judicial Procedure sets out the rights of the aggrieved party to initiate a prosecution:

> **Chapter 20, Section 5** An aggrieved person may report an offence for prosecution with any prosecutor or police authority. If the accusation has been made to an authority at a place other than one in which the prosecution may be instituted, the accusation shall be transmitted immediately to the authority at that other place.
>
> **Chapter 20, Section 8** The aggrieved person may not institute a prosecution for an offence falling within the domain of public prosecution unless he has reported the offence for prosecution and the prosecutor has decided not to institute a prosecution. When a prosecutor has instituted a prosecution, the aggrieved person may support the prosecution; he may also appeal to a superior court. The condition stated in the first paragraph does not limit the right of an aggrieved person to institute a prosecution for false or unjustified prosecution, false accusation, or any other untrue statement concerning an offence. The aggrieved person is the person against whom the offence was committed or who was affronted or harmed by it.

Where victims seek a private settlement with their alleged offender they may no longer report the offence for prosecution, thereby limiting their ability to seek out a prosecution only to join the prosecution as an auxiliary prosecutor:

> **Chapter 20, Section 12** When the aggrieved person, by settlement out of court or otherwise, has promised not to report or institute a prosecution, or when the aggrieved person has withdrawn his accusation or prosecution, he may thereafter neither report the offence institute a prosecution. If the offence falls within the domain of public

prosecution only upon accusation by an aggrieved person, and the promise not to accuse was made or the accusation withdrawn before the institution of a public prosecution, the offence may not subsequently be subject of public prosecution.

The Code of Judicial Procedure therefore provides a foundation for auxiliary prosecution by the aggrieved person. There are three types of aggrieved person or victim in the Swedish justice system. These include a brottsoffer, or a victim in a broad sense; *a målsägande*, or an aggrieved person seeking a compensation claim who may also appear as auxiliary prosecutor; and an alternative to the second term, *a målsägande*, who does not seek formal standing rights at trial but who takes an interest in proceedings in an emotional sense (Brienen and Hoegen, 2000: 890). In practice, therefore, the aggrieved party is distinct from the aggrieved person, because party standing grants participatory rights at trial, while the aggrieved person maintains an interest in the outcome of the matter. The aggrieved party may seek party standing by requesting leave from the court. Where granted, the aggrieved party may make submissions and question witnesses during the preliminary examination and during the trial. The *målsägande* may support the state prosecutor, or present submissions alongside the state. Where the state declines to prosecute, the aggrieved party may bring a private prosecution that may involve the appointment of a private counsel.

Counsel is provided for the assistance of victims, who may be publicly funded in certain cases of serious interpersonal or sexual violence. The aggrieved person has the right to a publicly funded advisor, or *målsägandebiträde*, for serious offences (as to assistance offered by Swedish support organisations, see Jägervi and Svensson, 2015). This provides a complementary manner of representation that builds upon the rights of the *målsägande*. The role of the *målsägandebiträde* is to safeguard the aggrieved person during the trial phases. The *målsägandebiträde* may go farther than court assistance, however, and may discuss matters relevant to the safety of the victim with the police and other authorities. The *målsägandebiträde* may also provide assistance with compensation, and can seek to adhere a claim in court:

> **Chapter 20, Section 15** An aggrieved person, who is examined in aid of the prosecution's case, may be accompanied at the examination by a suitable person as support (supporting person) during the trial. A supporting person known to the court shall, if possible, be given notice of the trial. In certain cases, counsel for the aggrieved person can be appointed pursuant to the Act concerning Counsel for the Aggrieved person. Counsel for the aggrieved person shall be summoned to the main hearing, or other sessions of the court, at which the aggrieved person or the legal representative of the aggrieved person is to be examined.

Private prosecutions may also be initiated other than by the aggrieved person:

> **Chapter 20, Section 16** When by an act or ordinance the prosecution of an offence may be instituted by a private person other than the aggrieved person, he shall be regarded as the aggrieved person in relation to matters concerning the right to report and prosecute an offence and to institute a prosecution.

Death cases allow the kin of the victim to act as the aggrieved person for the purpose of attaining standing before the courts:

> **Chapter 20, Section 13** When a criminal act has resulted in the death of a person, the decedent's surviving spouse, direct heir, father, mother or sibling succeeds to the right

of the aggrieved person to report the offence or prosecute the offence. When the person against whom the offence was committed, or who was affronted or harmed by it, dies, the persons related to him as aforesaid have the same right to report or prosecute the offence if the circumstances do not indicate that the deceased would have chosen not to report or prosecute the offence.

Claims for compensation adhered to the main trial proceedings are also permitted:

> **Chapter 22, Section 1** An action against the suspect or a third person for a private claim in consequence of an offence may be conducted in conjunction with the prosecution of the offence. When the private claim is not entertained in conjunction with the prosecution, an action shall be instituted in the manner prescribed for civil actions.
>
> **Chapter 22, Section 2** When a private claim is based upon an offence subject to public prosecution, the prosecutor, upon request of the aggrieved person, shall also prepare and present the aggrieved person's action in conjunction with the prosecution, provided that no major inconvenience will result and that the claim is not manifestly devoid of merit. If the aggrieved person desires to have his claim entertained together with the prosecution, he shall notify the investigation leader or the prosecutor of the claim and state the circumstances upon which it is based.

At trial, counsel has the capacity to call and examine witnesses, and opposing counsel may cross-examine witnesses. The presiding judge may also ask questions. This mode of examination departs from narrative evidence and results in differences between the prosecution and defence case, as found in adversarial trials. The *målsägandebiträde* may need to present at trial to make submissions for the aggrieved person, where they may raise objections, cross-examine the accused, or call witnesses of their own. They may also make general submissions regarding liability for damages or compensation and may also make submissions as to sentencing (Brienen and Hoegen, 2000: 890). The Swedish process integrates aspects of the inquisitorial and adversarial traditions in the trial phase in particular. However, the victim or aggrieved person or party is well positioned throughout to draw from the traditions of the continental European approach of providing the victim extended rights to criminal justice.

The Netherlands

The Dutch Penal Code of 1881, or *wetboek van strafrecht*, as amended, sets out the main criminal offences that apply in the Netherlands. The Dutch Code for Criminal Procedure of 1838, or *wetboek van strafvordering*, as amended, otherwise sets out the rights of the victim to access justice. While prosecutions will be initiated by the Public Prosecution Service under Dutch law, the victim is entitled to auxiliary and adhesive procedures alongside the state prosecution in accordance with reforms introduced in 2011 (see Ezendam and Wheldon, 2014: 63–64). These reforms were central to the ratification of the CEU FD of 2001 into law.

Dutch criminal procedure requires that criminal proceedings be initially brought before the district courts. Matters may be progressed to the courts of appeal and the Supreme Court, or *Hage Raad*. For criminal matters, the district courts are divided into the sub-district sector, or *kantongerecht*, and the criminal law sector, or *rechtbanken*. Felonies are tried in the criminal law sector, while misdemeanours are heard in the sub-district sector. The sub-district sector ensures a measure of access to justice by dealing with matters in a less formal way, before a single judge. Minor criminal matters are disposed of in this way, and may involve police matters or cases where the public prosecutor proposes a settlement with the offender. If a settlement is rejected by the offender the matter will proceed before a single judge. Settlements may include payment of compensation to the victim. There is a hearing following the examination of the case file, where the sub-district judge delivers an ex tempore judgement immediately following the hearing. The criminal law sector hears all matters that are not dealt with by the sub-district sector. These matters may be heard by a single judge, or a full-bench panel consisting of three judges. The full-bench panel will hear more complex and serious cases, or all cases in which the prosecution seeks a sentence greater than one year's imprisonment. Appeals from the sub-district court will proceed before the district court, while matters heard before the criminal law sector will be appealable to the courts of appeal. The Supreme Court may hear appeals on questions of law only, with the facts being established at trial in the lower court.

The victim gains the right to participate in the trial by virtue of his or her injured status under the Code for Criminal Procedure:

> **Section 51a** 1. A person who has incurred financial loss or another loss as a direct result of a criminal offence shall be deemed a victim. The legal person which has suffered financial loss or another loss as a direct result of a criminal offence shall be considered as equivalent to the victim. 2. The public prosecutor shall be responsible for ensuring that the victim is treated appropriately. 3. At the victim's request, the police and the public prosecutor shall keep the victim informed on the commencement and progress of the case against the suspect. In particular, the police shall at least provide written notification of discontinuance of the investigation or the forwarding of an official report against the suspect. The public prosecutor shall give written notification of the commencement and continuation of the prosecution, of the date and time of the court session and of the final judgment in the criminal case against the suspect. In cases designated for that purpose and in any case, if it concerns a serious offence as referred to in section 51e(1), he shall also, where requested, notify the release of the suspect or the convicted offender. 4. At the victim's request, information on how he can obtain compensation shall also be provided to him.

Once recognised as a victim for the purpose of proceedings, the victim or injured person will gain rights to access the case file. Access is granted on the basis that the victim may add relevant documents to assist with his or her claim for compensation:

> **Section 51b** 1. At the victim's request, the public prosecutor shall grant him permission to inspect the case documents of relevance to him. During the court hearing this leave shall be granted by the court of first instance, before which the case is being prosecuted, and for the rest by the public prosecutor. 2. The victim may request the public prosecutor to add to the case file documents that he considers relevant for the assessment of the case against the suspect or his claim against the suspect. 3. The public prosecutor may refuse to add documents or permit inspection thereof if he is of the opinion that the documents cannot be regarded as case documents or if he considers the addition of said documents or their inspection to be incompatible with the interests referred to in section 187d(1). 4. The public prosecutor shall require written authorisation for the

application of subsection (3), to be granted by the examining magistrate on his application. The public prosecutor shall notify his decision in writing to the victim. 5. The manner in which case documents are to be inspected shall be arranged by Governmental Decree. 6. The victim may obtain copies of the documents he has been permitted to inspect at the court registry in accordance with the provisions by or pursuant to section 17 of the Act on Remunerations in Criminal Cases [Wet Tarieven in Strafzaken]. Section 32(2) to (4) inclusive shall apply mutatis mutandis.

The victim may gain legal representation to assist with his or her claim:

Section 51c 1. The victim may have legal representation. 2. The victim may be represented at the court session by a lawyer, provided this lawyer declares that he has been given express authorisation, or by an authorised representative who has been given a special written power of attorney for that purpose. 3. If the victim is not fluent or sufficiently fluent in the Dutch language, he may have the assistance of an interpreter.
Section 51d Sections 51a to 51c inclusive shall apply mutatis mutandis to the surviving relatives within the meaning of section 51e(3) and (4), and to the persons referred to in section 51f(2).

Crimes are investigated by the police, but the more serious offences are handed over to an examining magistrate, or *rechter-commissaris*, who conducts a preliminary judicial investigation, the *gerechtelijk vooronderzoek*. Preliminary judicial investigations may be at the behest of the public prosecutor or the examining magistrate themselves. The examining magistrate will exercise supervision over the coercive measures required to procure evidence during this phase, ultimately advising the public prosecutor as to whether they can proceed to trial (Brienen and Hoegen, 2000: 647). The investigative magistrate will also direct the police investigation. The pretrial phase thus attains an inquisitorial character only in so far as the coercive measures of the investigative magistrate are concerned; otherwise the accused is able to challenge decisions made. The public prosecutor may summon the accused at the end of the investigation where a decision is made to out the accused on trial.

The trial phase is more accusatorial. Trials are largely based on the case file formed during the pretrial phase. Unless one of the parties seeks to call further witnesses, or adduce more evidence, the matter will be largely determined by reference to the file. Although witnesses are increasingly called and examined in court, Dutch trials are substantially shorter than in most adversarial jurisdictions out of use of the case file (Brienen and Hoegen, 2000: 648). At trial, the accused has a right to remain silent. After the indictment is read by the public prosecutor, further witnesses may be called and examined. Victims may participate at this point, where they have a compensation claim or wish to clarify issues before the court. The defence then has the ability to ask questions of witnesses, to make submissions, and to present their closing remarks. Once the defence closes any case in response, the court will pronounce guilt.

Although the victim is granted the right to join the prosecution, this tends to be limited to compensation claims as the prosecution is conducted by the public prosecutor, who is charged with the duty to support the victim during trial pursuant to section 51a of the Code for Criminal Procedure. The victim gains further rights to make a statement to the court for serious offences, which may include reference to the impact of the crime upon the victim and his or her family. The victim's kin also gain rights to address the court usually in death cases. These rights may be exercised by the victim's counsel:

Section 51e 1. The right to make a verbal statement at the court session may be exercised if the offence as charged in the indictment is a serious offence which carries a statutory term of imprisonment of at least eight years, or any of the serious offences referred to in sections 240b, 247, 248a, 248b, 249, 250, 285, 285b, 300(2) and (3), 301, (2) and (3), 306 to 308 inclusive and 318 of the Criminal Code and section 6 of the Road Traffic Act 1994 [Wegenverkeerswet 1994]. 2. The victim, the father or the mother of a minor victim who has a close relationship with that victim and persons who take care of or raise that victim as part of their family and have a close and personal relationship with the child, may, jointly or each separately, make a statement about the impact that the criminal offences referred to in subsection (1) have had on them at the court session. The person concerned shall notify in writing his intention to make such statement to the public prosecutor before the start of the court session so that the public prosecutor is able, in good time, to invite him to appear at the court session. The presiding judge may, ex officio or on application of the public prosecutor, deny or restrict the right of the father or mother or caretakers, referred to in the first sentence, to make a verbal statement, if he determines that this would be contrary to the minor victim's best interests. 3. The right to make a verbal statement at the court session, referred to in subsection (1), may also be exercised by a surviving relative who has made it known that he wishes to make a statement about the impact that the victim's decease has had on him at the court session. The surviving relative who wishes to exercise the right to make a verbal statement at the court session shall notify this intention in writing before the start of the court session so that the public prosecutor is able, in good time, to invite him to appear at the court session. 4. The surviving relatives, who are eligible to be called to appear at the court session under subsection (3), shall include: a. the spouse or civil registered partner or other partner, and b. the relatives by consanguinity in the direct line and those up to and including the fourth degree of the collateral line. If more than three surviving relatives, referred to in (b), have indicated that they wish to exercise their right to make a verbal statement, and they fail to agree among themselves which of them will address the court, the presiding judge shall decide which three persons may exercise the right to make a verbal statement. 5. The victims or surviving relatives who may exercise the right to make a verbal statement shall include the minor who has reached the age of twelve years. This shall also apply for the minor who has not yet reached that age and who can be deemed capable of reasonably assessing his interests in that respect. 6. If the victim or a surviving relative has not yet reached the age of twelve years, the right to make a verbal statement at the court session may be exercised by his legal representatives insofar as this representation is not contrary to the minor's best interests. The legal representatives may also, jointly or each separately, make a statement about the impact the criminal offences referred to in subsection (1) have had on them. The presiding judge may, ex officio or on application of the public prosecutor, decide to deny the legal representative the right to make a verbal statement at the court session, if he determines that this would be contrary to the minor's best interests. 7. If the victim or the surviving relative is actually incapable of exercising the right to make a verbal statement, the person referred to in subsection (4)(a) and one of the persons referred to in subsection (4)(b) may exercise the right to make a verbal statement about the impact the criminal offence has had on this victim or surviving relative at the court session.

The power to claim compensation and to adhere that claim to the main prosecution at trial is provided for under the Code for Criminal Procedure, rights simultaneously exercisable by the victim's kin:

> **Section 51f** 1. The person who has incurred direct damage as a result of a criminal offence may join the criminal proceedings in his capacity as injured party and claim compensation. 2. If the person referred to in subsection (1) has died as a result of the criminal offence, his heirs may also join the criminal proceedings in regard of their claim acquired under universal title and the persons, referred to in section 6:108(1) and (2) of the Civil Code [Burgerlijk Wetboek] in regard of the claims referred to in that section. 3. The persons referred to in subsections (1) and (2) may also join the criminal proceedings for a part of their claim. 4. Those persons who require legal representation or must be represented in order to appear in civil court proceedings shall also require legal representation or representation in order to be able to join the criminal proceedings in accordance with subsection (1). An authorisation of the single judge division of the Sub-District Court Sector, as referred to in section 1:349(1) of the Civil Code, shall not be required for that representative. The provisions pertaining to legal representation or representation, necessary in civil cases, shall not apply to the defendant. 5. If the public prosecutor institutes or continues prosecution, he shall notify the injured party thereof in writing as soon as possible. If the case is to be tried at a court session, the public prosecutor shall notify the date and time of the court session to the injured party as soon as possible.

Mediation between the accused and victim may be encouraged where appropriate and any agreement reached placed before the court prior to sentencing:

> **Section 51h** 1. The Public Prosecution Service shall see to it that the police inform the victim and the suspect of the option of mediation at the earliest possible stage. 2. If mediation between the victim and the suspect has resulted in an agreement, the court shall, if it imposes a punishment or measure, take this agreement into account. 3. The Public Prosecution Service shall encourage mediation between the victim and the convicted offender, after it has made certain that the victim agrees to such mediation. 4. Further rules pertaining to mediation between the victim and the suspect or between the victim and the convicted offender may be set by Governmental Decree.

Restorative practices and modes of intervention may be available for less serious offences where the victim and suspect have agreed to the harm caused. The nature of the agreement between victim and accused will be taken into account by the court during sentence.

Austria

The substantive criminal law of Austria is contained in the Penal Code of Austria of 1974, or *Strafgesetzbuch*, as amended. The Penal Code of Austria is divided into public law that prescribes criminal acts and penalties. However, criminal law also contains non-criminal actions and penalties, dealt with by administrative law, which contain a range of disciplinary penalties. Thus, it is necessary to differentiate the judicial and administrative criminal law, because the former will be disposed of in the criminal courts while the latter will be determined by the administrative authorities. The Austrian Code of Criminal Procedure of

1975, or *Strafprozeßordnung*, as amended, sets out court processes relevant to the disposal of criminal matters. The Code of Criminal Procedure also contains various provisions that set out the general rights of victims, define the victim or types of victims recognised under Austrian law, and allow for the participation and standing of the victim in Austrian courts.

The provisions of the Code of Criminal Procedure regulate the court processes that determine how a matter is proceeded with and disposed of, including the extent of any victim involvement. Austrian criminal procedure is defined by its reference to the discretion of the state prosecutor to determine the appropriate charge, to proceed upon relevant charges, and to provide the trial court with the evidence gathered during the pretrial process. The Code also prescribes that criminal proceedings ought to be held in camera in exceptional circumstances only, that court processes must proceed before an appropriately appointed judge, where relevant matters proceed before judge and jury, and that judges act independently throughout proceedings (Brienen and Hoegen, 2000: 64–66).

The examining magistrate, or *Untersuchungsrichter*, will conduct an investigation into a reported offence as referred by the state prosecutor, having been informed of an offence by the police. Where matters proceed before a jury, the preliminary investigation must be complete with a recommendation to proceed with the matter before any trial may take place. For other matters not proceeded with by way of jury trial, the public or private prosecutor may proceed with the matter before the investigation is complete (should one be initiated). The examining magistrate will close the investigation once sufficient evidence has been gathered to proceed to trial. Otherwise they may terminate the investigation where the state or private prosecutor seeks to withdraw the charge. Where the matter is serious enough to proceed before the regional court (see ahead), an indictment is drafted and intermediary proceedings are held to determine the dates of the trial, who is to be summoned to court, and any request for further evidence or investigation of the facts.

The courts of ordinary jurisdiction hear matters not dealt with by the public law courts, which include criminal cases. For criminal matters, the court that disposes of minor offences is the district court, or *Bezirksgerichte*. The district courts deal with cases where the offence carries a fine or a term of imprisonment of a year or less. More serious matters are heard by the regional courts sitting as courts of first instance, or *Landesgerichte*. Depending on type of offence, matters come within the jurisdiction of the district court or a regional court. Matters are heard before a single judge in the district court. The constitution of the regional court differs on the basis of the offence and penalty. The court will be constituted as a *Schoeffengericht*, with two professional and two lay judges, for offences that carry a sentence of five years or more. The court will be constituted as a *Schwurgericht*, with three professional judges and a jury of eight people, for offences involving murder or armed robbery, or for offences that carry life imprisonment (Brienen and Hoegen, 2000: 65). The jury decides guilt but also decides the relevant sentence in consultation with the professional judges.

Regional courts may also hear matters referred to them by the district court as a court of second instance, sitting as a bench of three professional judges. Appeals are always heard in one of the four province courts, of Vienna (for Vienna, Lower Austria, and Burgenland), Graz (for Styria and Carinthia), Linz (for Upper Austria and Salzburg), and Innsbruck (for Tyrol and Vorarlberg). The Supreme Court, or *Oberster Gerichtshof*, is the highest court in criminal matters. It is a final court of appeal, or court of last instance, sitting in panels of five for criminal matters. The Supreme Court will hear appeals only to nullify a verdict of the *Schoeffengericht* or the *Schwurgericht*. Appeals against sentence alone will proceed before the regional courts of second instance. The constitutional court, or *Verfassungsgerichtshof*, may provide guidance where a matter of constitutional significance is raised, or where a criminal law is challenged as unconstitutional. Issues relevant to criminal law and procedure may arise where a law limits the civil rights of citizens in accordance with the Austrian Constitution.

At trial, once the presiding judge opens proceedings, the accused may be questioned by the judge, the prosecution, defence counsel, and counsel for the victim or civil claimant. All other witnesses proceed in this order, including any expert witnesses called to give evidence. Witnesses are examined by counsel so that proceedings gain an adversarial character, despite involvement from the bench. Closing remarks are then made by the prosecution and defence. The verdict is received by the presiding judge. Reform of the Code of Criminal Procedure introduced the victim as an adhesive prosecutor with the capacity to act as a private prosecutor where the state prosecution is withdrawn. The victim has the right to participate in the investigation, and attains standing before the court in criminal proceedings. Victims are also able to adhere themselves to proceedings as civil claimants. The victim has a right to legal advice and support, who may act for the victim in proceedings as a subsidiary or accessory prosecutor. The victim also bears the right to appeal those verdicts relevant to his or her interests.

Part 1 of the Code of Criminal Procedure covers general matters and principles of proceedings (for translation of the Code, see Witzleb, 2016). Chapter 1 of the Code, the criminal proceeding and its principles, provides a right to a fair hearing. This includes rights in support of the victim, to be informed about such rights, including their reason and purpose. Fair trial rights are also extended to all parties participating in proceedings, including the victim and accused. Service rights to dignified treatment are also provided for the accused:

> **Section 6** (1) The suspect has the right to contribute to the whole proceeding and the obligation to be present during the trial. He is to be treated with respect for their personal dignity. (2) Every person involved in the proceeding or affected by the exercise of coercive measures has the right to a fair hearing and to be informed about the reason and purpose of procedural steps affecting them as well as about their significant procedural rights. The suspect has the right to be fully informed of all grounds for suspicion against them and be given complete opportunity to refute these and to justify himself.

Victim participation is provided under section 10 of the Code of Criminal Procedure. This section provides for participation through access to information, for the personal dignity of the victim, with regard to the need to protect the intimate sphere of the victim's life. The identity of the victim and exhibits such as photographs which may disclose identification particulars are to be handled with respect for the victim's dignity. This right of participation extends to all authorities and institutions taking part in the criminal proceeding:

> **Section 10** (1) Victims of crime are entitled in accordance with the provisions of Chapter 4 to participate in the criminal proceeding. (2) The criminal police, the public prosecutor and the court are obliged to have reasonable regard for the rights and interests of victims of crime and to inform all victims of their significant procedural rights as well as of the possibility of receiving compensation and support. (3) All authorities, institutions and persons taking part in the criminal proceeding shall treat victims during the proceeding with respect for their personal dignity and for their interest in protecting their intimate sphere of life. This applies in particular to the disclosure of photographs and the distribution of personal information which can reveal the identity to a wider range of persons, if this is not required for reasons of the administration of criminal

justice. When making decisions to discontinue the proceeding, the public prosecutor and the court shall always consider the victim's interests in reparation and promote it as far as possible.

Chapter 4 of the Code of Criminal Procedure refers to victims and their rights according to the harms committed against them. Division 1 provides for general matters, which includes the definition of victim:

> **Section 65** For the purposes of this statute, 1. 'Victim' is a. every person who through an intentionally committed crime may have been exposed to violence or a dangerous threat, or whose sexual integrity may have been infringed upon, b. the spouse, the registered partner, the de facto partner, the relatives in ascendant or descendant line, the brother or sister of a person whose death may have been caused by a crime, or other family members who witnessed the crime, c. every other person who through a crime may have suffered harm or loss or who may have been otherwise affected in their criminally protected interests, 2.'Private participant' is every victim who declares their participation in a proceeding in order to claim compensation for harm or loss suffered, 3. 'Private prosecutor' is every person who applies to the court for the prosecution, or otherwise applies for a trial, of a crime that is not subject to public prosecution (section 71), 4. 'Subsidiary prosecutor' is every private participant who maintains a prosecution withdrawn by the public prosecutor.

Division 2 of chapter 4 of the Code of Criminal Procedure deals with victims and private participants. Victim rights are prescribed and set out according to discrete rights and powers exercisable at each stage of proceedings. Significantly, section 66(2) provides that victims are to be provided psychosocial and legal process support to the extent necessary to protect the procedural rights of the victim, with highest possible regard to the victim's personal involvement in the trial:

> **Section 66** (1) Regardless of their position as private participants, victims have the right: 1. to be represented (section 73), 2. to access the files (section 68), 3. prior to interview to be informed about the subject-matter of the proceeding and about their significant rights (section 70(1)), 4. to be advised of the progress of the proceeding (sections 177(5), 194, 197 (3), 206 and 208(3)), 5. to receive translation assistance; section 56 applies in analogy,[4] 6. to participate in an interview of witnesses and suspects through video-link (section 165) and in a reconstruction of the crime (section 150(1)), 7. to be present at the trial and to ask questions of the accused, witnesses and experts as well as to be heard in relation to their claims, 8. to request the continuation of a proceeding discontinued by the public prosecutor (section 195). (2) Victims as defined in section 65 No. 1 a) or b) shall receive on demand psychosocial and legal process support to the extent necessary for the protection of their procedural rights with highest possible regard to their personal involvement. Psychosocial process support comprises the preparation of the affected person for the proceeding and the associated emotional strain as well as accompanying them for interviews during the criminal investigation and examinations during trial; legal process support [comprises] legal advice and representation by a legal practitioner. The Federal Minister for Justice is authorised to contractually engage institutions, which are proven to be suitable, to provide process support to victims as defined in section 65 No. 1 a) or b) provided the legal conditions are met.

The right to information during the investigative phase is granted in accordance with the victim's need for process support, with further particular rights provided to victims of domestic violence or interpersonal violence or where a family death has occurred. The right to be informed of unsupervised leave of a prisoner from prison, or of permanent or actual release from prison, is also granted:

> **Section 70** (1) As soon as a criminal investigation is opened against an identified suspect, the criminal police or the public prosecutor shall inform victims of their significant rights (sections 66 and 67). This may be postponed only for as long as is necessary to avoid prejudice to the purpose of the investigation. Victims as defined in section 65 No. 1 a) or b) shall be informed of the conditions of receiving process support no later than before their first questioning. Victims of domestic violence (section 38a of the SPG)[5] or victims as defined in section 65 No. 1 a) shall furthermore be informed no later than their interview according to section 177(5)[6] as well as in relation to their right to be advised, on application, without undue delay of the first unsupervised leave from prison or of the imminent or actual release of the prisoner (section 149(5) of the StVG).[7] (2) Victims whose sexual integrity may have been violated shall furthermore be informed no later than before their first questioning of their following rights: 1. to demand questioning in the criminal investigation by a person of their gender if possible, 2. to refuse to answer questions concerning circumstances of their intimate sphere of life or concerning details of the crime, if they find their description unacceptable (section 158(1) No. 2), 3. to demand to be questioned during the criminal investigation and during trial in a considerate manner (sections 165, 250(3)), 4. to demand the exclusion of the public from the trial (section 229(1)).

Under the Code of Criminal Procedure, chapter 5, common provisions, division 5, decisions and complaints, a complaint may be made by the victim where his or her rights have otherwise been denied or where the matter is discontinued by the public prosecutor:

> **Section 87** (1) Unless the statute provides otherwise, a judicial decision can be complained against to the court of appeal by the public prosecutor, by the suspect as far as their interests are immediately affected, as well as by any other person whose rights have been immediately denied or who has incurred an obligation through a judicial decision or who is affected by a coercive measure, and, if the decision consists of the discontinuation of the proceedings, by the private participant. (2) The public prosecutor also has the right to a complaint if their applications in accordance with section 101(2)[8] have not been dealt with. Furthermore, any person who alleges that the court, in taking the evidence, infringed upon a subjective right of that person (section 106(1)), has a right to a complaint. (3) A complaint has suspensive effect only if expressly provided for in the statute.

Part 2 of the Code of Criminal Procedure provides for the criminal investigation. Chapter 8 detailed rights during investigatory measures and the taking of evidence, wherein division 9 specifically deals with the visual inspection and reconstruction of the crime:

> **Section 150** (1) The public prosecutor, the suspect, the victim, the private participant and their representatives shall be given the opportunity to participate in the reconstruction of the crime. They have the right to ask questions and to demand supplementary investigations and determinations. If the criminal police is not involved in conducting

the reconstruction, it shall be notified of the event. (2) The suspect can be temporarily excluded from the participation if their presence could jeopardise the purpose of the proceeding or particular interests so require (section 250(1)). The victim and the private participant can be temporarily denied involvement if there is a concern that their presence could influence the suspect or witness in making a free and complete statement. In these cases, the participant concerned shall be given a copy of the record without delay. The participation of the defence lawyer shall not be curtailed in any case. In other respects, section 97 applies.[9]

Division 10 of part 2, chapter 8, provides rights in respect to enquiries and interviews. The victims retain the power to be exempted from making a witness statement:

Section 156 (1) The following persons are exempt from the duty to make a witness statement: 1. Persons who are supposed to make a statement in a proceeding against a family member (section 72 of the StGB),[10] whereby the characteristic of being a family member due to marriage or registered partnership is retained for the purpose of determining the right to refuse to make a witness statement even when the marriage or registered partnership no longer exists; 2. Persons who may be injured by the crime allegedly committed by the suspect and are under 14 years of age at the time of interview or may be injured in their sexual sphere, if the parties had the opportunity to participate in an interview through video-link (sections 165, 247). (2) In accordance with subsection 1 no. 1, an adult person who participates in the proceeding as a private participant (section 67) is not exempt from making a witness statement. (3) If in a proceeding against more than one suspect, the exemption from making a witness statement exists in relation only to one of the suspects, the witness is exempt in relation to the other suspects only if the statements cannot be separated. The same applies if the reason for the exemption only relates to one of a number of matters.

Part 4 of the Code of Criminal Procedure provides trial and appeal rights. Chapter 14 of part 4 provides rights before the state court as a court of lay assessors and appeal against its judgements. The victim is provided certain rights to contest the acquittal of the accused where the victim acts as a private participant, where the acquittal has affected his or her civil claim. Subsection 282(1) refers to standing in relation to appeals in favour of the accused on questions of law regarding the proceeding or the judgement, while subsection 282(2) provides the private participant substantive rights to challenge the acquittal:

Section 282(2) If detrimental to the accused, the complaint of nullity[11] can only be brought by the public prosecutor or the private prosecutor as well as by the private participant, by the latter however only in the case of acquittal and on the ground of section 281(1) no. 4.[12] The private participant can furthermore assert the aforementioned ground of nullity only as far as he was through the acquittal referred to civil proceedings and it is apparent that the dismissal of an application he made at trial may have had a prejudicial influence on his civil claim.

The right to claim compensation is also provided for:

Section 67 (1) Victims have the right to claim compensation for the damage suffered as a result of the crime or for the infringement of their legal interests protected by criminal law. The extent of the damage or infringement is to be determined by the court acting of its own motion, as far as this is possible from the findings in the criminal proceeding or through simple further inquiries. If an expert is appointed to assess a physical injury or damage to health, he shall be instructed also to determine the periods of pain. (2) Victims obtain the status of private participants through declaration. Unless this is evident, they shall in the declaration give reasons for their entitlement to participate in the proceeding and for their claim for compensation. (3) A declaration pursuant to subsection 2 shall be submitted to the criminal police or the public prosecutor; after charges are filed, it shall be submitted to the court. It may not be made after the hearing of evidence is concluded; at that point, the amount of damages claimed must also be quantified. The declaration can be withdrawn at any time. (4) The declaration shall be dismissed if: 1. it is evidently without cause, 2. it is made late (subsection 3) or 3. the amount of damages has not been quantified within time. (5) The dismissal of a declaration pursuant to subsection 4 lies in the responsibility of the public prosecutor and, after charges are filed, of the court, respectively. (6) Apart from the rights of victims (section 66), private participants also have the right, 1. to apply for the taking of evidence (section 55), 2. to maintain the charge pursuant to section 72, after it has been withdrawn by the public prosecutor, 3. to make a complaint against the discontinuation of the proceeding ordered by the court pursuant to section 87, 4. to be summonsed to the trial and to be given the opportunity, after the final plea of the public prosecutor to make and give reasons for their claim, 5. to bring an appeal in relation to their private law claim pursuant to section 366. (7) Unless private participants are granted legal process support (section 66(2)), they shall be granted procedural support through the assignment of a legal practitioner free of charge, provided that representation through a legal practitioner is required for the administration of justice, in particular for the purposes of enforcing their legal entitlements without the need for a subsequent civil proceeding, and they are unable to afford the cost of legal representation without experiencing hardship in meeting their basic living expenses. Basic living expenses are the expenses a person requires for a simple lifestyle for themselves and their dependent family members. The provisions of sections 61(4) and 62(1), (2) and (4) apply in analogy to the assignment and appointment of such a legal representative.

Compensation is available even where a charge is withdrawn by the public prosecutor. The victim may present evidence in support of his or her claim. Private participants may be entitled to legal process support under section 66(2); however, they will be assigned a publicly funded legal practitioner where they have otherwise not received section 66(2) support. Such support is provided on the assumption that the victim requires representation through a legal practitioner, for the administration of justice, and in particular, to enforce the legal entitlements of the victim without the need for subsequent civil proceedings.

Adversarial systems

Adversarial systems of justice are characterised by an accusatorial, common law process dependent on the testing of the state or Crown case. This tends to occur through an independent prosecutor, who is briefed by the police, who brings charges against an accused. The accused may remain silent until proven guilty. The accused has the right to counsel in pursuit of the right to test the prosecution case. The defence is not compelled to offer any evidence at trial, although most do so in order to enhance their changes of acquittal.

Most though not all jurisdictions that adhere to an adversarial model utilise a jury system of around twelve laypeople who take on the role of arbiters of fact. In adversarial proceedings the judge is arbiter of law, is independent of counsel, and will intervene only to restore control of proceedings or where the interests of justice so necessitate. Judges will generally refrain from asking questions or leading witnesses, but will open and close proceedings by summarising relevant facts and stating the law to the jury.

The development of systems of adversarial justice has seen victims removed to the periphery of justice. Unlike continental European systems of civil law, victims in adversarial, common law states have few rights at trial. Although the right to private prosecution exists, few victims exercise it. However, the movement towards the ratification of international and regional instruments, or otherwise through processes of policy transfer or law reform, has seen many adversarial countries substantially develop their victim rights record.

England and Wales

The criminal law of England and Wales is set out across a number of statutes as derived from the common law and as added to by amending legislation over time. Most older common law offences have now been abolished or abrogated from the common law, and replaced with statutory alternatives. The statute that contains the main indictable offences against the person is the *Offences Against the Person Act 1861* (UK). Associated legislation that sets out other relevant criminal offences includes the *Sexual Offences Act* 2003 (UK), *Theft Act 1968* (UK), and *Criminal Justice Act 1993* (UK), which deals with drug trafficking, proceeds and profit of crime, financing of terrorism, and insider dealing. The *Criminal Justice Act 1988* (UK) sets out limited criminal offences aside from the rules of evidence as they relate to the criminal trial, the confiscation of the proceeds of crime, and the jurisdiction of the Criminal Injuries Compensation Board. Other major instruments which set out relevant court processes, including investigative and pretrial processes, include the *Police and Criminal Evidence Act 1984* (UK), *Criminal Justice and Public Order Act 1994* (UK), and *Bail Act 1976* (UK), regarding police powers, search and seizure of evidence, pretrial detention and application for bail respectively. The *Crime and Courts Act 2013* (UK) creates the National Crime Agency, sets out rules on filming court proceedings, and amends the law of self-defence. The *Youth Justice and Criminal Evidence Act 1999* (UK) contains provisions regarding criminal procedure relevant to young persons, and the *Criminal Justice Act 2003* (UK) contains provisions regarding out-of-court and documentary evidence. Otherwise, criminal procedure in England and Wales is a matter for court rules and practice directions, issued to practitioners appearing before the relevant courts. The consolidated rules are published under section 69 of the *Courts Act 2003* (UK) as the Criminal Procedure Rules.

The courts of England and Wales range from those dealing with matters summarily before a magistrate sitting alone, the magistrates' court, to those that deal with all indictable offences, the crown court, including the Central Crown Court or Old Bailey in London. Matters are appealable to the Court of Appeal of England and Wales (Criminal Division), the decisions of which may be further appealed to the Supreme Court of the UK, or formerly, the House of Lords.

In the case of *Attorney-General's Reference (No. 3 of 1999)* [2000] UKHL 63, Lord Steyn refers to the importance of the victim as one of the stakeholders of justice, at par. [25]:

> The purpose of the criminal law is to permit everyone to go about their daily lives without fear of harm to person or property. And it is in the interests of everyone that serious

crime should be effectively investigated and prosecuted. There must be fairness to all sides. In a criminal case this requires the court to consider a triangulation of interests. It involves taking into account the position of the accused, the victim and his or her family, and the public.

Provisions for the inclusion of the victim in court proceedings are dispersed across different processes and courts, usually in terms of the different phases of the criminal trial process. This is consistent with the way victim rights are peripheral to common law systems of criminal justice. As such, there is no overarching criminal code or procedure that grants victims substantive or enforceable rights of universal application. Rather, specific processes and opportunities for victim participation must be interrogated in order to identify the rights framework of victims in common law, adversarial countries, such as England and Wales. Within this context belies the movement towards non-enforceable declarations and charters of victim rights (extracted in Chapter 2 at 2.4, 3.5, 4.5, 6.8, 8.4). Such non-enforceable instruments affording victim rights to treatment, information, or limited participation are common in the adversarial, common law jurisdictions that have a history of excluding victim participation. Tracing the role of the victim in a procedural sense is therefore a matter of discrete investigation and articulation of the various laws and processes that combine to offer victims different, at times conflicting, levels of participation.[13]

The rights of the victim in the pretrial process, including during investigation and during pretrial processes in court, were covered in Chapter 3. These rights are largely identified as limited in that they do not always grant victims substantive rights that can be enforced against the state or accused. For instance, the victim is entitled to various pretrial rights of consultation during the investigative and arrest process, under the Victims' Code (see CPS, 2013a, 2013b) and the *Directors Guidance on Charging* (see CPS, 2013c). In Chapter 3, the victims' right to review was also covered in terms of the emerging EU framework under the CEU DVC of 2012 and its ratification into domestic legal processes through the case of *R v Killick* [2011] EWCA Crim 1608 and the *Victims Right to Review Guidance* published in July 2014 (CPS, 2014).

Moreover, much of the development of victim rights in England and Wales concerns rights and powers intended to protect vulnerable and child victims from secondary victimisation at trial. The case of *R v Camberwell Green Youth Court* [2005] 1 All ER 999 assesses section 21 of the *Youth Justice and Criminal Evidence Act 1999* (UK), which examines the extent to which a court may depart from standards of the fair adversarial trial to support protective measures for young or vulnerable witnesses. Although the court recognises the right of the accused to examine witnesses consistent with adversarial processes, *R v Camberwell Green Youth Court* assesses the extent to which section 21 complies with the fair trial requirements of Article 6 of the ECHR by setting up special measures for vulnerable victims. Section 21 enables young witnesses to sexual offences and violence to provide their evidence by live television link or video recording, and does so without the requirement to assess compelling circumstances that may be relevant to each matter. Lady Hale of Richmond refers to the jurisprudence of the ECtHR and rules the following at par. [49]:

> It is difficult to see anything in the provisions of the 1999 Act with which we are concerned which is inconsistent with these principles. All the evidence is produced at the trial in the presence of the accused, some of it in pre-recorded form and some of it by contemporaneous television transmission. The accused can see and hear it all. The accused has every opportunity to challenge and question the witnesses against him at

the trial itself. The only thing missing is a face to face confrontation, but the appellants accept that the Convention does not guarantee a right to face to face confrontation. This case is completely different from the case of anonymous witnesses. Even then the Strasbourg Court has accepted that exceptions may be made, provided that sufficient steps are taken to counter-balance the handicaps under which the defence laboured and a conviction is not based solely or decisively on anonymous statements (see *Doorson v Netherlands* [1996] 22 EHRR 330, 350, para 72; *Van Mechelen v Netherlands* [1997] 25 EHRR 647, 673, paras 54, 55; *Visser v Netherlands*, Application No 26668/95, Judgment 14 February 2002, para 43).

The modification of the criminal trial to grant victims and witnesses protective or special measures is therefore not consistent with the fair trial rights of the accused so long as sufficient steps are taken. In the same case, Lord Roger of Eearlsferry argued that the ECtHR has not required that Article 6 mandates that the accused be in the same room as the witness testifying, so long as the accused is given an appropriate opportunity to cross-examine the witness in a way that maintains the victim's recourse to privacy. Section 23 of the *Criminal Justice Act 1988* (UK) (Section 21 is now repealed; see *Criminal Justice Act 2003* (UK) section 116) granted a right to tender hearsay evidence where the victim could be classed as a 'frightened witness' (see contra Requa, 2010). *R v Sellick and Sellick* [2005] 2 Cr App R 15 held where a victim was in fear of the accused, he or she may testify by statement without the need to be present in court. This necessarily limited the accused's ability to cross-examine the witness in court. The court ruled that this may occur even where the statement was substantially determinative in the case. Lord Justice Waller, with whom Mr Justice Owen and Mr Justice Fulford agreed, held the following, dismissing the appeal at par. [57]:

> Our view is that certainly care must be taken to see that sections 23 and 26, and indeed the new provisions in the *Criminal Justice Act 2003*, are not abused. Where intimidation of witnesses is alleged the court must examine with care the circumstances. Are the witnesses truly being kept away by fear? Has that fear been generated by the defendant, or by persons acting with the defendant's authority? Have reasonable steps been taken to trace the witnesses and bring them into court? Can anything be done to enable the witnesses to be brought to court to give evidence and be there protected? It is obvious that the more 'decisive' the evidence in the statements, the greater the care will be needed to be sure why it is that a witness cannot come and give evidence. The court should be astute to examine the quality and reliability of the evidence in the statement and astute and sure that the defendant has every opportunity to apply the provisions of Schedule 2. It will, as section 26 states, be looking at the interests of justice, which includes justice to the defendant and justice to the victims. The judge will give warnings to the jury stressing the disadvantage that the defendant is in, not being able to examine a witness.

Where concerns exist as to the reliability of documentary evidence the court will act to restrict admissibility. *R v Martin* [2003] 2 Cr App R 21 held that where the accused is unfit to stand trial, and cannot testify to his defence, documentary evidence prejudicial to the accused would not be admissible where cross-examination of their content was not possible. Lord Justice Potter, Mr Justice Mackay, and His Honour Judge Mellor held the following at par. [61]:

> we find ourselves unable to support the judge's exercise of his discretion to admit the statement of Tamba Bona. It is not in dispute that the entire case for the prosecution

rested upon Tamba Bona's statement. Thus, while it was plainly in the interests of justice so far as the prosecution was concerned that the statements should be before the jury, it was also in the interests of justice from the point of view of the defendant that he should not be unduly disadvantaged by admission of the statements in circumstances where they could not be made the subject of cross-examination.

There are different 'special measures' presently available to vulnerable and intimidated victims and witnesses, specifically the use of screens, live TV link, giving evidence in private (though this is restricted to sexual offences and those involving intimidation), having counsel remove wigs and gowns, and the use of video recorded interviews as evidence-in-chief.[14]

The *Criminal Justice Act 2003* (UK) was amended in 2003 to allow evidence by statement where a witness may otherwise be unsuitable for cross-examination. Section 116(1) allows the tenure of a statement, not given in oral evidence in the proceedings, if (a) oral evidence given in the proceedings by the person who made the statement would be admissible as evidence of that matter, (b) the person who made the statement (the relevant person) is identified to the court's satisfaction, and (c) any of the five conditions mentioned in subsection (2) is satisfied. Subsection 2(e) provides the condition:

> that through fear the relevant person does not give (or does not continue to give) oral evidence in the proceedings, either at all or in connection with the subject matter of the statement, and the court gives leave for the statement to be given in evidence.

The introduction of section 116 of the *Criminal Justice Act 2003* (UK) extended the range of circumstances under which statements were admissible. Unlike former provisions under section 23 of the *Criminal Justice Act 1988* (UK), section 116 includes oral and written evidence. Statements may be drafted by someone other than the police, and the term 'fear' is to be read broadly enough to allow a range of reasons for testifying in open court. As Lord Justice Waller put it in *Sellick*, at par. [53]:

> In our view, having regard to the rights of victims, their families, the safety of the public in general, it still cannot be right for there to be some absolute rule that, where compelling evidence is the sole or decisive evidence, an admission in evidence of a statement must then automatically lead to a defendant's Article 6 rights being infringed. That would lead to a situation in which the more successful the intimidation of the witnesses, the stronger the argument becomes that the statements cannot be read. If the decisive witnesses can be 'got at' the case must collapse. The more subtle and less easily established intimidation provides defendants with the opportunity of excluding the most material evidence against them. Such an absolute rule cannot have been intended by the European Court in Strasbourg.

Adherence to these special provisions for victims has been affirmed by the lord chief justice of England and Wales. In *Criminal Practice Directions Amendment No. 2* [2014] EWCA Crim 1569, Lord Thomas of Cwmgiedd CJ amended the *Criminal Practice Directions 2014*, which sets out the criminal procedure of vulnerable witnesses at 3E.4:

> All witnesses, including the defendant and defence witnesses, should be enabled to give the best evidence they can. In relation to young and/or vulnerable people, this may mean departing radically from traditional cross-examination. The form and extent

of appropriate cross-examination will vary from case to case. For adult non vulnerable witnesses an advocate will usually put his case so that the witness will have the opportunity of commenting upon it and/or answering it. When the witness is young or otherwise vulnerable, the court may dispense with the normal practice and impose restrictions on the advocate 'putting his case' where there is a risk of a young or otherwise vulnerable witness failing to understand, becoming distressed or acquiescing to leading questions. Where limitations on questioning are necessary and appropriate, they must be clearly defined. The judge has a duty to ensure that they are complied with and should explain them to the jury and the reasons for them. If the advocate fails to comply with the limitations, the judge should give relevant directions to the jury when that occurs and prevent further questioning that does not comply with the ground rules settled upon in advance. Instead of commenting on inconsistencies during cross-examination, following discussion between the judge and the advocates, the advocate or judge may point out important inconsistencies after (instead of during) the witness's evidence. The judge should also remind the jury of these during summing up. The judge should be alert to alleged inconsistencies that are not in fact inconsistent, or are trivial.

Special measures for child victims, including the ability to depart from standard adversarial processes for vulnerable adults, grant the victim new rights of participation in accordance with international norms of victim rights traced in Chapter 2. The continued development of the provisions for out-of-court evidence indicates that this is an area of expanding rights for victims of crime. Henderson (2014: 95) argues the victims may be better supported if the chances of miscommunication are avoided by developing questions based on the developmental needs of witnesses, by limiting suggestive questions, and by limiting cross-examination of the witness (also see Starmer, 2014; Hoyano, 2015; the law of Scotland has also been recently modified to better accommodate child and vulnerable witnesses; see Raitt, 2013 and the discussion in the next section). Lady Justice Hallett DBE in *R v Lubemba* [2014] EWCA Crim 2064 considered the extent to which traditional trial processes ought to be modified to accommodate the examination of vulnerable witnesses through special hearings as a standard measure, at par. [42]:

> The court is required to take every reasonable step to encourage and facilitate the attendance of vulnerable witnesses and their participation in the trial process. To that end, judges are taught, in accordance with the Criminal Practice Directions, that it is best practice to hold hearings in advance of the trial to ensure the smooth running of the trial, to give any special measures directions and to set the ground rules for the treatment of a vulnerable witness. We would expect a ground rules hearing in every case involving a vulnerable witness, save in very exceptional circumstances. If there are any doubts on how to proceed, guidance should be sought from those who have the responsibility for looking after the witness and or an expert.

The courts of England and Wales have also increasingly sought to include victim interests in sentencing. Chapter 3 considered the inclusion of victim rights and interests in compensation and restitution under the *Powers of Criminal Courts (Sentencing) Act 2000* (UK), sections 130, 148–149, and in the Australian context under the *Criminal Law (Sentencing) Act 1988* (SA), section 53. In both jurisdictions, sentencing courts may go beyond the normal capacity to determine a compensation award where otherwise not determined by the executive. Here, the courts have a capacity to include the compensation or restitution claim as part of an offender's sentence.

However, despite the ability to compensate the victim as part of sentencing proceedings and as relevant to the sentence of the accused, the capacity for the offender to indeed pay the amount awarded remains an important determinant in the amount awarded against an accused. Moreover, the sum arrived at may be independent of other orders, including the confiscation of assets. There are, however, limits to the extent to which the court will allow a double counting of restitution. *Mohid Jawad v The Queen* [2013] EWCA Crim 644 ruled that the offender should not have to repay a victim where the offender was already subject to a confiscation order that would lead to the double counting of moneys owed. In this case, however, the court ruled that the sentence was not disproportionate unless the offender could prove that he or she would be required to repay both amounts. The court also clarified that section 130 of the *Powers of Criminal Courts (Sentencing) Act 2000* (UK) provided for a civil award although it was available to a sentencing court as an ancillary order, at par. [12]:

> A compensation order and a POCA [Proceeds of Crime Act] confiscation order are two very different things. They derive from quite separate statutes and they serve different purposes. The power to make a compensation order is now derived from section 130 Powers of Criminal Courts (Sentencing) Act 2000. Historically the power existed long before any proceeds of crime legislation and has not been modified as a result of it. A POCA confiscation order is designed to remove from the defendant the fruits of crime. A compensation order has a different purpose; it is designed as a limited and summary method of ordering the defendant to repay the loser and is available to short-circuit a civil action against the defendant in a straightforward case. Because the two orders serve different purposes, it has been held on several occasions in the past that there is no obstacle to making both orders in the same case.

Reforms to the law of England and Wales demonstrate how the victim is being increasingly credited with rights and powers that may be substantially enforced in the court. However, there are limits to which the victim is empowered in the context of fair trial rights and processes that grant the accused access to justice. This necessarily includes access to evidence with a view that the accused may critically examine the content of statements tendered. Departure from the standard adversarial criminal process is significant in terms of the degree and scope of rights now afforded to the victim in the context of a justice tradition that has ill afforded rights of victim participation.

England's decision to leave the European Union in the poll of June 2016 may have ramifications for the continued development of English law and policy towards the continental European standards of victim participation. However, even without the guidance of framework directives and other regional EU instruments, English law and policy are likely to continue to develop in a way that increasingly accommodates the victim into justice processes.

Scotland

The criminal law of Scotland is contained in the common law, which is also supplemented by statute – namely the *Criminal Law (Consolidation) (Scotland) Act 1995* (Scot) and other Acts, including the *Sexual Offences (Scotland) Act 2009* (Scot). Criminal procedure is principally provided under the *Criminal Procedure (Scotland) Act 1995* (Scot) and other Acts, but also the *Victims and Witnesses (Scotland) Act 2014* (Scot), the *Sexual Offences (Procedure and Evidence) (Scotland) Act 2002* (Scot), and the *Vulnerable Witnesses (Scotland) Act 2004* (Scot).

The criminal courts of Scotland exercise summary and indictable justice. The justice of the peace courts are local courts that exercise a summary jurisdiction over minor offences heard by a lay magistrate sitting alone, without a jury. The lay magistrate may impose sentences of up to sixty days' imprisonment. The sheriff court also exercises a summary jurisdiction for matters not dealt with before the justice of the peace courts. The sheriff court may also sit solemn – that is, with a lay jury of up to fifteen people. When the sheriff court sits solemn, it may impose a maximum sentence of five years on an accused. Higher sentences may be passed where matters proceed before the high court of justiciary, where a jury of fifteen may decide more serious indictable offences. Summary matters from the justice of the peace courts and the sheriff court may be appealed to the sheriff court of appeal. Appealable matters from the sheriff court of appeal or matters on indictment from the sheriff court and high court of justiciary may be appealed to a two- or three-judge panel of the high court of justiciary, depending on whether it is an appeal against sentence or conviction respectively.

The *Victims and Witnesses (Scotland) Act 2014* (Scot) was passed in 2013 to introduce a number of reforms to Scotland's justice system to establish a range of victim rights and powers. These reforms include: establishing a duty for justice agencies to provide clear standards of service for victims and witnesses; granting victims and witnesses a right to prescribed information regarding their court matter; establishing initiatives to support vulnerable victims and witnesses during court proceedings (including lowering the age of child witnesses to those under eighteen rather than sixteen, as previously prescribed, and establishing categories of victims as inherently vulnerable to grant those victims access to special measures when giving evidence in court); establishing a 'victim surcharge' on fines paid to pay for the support of victims; establishing a restitution scheme for accused persons who assault police officers, facilitating the recovery of such victims; and granting victims the ability to make an oral statement regarding the release of life sentence prisoners.[15]

The criminal procedure and law of evidence of Scotland allow victims to obtain counsel beyond the pretrial hearing for subpoenaing of evidence of the victim's sexual history in rape cases.[16] The victim's ability to consult a lawyer is now granted in so far as senior office holders within the executive and judiciary are bound to uphold the general principles owed to victims and witnesses when undertaking their functions of office. These principles cover different phases of the trial process but also include the main trial, where victims will be called to give evidence. Section 1(3) of the *Victims and Witnesses (Scotland) Act 2014* (Scot) prescribes the following:

> **Section 1(3)** The principles are: (a) that a victim or witness should be able to obtain information about what is happening in the investigation or proceedings, (b) that the safety of a victim or witness should be ensured during and after the investigation and proceedings, (c) that a victim or witness should have access to appropriate support during and after the investigation and proceedings, (d) that, in so far as it would be appropriate to do so, a victim or witness should be able to participate effectively in the investigation and proceedings.

The use of counsel to assist vulnerable victims of sexual assault has a history in the legislative changes introduced under the *Sexual Offences (Procedure and Evidence) (Scotland) Act 2002* (Scot) (see section 294 of the *Criminal Procedure (Scotland) Act 1995* (Scot)) and the *Vulnerable Witnesses (Scotland) Act 2004* (Scot). These statutes gave special recognition to the secondary harm occasioned to sex offences victims when giving evidence at trial out of the general practice of cross-examining victims on their personal character and sexual history. Rights were granted to limit pretrial discovery of evidence regarding the sexual history or general character of the victim.[17] Victims were able to seek assistance from a lawyer where an application was to be challenged in court (see Raitt, 2010, 2013). The *Victims and Witnesses (Scotland) Act 2014* (Scot) develops the restrictions put in place by the 2002 Act by seeking continued support for victims who are deemed to be vulnerable at trial. The reforms in Scotland, however, go beyond the provision of pretrial counsel provided in other jurisdictions (see USA, below) out of the reforms implemented by the 2014 Act requiring continued support for victims during the trial. Allowing counsel in the trial phase has proven controversial, and debate ensues to the extent to which this unsatisfactorily interferes with the due process rights of the accused (see Hoyano, 2015: 119).

The use of counsel as a support mechanism for victims may be warranted out of the recognition afforded to victims under the *Victims and Witnesses (Scotland) Act 2014* (Scot).[18] The proposal to expand the availability of counsel for victims, even in a limited capacity as a support person to ensure protective measures are made available and effectively implemented at trial, is, however, contentious. Chalmers (2014: 186; also see Munro, 2014: 158–160) makes the case that counsel for vulnerable victims would not necessarily obtain standing before the court as equal to the prosecution and defence. Rather, such counsel would provide access to justice for victims in a way that is recognised elsewhere, including Ireland and Canada:

> As this makes clear, what is contemplated here is not any sort of status as an equal party with the prosecutor; it is instead a right to make representations at certain specific points. It bears similarities to the limited rights to representation which have been recognised in Canada (in respect of disclosure of personal records) and Ireland (in respect of applications to lead sexual history evidence).

The *Victims and Witnesses (Scotland) Act 2014* (Scot) provides other rights, including the right encouraged under the CEU DVC of 2012, including the right to review the prosecution's decision not to proceed with a matter, victim statements, access to restorative intervention, adequate compensation for victims, and the victim's right to information.

Ireland

Criminal law in Ireland flows from the common law and a number of statutes, including the *Offences Against the Person Act 1861* (Ire), the *Criminal Justice Act 1964* (Ire), the *Non-Fatal Offences Against the Person Act 1997* (Ire), the *Criminal Law (Jurisdiction) Act 1976* (Ire), the *Criminal Law (Sexual Offences) Act 1993* (Ire), the *Criminal Law (Sexual Offences) Act 2006* (Ire), the *Misuse of Drugs Act 1977* (Ire), the *Criminal Justice (Drug Trafficking) Act 1996* (Ire), the *Criminal Justice (Theft and Fraud Offences) Act 2001* (Ire), and the *Criminal Law Act 1976* (Ire). Criminal procedure is contained in the *Bail Act 1997* (Ire) (cf. *Bail Bill 2015* (Ire)), the *Criminal Justice Act 1984* (Ire), the *Criminal Law Act 1997* (Ire), the *Criminal Law (Rape) Act 1981* (Ire), the *Criminal Procedure Act 1967* (Ire), the *Criminal Evidence Act 1992* (Ire), and the *Criminal Justice Act 2006* (Ire).

The criminal courts of Ireland consist of the district court, where matters are heard summarily before a judge sitting alone, the circuit criminal court, which hears less serious indictable offences before judge and jury, and the high court, which sits as the central criminal court, where serious matters such as murder, rape, treason, and piracy are dealt with before judge and jury. Decisions of the district court are appealable to the circuit criminal court. Decisions of the trial courts are appealable to the court of appeal in the first instance, which may then be subject to further appeal to the Supreme Court of Ireland. Common law offences are classed as indictable offences, although modern offences passed by the Parliament of Ireland, the Oireachtas, distinguish between summary and indictable offences and how they may be disposed of before the courts. Article 38.2 of the Constitution of Ireland prescribes that minor offences may be tried in summary courts. When a case is disposed of summarily before the district court, the judge is restricted to a maximum sentence of one year for any individual offence, or a maximum of two years for cumulative offences, pursuant to section 11 of the *Criminal Justice Act 1984* (Ire). There are several offences that are strictly indictable, and include those serious indictable offences prescribed under the *Criminal Procedure Act 1967* (Ire) and the *Criminal Law (Rape) (Amendment) Act 1990* (Ire). Ireland has also utilised commissions of inquiry to uncover evidence of institutional abuse of children, as discussed in Chapter 3.

Ireland has made several recent reforms to accommodate the rights of victims but most recently under the *Criminal Justice (Victims of Crime) Bill 2015* (Ire). The Bill is prefaced with the 2012 directive of the EU – specifically:

> An Act to give effect to certain provisions of Directive 2012/29/EU of the European Parliament and of the Council of 25 October 2012 establishing minimum standards on the rights, support and protection of victims of crime, and replacing Council Framework Decision 2001/220/JHA and to provide for related matters.

The Bill sets out the statutory rights of victims, which include substantive and enforceable rights in addition to rights to access information and be kept informed of relevant developments regarding a matter before the courts. The Bill includes the right to be informed when the director of public prosecutions decides not to proceed with a prosecution, and further provides an entitlement to review that decision. Victims also gain the right to specific information from the police, or *Garda Síochána*, when an offence is reported. Further rights regarding the prisoner release are also provided. The Bill also provides for the assessment of protective measures for individuals subject to repeat victimisation or retaliation. The Bill further provides for the statutory requirement that victims be assessed with regard to their entitlement to special measures, such as out-of-court or documentary evidence, in terms of pending criminal proceedings.

Head 2 of the Bill provides the definition of victim:

> 'victim' means (a) a natural person who has suffered harm, including physical, mental or emotional harm or economic loss which was directly caused by a criminal offence perpetrated against him or her, or (b) a family member of a person whose death was directly caused by a criminal offence and who have suffered harm as a result of that person's death, whether or not, in either case, a complaint alleging the commission of an offence has been made or any offender has been identified, apprehended, charged or convicted in relation to the offence.

Select rights that set out substantive rights to justice include those available in the investigative, trial, and sentencing phase of criminal proceedings. The pretrial, investigative rights are mindful of the fact that most victims are unfamiliar with criminal justice processes and will require basic information as to services provided. Access to compensation and expense reimbursement and the right to inform the trial court of the effect of the offence (pursuant to Head 9, Victim Personal Statement) are also provided for:

> **Head 4** Information to be provided to victims. Provide that: A person who contacts a member of the Garda Síochána stating that he or she or another person has been the victim of a criminal offence shall be offered information concerning the following; (a) procedures for making a complaint alleging an offence. (b) services which provide support for victims of crime. (c) the role of the victim in the criminal justice process. (d) protection measures available for victims. (e) services providing legal advice and legal aid. (f) The Criminal Injuries Compensational Tribunal and the power of a court to make a compensation order under section (6) of the *Criminal Justice Act 1993*. (g) entitlement to interpretation and translation or other linguistic assistance. (h) procedures for victims who are resident outside the State. (i) entitlement to expenses arising from participation in the criminal justice process. (j) entitlement of a victim to inform the court of trial how he or she has been affected by the offence. (k) the procedure to obtain information from the Irish Prison Service on the release of a prisoner. (l) available grievance procedures.

The Bill also takes a novel approach to the assessment of the needs of the victim, rather than assuming what the victim must need, or as provided by standard welfare measures:

> **Head 6** Assessment of a victim where a complaint has been made. Provide that: (1) The member of the Garda Síochána taking a complaint or another appropriate member shall assess, in consultation with the victim; (i) the measures, if any, that may be necessary for protection of the victim from any secondary or repeat victimisation, intimidation or retaliation, and (ii) if the victim would, in the course of the investigation of the offence alleged, benefit from any measure provided for in section 15, (3) If the member assesses under (1) (i) that measures may be necessary for the protection of the victim, he or she shall report this to the District Officer of the Garda Síochána District to which he or she is attached for any action deemed necessary. Protection measures may include advice as to personal safety, protection of property, availability of protection or barring orders, seeking to remand an offender in custody or seeking conditions on bail, if granted, to prevent contact with the victim or any other measure to prevent secondary victimization, retaliation or intimidation. (4) If the member assesses under (1) (ii) that, in the course of the investigation of the offence alleged, the victim would benefit, in whole or in part, from any measure provided for in section 15, he or she shall inform the District Officer of the Garda Síochána District to which he or she is attached accordingly. (5) If the member assesses under (1) (iii) that, in the event of the victim being required to give evidence in the trial of any offender charged with the alleged offence, he or she would benefit from any measure provided for in section 16, he or she shall inform the District Officer of the Garda Síochána District to which he or she is attached who shall include the information in any file sent to the Director of Public Prosecutions concerning the offence alleged in the complaint. (6) (a)Where it appears to the member of the Garda Síochána conducting the assessment that the capacity of the victim to contact a service supporting victims of crime is limited and that he or she might benefit from contact with such a service,

and the victim so consents, or (b) if the victim requests the member of the Garda Síochána taking the complaint or conducting the assessment, as the case may be, to contact a service supporting victims of crime on their behalf, the appropriate member of the Garda Síochána shall so inform that service. And (iii) if, in the event of the victim being required to give evidence in the trial of any offender charged with the alleged offence, he or she would benefit from any measure provided for in section 16. (2) The scope of the assessment shall have regard to; (a) the personal characteristics of the victim, including his or her age, gender and gender identity or expression, ethnicity, race, religion, sexual orientation, physical or mental health issues and ability to communicate. (b) the type and nature of the offence alleged (c) the severity of the offence (d) the degree of harm suffered by the victim, and (e) the circumstances of the commission of the offence alleged (f) the relationship, if any, between the victim and the alleged offender.

Where victims are required to be interviewed they may be supported by a personal representative. However, it is significant that the Bill recognises the role of private counsel for victims in this context:

Head 12 Attendance at interviews. Provide that; A victim may be accompanied by a person of his or her choice and by his or her legal representative, if any, when being interviewed by a member of the Garda Síochána in relation to a complaint, unless the member reasonably believes that the presence of the legal representative or the person would hinder the proper conduct of the interview or would prejudice the investigation or the criminal proceedings.

Special measures available to victims during trial build upon rights established under the *Sex Offences Act 2001* (Ire), which allows a sex offences victim to obtain counsel to challenge applications for the use of evidence that may establish the sexual history of the victim. Head 16 provides for protective measures during court appearances where the victim will give evidence.

Head 16 Special measures during trial. Provide that: (1) In any proceedings for an offence where a victim is required to give evidence, the Court may, on the application of the prosecutor, where it is satisfied that the victim by reason of any of the following: (a) his or her personal characteristics (b) the type and nature of the offence alleged (c) the degree of harm suffered by him or her as a result of the offence alleged (d) the relationship, if any, between him or her and the accused (e) The nature of the evidence he or she is to give (f) any behaviour towards him or her on the part of: (i) the accused (ii) members of the family of or associates of the accused should be permitted to give evidence other than viva voce in open court and, if it is further satisfied that no injustice would thereby be caused to the defendant, shall direct that the evidence be given under such provision as it considers appropriate of Part III of the *Criminal Evidence Act 1992*, as amended. (2) A court may, if it does not make a direction under (1), if it is satisfied that by reason of any of the matters referred to in (1) (a) to (f) it is appropriate to do so, exclude from the court while the victim is giving his or her testimony all persons except officers of the court, persons directly concerned in the proceedings, bona fide representatives of the media and such other persons (if any) as the court may in its discretion permit.

The Bill retains access for the media where the general public is excluded for protection of the victim. This is a questionable inclusion, given the potential damage media reporting may do when sensitive victim issues are put to the court and then reported. The Bill further provides for restorative justice intervention as provided by the CEU DVC of 2012:

> **Head 28** Restorative Justice Schemes. Provide that: Where any agency or body listed in the Schedule to this Bill provides or enables any restorative justice service, [other than those provided for in the *Children Act 2001* (as amended)], it shall ensure that; (a) the restorative justice services are used only if they are in the interest of the victim, subject to any safety considerations, and are based on the victim's free and informed consent, which may be withdrawn at any time; (b) before agreeing to participate in the restorative justice process, the victim is provided with full and unbiased information about that process and the potential outcomes as well as information about the procedures for supervising the implementation of any agreement; (c) the offender accepts responsibility for his or her criminal behaviour (d) any agreement is arrived at voluntarily and may be taken into account in any further criminal proceedings; (e) discussions in restorative justice processes that are not conducted in public are confidential and are not subsequently disclosed, except with the agreement of the parties.

The Joint Committee on Justice, Defence and Equality of the Parliament of Ireland considered the Bill in October 2015, and made recommendations that certain provisions be funded, and that a previous report informing the rights of sex offences victims be recommissioned (see SAVI Report, 2002). The omission of secondary victims or witnesses was also noted and, where possible, victims should be informed of delays or withdrawal of proceedings in order to limit further harm and to provide for other actionable rights. Note that other rights encouraged by the CEU DVC of 2012 are provided under the 2015 Bill, including the victim's right to review under Heads 13 and 14.[19]

United States of America

The USA has a substantial criminal code at the federal level, together with its own federal court and prison system. The states also have jurisdiction over criminal matters, with their own criminal codes and prison systems. This section will focus on the federal level and the rights of victims under the *Crime Victim Rights Act 2004* (US) as amending the USC and expanding on previous attempts to provide victim rights in the criminal justice process under the *Victims' Rights and Restitution Act 1990* (US), amending the USC, 42 USC §§ 10601, 10606–07. The *Crime Victim Rights Act 2004* (US) amendments, 18 USC § 3771, now constitutes the principal criminal code consolidating criminal law and procedure for federal offences and courts (see Cassell, 2012; Cassell, Mitchell, and Edwards, 2014).

The federal courts of the USA provide for a trial court in the federal district courts. Matters are disposed of before this court before judge and jury, with the exception of pretrial matters dealt with by a federal magistrate. A federal magistrate may issue warrants, conduct preliminary hearings, grant bail, and decide motions to determine whether the accused is able to discover evidence against the victim. There are ninety-four district courts throughout the USA, and the decisions of the court appealable to the United States courts of appeals, of which the ninety-four districts are organised into twelve circuits, with one United States Court of Appeals for the Federal Circuit. The federal circuit also includes specialty courts that may deal with criminal matters, such as the United States Court of Appeals for the

Armed Forces, which deals with military cases. Decisions of the circuit courts of appeals may be further appealed to the Supreme Court of the United States with the leave of the court.

The USA provides detailed rights at the federal level under the USC (see Cassell, 2005). With regard to victim's pretrial rights to challenge the accused's access to their private counselling or medical records for the purpose of obtaining evidence damaging to the character of the victim, see the Federal Rules of Evidence 28 USC Article IV § 412(c), which provides rules that afford protection to victims that may also allow victims to access counsel to protect those rights.[20]

In 2004, the *Crime Victim Rights Act 2004* (US) amended the USC with respect to the provision of an enforceable charter of rights for victims in federal cases. The non-enforceable charter was replaced with 18 USC § 3771, which grants victims the following rights of substantive participation in the pretrial and trial process:

> **18 USC § 3771** Crime Victims' Rights: (a) Rights of Crime Victims: A crime victim has the following rights: (1) The right to be reasonably protected from the accused; (2) The right to reasonable, accurate, and timely notice of any public court proceeding, or any parole proceeding, involving the crime or of any release or escape of the accused; (3) The right not to be excluded from any such public court proceeding, unless the court, after receiving clear and convincing evidence, determines that testimony by the victim would be materially altered if the victim heard other testimony at that proceeding; (4) The right to be reasonably heard at any public proceeding in the district court involving release, plea, sentencing, or any parole proceeding; (5) The reasonable right to confer with the attorney for the Government in the case; (6) The right to full and timely restitution as provided in law; (7) The right to proceedings free from unreasonable delay; and (8) The right to be treated with fairness and with respect for the victim's dignity and privacy.

The rights as phrased under the USC are strictly enforceable, as even rights that are traditionally not enforceable, such as the right to dignified treatment, is placed in the context of fairness and privacy, both terms of art in criminal litigation and as recognised under international and regional resolution (as may be applicable in the context of the legal system of the USA).[21] However, much of the litigation that has resulted since the amendment of the USC has involved pretrial litigation where the right of the victim to confer with the state attorney has been denied altogether, or not proceeded with in a way that gives full realisation to the rights granted under 18 USC § 3771(4),(5). Victims in federal proceedings may seek remedy where they are denied their right to confer with the state attorney under § 3771(a) (5). Relief may be sought by writ of mandamus, which is an order quashing the original plea deal made, referring the attorney back to the rights under 18 USC § 3771 to consult with victims and make the decision in accordance with the requirements of the Federal Code (see Beloof, 2005; Cassell, 2010; Cassell, Mitchell, and Edwards, 2014). What constitutes appropriate consultation for the purpose of the right afforded is often a matter of contest between states and victim rights groups.

The right to proceed to have a government decision subject to judicial review and remedied by writ of mandamus is provided for under the USC. Section 18 USC § 3771(c)(3) Motion for Relief by Writ of Mandamus provides the following:

> The rights described in subsection (a) shall be asserted in the district court in which a defendant is being prosecuted for the crime or, if no prosecution is underway, in the

district court in the district in which the crime occurred. The district court shall take up and decide any motion asserting a victim's right forthwith. If the district court denies the relief sought, the movant may petition the court of appeals for a writ of mandamus. The court of appeals may issue the writ on the order of a single judge pursuant to circuit rule or the Federal Rules of Appellate Procedure. The court of appeals shall take up and decide such application forthwith within 72 hours after the petition has been filed. In no event shall proceedings be stayed or subject to a continuance of more than five days for purposes of enforcing this chapter. If the court of appeals denies the relief sought, the reasons for the denial shall be clearly stated on the record in a written opinion.

Several cases have emerged as authority for the substantive rights of the victim in federal criminal cases. *In re Dean* (2008) 527 F 3d 39 provides the foundational precedent for the test for the availability of a writ of mandamus in the federal courts. This order may be granted where the victim is denied rights under § 3771 but only where specific circumstances warrant the granting of the writ (see Beloof, 2005; Cassell, 2010). The court determined that circumstances are limited to those where the petitioner has no other adequate means to attain relief, where the petitioner has demonstrated a right to the issuance of a writ that is clear and indisputable, and where the issuing court, in the exercise of its discretion, is satisfied that the writ is appropriate in the circumstances. The issuing of a writ of mandamus is therefore seen to be an extraordinary remedy, and will be granted in compelling circumstances. Nevertheless, the circuit courts of appeals will grant intervention where the rights of the victim have been clearly and indisputably denied under 18 USC § 3771.The case of *In re Antrobus* (2008) 519 F 3d 1123 maintains this standard, holding that the granting of the writ should be exceptional and that victims should be granted relief only where it can be shown that the original court made a clear and indisputable error.

However, the court of appeals for the fifth circuit in *Re: Jewell Allen, et al.* (2014) 12–40954 (5th Cir. 2014) provided such relief, directing the district court to consider the victim status of the petitioners, at pars [4]–[6]:

> As recognized by the court below, Petitioners have a right to file their own motion to be declared crime victims under the CVRA, and it is clear and indisputable that no time bar prevented the district court from considering the novel arguments raised by pro bono counsel in its motion below. Here, where Petitioners raise arguments not previously raised by the Government during the time the Government represented their interests, and where Petitioners have been able to retain counsel, issuance of a writ is appropriate.
>
> Accordingly, we direct the district court to consider the arguments raised by pro bono counsel below in Petitioners' motion to be afforded crime victim status under the CVRA.
>
> It is ordered that the petition for writ of mandamus pursuant to the Crime Victims' Act is granted to the extent that the district court must hear all new victim status arguments being submitted pre-sentencing by pro bono counsel.

The court of appeals for the armed forces in *LRM v Kastenberg* (2013) 13–5006/AF (CAAF 2013) considered the issuance of a writ of mandamus and the role of the victim in hearings for its petitioning at 15–16:

> Furthermore, while the military judge suggests that LRM's request is novel, there are many examples of civilian federal court decisions allowing victims to be represented

by counsel at pretrial hearings. Although not precedent binding on this Court, in the United States Court of Appeals for the Fifth Circuit, for example, victims have exercised their right to be reasonably heard regarding pretrial decisions of the judge and prosecutor 'personally [and] through counsel.' *In re Dean*, 527 F.3d 391, 393 (5th Cir. 2008). The victims' 'attorneys reiterated the victims' requests' and 'supplemented their appearances at the hearing with substantial post-hearing submissions.' Id.; see also *Brandt v Gooding*, 636 F.3d 124, 136–37 (4th Cir. 2011) (motions from attorneys were 'fully commensurate' with the victim's 'right to be heard.').

Similarly, in United States v Saunders, at a pretrial Fed. R. Evid. 412(c)(1) hearing, 'all counsel, including the alleged victim's counsel, presented arguments.' 736 F. Supp. 698, 700 (E.D. Va. 1990). In *United States v Stamper*, the district court went further and, in a pretrial evidentiary hearing, allowed counsel for 'all three parties,' including the prosecution, defense, and victim's counsel, to examine witnesses, including the victim. 766 F. Supp. 1396, 1396 (WDNC 1991).

Litigation for restitution of child victims in child abuse or exploitation cases demonstrates the use of victim rights under the USC to effect remedy and restitution from offenders who possess child exploitation material where the victim brings a claim against the accused for damage that the victim has incurred as a result of the dissemination and viewing of such material. Despite some attempt to argue against the remoteness of damage incurred against such victims by the distribution of exploitation material, the federal courts allow such claims under the heads of loss set out under 18 USC § 2259(b)(3):

18 USC § 2259(b)(3) Definition: For purposes of this subsection, the term 'full amount of the victim's losses' includes any costs incurred by the victim for: (A) medical services relating to physical, psychiatric, or psychological care; (B) physical and occupational therapy or rehabilitation; (C) necessary transportation, temporary housing, and child care expenses; (D) lost income; (E) attorneys' fees, as well as other costs incurred; and (F) any other losses suffered by the victim as a proximate result of the offense.

Where an accused is in possession of limited material the liability for restitution is generally calculated in accordance with the harm the accused proximately caused, and not for the entirety of the injury cause by others. The matter of *United States v Monzel* (2011) 641 F 3d 528 determined that in such instances, the accused causes the victim a discrete injury, at 538:

Because restitution awards under § 2259 are limited to harms the defendant proximately caused, we cannot say that Amy is clearly and indisputably entitled to the full $3,263,758 she seeks. Although the government submitted evidence that Amy suffered losses stemming from her sexual exploitation as a child, see Mot. for Restitution at 6–7; Gov't's Mem. of Law Regarding the Victims' Losses at 6–15, and argued persuasively that possession of child pornography causes harm to the minors depicted, Mot. for Restitution at 9–12; see also *New York v Ferber*, 458 U.S. 747, 758–60, 102 S.Ct. 3348, 73 L.Ed.2d 1113 (1982), it made no showing as to the amount of Amy's losses traceable to Monzel. Whatever else may be said of his crime, the record before us does not establish that Monzel caused all of Amy's losses.

Despite the line of authority necessitating proximate cause of injury in order to determine the quantum of damages owed to the victim, Cassell, Marsh and Christiansen (2013: 42) note, however, 'The injury to victims of child pornography via possession and distribution manifests itself in the same way as multiple tortfeasors.' The attribution of damages to the proximate harm caused to the victim therefore remains contentious despite the intention of the 2004 amendments to the USC providing added recourse to justice for victim of crime.

In the context of the international movement towards the provision of victim rights and the granting of counsel in appropriate circumstances, the federal courts are aware of the significance of the right to grant the victim standing before the courts. While other jurisdictions debate whether such rights should be granted to any extent, victims seeking to exercise their rights under the USC have a right to appear in hearings to challenge the substantive outcome of pretrial decisions and orders for restitution. As *United States v Monzel* demonstrates, standing rights do not guarantee an outcome in the victim's best interests. The threshold for the writ of mandamus has also been criticised as unduly high (see Cassell, Mitchell, and Edwards, 2014), where such writs may be granted only where no other adequate means of relief may be attained. This may thwart the principles of open access to justice upon which the 2004 reforms were based. However, the USC provisions go well beyond the non-enforceable rights prescribed by such comparable common law, adversarial jurisdictions that have generally non-enforceable declarations and charters. Although there are limited rights for victims to be heard under the NSW and South Australian declarations, these rights are subject to a non-enforcement clause that victims may not appeal to a court to seek relief, otherwise than by existing common law process.

Australia

The criminal law of Australia is a matter for eight state and territory jurisdictions, in addition to a limited federal jurisdiction exercised by the Commonwealth. The states of NSW, Victoria, and South Australia retain a common law jurisdiction, while Queensland, Tasmania, the Northern Territory, the Austrian Capital Territory, and Western Australia exercise a code jurisdiction. The main difference between common law and code jurisdictions is that despite some codification of the principles of common law liability in statute by the common law states, code jurisdictions have sought to codify all principles of criminal liability, as enumerated in statutory form. In NSW, the main statutory instruments prescribing statutory offences are the *Summary Offences Act 1988* (NSW) for offences disposed of summarily, and the *Crimes Act 1900* (NSW) for offences to be tried on indictment. Elements of offences and certain defences are generally left to the common law. The *Criminal Procedure Act 1986* (NSW) sets out processes by which certain indictable offences may be disposed of summarily. The other states and territories have similar arrangements allowing disposal of indictable matters in summary courts. Criminal procedural rules and statutes also provide for victim participation in court, although this is variable by state and jurisdiction. Adjunct proceedings for preventive detention of risky offenders are also provided.[22] Royal commissions have also been used as an investigative vehicle where a particular matter warrants close examination. Recently, this method has been used to investigate systemic child abuse under the RCIRCA.

The court system of the states and territories exercising a criminal jurisdiction generally consists of lower local courts through to the state supreme courts. In NSW, the local court determines matters summarily before a magistrate sitting alone. Indictable matters are heard before the district court, with more serious offences being disposed of before the supreme court. Appeals from the local court lie to the district court. Appeals from the trial courts, with leave on fact or of by law of right, lie to the court of criminal appeal. With leave, matters may be further appealed to the federal supreme court, the High Court of Australia.

The victim's right to information and services and for limited participation has been extracted in Chapter 2 (see extracts 2.1–2.6). These rights may be further clarified in the context South Australian law, which provides victims with several key rights that are well positioned against the normative rights covered in Chapter 2. These rights are provided for under the *Victim of Crime Act 2001* (SA), sections 6–14 (cf. *Victims Rights Act 1996* (NSW), now under section 6 of the *Victims Rights and Support Act 2013* (NSW)), and include the right: to fair and dignified treatment; to have perceived need for protection taken into account in bail proceedings; to information; to be advised on role as witness; with regard to a serious offence, an entitlement to be consulted in relation to certain decisions; to be present in court; to have impact of offence considered by sentencing court and to make submissions on parole; to allow the victim to request consideration of a criminal appeal; to be informed about access to health and welfare services; for compensation and restitution; to have property returned; and to have the victim's privacy protected (see O'Connell, 2015; Holder, 2015).

Despite various declarations or charters of rights across Australia, victim rights tend to be restricted out of a general lack of enforceability in criminal or civil proceedings (McEwin, 2014). The *Victim of Crime Act 2001* (SA) provides the following:

Section 5 Reasons for declaration and its effect: (1) In this Part, Parliament seeks to declare the principles that should govern the way victims are dealt with by public agencies and officials. (2) The need for the declaration arises out of national and international concern about the position of victims of crime. (3) The principles: (a) are not enforceable in criminal or civil proceedings; and (b) do not give rise to any right to damages for breach; and (c) do not affect the conduct of criminal proceedings. (4) However, public agencies and officials are authorised and required to have regard, and to give effect, to the principles so far as it is practicable to do so having regard to the other obligations binding on them.

The general lack of enforceability against the accused or state must be read against limited rights granted through the office of the commissioner for victims' rights to access pre- and post-trial decision-making and justice processes. Sections 32A, together with rights to consultation and consideration under sections 9A and 10A of the *Victim of Crime Act 2001* (SA) (see *Statutes Amendment (Victims of Crime) Act 2007* (SA); *Statutes Amendment (Victims of Crime) Act 2009* (SA); also see *Victims of Crime (Commissioner for Victims' Rights) Amendment Act 2007* (SA)), grant the victim a degree of participation, despite being limited by the section 5 requirement that rights are not enforceable under civil law.[23] The operation of the rights of victims in South Australia therefore flows through an administrative context of public stakeholders, who are obliged to uphold the declaration of victim rights despite any failure to implement the requirements of the declaration, not being subject to remedy in court. However, the commissioner for victims' rights does have statutory independence and victims have an associated power to representational rights which may be exercised through the commissioner or, alternatively, through counsel. It is therefore the combination of rights available under section 16E, 32A, together with the consultative rights under sections 9A and 10A, that provides some degree of substantive right to participation for South Australian victims.

The independence of the commissioner for victims' rights is provided for under the *Victims of Crime Act 2001* (SA) as follows:

Section 16E Independence of Commissioner: (1) Subject to this section, the Commissioner is entirely independent of direction or control by the Crown or any Minister or officer of the Crown; (2) The Attorney-General may, after consultation with the Commissioner, give directions and furnish guidelines to the Commissioner in relation to the carrying out of his or her functions; (3) Directions or guidelines under this section, (a) must, as soon as practicable after they have been given, be published in the Gazette; and (b) must, within 6 sitting days after they have been given, be laid before each House of Parliament.

The right to act independently is significant where a victim may request the commissioner's assistance to represent his or her right to consider a request or consult under the *Victims of Crime Act 2001* (SA). A measure of substantive participation may thus be afforded where a victim makes such a request:

> **Section 32A** Victim may exercise rights through an appropriate representative: (1) Rights granted to a victim under this, or any other, Act may be exercised on behalf of the victim by an appropriate representative chosen by the victim for that purpose. Note: Such rights would include (without limitation) the right to request information under this or any other Act, the right to make a claim for compensation under this or any other Act and the right to furnish a victim impact statement under the Criminal Law (Sentencing) Act 1988; (2) This section does not apply to rights, or rights of a kind, prescribed by the regulations; (3) In this section: 'appropriate representative', in relation to a victim, means any of the following: (a) an officer of the court; (b) the Commissioner for Victims' Rights or a person acting on behalf of the Commissioner for Victims' Rights; (c) an officer or employee of an organisation whose functions consist of, or include, the provision of support or services to victims of crime; (d) a relative of the victim; (e) another person who, in the opinion of the Commissioner for Victims' Rights, would be suitable to act as an appropriate representative.

The victim's right to consult with the prosecutor regarding charging of the suspect, to change or amend the original charge, not to proceed with a charge, or to investigate the offender's capacity to stand trial is provided for under the *Victims of Crime Act 2001* (SA). This section grants this right for serious offences, usually of interpersonal violence, in the following terms:

> **Section 9A** Victim of serious offence entitled to be consulted in relation to certain decisions. A victim of a serious offence should be consulted before any decision is made: (a) to charge the alleged offender with a particular offence; or (b) to amend a charge; or (c) to not proceed with a charge; or (d) to apply under Part 8A of the Criminal Law Consolidation Act 1935 for an investigation into the alleged offender's mental competence to commit an offence or mental fitness to stand trial.

The right to ask that a matter be appealed following trial is also provided as a corollary right to be consulted with regard to pretrial prosecutorial decisions. This is not a consultative right, but the right to request consideration to appeal an outcome that the prosecutor would ordinarily be able to appeal. Although consultation is not provided for under the section, the victim's request must be given 'due consideration'. What this specifically entails has not yet been the subject of litigation, but this would arguably involve more than being informed of reasons why the prosecution is not proceeding with an appeal, or an appeal on limited issues. The engagement of the victim in a process that explains to the victim the reasoning of the prosecution would ensure that the consideration is indeed 'due consideration', per the section:

> **Section 10A** Victim may request consideration of appeal (1) A victim who is dissatisfied with a determination made in relation to the relevant criminal proceedings (being a determination against which the prosecution is entitled to appeal) may request the prosecution to consider an appeal against the determination. (2) A request under this section must be made within 10 days after the making of the determination. (3) The prosecution must give due consideration to a request made under this section.

The rights granted to the victim under sections 9A and 10A are significant in that few jurisdictions in Australia provide victims such substantive rights of participation. The rule against enforcement notwithstanding, the victim does gain some access to the decision-making process of the state. The victim's perspective may enhance justice outcomes for victims by requiring the public prosecutor to acknowledge and take heed of the rights of the victim in so far as they can be factored into a decision that must be made from the community's perspective. This is a process where it may be desirable for victims to exercise their representational rights under section 32A. The commissioner for victims' rights or another person, including legal counsel, may be able to assist the victims with a 9A or 10A request. As these are ultimately non-enforceable rights, the commissioner or counsel acting for a victim would be able to ensure open communication and access to the level of justice that the rights are designed to provide. As these rights are ultimately non-enforceable, however, they are illusory to the extent that they indicate that the victim gains some degree of standing as a stakeholder in the pre- and post-trial decision-making process, but in an opaque way (see Beloof, 2005). The provision of access to representation for non-enforceable rights renders these rights ambiguous and potentially not in full compliance with the international trend to offer victims rights of substantive import.

An alternative approach is adopted in NSW. The *Crimes (Sentencing Procedure) Act 1999* (NSW), section 35A, requires that victims and the police be consulted with regard to charge negotiations. This is a right that, where exercised, must be certified to the court prior to the sentencing process: see *Chen v R* [2015] NSWCCA 277; *McDonald v R* [2014] NSWCCA 127. The section provides that where a plea deal is arranged that the police and victim be consulted as to their views on the charges reached. This does not give the victim or the police control over the decision to negotiate the outcome; however, it does provide for a process of consultation that allows the victim to be included in the decision-making process. Ultimately, section 35A seeks to identify the agreed facts to all stakeholders such that 'a fair and accurate account of the objective criminality of the offender' is reached, with all parties having been consulted with the view to settling different perspectives on the offering of a charge consistent with objective criminality of the offender:

> **Section 35A** Consultation with victim and police in relation to charge negotiations (1) In this section: 'charge negotiations' means negotiations between the prosecution and an offender with respect to a plea of guilty in relation to an offence other than the offence or offences with which the offender has been charged or committed for trial, 'prosecution guidelines' means prosecution guidelines in relation to charge negotiations issued by the Director of Public Prosecutions, 'requisite consultation' means consultation with the victim and the police officer in charge of investigating an offence that complies with the applicable prosecution guidelines, victim' has the same meaning

as it has in section 26. (2) A court must not take into account offences specified in a list of additional charges under section 32 in relation to an offence, or any statement of agreed facts, that was the subject of charge negotiations unless the prosecutor has filed a certificate with the court verifying that: (a) the requisite consultation has taken place or, if consultation has not taken place, the reasons why it has not occurred, and (b) any statement of agreed facts arising from the negotiations tendered to the court constitutes a fair and accurate account of the objective criminality of the offender having regard to the relevant and provable facts or has otherwise been settled in accordance with the applicable prosecution guidelines. (3) The certificate must be signed by or on behalf of the Director of Public Prosecutions or by a person, or a person belonging to a class of persons, prescribed by the regulations. (4) A certificate is taken to be signed on behalf of the Director of Public Prosecutions if it is signed by a person who is authorised to do so by means of a written order signed by the Director of Public Prosecutions or who belongs to a class of persons so authorised. (5) The court may require the prosecution to explain the reason for a failure to file a certificate when it is required by this section to do so.

The law of NSW also provides a charter of rights for victims of crime under section 6 of the *Victims Rights and Support Act 2013* (NSW), which, like South Australia, is also non-enforceable. However, ancillary rights, such as section 35A, that connect stakeholders in new ways by requiring consultations to be certified prior to sentence meet the objects of the inclusion of the victim in relevant decision-making processes without compromising the requirement that justice serve the community's best interests. The rights extracted in Chapter 2 at 5.8 provide for levels of participation in the pretrial and sentencing process. Despite criticism that these rights are illusory, declaratory non-enforceable rights are potentially useful as an important complement to victim rights that offer substantive participation in relevant decision-making processes. Sections 35A, 9A, and 10A of the 1999 and 2001 Acts respectively provide an example of the movement towards substantive participation in South Australia and NSW that attempts to conform with broader requirements that criminal justice decisions accord with the state prerogative to control crime.

Other substantive provisions for victims in the Australian criminal justice system include access to counsel in the pretrial context, discussed in Chapter 3. Section 299A of the *Criminal Procedure Act 1986* (NSW) provides for the standing of the victim in pretrial applications for the discovery of confidential counselling notes. *PPC v Williams* [2013] NSWCCA 286 indicates that the victim may retain counsel where he or she seeks to challenge the discovery of medical or counselling communications, which would ordinarily be private records of the patient.[24] The victim gains standing as a direct participant in criminal justice proceedings for the purpose of bringing this challenge. Where confidential records are the subject of an application for discovery by the accused, NSW Legal Aid now grants victims access to publicly funded counsel under the Sexual Assault Communication Privilege Service.

The sentencing process also provides access to justice for victims of crime in Australia. The states and territories allow VIS in most summary and indictable matters disposed of before the courts. Increasingly, Australian sentencing courts have acknowledged the admissibility of VIS as a relevant form of evidence. While VIS were generally taken into account for non-fatal offences to the person, and were seen to be especially relevant for sex offences victims, where the impact of the crime develops over time, courts were more reluctant to draw from the content of a VIS in homicide cases out of adherence to the principle of quality in death. This is a principle long resolved in the victim's favour across the rest of the common law world. In 2014, NSW abandoned its adherence to this outmoded rule, allowing courts to use the content of a VIS to inform sentencing outcomes in death cases.[25] The 2014 amendment rejected the approach formerly adopted, providing a total prohibition on the use of VIS as substantive evidence in sentencing outcomes.[26] Section 28(4) of the *Crimes (Sentencing Procedure) Act 1999* (NSW) provides the following:

> A victim impact statement given by a family victim may, on the application of the prosecutor and if the court considers it appropriate to do so, be considered and taken into account by a court in connection with the determination of the punishment for the offence on the basis that the harmful impact of the primary victim's death on the members of the primary victim's immediate family is an aspect of harm done to the community.

The accused's recourse to justice is protected by the requirement that a family VIS can be tendered where the prosecutor and court so agree. As a rule, a VIS is also admissible under the law of evidence, which will generally have the effect of limiting harm to those that can be established beyond reasonable doubt. These protections, however, ensure the validity and integrity of the process of submitting a VIS, and ensure that victims gain a substantive right to justice by enabling the court to utilise the content of a VIS, rather than just accepting the VIS as evidence that could not be taken into account.[27] Courts will continue to exercise the usual discretion to take account of harm as is relevant to a sentencing decision, as required under sentencing law. The admissibility and potential use of the VIS across most offences now provide for a more transparent and comprehensive framework of rights for victims in NSW, which also brings NSW in line with international standards.

Victims possess general rights to compensation and restitution in accordance with international standards. Restitution is used where the victim or state can recover assets from the accused. The process may also be relevant to a process of restorative intervention where an offender contributes to the restoration of damaged property. In South Australia, restitution may also be factored into sentence. In the matter of *Brooks v Police* [2000] SASC 66, Bleby J indicates that the desire to offer a payment or service to the victim is indicia of contrition, which is materially relevant to sentence:

> It can be seen that the Sentencing Act gives some prominence to the question of compensation to victims . . . where a defendant exhibits genuine contrition borne out of a desire to pay compensation, but does not have the means to pay it (usually because the defendant never has had the means), and where it can be seen that some payment, periodic or otherwise, which the defendant can afford, may well have some therapeutic benefit in the rehabilitation of the offender, it can become a useful sentencing tool. This is so particularly where the alternative of imprisonment will mean loss of a job, a negation of any ability to pay compensation or to reimburse the Attorney-General, and a denial of any opportunity to the offender to become a useful member of the community.

Restorative justice programmes are now well placed within the Australian justice context. All jurisdictions offer restorative intervention for young and adult offenders. Indigenous programmes are also available. Forum and circle sentencing are available in the local court of NSW for prescribed offences, usually of lower-order offences of interpersonal violence. Forum and circle sentencing replace the sentence hearing for a circle of justice stakeholders, including the victim, should he or she wish to participate. Circle sentencing is adapted especially for Aboriginal offenders (see Judicial Commission NSW, 2003; CIRCA and BOCSAR, 2008; NSWLRC, 2013; for forum sentencing, see Rossner, Bruce, and Meher, 2013). Youth justice conferencing is a mode of alternative intervention that diverts young offenders from the criminal justice system. The *Young Offenders Act 1997* (NSW) diverts young offenders by offering warnings and cautions for minor offences, and the possibility of a conference inclusive of the police and victim where the matter otherwise goes to court (Juvenile Justice NSW, 2010). Restorative processes have reformed the traditional role of stakeholders in court proceedings in Australia. The availability of restorative justice and diversionary programmes for young and adult offenders provides an important adjunct to the criminal justice process that attempts to restore victims and offenders and reduce recidivism by removing offenders from traditional penal systems by encouraging rehabilitation and restoration in alternative justice programmes (Pena and Carayon, 2013; also see Christie, 2015). The use of problem-solving justice in the context of a neighbourhood or community courts also demonstrates the reinvestment of resources into new court models that seek to connect offenders, victims, the community, and traditional justice stakeholders in new ways. In 2007, the Neighbourhood Justice Centre was established in Collingwood, Melbourne, under the *Courts Legislation (Neighbourhood Justice Centre) Act 2006* (Vic). Murray (2009: 82) sees the guiding principles of access to justice and therapeutic jurisprudence as reshaping the traditional boundaries between stakeholders, services, and the courts:

> These guiding principles of therapeutic jurisprudence and restorative justice can typically shape neighbourhood courts in at least three key ways. Firstly, they enable neighbourhood courts to potentially experiment with less traditional curial methods to try to bring about more desirable legal outcomes. Secondly, neighbourhood courts are single-minded in their desire to attract judicial officers and community agencies that are able to serve the community and command its respect. The way the judicial officer interacts with defendants and develops supportive relationships becomes very important in this process as the dynamic between the bench and the community is reconceptualised. Thirdly, therapeutic jurisprudence and restorative justice can facilitate more problem-oriented and interdisciplinary approaches. In so doing, the neighbourhood courts are able to draw upon the support of the agencies linked with the court allowing it to undertake a broader policy role.

The use of the royal commission as a vehicle through which to investigate significant and widespread injustice has also provided important access to justice for victims of sexual violence in the Australian justice context. The investigation of systemic child abuse under the RCIRCA is discussed in Chapters 1 and 3.

Canada

The criminal law of Canada flows from its federal jurisdiction and is enumerated in the Canadian Criminal Code (RSC 1985 C-46). The criminal courts of Canada consist of provincial and territorial courts, which hear minor offences without a jury, and the provincial and territorial superior courts, which sit as trial courts and hear serious offences. Matters may be appealed to the provincial and territorial courts of appeal, whose decision may be further appealed to the Supreme Court of Canada. Criminal procedure in the Canadian court is established under the Canadian Criminal Code.

In 2015, Canada introduced the *Victims Bill of Rights Act 2015* (Can), enacting the *Canadian Victims Bill of Rights* (SC 2015, chapter 13, section 2). Extracts from the *Canadian Victims Bill of Rights* make up the normative framework of victim rights presented in Chapter 2 (extracted in Chapter 2 at 1.3, 2.3, 3.4, 4.4, 5.6, 6.7, 7.6). The Act does several things in addition to setting out a federal bill of rights for victims of crime. The Act amends the Canadian Criminal Code to grant victims access to information and protection and to provide victims with increased opportunities to participate at trial and during sentencing; assumes that an accused's spouse is competent and can be compelled to give evidence in criminal proceedings under the Canada Evidence Act; and amends the *Corrections and Conditional Release Act 1992* (Can) to grant victims access to information on the offender.

The *Canadian Victims Bill of Rights* provides several rights for victims, some of which existed before the enactment of the Bill. These rights may be generally grouped as including the right to information (e.g., bail orders, conditional sentence orders, and probation orders regarding the offender), the right to protection (e.g., victims have the right to have reasonable and necessary measures taken by authorities to protect them against intimidation and retaliation), the right to participation (e.g., victims have a right to present a victim impact statement and to have it considered), and the right to restitution (victims possess the right to have the court consider making a restitution order against the offender, and the court must turn its mind to the making of such an order). Several of these rights are expressed in terms of amendments to the Canadian Criminal Code, as set out ahead.

Much like the charters and declarations of England and Wales, New Zealand, South Africa, and as found across the Australian states and territories, the *Canadian Victims Bill of Rights* in non-enforceable. Heralded as placing victims at the heart of the Canadian justice system, the *Canadian Victims Bill of Rights* has been criticised as lacking any enforcement mechanisms that would see victims gain substantive rights and powers in the justice system. In a comment in the *National Post*, Perrin (2014) is critical of the remit of the Bill of Rights and the remedies available to victims:

> Bill C-32 should be amended to enhance the status of victims and remedies available to them. While victims should not be parties to criminal proceedings, they should have a general right to observe them. They should also be able to make their views or concerns known to the court in relation to their rights, as appropriate, and have standing to request that a court give effect to their rights under the Canadian Victims Bill of Rights related to judicial proceedings in that court.

A complaints mechanism is also provided under clause 25. Where a right is infringed or not provided for, clause 25 requires that all federal departments dealing with victims must provide a review of the complaint, with the undisclosed power to make recommendations and remedy such infringements and denials. Clause 28 makes clear that such complaints are not legal actions granting the victim rights against the state or accused. Thus, no cause of action or right to damages arises from an infringement or denial of a right. Clause 29 provides that no appeal lies from any decision or order solely on the grounds that a right has been infringed or denied. This effectively limits the Bill of Rights to service-level rights that encourage modes of treatment alone.

The lack of enforcement and standing provided to victims under the *Canadian Victims Bill of Rights* is reminiscent of the Ontario government's attempt to pass legislation setting out the rights of victims under *An Act Respecting Victims of Crime* (SO 1995, chapter 6) enacting the *Victims Bill of Rights* in 1995. The Ontario Superior Court of Justice in *Vanscoy v Ontario* [1999] OJ 1661 (QL) reviewed the legislation and found that the Act did not intend to create any new rights for victims and that the Act was 'a statement of principle and social policy, beguilingly clothed in the language of legislation. It did not establish any statutory rights for the victims of crime' (par. 22). In this case, the accused killed Vanscoy's daughter, entering into a plea bargain that the original charge of attempted murder be withdrawn for aggravated assault, with the Crown and defence agreeing that the accused receive a two-year sentence. In *Vanscoy v Ontario*, the applicant sought a judicial declaration that the plea deal reached by the Crown violated their rights under the *Victims Bill of Rights*. The application failed because the 1995 Act never established rights of a kind that could be enforced against the state.

However, not all rights as expressed in the *Victims Bill of Rights Act 2015* (Can) will require enforcement. Several of these rights involve amendments to existing laws and policies. The *Victims Bill of Rights Act 2015* (Can) also amended the Canadian Criminal Code with respect to several important rights. Several of these involve the reorganisation or restatement of existing rights and duties owed to victims by the prosecution or state. These include:

- the definition of victim (clause 3): the definitions of the term *victim* in the *Canadian Victims Bill of Rights* and in the Code differ. The CVBR definition appears to apply both to immediate victims and to other persons, such as family members, who have suffered physical or emotional harm, property damage, or economic loss as the result of the commission or alleged commission of an offence. Under the Code, persons other than those against whom an offence has been committed are considered to be victims only in specified circumstances.

- persons who may act on a victim's behalf (clause 4): a spouse (married or common law), relative, dependant, or individual who has custody or is responsible for the care or support of the victim or of a dependant of the victim may exercise the rights of the victim if the latter is deceased or incapacitated.

- right to information (clauses 20, 27, 32, and 33): victims may request copies of judicial interim release orders (bail orders), conditional sentence orders, restitution orders, and probation orders. Courts making restitution orders are currently required to notify the person to whom the restitution is ordered to be paid. The Bill provides that a public authority responsible for enforcing the restitution order must also be notified of the order. Although such orders are presumed to be available to the public at courthouses across the country, these amendments provide specific rights of access.

- informing the victim of guilty plea agreements (clause 21): requires a judge, after accepting a guilty plea, to ask the prosecutor if reasonable steps were taken to inform the victim of a plea agreement in cases of murder or 'serious personal injury offences'; it includes the offences of sexual assault, sexual assault with a weapon, threats to a third party, and causing bodily harm or aggravated sexual assault, as well as attempts to commit those offences. A duty to inform the victim is imposed upon the prosecutor, who must, as soon as is feasible, take reasonable steps to inform the victim of the agreement and the acceptance of the plea. However, neither the failure of the court to inquire of the prosecutor nor the failure of the prosecutor to take reasonable steps to inform the victims of the agreement affects the validity of the plea.

- right to protection (clauses 5–10): records that contain personal information about the victim or other witnesses in the possession of someone other than the Crown prosecutor or the defence, such as medical, psychiatric, therapeutic, counselling, education, employment, child welfare, adoption, and social services records, as well as personal journals and diaries, are protected. In criminal prosecutions, although the Crown prosecutor has an obligation to disclose investigative files to the accused, third parties in possession of records do not have the same obligation. The Code provides a two-stage procedure for the disclosure of personal information records: the first stage involves a determination as to whether the records ought to be produced to the court, and the second stage involves a determination as to whether the court will order that the records be disclosed to the accused. Although the right to make full answer and defence under sections 7 and 11(d) of the *Canadian Charter of Rights and Freedoms* of the Constitution of Canada is a core principle of justice, in the context of the production of records in sexual offence cases it does not automatically entitle the accused to gain access to information contained in the private records of complainants and witnesses. Clause 5 lists the types of offences for which complainants' records held by a third party may not be disclosed to an accused, except in accordance with set procedure. Complainants, witnesses, and persons in possession or control of such records are entitled to make submissions. The bill gives the court the duty to inform these persons of their right to be represented by counsel during the proceedings. Representation by independent counsel can make a significant difference in the ability of victims and other persons to navigate the third-party records application process, to assess any privacy or security risks that the process may create, and to make informed choices about how to proceed. The Bill also amends the Code to include the security interests of the complainant, witness, or other persons to whom a personal record relates.

- testimonial aids for witnesses (clauses 14–15): The bill extends the availability of testimonial aids to victims and witnesses by expanding the types of supports and procedural protections, as well as the categories of persons who may benefit from such protections, provided that certain criteria are met. These amendments build upon previous Canadian Criminal Code amendments that extended the availability of testimonial aids for witnesses in order to encourage victims and witnesses to participate in the criminal justice process.

- excluding the public in criminal proceedings (clause 13): The judge may order the exclusion of the public if such an order is in the interests of public morals, the maintenance of order, or the proper administration of justice, or is necessary to prevent injury to international relations, national defence, or national security. Excluding the public allows a court to control the publicity of its proceedings with a view to protecting the innocent and safeguarding privacy interests.

- support persons for witnesses (clause 14): If the witness is under the age of eighteen years or has a mental or physical disability, the judge must make the order under this section, as requested, unless he or she is of the opinion that the order would interfere with the proper administration of justice. For other witnesses, the judge can authorise a support person to be present and close to the witness when he or she testifies, if the judge is of the opinion that the order is necessary to obtain a full and candid account. Additional factors are to be considered by the court in determining whether to make such an order; these factors include whether the witness needs the order for his or her security or for protection from intimidation or retaliation; society's interest in encouraging the reporting of offences; and the participation of victims and witnesses in the criminal justice process.

- witness testimony (clause 15): Witness testimony to be given, in certain cases, outside of the courtroom or behind a screen or other device that allows the witness not to see the accused. However, witnesses cannot testify outside the courtroom unless facilities are available to allow the accused, the judge, and the jury to watch the testimony by closed-circuit television or other arrangement and the accused has a means of communicating with counsel while watching the testimony. In cases involving witnesses under the age of eighteen years or who may have difficulty communicating their testimony because of a mental or physical disability, the provision effectively creates a presumption that the order will be granted, unless the judge is of the opinion that the order would interfere with the proper administration of justice.

- cross-examination by the accused (clause 16): Allows for a court order prohibiting a self-represented accused from personally cross-examining a witness in certain cases. When such an order is made, the court must also make an order appointing counsel for the purpose of cross-examination. The judge must make the order unless the proper administration of justice requires that the accused personally cross-examine the witness.
- non-disclosure of the identity of witnesses (clause 17): Creates a new type of court order directing that any information that could identify the witness not be disclosed in the course of the proceedings when such an order is in the interest of the proper administration of justice. Under this new measure, the identity of a witness would not be disclosed to the accused or his or her defence lawyer, or to the general public.
- publication bans (clauses 18 and 19): A court can order a publication ban, which is an order that the identity of a complainant or a witness (or information that could identify him or her) not be published, broadcasted, or transmitted in any way. The power of a court to regulate the publicity of its proceedings serves to protect privacy interests, especially those of witnesses and victims.
- offence of intimidation of a justice system participant (clause 12): Section 423.1 of the Canadian Criminal Code criminalises intimidation that is intended to provoke a state of fear in a group of persons or the general public in order to impede the administration of criminal justice; a justice system participant in order to impede him or her in the performance of his or her duties; or a journalist in order to impede him or her in the transmission to the public of information in relation to a criminal organisation. Clause 12 amends the offence of intimidation of a justice system participant to extend the liability for the commission of the offence to any form of conduct that is intended to provoke a state of fear described earlier.
- participatory rights in bail hearings (clause 20): Measures to protect the safety of victims of crime in bail proceedings include requiring justices to consider no-contact conditions and any other conditions necessary to ensure the safety and security of victims. When considering whether detention is necessary for the protection or safety of the public, justices must specifically consider whether detention is necessary for the protection or safety of any victim of or witness to the offence. During bail hearings, justices must consider any evidence submitted regarding the need to ensure the safety or security of any victim or witness to an offence. A justice who makes an order in respect of bail shall include in the record of the proceedings a statement that he or she considered the safety and security of every victim of the offence when making the order.
- sentencing – the protection of society (clause 23): The protection of society to the provision that specifies the fundamental purpose of sentencing. A codification of an existing purpose of sentencing as existing case law recognises the protection of society as the fundamental purpose of any sentence of whatever kind.
- sentencing – harm done to victims and the community (clause 23): Modifies the objectives of sentencing to specify that denunciation includes denunciation of the harm

caused by the unlawful conduct to both victims and the community. Although the addition of the harm done to the community will be a factor to be considered in all cases, it will be particularly relevant in cases involving offences for which the victim is society at large rather than identifiable individuals (e.g., drug offences and criminal organisation offences).

- sentencing – sanctions other than imprisonment must be consistent with the harm done to victims or to the community (clause 24): The harm done to victims or to the community shall be considered in the determination of whether sanctions other than imprisonment are appropriate in a particular case.
- sentencing – victim impact statements (clause 15): Every victim has the right to present a victim impact statement to the appropriate authorities in the criminal justice system and to have it considered. According to case law, the nature of the information that can be included in a VIS is restricted by the principle that fairness in the sentencing process is of fundamental importance. As such, the content of a VIS is restricted to personal statements of harm and loss that do not include criticisms of the offender or a retelling of the crime. Compare VIS to the amendment of the Canadian Criminal Code regarding the submission of a community impact statement (CIS) (cf. CPS, 2015).
- sentencing – method of submission and presentation process (clauses 25, 22, and 36): Victims can either read their statement aloud during sentencing proceedings or present it in any other manner that the court considers appropriate Clause 25 specifies different ways in which the statement may be presented that afford the victim support and privacy: the victim can read the statement in the presence of a support person, or read it outside the courtroom or behind a screen (with a means, such as closed-circuit television, of allowing for the court and the offender to watch the presentation). The victim, or the victim's representative, may bring a photograph of the victim to court when presenting the VIS, unless to do so would disrupt court proceedings. The new provisions specify that the court shall take into account the portions of the statement that it considers relevant in sentencing the offender and disregard any other portion. Victims may also provide a VIS at a disposition hearing if the accused has been found to be not criminally responsible because of a mental disorder.
- sentencing – community impact statements (clauses 11, 26, and 35): Community impact statements constitute a means by which the court may ascertain the impact of the harm against the community. Community impact statements may be applicable in sentencing hearings for all criminal and regulatory prosecutions. Under new Section 722.2 of the Code, the court is required to consider any statement made by an individual on a community's behalf describing the harm or loss suffered by the community resulting from the offence and the impact of the offence on the community. Unlike a VIS, a CIS can be used in sentencing proceedings for offences, such as drug offences and criminal organisation offences, that have no identifiable individual victim.
- sentencing – victim surcharge (clause 28): The victim surcharge is a financial penalty imposed under section 737 of the Canadian Criminal Code on offenders at the time of sentencing. It is added to any other penalty imposed by the court upon conviction for an offence under the Code.
- sentencing – consideration of restitution order now mandatory (clause 29): Requires the court to consider making a restitution order if an offender is convicted or given a conditional or absolute discharge. The court must always consider whether a restitution

- order is appropriate prior to sentencing or when an absolute or conditional discharge is granted and, where restitution is not granted, include the reasons in the court record.
- payment (clause 30): An offender's financial means or ability to pay does not prevent a restitution order being made.
- enforcement of restitution (clauses 30–31): When making a restitution order the court may make the order in favour of a public authority that would then be responsible for enforcing the order and remitting the amount to the person who made the request for restitution.
- amendments to the *Canada Evidence Act 1985* (Can) (RSC, 1985, chapter C-5) (clause 52): Abrogation of the rule of spousal incompetency. The common law rule of spousal incompetence would be abolished and spouses will be competent and compellable by the prosecution to testify against the other spouse. However, spousal privilege under Section 4(3) remains, so a husband would continue not to be compellable to disclose communications made by his wife during the marriage and vice versa.

Although the *Canadian Charter of Rights and Freedoms* does not directly relate to the expression of victim rights and interests, the courts have considered victims' rights under several provisions.[28] These include section 7 (right to life, liberty and security of the person), section 8 (right to privacy), sections 15 and 28 (right to equality), and section 1 (providing for reasonable limits as long as they are prescribed by law and can be shown to be demonstrably justified in a free and democratic society). However, victim rights under the *Canadian Charter of Rights and Freedoms* remain relatively limited and the court must find a reason to extend the principles to victims. In so doing, the court must carefully balance the interests of the victim with those of the state.

New Zealand

Criminal law in New Zealand flows from the common law but is now substantially contained in the *Crimes Act 1961* (NZ). Summary offences are provided under the *Summary Offences Act 1981* (NZ). The *Criminal Procedure Act 2011* (NZ) prescribes court processes, modes of offence disposal, and rights of victims and witnesses relevant to the criminal trial. While New Zealand has not directly incorporated the ICCPR into law, it has taken measures to enact into several fundamental rights and freedoms under the *New Zealand Bill of Rights Act 1990* (NZ). The criminal courts of New Zealand consist of the district court, high court, court of appeal, and the Supreme Court of New Zealand. Summary matters are dealt with in the district court, which may also hold jury trials for more serious offences. Serious offences are disposed of before judge and jury in the high court. Appeals lie to the court of appeal and then on further appeal to the Supreme Court.

The *Victims' Rights Act 2002* (NZ) consolidates a range of rights and powers available to victims in New Zealand. The 2002 Act also sets out the provisions relating to treatment and rights of victims generally. Section 10 restricts liability as non-enforceable rights for victims. These rights are further enumerated in the draft Victims' Code (NZ), which in April 2015, was open for consultation. In September 2015, the Ministry of Justice launched a finalised version of the Victims' Code (NZ). The Victims' Code (NZ) provides information on: the rights of victims; services available to victims from government and other organisations; government agencies' duties and responsibilities when dealing with victims; and guidance on standards of service that victims can expect from providers of services, and outlines how victims can make a complaint.

The following eight general principles are provided:

- Safety: Services should be provided in a way that minimises any potential harm you and your family/whānau might suffer, and prioritises your safety.
- Respect: Providers should treat you with respect, courtesy and compassion. They should respect your cultural, religious, ethnic and social needs, values and beliefs.
- Dignity and Privacy: Providers should treat you with dignity and protect your privacy.
- Fair Treatment: Providers should respond appropriately to your needs, and should provide their services in a timely and straight-forward manner.
- Informed Choice: Providers should ensure they properly understand your situation and clearly explain the options for getting help. This includes the timeframe in which you can receive their services. They should give honest and accurate answers to any questions you may have about their services.
- Quality Services: Providers should treat you with care and consideration. They should work together to make sure you receive quality and continuity of services.
- Communication: Providers should give you information in a way that is easy to understand. You and your providers should communicate with each other openly, honestly and effectively.
- Feedback: Providers should let you know how you can give feedback and/or make a complaint, and should make it easy for you to do so.

Victims are also entitled to other rights as provided for under a range of statutes, including the *Privacy Act 1993* (NZ), the *Bill of Rights Act 1990* (NZ), the *Sentencing Act 2002* (NZ), and the *Bail Act 2000* (NZ).

The Victims' Code (NZ) presently provides eleven rights to justice for victims of crime:

- Right 1: to be given information about programmes, remedies and services
- Right 2: to be given information about investigation and criminal proceedings
- Right 3: to make a victim impact statement
- Right 4: to express your views on name suppression
- Right 5: to speak official languages in court
- Right 6: to get back property held by the state.

Rights 7 to 10 apply to victims of sexual offending or serious assault, including where a person is killed or becomes unable to look after him- or herself:

- Right 7: to be informed about bail and express your views
- Right 8: to receive information and notifications after sentencing
- Right 9: to have a representative receive notifications
- Right 10: to make a submission relating to parole or extended supervision orders.

Right 11 refers to processes relevant to the youth justice system. It is a right provided to victims of youth offending:

- Right 11: family group conferences.

Government agencies with criminal justice responsibilities have additional duties towards victims. These include: police must tell the victim if they are seeking an alternative to filing a charge in the youth court and what other options are available to the police for responding to the offending; where the victim wants to meet the offender, the victim should be given information on restorative justice and help to make the meeting happen; prosecuting agencies (including the police, court staff, and corrections) should contact you and any other victims of a crime to discuss giving evidence; prosecuting agencies should contact the victim of a sexual offence, or the family member of a victim who has died, and should help minimise distress; prosecuting agencies should tell the victim if an offender has asked for name suppression; and agencies must make sure the victim's contact information is kept confidential, and copies of any victim impact statements are returned to the court.

The rights of victims across New Zealand are also supported by a number of rights that exist as a matter of criminal process. The *Criminal Procedure Act 2011* (NZ) provides the following:

> **Section 26** Private prosecutions (1) If a person who is proposing to commence a private prosecution seeks to file a charging document, the Registrar may: (a) accept the charging document for filing; or (b) refer the matter to a District Court Judge for a direction that the person proposing to commence the proceeding file formal statements, and the exhibits referred to in those statements, that form the evidence that the person proposes to call at trial or such part of that evidence that the person considers is sufficient to justify a trial. (2) The Registrar must refer formal statements and exhibits that are filed in accordance with subsection (1)(b) to a District Court Judge, who must determine whether the charging document should be accepted for filing. (3) A Judge may issue a direction that a charging document must not be accepted for filing if he or she considers that: (a) the evidence provided by the proposed private prosecutor in accordance with subsection (1)(b) is insufficient to justify a trial; or (b) the proposed prosecution is otherwise an abuse of process. (4) If the Judge determines under subsection (2) that the charging document should not be accepted for filing, the Registrar must: (a) notify the proposed private prosecutor that the charging document will not be accepted for filing; and (b) retain a copy of the proposed charging document. (5) Nothing in this section limits the power of a Registrar to refuse to accept a charging document for want of form.

> **Section 96** Restriction on who may take oral evidence of complainant in case of sexual nature. Despite section 95(1), the oral evidence of a complainant may be taken only by a Judge if the defendant is charged with an offence specified in section 93(1).

The *Evidence Act 2006* (NZ) provides specific rights exercisable on direction from the Crown or court:

> **Section 103** Directions about alternative ways of giving evidence (1) In any proceeding, the Judge may, either on the application of a party or on the Judge's own initiative, direct that a witness is to give evidence in chief and be cross-examined in the ordinary way or in an alternative way as provided in section 105. (2) An application for directions under subsection (1) must be made to the Judge as early as practicable before the proceeding is to be heard, or at any later time permitted by the court. (3) A direction under subsection (1) that a witness is to give evidence in an alternative way, may be made on the grounds of: (a) the age or maturity of the witness; (b) the physical, intellectual, psychological, or psychiatric impairment of the witness; (c) the trauma suffered by the witness; (d) the witness's fear of intimidation; (e) the linguistic or cultural

background or religious beliefs of the witness; (f) the nature of the proceeding; (g) the nature of the evidence that the witness is expected to give; (h) the relationship of the witness to any party to the proceeding; (i) the absence or likely absence of the witness from New Zealand; (j) any other ground likely to promote the purpose of the Act. (4) In giving directions under subsection (1), the Judge must have regard to: (a) the need to ensure: (i) the fairness of the proceeding; and (ii) in a criminal proceeding, that there is a fair trial; and (b) the views of the witness and: (i) the need to minimise the stress on the witness; and (ii) in a criminal proceeding, the need to promote the recovery of a complainant from the alleged offence; and (c) any other factor that is relevant to the just determination of the proceeding.

Section 105 Alternative ways of giving evidence (1) A Judge may direct, under section 103, that the evidence of a witness is to be given in an alternative way so that: (a) the witness gives evidence: (i) while in the courtroom but unable to see the defendant or some other specified person; or (ii) from an appropriate place outside the courtroom, either in New Zealand or elsewhere; or (iii) by a video record made before the hearing of the proceeding; (b) any appropriate practical and technical means may be used to enable the Judge, the jury (if any), and any lawyers to see and hear the witness giving evidence, in accordance with any regulations made under section 201; (c) in a criminal proceeding, the defendant is able to see and hear the witness, except where the Judge directs otherwise: (d) in a proceeding in which a witness anonymity order has been made, effect is given to the terms of that order. (2) If a video record of the witness's evidence is to be shown at the hearing of the proceeding, the Judge must give directions under section 103 as to the manner in which cross-examination and re-examination of the witness is to be conducted. (3) The Judge may admit evidence that is given substantially in accordance with the terms of a direction under section 103, despite a failure to observe strictly all of those terms.

Restorative interventions, including those that allow the input of the victim directly, are recognised under section 10(4) of the *Sentencing Act 2002* (NZ). This section provides that:

Without limiting any other powers of a court to adjourn, in any case contemplated by this section a court may adjourn the proceedings until: (a) compensation has been paid; or (b) the performance of any work or service has been completed; or (c) any agreement between the victim and the offender has been fulfilled; or (d) any measure proposed under subsection (1)(d) has been completed; or (e) any remedial action referred to in subsection (1)(e) has been completed.

India

The criminal law of India is divided amongst three statutes – specifically, the *Indian Penal Code Act 1860* (Ind), the *Code of Criminal Procedure Act 1973* (Ind), and *Indian Evidence Act 1872* (Ind). The latter two Acts provide for a criminal process which contains reference to rights and powers exercisable in court to protect witnesses (see Gaur, 2011; Kelkars, 2014; see, generally, Jaishankar, 2014: 71–74). The Constitution of India may also provide some basis for victim rights, at least in terms of arguing for a reform agenda to redress gaps and failings, or for the ratification of international resolutions and agreements. The criminal courts of India comprise the sessions courts for both metropolitan and district courts. Matters may be appealed to the high court and then to the Supreme Court of India. Jury trial was abolished in 1960 following acquittal of the accused in *KM Nanavati v State of Maharashtra* [1962] AIR 605 in questionable circumstances.

India has recently embarked upon a significant reform agenda to realise the rights of victims in a number of key respects. The amendments introduced by the *Code of Criminal Procedure (Amendment) Act 2008* (Ind) and the *Criminal Law (Amendment) Act 2013* (Ind) further progress the interests of the victim by providing access to counsel to assist the prosecution, to victim support when making a complaint, and to increased rights to victims' compensation.

India has been criticised as maintaining limited access to justice for victims of crime. Not only are victims excluded from the courts but also the independence of the judge and the adversarial tradition of examination through counsel further limit victim protection and participation where a codified criminal procedure otherwise fails to recognise the special and vulnerable status of certain victims, including sex offences victims (Singh, 1985; Chockalingam, 2000; Bajpai, 2006). However, it is unfair to present India as a country lacking a victim rights framework. Rather, the foundational aspects of victim rights and the support of the vulnerable must be identified across a number of instruments and judgements that create a basis for the development and expression of rights for victims of crime.

Central to this process of reform, the high courts and the Supreme Court of India have raised the awareness of the plight of victims and the need for an integrated approach to victim rights by delivering judgements across several key areas of victim interests, including: restitution to victims (see *Sukhdev Singh v State of Punjab* [1982] SCC [Cr] 467; *Balraj v State of UP* [1994] SCC (Cr) 823; *Giani Ram v State of Haryana* [1995] AIR 1995 SC 2452; *Baldev Singh v State of Punjab* [1996] AIR 1996 SC 372), the status of rape victims in court (see *Bodhisattwa Gautam v Subhra Chakraborty* [1996] AIR 1996 SC 922; *Pravin v The State of Maharashtra* [2012] HC (Bombay) 249), and state compensation for victims following a crime (see *Rudul Sah v State of Bihar* [1983] AIR 1983 SC 1086; *Saheli, a Women's Resources Centre through Mrs. Nalini Bhanot v Commissioner of Police, Delhi Police* [1990] AIR 1990 SC 513; *DK Basu v State of West Bengal* [1997] AIR 1997 SC 61). Incremental policy and legislative reform has also been central to the development of a victim rights framework. Of particular note discussed in this section are the Justice Malimath Committee on Reforms of Criminal Justice System (Government of India, 2003) and the *National Commission for Protection of Child Rights* (NCPCR), together with key legislative reforms, including the *Protection of Women from Domestic Violence Act 2005* (Ind), the *Maintenance and Welfare of Parents and Senior Citizens Act 2007* (Ind), and the *Prevention of Caste-Based Victimization and Protection for Victims: The Scheduled Castes and the Scheduled Tribes (Prevention of Atrocities) Act 1989* (Ind).

The Constitution of India provides several key rights that may provide for a foundation of rights for victims:

Article 21A The State shall provide free and compulsory education to all children of the age of six to fourteen years in such manner as the State may, by law, determine.

Article 38 State to secure a social order for the promotion of welfare of the people: (1) The State shall strive to promote the welfare of the people by securing and protecting as effectively as it may a social order in which justice, social, economic and political, shall inform all the institutions of the national life. (2) The State shall, in particular, strive to minimise the inequalities in income, and endeavour to eliminate inequalities in status, facilities and opportunities, not only amongst individuals but also amongst groups of people residing in different areas or engaged in different vocations.

Article 41 Right to work, to education and to public assistance in certain cases: The State shall, within the limits of its economic capacity and development, make effective provision for securing the right to work, to education and to public assistance in cases of unemployment, old age, sickness and disablement, and in other cases of undeserved want.

Access to justice is a real concern across a large, diverse population, where religious sanction and gendered practice manifest in modes of victimisation that are not always reported. Incomplete policing and prosecution of gendered crime, and crime in the context of the marital union, continue to be of significant concern. However, India does provide a series of offences to allow for the prosecution of the abuse of women, as provided under the *Indian Penal Code Act 1860* (Ind):

Section 498A Husband or relative of husband of a woman subjecting her to cruelty. Whoever, being the husband or the relative of the husband of a woman, subjects such woman to cruelty shall be punished with imprisonment for a term which may extend to three years and shall also be liable to fine. Explanations: For the purposes of this section, 'cruelty' means: any willful conduct which is of such a nature as is likely to drive the woman to commit suicide or to cause grave injury or danger to life, limb or health (whether mental or physical) of the woman; or harassment of the woman where such harassment is with a view to coercing her or any person related to her to meet any unlawful demand for any property or valuable security or is on account of failure by her or any person related to her to meet such demand.

Section 304B Dowry death. Where the death of a woman is caused by any burns or bodily injury or occurs otherwise than under normal circumstances within seven years of her marriage and it is shown that soon before her death she was subjected to cruelty or harassment by her husband or any relative of her husband for, or in connection with, any demand for dowry, such death shall be called 'dowry death', and such husband or relative shall be deemed to have caused her death. Explanations: For the purposes of this sub-section, 'dowry' shall have the same meaning as in section 2 of the Dowry Prohibition Act, 1961 (28 of 1961). Whoever commits dowry death shall be punished with imprisonment for a term which shall not be less than seven years but which may extend to imprisonment for life.

The case of *State of UP v Damodar and Anr* (2015) ILC-2015-SC-CRL-May-2, brought before the Supreme Court of India under sections 498A and 304B of the *Indian Penal Code Act 1860* (Ind), involving the acquittal of the accused following the dowry death of the victim, resulted in the matter being remanded back to the high court after it was determined that it was improbable that the falling of a lamp on the mattress of the victim would in itself result in the death of the victim by burns, where others were present to douse the fire. *Sandeep and Anr v State of Haryana* (2015) ILC-2015-SC-CRL-May-17 involves the use of a statement made by the victim prior to her death, as recorded by a judicial magistrate in the presence of a doctor, who had attested to the victim's capacity to make the statement. The victim stated that she had been initially kept properly by her husband but, being unable to bring sufficient dowry, began to be subject to harassment and beatings by the accused and his family. The Supreme Court ruled that the conviction of the appellants was correct and justified in the circumstances. In *Basisth Narayan Yadav v Kailash Rai and Ors* (2015) ILC-2015-SC-CRL-Jul-9, the Supreme Court of India set aside the acquittal of the accused where the death of the victim had occurred within seven years of the marriage, as a result of burn injuries following demands of dowry and as accompanied with physical and mental cruelty of the victim. The autopsy revealed the physical assault on the victim prior to her death. In such instances, the burden of proof falls to the accused to explain the death, who submitted that the victim sustained burns from a stove while cooking. However, as the victim did not receive medical treatment and because there was no explanation given as to why the victim's body was left unattended to the next day, the court ruled that the accused serve out their custodial sentences as ordered by the trial court.

Other offences contained under the *Indian Penal Code Act 1860* (Ind) seeking to protect the autonomy and status of women in India include those that criminalise the attempt to procure a miscarriage, or death in the attempt to procure the same:

Section 313 Causing miscarriage without woman's consent. Whoever commits the offence defined in the last preceding section without the consent of the woman, whether the woman is quick with child or not, shall be punished with imprisonment for life, or with imprisonment of either description for a term which may extend to ten years, and shall also be liable to fine.

Section 314 Whoever, with intent to cause the miscarriage of woman with child, does any act which causes the death of such woman, shall be punished with imprisonment of either description for a term may extend to ten years, and shall also be liable to fine. If act done without woman's consent: And if the act is done without the consent of the woman, shall be punished either with [imprisonment for life] or with the punishment above mentioned.

The *Evidence Act 1872* (Ind) provides limited protections for victims and witnesses, but relevant sections do regulate the questions which may be asked of witnesses, and seek to limit offensive and indecent questions. These powers give the judge sufficient discretion to limit questioning of vulnerable witnesses, such as sex offences victims, although this power is also provided by *Bodhisattwa Gautam v Subhra Chakraborty* (1996) AIR 1996 SC 922:

Section 148 Court to decide when question shall be asked and when witness compelled to answer. If any such question relates to a matter not relevant to the suit or proceeding, except in so far as it affect the credit of the witness by injuring his character, the Court shall decide whether or not the witness shall be compelled to answer it, and may, if it thinks fit, warn the witness that he is not obliged to answer it. In exercising its discretion, the Court shall have regard to the following considerations: Such questions are proper if they are of such a nature that the truth of the imputation conveyed by them would seriously affect the opinion of the Courts as to the credibility of the witness on the matter to which testifies; such questions are improper if the imputation which they convey relates to matters so remote in time, or of such a character, that the truth of the imputation would not affect, or would effect in a slight degree, the opinion of the Court as to the credibility of the witness on the matter to which he testifies; such questions are improper if there is a great disproportion between the importance of the imputation made against the witness's character and the importance of his evidence; the Court may, if it sees fit, draw, from the witness's refusal to answer, the inference that the answer if given would be unfavourable.

Section 149 Question not to be asked without reasonable grounds. No such question as is referred to in section 148 ought to be asked, unless the person asking it has reasonable grounds for thinking that the imputation which it conveys is well-founded. Illustrations: A barrister is instructed by an attorney or vakil that an important witness is a dakait. This is a reasonable ground for asking the witness whether he is a dakait. A pleader is informed by a person in court that an important witness is a dakait. The informant, on being questioned by the pleader, gives satisfactory reasons for this statement. This is a reasonable ground for asking the witness whether he is a dakait. A witness, of whom nothing whatever is known, is asked at random whether he is a dakait. There are here no reasonable grounds for the question. A witness, of whom nothing whatever is known, being questioned as to his mode of life and means of living, gives unsatisfactory answers. This may be a reasonable ground for asking him if he is a dakait.

In *Abdul Waheed v State of UP* (2015) ILC-2015-SC-CRL-Sep-27, the Supreme Court of India upheld *inter alia* the conviction of the accused where they sought to challenge the testimony of eye witnesses who witnessed the acts of the accused. This elevated the witnesses to that of 'injured witness', which allows the court to accept their testimony unless cogent and convincing doubts emerge.

Section 151 Indecent and scandalous questions. The Court may forbid any questions or inquiries which it regards as indecent or scandalous, although such questions or inquiries may have some bearing on the questions before the Court, unless they relate to facts in issue, or to matters necessary to be known in order to determine whether or not the facts in issue existed.

Section 152 Questions intended to insult or annoy. The Court shall forbid any question which appears to it to be intended to insult or annoy, or which, though proper in itself, appears to the Court needlessly offensive in form.

In 1996, the Law Commission of India made several recommendations to encourage the state to provide financial assistance to victims out of public funds, where the offender is acquitted or where the victim makes a valid complaint despite the offender remaining at large (Law Commission of India, 1996). The Justice Malimath Committee Report on Reforms of Criminal Justice System further argued that victims should have participatory rights in the criminal justice system, including the right to participate in court and to proper compensation. Recommendations were made that included that the victim's legal counsel should have the right to standing as a party in every criminal proceeding where the offence carries a term of imprisonment of seven years or more; that, subject to the leave of the court, approved voluntary rights groups should have the capacity to intervene in proceedings on behalf of the victim or victims; the right to implead in court proceedings; that the victim should be able to appoint an advocate paid out of public funds where the victim is unable to afford counsel; that the victim's participatory rights during the criminal trial ought to include a right to adduce evidence; to question witnesses; to be kept informed of the status of the investigation, and seek a direction from the court as to the need for further investigation; to have standing rights in court regarding bail and a withdrawal of prosecution; to advance arguments following the close of the prosecutor's case; to seek appeal against any adverse order, including the acquittal of the accused, a plea deal leading to convicting for a lesser offence, imposing an inadequate sentence, or granting inadequate compensation to victims; services should be extended to victims and may include psychiatric and medical assistance, interim compensation orders, and procedural protections against secondary victimisation; as provided by the Law Commission of India, compensation ought to be a state obligation for all serious offences, as prescribed by statute; and that compensation should provide for a statutory fund administered by independent authority (Government of India, 2003).

Several of these concerns have, however, been addressed following passage of the *Code of Criminal Procedure (Amendment) Act 2008* (Ind) and the *Criminal Law (Amendment) Act 2013* (Ind). As such, section 2(w)(a) of the Code of Criminal Procedure now provides that a guardian or legal heir of the victim is a 'victim', which confers on him or her the rights equivalent to those of the victim.[29] Section 24(8) of the Code of Criminal Procedure enabled victims to retain counsel of their choosing, to assist the public prosecutor.[30] Section 26(A) of the Code of Criminal Procedure provides that offence under section 376(A)–(D) of the Indian Penal Code shall be tried, as far as practicable, by a court presided over by a female judge.[31] Section 327 of the Code of Criminal Procedure was amended with respect to in camera proceedings and bans on the publication of details of rape trials, unless assurances can be made as to the confidentiality of the names and addresses of the parties.[32] Section 157 of the Code of Criminal Procedure now provides that the complaint made by a rape victim will be recorded at the residence of the victim, or otherwise in a place of her choosing and, as far as is practicable, by a female police officer. The complaint may be made in the presence of the victim's parent or guardian or nearest relative. Alternatively, a social worker may be present to assist the victim. Section 173(1A) of the Code of Criminal Procedure now provides that the agency investigating an allegation of child rape has three months in which to complete the investigation. Section 357A of the Code of Criminal Procedure now provides that a statutory scheme be established to provide for victim compensation, for victims who have suffered loss or injury because of a crime.[33]

Other relevant legislation recently amending the criminal law and procedure of India include the *Protection of Women from Domestic Violence Act 2005* (Ind), the *Maintenance and Welfare of Parents and Senior Citizens Act 2007*, and the *Prevention of Caste-Based Victimization and Protection for Victims: The Scheduled Castes and the Scheduled Tribes (Prevention of Atrocities) Act 1989* (Ind). Restorative justice is also increasingly utilised as an informal adjunct to criminal proceedings in India, in so far as traditional sources of customary law and practice have become enshrined into law under the *Gram Nyayalayas Act 2008* (Ind). This Act recognises the Panchayat system of informal justice founded in village rule, where disputes may be heard by communal elders, usually in rural locations (see Hardgrav, and Kochanek, 2008; Latha and Thilagaraj, 2013: 312–313).

South Africa

Criminal law in South Africa manifests in the common law but is also developed by statute. Amending legislation informs and develops the substantive criminal law, and its means of disposal, pursuant to the *Criminal Procedure Act 1977* (SthA), which also sets out the relative substantive offences and alternative offences where the former cannot be proven in court (see Kemp, Walker, Palmer, Baqwa, Gevers, Leslie, and Steynberg, 2012). The *Criminal Procedure Act 1977* (SthA) also provides for criminal procedure relevant to criminal trials and the appeals process. The jury trials have been abandoned in South Africa for professional and lay judges, the latter being known as assessors. The process was most notably demonstrated in the high-profile case against Oscar Pistorius (see *Director of Public Prosecutions, Gauteng v Pistorius* [96/2015] [2015] ZASCA 204; [2016] 1 All SA 346).

The criminal courts of South Africa consist of the district magistrates' courts and the regional magistrates' courts. These courts hear and determine matters before a single magistrate. Trials are heard in the high court of South Africa, which may also hear appeals from the magistrates' courts. The supreme court of appeal will hear appeals on matters of fact or law arising out of the trial court. The Constitutional Court of South Africa may hear appeals on matters of constitutional significance as relevant to criminal law and procedure, or sentencing.

The National Development Plan 2030 of the South African Government (2013) provides a proposal for the development of safe communities, of interest to victims generally. The plan contains a longer-term vision for the government of South Africa to provide for a safer community by 2030. This plan is founded on a criminal justice system responsive to the needs of victims and the community, and requires the assistance of the police, judiciary, and correctional services in order for crime to be apprehended and prosecuted in a way that develops and maintains a stronger society. Other connected areas of development, including housing, the economy, and infrastructure, are also identified. This plan is, however, a board blueprint for the future and provides little detail of the immediate policy directives of the government of South Africa.

The Service Charter for Victims of Crime in South Africa or Victims' Charter (SthA) was developed in 2004 to set minimum service rights for victims of crime. The Victims' Code (SthA) was a collaborative effort of several stakeholder organisations that make up the South African criminal justice system. These stakeholders include the Gender Directorate in the Department of Justice, and the Departments of Constitutional Development, Social Development, Correctional Services, Education, and Health. Additional stakeholders include the National Prosecuting Authority (NPA), the South African Police Service, the South African Law Reform Commission, the South African Human Rights Commission, the Office of the Public Protector, the Independent Complaints Directorate, members of the Magistrates' and Judicial Service Commissions, and members of Tshwane Metro Police.

The rights provided for under the Victims' Code (SthA) include many of these that correspond to the normative rights identified in Chapter 2. The specific rights include the right to:

- be treated with fairness and with respect for dignity and privacy
- offer information
- receive information
- protection
- assistance
- compensation
- restitution.

The National Implementation plan for the Service Charter for Victims of Crime 2007 provides for the implementation of the Victims' Code (SthA) across several departments and organisations central to the interests of the victim in a justice or welfare context. The departments directly mentioned in the plan include many of those involved in the drafting of the Victims' Code (SthA) in 2004, and for which a five-year implementation plan was presented for public exposure, including the Departments of Justice and Constitutional Development, National Prosecuting Authority, South African Police Service, Correctional Services, Social Development, and Health. The implementation plan for the National Prosecuting Authority demonstrates how there has been consideration as to the inclusion of the victim across a range of policy areas, spanning restorative justice, community justice, and prosecution-guided investigations. The Prosecution Guidelines of the National Prosecuting Authority (NPA, 2014) provide some detail as to the consideration of the victim in the decision to prosecute and related matters. However, little is said of the alternative policy directives referred to under the implementation plan and how these may connect to the decision to prosecute in the first instance.

The *Criminal Procedure Act 1977* (SthA) provides for various powers for victims in the context of procedural rights to private prosecution and other protections afforded during the criminal trial. The right to services while participating in the trial process is prescribed for by statute:

> **Section 191A** Witness services. (1) The Minister has the power to determine services to be provided to a witness who is required to give evidence in any court of law. (2) The Minister may make regulations relating to: (a) the assistance of, and support to, witnesses at courts; (b) the establishment of reception centres for witnesses at courts; (c) the counselling of witnesses; and (d) any other matter which the Minister deems expedient to prescribe in order to provide services to witnesses at courts.

South Africa has a substantial number of rights and powers in support of private prosecution which, for a common law state, demonstrate a significant emphasis on the power of the victim to bring an offender to justice. The power to proceed through counsel is provided for, but only in so far as private prosecution is concerned:

> **Section 172** Parties may examine witness. Any party to proceedings in which a commission is issued under section 171, may: (a) transmit interrogatories in writing which the court issuing the commission may think relevant to the issue, and the magistrate to whom the commission is issued, shall examine the witness upon such interrogatories; or (b) appear before such magistrate, either by a legal representative or, in the case of an accused who is not in custody or in the case of a private prosecutor, in person, and examine the witness.

The prosecution may be brought in the name of the private prosecutor as represented by their personal counsel, but the prosecution will otherwise proceed as though it was an action of the state. This means that once initiated, the private prosecutor has the same function at trial as a state attorney:

> **Section 7** Private prosecution on certificate nolle prosequi. (1) In any case in which a Director of Public Prosecutions declines to prosecute for an alleged offence: (a) any private person who proves some substantial and peculiar interest in the issue of the trial arising out of some injury which he individually suffered in consequence of the commission of the said offence; (b) a husband, if the said offence was committed in respect of his wife; (c) the wife or child or, if there is no wife or child, any of the next of kin of any deceased person, if the death of such person is alleged to have been caused by the said offence; or (d) the legal guardian or curator of a minor or lunatic, if the said offence was committed against his ward, may, subject to the provisions of section 9 and section 59 (2) of the Child Justice Act, 2008, either in person or by a legal representative, institute and conduct a prosecution in respect of such offence in any court

competent to try that offence. (2) (a) No private prosecutor under this section shall obtain the process of any court for summoning any person to answer any charge unless such private prosecutor produces to the officer authorized by law to issue such process a certificate signed by the attorney-general that he has seen the statements or affidavits on which the charge is based and that he declines to prosecute at the instance of the State. (b) The attorney-general shall, in any case in which he declines to prosecute, at the request of the person intending to prosecute, grant the certificate referred to in paragraph (a). (c) A certificate issued under this subsection shall lapse unless proceedings in respect of the offence in question are instituted by the issue of the process referred to in paragraph (a) within three months of the date of the certificate. (d) The provisions of paragraph (c) shall apply also with reference to a certificate granted before the commencement of this Act under the provisions of any law repealed by this Act, and the date of such certificate shall, for the purposes of this paragraph, be deemed to be the date of commencement of this Act.

Section 8 Private prosecution under statutory right. (1) Any body upon which or person upon whom the right to prosecute in respect of any offence is expressly conferred by law, may institute and conduct a prosecution in respect of such offence in any court competent to try that offence. (2) A body which or a person who intends exercising a right of prosecution under subsection (1), shall exercise such right only after consultation with the attorney general concerned and after the attorney-general has withdrawn his right of prosecution in respect of any specified offence or any specified class or category of offences with reference to which such body or person may by law exercise such right of prosecution. (3) An attorney-general may, under subsection (2), withdraw his right of prosecution on such conditions as he may deem fit, including a condition that the appointment by such body or person of a prosecutor to conduct the prosecution in question shall be subject to the approval of the attorney-general, and that the attorney-general may at any time exercise with reference to any such prosecution any power which he might have exercised if he had not withdrawn his right of prosecution.

Section 10 Private prosecution in name of private prosecutor. (1) A private prosecution shall be instituted and conducted and all process in connection therewith issued in the name of the private prosecutor. (2) The indictment, charge-sheet or summons, as the case may be, shall describe the private prosecutor with certainty and precision and shall, except in the case of a body referred to in section 8, be signed by such prosecutor or his legal representative. (3) Two or more persons shall not prosecute in the same charge except where two or more persons have been injured by the same offence.

Section 12 Mode of conducting private prosecution. (1) A private prosecution shall, subject to the provisions of this Act, be proceeded with in the same manner as if it were a prosecution at the instance of the State: Provided that the person in respect of whom the private prosecution is instituted shall be brought before the court only by way of summons in the case of a lower court, or an indictment in the case of a superior court, except where he is under arrest in respect of an offence with regard to which a right of private prosecution is vested in any body or person under section 8. (2) Where the prosecution is instituted under section 7 (1) and the accused pleads guilty to the charge, the prosecution shall be continued at the instance of the State.

Section 15 Costs of private prosecution. (1) The costs and expenses of a private prosecutor shall, subject to the provisions of subsection (2), be paid by the private prosecutor.

(2) The court may order a person convicted upon a private prosecution to pay the costs and expenses of the prosecution, including the costs of any appeal against such conviction or any sentence: Provided that the provisions of this subsection shall not apply with reference to any prosecution instituted and conducted under section 8: Provided further that where a private prosecution is instituted after the grant of a certificate by an attorney-general that he declines to prosecute and the accused is convicted, the court may order the costs and expenses of the private prosecution, including the costs of an appeal arising from such prosecution, to be paid by the State.

Victims are also entitled to protective mechanisms where they are present as a sex offences victim and required to give evidence:

Section 227 Evidence of character and previous sexual experience. (1) Evidence as to the character of an accused or as to the character of any person against or in connection with whom a sexual offence as contemplated in the Criminal Law (Sexual Offences and Related Matters) Amendment Act, 2007, is alleged to have been committed, shall, subject to the provisions of subsection (2), be admissible or inadmissible if such evidence would have been admissible or inadmissible on the 30th day of May, 1961. (2) No evidence as to any previous sexual experience or conduct of any person against or in connection with whom a sexual offence is alleged to have been committed, other than evidence relating to sexual experience or conduct in respect of the offence which is being tried, shall be adduced, and no evidence or question in cross examination regarding such sexual experience or conduct, shall be put to such person, the accused or any other witness at the proceedings pending before the court unless: (a) the court has, on application by any party to the proceedings, granted leave to adduce such evidence or to put such question; or (b) such evidence has been introduced by the prosecution. (3) Before an application for leave contemplated in subsection (2) (a) is heard, the court may direct that any person, including the complainant, whose presence is not necessary may not be present at the proceedings. (4) The court shall, subject to subsection (6), grant the application referred to in subsection (2) (a) only if satisfied that such evidence or questioning is relevant to the proceedings pending before the court. (5) In determining whether evidence or questioning as contemplated in this section is relevant to the proceedings pending before the court, the court shall take into account whether such evidence or questioning: (a) is in the interests of justice, with due regard to the accused's right to a fair trial; (b) is in the interests of society in encouraging the reporting of sexual offences; (c) relates to a specific instance of sexual activity relevant to a fact in issue; (d) is likely to rebut evidence previously adduced by the prosecution; (e) is fundamental to the accused's defence; (f) is not substantially outweighed by its potential prejudice to the complainant's personal dignity and right to privacy; or (g) is likely to explain the presence of semen or the source of pregnancy or disease or any injury to the complainant, where it is relevant to a fact in issue. (6) The court shall not grant an application referred to in subsection (2) (a) if, in its opinion, such evidence or questioning is sought to be adduced to support an inference that by reason of the sexual nature of the complainant's experience or conduct, the complainant (a) is more likely to have consented to the offence being tried; or (b) is less worthy of belief. (7) The court shall provide reasons for granting or refusing an application in terms of subsection (2) (a), which reasons shall be entered in the record of the proceedings.

The assistance of an intermediary may also be provided for:

Section 170A Evidence through intermediaries. (1) Whenever criminal proceedings are pending before any court and it appears to such court that it would expose any witness under the biological or mental age of eighteen years to undue mental stress or suffering if he or she testifies at such proceedings, the court may, subject to subsection (4), appoint a competent person as an intermediary in order to enable such witness to give his or her evidence through that intermediary. (2) (a) No examination, cross-examination or re-examination of any witness in respect of whom a court has appointed an intermediary under subsection (1), except examination by the court, shall take place in any manner other than through that intermediary. (b) The said intermediary may, unless the court directs otherwise, convey the general purport of any question to the relevant witness. (3) If a court appoints an intermediary under subsection (1), the court may direct that the relevant witness shall give his or her evidence at any place: (a) which is informally arranged to set that witness at ease; (b) which is so situated that any person whose presence may upset that witness, is outside the sight and hearing of that witness; and (c) which enables the court and any person whose presence is necessary at the relevant proceedings to see and hear, either directly or through the medium of any electronic or other devices, that intermediary as well as that witness during his or her testimony. (4) (a) The Minister may by notice in the Gazette determine the persons or the category or class of persons who are competent to be appointed as intermediaries. (b) An intermediary who is not in the full-time employment of the State shall be paid such travelling and subsistence and other allowances in respect of the services rendered by him or her as the Minister, with the concurrence of the Minister of Finance, may determine.

The case against Oscar Pistorius having shot dead his girlfriend, Reeva Steenkamp, thinking that she may be an intruder in their home, garnered international attention and provides a window through which the South African trial process may be viewed. Pistorius was convicted of the lesser offence of culpable homicide; however, on appeal, the Supreme Court of Appeal of South Africa per Leach JA, with whom the court agreed, substituted the verdict of murder, finding that the accused possessed the requisite intent and that relevant defences did not apply (see *Director of Public Prosecutions, Gauteng v Pistorius* [96/2015] [2015] ZASCA 204; [2016] 1 All SA 346; sections 258, 259 of the *Criminal Procedure Act 1977* (SthA)). The court on appeal rejected the contention that the evidence did not support a murder conviction and also dismissed the relevance defence raised by the accused at pars [31] and [51]:

This finding goes to the heart of the first question of law reserved ie whether the principles of *dolus eventualis*, including so-called '*error in objecto*', were properly applied. In this regard, it is necessary to stress that although a perpetrator's intention to kill must relate to the person killed, this does not mean that a perpetrator must know or appreciate the identity of the victim. A person who causes a bomb to explode in a crowded place will probably be ignorant of the identity of his or her victims, but will nevertheless have the intention to kill those who might die in the resultant explosion.

. . .

In these circumstances I have no doubt that in firing the fatal shots the accused must have foreseen, and therefore did foresee, that whoever was behind the toilet door might die, but reconciled himself to that event occurring and gambled with that person's life. This constituted *dolus eventualis* on his part, and the identity of his victim is irrelevant to his guilt.

As for Pistorius' reliance on self-defence on the basis that his honest belief, however erroneous, was that his or the victim's life was in danger, the court ruled the following, rejecting the claim, at par. [52]:

> The immediate difficulty that I have with the accused's reliance upon putative private defence is that when he testified, he stated that he had not intended to shoot the person whom he felt was an intruder. This immediately placed himself beyond the ambit of the defence, although as I have said, his evidence is so contradictory that one does just not know his true explanation for firing the weapon.

The trial against Pistorius became an international spectacle, with substantial media and public interest generating theories of Pistorius' liability, and the punishment he ought to face. The trial did demonstrate how the trial process may work to the exclusion of the victim and their family, in accordance with the adversarial method of testing evidence against the accused, although Reeva Steenkamp's family members were present in court throughout his trial and were often commented on by the observing media. In January 2016, counsel for Pistorius sought leave to appeal to the Constitutional Court of South Africa on the basis that the appeals court acted unlawfully and unconstitutionally by rejecting the factual findings of the original case. This application has since been denied, which means that Pistorius' conviction as revised by the Supreme Court of Appeal of South Africa stands.

Mixed and hybrid systems

Mixed and hybrid systems of justice are characterised by their development out of distinct legal traditions. Mixed and hybrid systems may result from processes of colonisation or settlement under a European, civil law model, as is the case in Brazil, or out of the influence of Anglo-American law following World War II, and then further strategic reform in the 2000s to better position to the victim, as is the case in Japan. Other countries could also feature here, adapting law and policy from different frameworks, through process of ratification of international human rights norms and policy transfer to articulate a role for the victim alongside other criminal justice stakeholders (Roberson and Das, 2016). Although a mixed or hybrid model of justice does not guarantee better or more integrated rights for the victim, the lack of national attachment to a particular justice tradition means that government and people are open to different modalities of reform that may be blocked in other systems.

Japan

The criminal law of Japan is contained in its penal code or *Keihō*, Law No. 45 of 1907 (Jpn). Japan's strategic reform of the criminal process from 2000 onwards to better include the victim evidences a purpose-driven shift from an adversarial process to one that includes the victim as a participant in proceedings. Japan's legal system may be appropriately characterised as a hybrid legal system because it is developed out of the European and Anglo-American systems, although it tends towards the Anglo-American adversarial model of justice. The movement towards greater victim participation was effected by the Fundamental Plan in

2005, and amendments to the Code of Criminal Procedure (Act No. 131 of 1948) (Jpn), following introduction of the Act to Amend Parts of the Code of Criminal Procedure and Others in Order to Protect Rights and Interests of Victims of Crime (*Hanzaihigaishatō no kenririeki no hogo wo hakarutame no keijisoshōhōtō no ichibu wo kaisesuru hōritsu*), Law No. 95 of 2007 (Jpn). This amendment provided for substantial levels of victim participation during the criminal trial, in addition to the removal of other restrictions (see Saeki, 2010). These reforms significantly changed the relationship between trial stakeholders, which complements changes to the jury trial introduced in 2004, which provided for lay panels to determine liability and, where convicted, to sentence the accused. Changes to the jury trial in Japan were also consolidated under the Code of Criminal Procedure (Jpn) as amended by the Act concerning Participation of Lay Assessors in Criminal Trials (*Saiban'in no sanka suru keiji saiban ni kansuru hōritsu*), Law No. 63 of 2004 (Jpn) (see Matsui, 2011; Fukurai, 2013; Johnson and Shinomiya, 2015).

The criminal court system of Japan comprises a court of first instance, the summary court, which hears and determines matters before a single judge without a jury. Modest penalties including fine or servitude with labour may be imposed by this court. The district court handles more serious offences, which are heard before a single judge unless the offence carries a substantial penalty, in which case the matter will be heard by a panel of three judges. An offence in which the general public has a strong interest will be disposed of under the Saiban-in system. This is the lay jury introduced in the 2004 reforms. The Saiban-ins comprise a panel of six selected from voter registration rolls, with three professional judges, similar to the lay panels used in Germany. The Saiban-in system is used where the public is likely to have a strong interest in the outcome of the prosecution, where the accused is charged with an offence punishable by death or imprisonment for life, or where the offence involves intentional conduct resulting in the victim's death, and where the minimum term is one year's imprisonment. Offences including homicides, robbery with injury or death, arson of inhabited buildings, and kidnapping for ransom may go before the lay and professional jury. The Saiban-ins are arbiters of fact while the professional judges determine points of law. The sentence, where the accused is convicted, is determined after consultation between the Saiban-ins and the professional judges (see contra. Wilson, 2009; Hans, 2014). A court of second instance, known as the court of appellate instance or high court, may hear appeals from the lower courts. Appeals will proceed before three judges based on non-compliance with procedural law in the trial procedure, an error in the interpretation or application of law in the judgement, excessive severity or leniency of the sentence, or an error in fact finding on the part of the trial court. The final court of appeals is the Supreme Court of Japan. The Supreme Court will hear appeals before a panel of five judges based on a violation of the Constitution of Japan, or an error in the interpretation of the Constitution, or due to an alleged conflict with a former precedent of the Supreme Court or high courts.

Victims lack the power of private prosecution and all offences must be brought to court by a public prosecutor. However, once initiated, the victim gains substantial powers to intervene and be heard in court proceedings in accordance with the reforms of 2007. The 2007 reforms to the Code of Criminal Procedure took effect in 2008. Following the granting of leave from the court, victims and family members may seek participant standing before the court. Victim participants may then ask questions of witnesses, make submissions, and address the court during closing arguments (see ahead). Amendment to the Code of Criminal Procedure in 2000 and 2004, the *Kensatsu shinsakaihō*, Law No. 147 of 1948 (Jpn), Prosecution Review Board Act, together with the *Keijisoshōhōtō no ichibu wo kaiseisuru hōritsu*, Law No. 62 of 2004 (Jpn), or an Act to Revise the Code of Criminal Procedure, made it possible to review the decision of a public prosecutor to not proceed with a matter. Where the public prosecutor refuses to bring charges in a case involving the death of the primary victim, a family member may appeal to the Prosecution Review Board (PRB). The decision of the PRB is binding, and where a prosecution decision not to proceed is reversed, private counsel will be briefed to continue with the prosecution case.

Victims now have greater access to the prosecution case file, and may draw upon the file to initiate a civil action against an accused. Article 250 of the Code of Criminal Procedure now delimits the time in which charges for homicide may be brought, removing the former restriction of twenty-five years. Article 290–2 provides that the names of victims can be removed from the indictment or writs of prosecution, preserving the victim's anonymity. Article 295 of the Code of Criminal Procedure further preserves anonymity by allowing the court to restrict the assessment of witness statements where the identity of the victim is likely to be disclosed. Once the trial commences, victims, their counsel, and other support persons may seek preferential seating in court, which the presiding judge must arrange pursuant to the Victim Protection Act (*Higaisha no hogo ni kansuru hōritsu*), Law No. 75 of 2000 (Jpn). Article 157–2 allows a support person to be present where the victim is called to testify in court. The support person is to provide emotional assistance but may not otherwise inform the victim's testimony. Under Article 157–3, physical shields and barriers may be erected to protect victims where they are distressed or intimidated or are otherwise of a frail mental condition. Article 157–4 allows the use of closed-circuit television (CCTV) to provide for out-of-court evidence.

Participatory rights are granted under several sections of the Code of Criminal Procedure. Article 292–2 of the Code of Criminal Procedure affords victims the benefit of stating their feelings regarding proceedings as a submission made to the court. Victims may retain legal counsel to assist with this submission. This power allows victims to give an opinion during proceedings, which may include a statement as to the charge, the evidence, or the conduct of proceedings. However, the privilege is not absolute. Rather, the victim must seek leave of the court after the prosecutor has responded to the request of the victim to give an opinion. The prosecution may contest the application where the opinion is repetitive, frivolous, vexatious, or irrelevant. Where the court denies the victim's request, the victim may file a statement of opinion in accordance with Article 134. Any opinion submitted to the court does not gain the weight of evidence before the court.

Victims of particularly serious offences may seek representation by counsel. Victims of homicide, bodily injury, rape, forced obscene acts, illegal imprisonment or detention, or negligent operation of motor vehicles resulting in death or injury may request representation through counsel under Article 316–33 of the Code of Criminal Procedure. The right to direct participation even through legal representation is not absolute, and the leave of the court must first be granted. The court will determine if victim participation is appropriate against the nature of the offence and the need to protect the interests of the victim during the trial. The prosecution and defence may respond to the victim's request to participate directly. Under Article 316–34, the victim may sit with the prosecution in court. Direct participation will entitle victims to make submissions as to their opinion on how the trial ought to be conducted, including statements regarding the use of evidence, final argument, or sentence that is sought. Article 316–36 allows the victim to examine witnesses and to challenge their credibility, while Article 316–37 extends this power to questions asked of the accused. Article 316–38 allows victims to state their opinion on the facts and law applied at trial, following close of the prosecutor's case. Article 5 of the Victim Protection Act (*Higaisha no hogo ni kansuru hōritsu*), Law No. 75 of 2000 (Jpn), allows a victim to be represented by counsel and to have a publicly funded lawyer should the victim not be able to afford a private attorney (see, generally, Anderson and Johnson, 2010).

The European system of reparations from the accused was also adopted in Japan, which was also influenced by the Anglo-American practice of seeking compensation following a conviction in criminal proceedings. Although compensation tends to be assessed in the Anglo-American or common law model from evidence adduced separately from trial, heard during sentencing or in a separate hearing, the European tradition of adhering a claim to the trial was integrated into the Japanese trial process in so far as it made possible the assessment of damages on the basis of evidence adduced at trial. Known as a 'damage order system', victims may seek damages at trial in order to overcome the burden of initiating separate proceedings in civil court. Article 13 of Law No. 75 of 2000 (Jpn) allows a court to record the details of a private settlement between offender and victim on the trial transcript. By recording the details of the agreement reached, the agreement becomes enforceable against the accused. Article 17 of Law No. 75 of 2000 (Jpn) empowers the victim to seek damages during the trial, so long as the original offence was intentional, such as in the case of rape, forcible obscene act, child abduction, abduction for ransom, and other like offences. Judges will assess liability for damages following conviction.

Brazil

Brazil is a federal republic constituted by twenty-seven states. Brazilian law has been influenced by various legal traditions, including Portuguese, French, Italian, and German civil law, such that it now represents a system of mixed legal traditions. Brazilian criminal law is codified under the *Código Penal* or Penal Code, Decree-Law No. 2,848 of December 7, 1940 (Brazil). The criminal procedure of the court of Brazil is contained in the *Código de Processo* or Code of Criminal Procedure, Decree-Law No. 3,689 of Oct. 3, 1941 (Brazil), as amended. The Brazilian criminal justice system is established under the *Constituição da República Federativa do Brasil* or Constitution of the Federal Republic of Brazil of 1988, which prescribes that there be rules on criminal and procedural matters, the judiciary, procedural guarantees, and juridical international cooperation. The Code of Criminal Procedure sets out rules regarding criminal investigation, prosecution, and trial processes, including provisions for victim participation during investigation and at trial. Rules that progress the standing of the victim in the Brazilian criminal justice system are also contained across a range of cognate statutes, such as the right to counsel, prescribed under Federal Law No. 1,060 of 1950 (Brazil) and Complementary Law No. 132 of 2009 (Brazil) (see, generally, Jaishankar, 2014: 69–71).

The criminal courts of Brazil comprise trial courts as found in each municipality. The trial courts will hear minor offences before a judge sitting alone. Jury trials will be held for more serious offences, including wilful crimes against the person, manslaughter, infanticide, abortion, and inciting suicide. Matters dealt with before the trial court may be appealed to the tribunal de justiça or courts of justice. Where the court of justice is constituted as an appeals court, three judges will be empanelled to hear the case. The federal courts may hear offences under the jurisdiction conferred on them by the Constitution of Brazil. These offences include political crimes, international drug trafficking, terrorism, and offences regarding immigration and border control. The federal court structure consists of varas federais or trial courts of first instance, and tribunais regionais federais, or regional federal courts of second instance. Non-constitutional federal and state matters may be appealed to the superior tribunal de justiça or superior court of justice where a question arises as to the interpretation of a federal law. The *Supremo Tribunal Federal* or Supreme Federal Court determines matters as to the validity of a law pursuant to the Constitution of Brazil, which may include appeals arising from second instance courts where the constitutionality of a ruling is in question.

Laws that protect the rights of victim in the Brazilian criminal justice system are largely contained in the Code of Criminal Procedure. In Brazil, a criminal action does not need to be initiated by the victim personally. The police will refer matters to the prosecution. Where the police refuse to act, the victim may seek to appeal to the chief of police under Article 5. For offences of interpersonal or sexual violence, however, Article 5 provides that the victim must first enter a complaint. The pretrial process is largely inquisitorial and the victim is generally excluded while the police and prosecution gather evidence and investigate the offence. Articles 125–127 (also see Articles 126 and 134 regarding the freezing of personal assets, and 135 and 140 regarding the payment of compensation to the victim) allow the court to seize assets of an accused on application of the prosecution, which may ultimately flow to the victim as restitution and compensation. Final removal of assets and payment to the victim must, however, follow conviction (see Articles 125–144A). Support services may also be available during the investigative phase. Article 7 of Federal Law No. 9,807 of 1999 (Brazil) may provide for victims of organised crime. The rights afforded include:

- transference of residence;
- monthly financial aid per person;
- food and clothing supplies;
- safety when traveling from one place to another;
- help in finding a new job;
- removal of public employees without loss of remuneration;
- social, psychological, and medical assistance;
- change of identity.

Persons who have suffered domestic violence may also be entitled to support under Articles 23–24 of Federal Law No. 11,340 of 2006 (Brazil). The statute identifies women of any 'sexual orientation', and is notable for recognising transgender rights of victims. The entitlements include the following:

- offenders may not be granted alternative, non-custodial sentences;
- the maximum sentence was increased from one to three years;
- increased police powers, including the removal of the offender from the home;
- proximity restrictions around the victim, including children of the victim.

Article 100 of the Code of Criminal Procedure provides that where the public prosecutor does not seek to prosecute, the victim may initiate a private prosecution. Article 24 provides that in such a case, the complaint must proceed from victims themselves, or their counsel, or where the victim is deceased or missing, his or her spouse or kin. Private prosecution is generally restricted to crimes against one's reputation, such as defamation and moral injury, property offences without violence, and fraud. The private prosecutor will pay costs associated with their case, unless public counsel is appointed, or where the judge appoints private counsel under Article 32. The public prosecutor may intervene in a private prosecution, and introduce evidence and make submissions under Articles 45–47. Alternatively, the public prosecutor may initiate the case against the accused, to be joined by the victim as accessory prosecutor. Brazil has ratified the Rome Statute into domestic law, adopting provisions of the statute under Decree No. 4,388 of 2002 (Brazil) into the Code of Criminal Procedure. Brazil has also ratified the Geneva Conventions under Decree No. 33,648 of 1953 (Brazil). Where international crimes against humanity are adopted into the penal code, they will be prosecuted publicly. It would be only where the public prosecutor chooses not to proceed with a matter that the victim is able to take up the prosecution privately. However, given the largess of expense and time of such cases, private prosecution of international war crimes is not feasible.

The trial process itself is adversarial in that counsel may examine and cross-examine witnesses. Although cross-examination is generally not recognised, witnesses are subject to examination in open court, which is counsel-led and may be aversive. The judge and victim may intervene and ask questions of witnesses as well (see Articles 156 and 229). Once the indictment is issued by the prosecution, the victim gains substantive rights to access the prosecution case. Article 5, LX, of the Constitution of Brazil grants the victim the right to access the evidence presented under the indictment. Under Article 201, the victim further gains the right to information on the trial, including hearing dates and changes to the detention status of the accused following conviction. Article 201 also provides the right to be heard at trial and to make submissions and offer evidence. Where the victim participates but without standing as an accessory or private prosecutor, he or she will be identified as an accusation assistant, which presents as a quasi-formal role that distinguishes the victim as a stakeholder with Article 201 rights. The rights of the accusation assistant are further articled under Articles 271, 157, 387, 403, 584, 598, and 927 as the right to:

- submit new evidence, including calling and examining witnesses (although note the prosecution is generally limited to a determined number of witnesses, which the victim must also observe);
- submit non-binding material to the court;
- directly question witnesses;
- propose an amended charge where a matter proceeds before a jury;
- make submissions and engage in oral argument across all phases through to sentencing;
- provide reasons in favour of an appeal, or respond to the defence's request to appeal;
- file interlocutory or supplementary appeals;
- make an open or closing statement;
- seek reparations during sentencing (with court tending towards an award for material rather than moral damages);
- compensation may be additionally sought, and may involve conversion of the accused's confiscated assets as reparation.

Article 201 of the Code of Criminal Procedure also grants the right to proceedings in camera, or the use of other appropriate measures as approved by the court, including the use of screens. Victims also have a right to in court support services, such as counselling and witness assistance, or the use of an intermediary to facilitate communication with the court, as deemed necessary by the judge. The victim has a further right to be physically separated from the accused in court under Article 202. Article 212 of the Code of Criminal Procedure prevents intimidation of victims and witnesses by authorising the use of CCTV to enable a witness or victim to give out-of-court evidence. Where denied the right to participate, say out of the interests of justice, fairness to the accused, or because the offence does not privilege the victim with such rights, the victim may seek a writ of mandamus from a superior court to enforce his or her right to participate.

Brazil has a reputation of ratifying international covenants and treaties. Reflecting on Brazil's compliance with the ICCPR, Wilks (2012: 138) indicates the need for continued reform in accordance with an integrated model of criminal procedural rights that are inclusive of those of the victim:

> It is the responsibility of judges to ensure that defendants, witnesses and victims are treated fairly and that those accused of having committed a criminal offence receive a fair trial. This involves ensuring that their rights are respected at all times, and that only evidence which has been properly obtained should be admissible in court. It also means ensuring that those responsible for upholding the law are themselves bound by its strictures. This may involve taking an assertive role to ensure that all testimony and evidence has been given freely and has not been obtained using coercive means. Judges should at all times be alert to the possibility that defendants and witnesses may have been subject to torture or other ill-treatment. If, for example, a detainee alleges that he or she has been ill-treated when brought before a judge at the end of a period of police custody, it is incumbent upon the judge to record the allegation in writing, immediately order a forensic medical examination and take all necessary steps to ensure the allegation is fully investigated. This should also be done in the absence of an express complaint or allegation if the person concerned bears visible signs of physical or mental ill-treatment.

The criminal justice system of Brazil borrows from continental European traditions in the context of a legal system increasingly developed out of ratification of human rights instruments and norms. Access to justice for victims and accused remains a significant challenge, however, in the context of a justice system that provides rights and powers but offers limited welfare and support to access those rights, at least evenly across the population.

Notes

1 Although contra see the criminal procedure of the Netherlands prior to 2011.
2 See section 397a of the German Criminal Code: 'Appointment of an Attorney as Counsel, (1) Upon application of the private accessory prosecutor an attorney shall be appointed as his counsel if he 1. has been aggrieved by a felony pursuant to sections 176a, 177, 179, 232 and 233 of the Criminal Code; 2. has been aggrieved by an attempted unlawful act pursuant to sections 211 and 212 of the Criminal Code or is a relative of a person killed through an unlawful act within the meaning of Section 395 subsection (2), number 1; 3. has been aggrieved by a felony pursuant to sections 226, 226a, 234 to 235, 238 to 239b, 249, 250, 252, 255 and 316a of the Criminal Code which has caused or is expected to cause him serious physical or mental harm; 4. has been aggrieved by an unlawful act pursuant to sections 174 to 182 and 225 of the Criminal Code and had not attained the age of 18 at the time of the act or cannot sufficiently safeguard his own interests himself; or 5. has been aggrieved by an unlawful act pursuant to sections 221, 226, 226a, 232 to 235, 237, 238 subsections (2) and (3), 239a, 239b, 240 subsection (4), 249, 250, 252, 255 and 316a of the Criminal Code and has not attained the age of 18 at the time of his application or cannot sufficiently safeguard his own interests himself. (2) Where the conditions for an appointment pursuant to subsection (1) have not been fulfilled, the private accessory prosecutor shall, upon application, be granted legal aid for calling in an attorney subject to the same provisions as apply in civil litigation if he cannot sufficiently safeguard his own interests or if this cannot reasonably be expected of him. Section 114, subsection (1), second part of the first sentence, and subsection (2) as well as section 121 subsections (1) to (3) of the Code of Civil Procedure shall not be applicable. (3) Applications pursuant to subsections (1) and (2) may already be made prior to the declaration of joinder. The presiding judge of the court seized of the case shall decide on the appointment

of the attorney, to which Section 142 subsection (1) shall apply *mutatis mutandis*, and on the granting of legal aid.

3 French Code for Criminal Procedure, Article 41–2: 'Prior to any public prosecution being instituted, the District prosecutor may propose, directly or through an authorised person, criminal mediation to an adult person who admits having committed one or more misdemeanours under articles 222–11, 222–13 (1 to 11), 222–16, 222–17, 222–18 (first paragraph), 227–3 to 227–7, 227–9 to 227–11, 311–3, 313–5, 314–5, 314–6, 321–1, 322–1, 322–2, 322–12 to 322–14, 433–5 to 433–7 and 521–1 of the Criminal Code, under the articles 28 and 32 (2°) of the Ordinance of 18 April 1939 fixing the regime of war materials, arms and munitions, under Article L. 1 of the Traffic Code and under Article L. 628 of the Public Health Code, which consists of one or more of the following orders; 1 the payment of a mediatory fine to the Public Treasury. The amount of such a mediatory fine, which may not exceed either €3,750 or half of the maximum fine for the offence, is fixed in accordance with the gravity of the facts as well as the income and expenses of the person. Its payment may be made by instalments in accordance with a schedule of payments fixed by the district prosecutor within a period which may not exceed one year. 2 to hand over to the State the thing which was used to or intended to commit the offence, or which is the product of it; 3 to surrender to the clerk's office of the district court the offender's driving licence for a maximum period of six months, or his hunting licence for a maximum period of four months; 4 to undertake for the benefit of the community unpaid work for a maximum of sixty hours, over a period which may not exceed six months; 5 the completion of a maximum of three months' training course or work experience with an organisation or service provider in health, social care or some other professional area over a period which may not exceed eighteen months. Where the victim is identified, and unless the offender establishes that the damage has been made good, the district prosecutor must propose to the offender that he make good the damage caused by his offence within a period which may not exceed six months. He informs the victim of this proposal. The district prosecutor's proposal for criminal mediation may be brought to the knowledge of the offender through a judicial police officer. Here it takes the form of written decision signed by the prosecutor, which specifies the nature and quantum of the measures proposed and which is endorsed on the file. Criminal mediation may be proposed in a public centre for legal advice. The person to whom criminal mediation is proposed is informed that he may be assisted by an advocate before giving his consent to the district prosecutor's proposal. This consent is recorded in an official record. A copy of the official record is given to him. Where the offender consents to the measures proposed, the district prosecutor seises the President of the district court by way of a petition seeking the approval of the mediation. The district prosecutor informs the offender of this and, where necessary, the victim. The President of the court may proceed to hear the offender and the victim, assisted, where necessary, by their advocates. Where the judge makes an order approving the mediation, the measures decided are put into effect; if not, the proposal becomes void. The decision of the President of the district court, which is notified to the offender and, where necessary, the victim, is not open to appeal. Where the person does not accept the mediation or where, after having given his consent, he does not fully implement the measures decided on, or where the approval required by the previous paragraph is not given, the district prosecutor decides what further action to take in the case. In the case of prosecution and conviction, account is taken, where appropriate, of the work already accomplished and sums already paid by the offender. The limitation period for prosecution is suspended between the dates when the district prosecutor proposes criminal mediation and the expiry of the time granted for the mediation to be carried out. The implementation of the criminal mediation extinguishes the prosecution. However, it does not negate the right of a civil party to issue a summons before the correctional court under the conditions laid down by the present Code. The court then rules only on the civil aspects of the case, on examining the file, which is open for discussion. Any criminal mediations carried out are recorded on certificate n 1 of the offender's criminal record. The conditions for the application of the present article are fixed by a Council of State decree.'

4 Section 56 deals with translation assistance to be provided to a suspect.

5 *Sicherheitspolizeigesetzv*, see *Security Police Act* (*Bundesgesetzblatt* – Federal Gazette (BGBl.) Nr. 566/1991, most recently amended through BGBl. I Nr. 97/2014 (VfGH)).

 6 Section 177(5) concern the victim's right to be informed about a release of a suspect from remand custody.
 7 *Strafvollzugsgesetz*, see *Execution of Sentences Act* (BGBl. Nr. 144/1969, most recently amended through BGBl. I Nr. 13/2015).
 8 Section 101 deals with applications by the public prosecutor during the criminal investigation which require judicial approval.
 9 Section 97 deals with the circumstances in which video and audio recordings of witness statements are permissible.
10 *Strafgesetzbuch*, see Austrian Criminal Code (BGBl. Nr. 60/1974, most recently amended through BGBl. I Nr. 112/2015).
11 The 'complaint of nullity' concerns alleged formal errors affecting the proceeding or the judgement.
12 Section 281(1) no. 4 deals with decisions by the court which violate fundamental rights or other fundamental principles of fair proceedings.
13 Also see Australia, South Africa, Canada, and New Zealand as jurisdictions that offer non-enforceable rights frameworks for victims of crime.
14 See *Youth Justice and Criminal Evidence Act 1999* (UK), sections 23–30. Also see Ministry of Justice (2011a), *Achieving Best Evidence in Criminal Proceedings: Guidance on Interviewing Victims and Witnesses, and Guidance on Using Special Measures*, Ministry of Justice, UK; also see Ministry of Justice (2012b, 2014).
15 See section 271H of the *Criminal Procedure (Scotland) Act 1995* (Scot): 'The special measures (1) The special measures which may be authorised to be used under section 271A, 271C or 271D of this Act for the purpose of taking the evidence of a vulnerable witness are: (a) taking of evidence by a commissioner in accordance with section 271I of this Act, (b) use of a live television link in accordance with section 271J of this Act, (c) use of a screen in accordance with section 271K of this Act, (d) use of a supporter in accordance with section 271L of this Act, (e) giving evidence in chief in the form of a prior statement in accordance with section 271M of this Act, and (f) such other measures as the Scottish Ministers may, by order made by statutory instrument, prescribe.'
16 See Chapter 3, Counsel for Victims of Crime, for a discussion of the victim's right to counsel in pretrial discovery matters.
17 See section 274 of the *Criminal Procedure (Scotland) Act 1995* (Scot): 'Restrictions on evidence relating to sexual offences. (1) In the trial of a person charged with an offence to which section 288C of this Act applies, the court shall not admit, or allow questioning designed to elicit, evidence which shows or tends to show that the complainer: (a) is not of good character (whether in relation to sexual matters or otherwise); (b) has, at any time, engaged in sexual behaviour not forming part of the subject matter of the charge; (c) has, at any time (other than shortly before, at the same time as or shortly after the acts which form part of the subject matter of the charge), engaged in such behaviour, not being sexual behaviour, as might found the inference that the complainer: (i) is likely to have consented to those acts; or (ii) is not a credible or reliable witness; or (d) has, at any time, been subject to any such condition or predisposition as might found the inference referred to in sub-paragraph (c) above. (2) In subsection (1) above: "complainer" means the person against whom the offence referred to in that subsection is alleged to have been committed; and the reference to engaging in sexual behaviour includes a reference to undergoing or being made subject to any experience of a sexual nature.'
18 See Chapter 6, England and Wales, for like issues regarding the modification of trial rights for child and vulnerable victims under the CEU DVC of 2012 and the jurisprudence of the ECtHR.
19 See the discussion of the victims' right to review, Chapter 6, England and Wales.
20 See Chapter 3, Counsel for Victims of Crime.
21 Several states have also ratified bills of victim rights. See, for example, Georgia's *Crime Victims Bill of Rights*, Georgia Code 2010, Title 17 Criminal Procedure, chapter 17, sections 17.17.1–17.17.16, which provides victims certain specified rights, including: the right to reasonable, accurate, and timely notice of any scheduled court proceedings or any changes to such proceedings; the right to reasonable, accurate, and timely notice of the arrest, release, or escape of the accused; the right not to be excluded from any scheduled court proceedings, except as provided by law; the right to be heard at any scheduled court proceedings involving

the release, plea, or sentencing of the accused; the right to file a written objection in any parole proceedings involving the accused; the right to confer with the prosecuting attorney in any criminal prosecution related to the victim; the right to restitution as provided by law; the right to proceedings free from unreasonable delay; and the right to be treated fairly and with dignity by all criminal justice agencies involved in the case.

22 See *Dangerous Prisoners (Sexual Offenders) Act* 2003 (Qld), *Dangerous Prisoners (Sexual Offenders) Amendment Bill 2007* (Qld), and Dangerous Prisoners (Sexual Offenders) Amendment Bill 2007 (Qld) (Explanatory Notes) as to the legislative framework that affords victims the capacity to make submissions to extend the detention of recidivist sex offenders. Also see *Habitual Criminals Act 1957* (NSW) and the *Crimes (High Risk Offenders) Act 2006* (NSW).

23 Although such rights may be enforced by process of judicial review in administrative law: *Maxwell v The Queen* (1996) 184 CLR 501.

24 Also see the discussion of *KS v Veitch (No. 2)* [2012] NSWCCA 266 in Chapter 3.

25 This amendment followed the controversial decision of the sentencing judge in *R v Loveridge* (2014) NSWCCA 120, where the New South Wales Court of Criminal Appeal (NSWCCA) revised the manifestly inadequate sentence handed down following trial. This case spawned a course of law reform that abolished the common law rule against family VIS in *R v Previtera* (1997) 94 A Crim R 76 VIS, but also included a mandatory minimum sentence for the newly prescribed offence, assault causing death (sections 25A, 25B *Crimes Act 1900* (NSW)), as introduced by the *Crimes and Other Legislation Amendment (Assault and Intoxication) Act 2014* (NSW). This Act also made changes to the *Crimes (Domestic and Personal Violence) Act 2007* (NSW) and the *Law Enforcement (Powers and Responsibilities) Act 2002* (NSW). The *Bail Act 2013* (NSW) was further reformed in 2014 to invoke stricter tests for the granting of bail out of similar concerns.

26 *Crimes (Sentencing Procedure) Amendment (Family Member Victim Impact Statement) Act 2014* (NSW). As of March 2015 no family impact statements have been explicitly referred to as representing harm to the community. Also see *Crimes (Sentencing Procedure) Amendment (Victim Impact Statements – Mandatory Consideration) Bill 2014* (NSW).

27 A VIS is now regarded as a source of evidence that may be adduced in sentencing proceedings in order to influence sentencing. This gives rise to substantive rather than procedural rights as the VIS can now influence the sentencing decision made.

28 Cf. *Charter of Human Rights and Responsibilities Act 2006* (Vic), which also omits any reference to victim rights.

29 *Code of Criminal Procedure (Amendment) Act 2008* (Ind) Amendment of section 2: 'In section 2 of the Code of Criminal Procedure, 1973 (hereinafter referred to as the Principal Act), after clause (w), the following clause shall be inserted, namely – "(wa) 'victim' means a person who has suffered any loss or injury caused by reason of the act or omission for which the accused person has been charged and the expression 'victim' includes his or her guardian or legal heir."'

30 *Code of Criminal Procedure (Amendment) Act 2008* (Ind) Amendment of section 24: 'In section 24 of the Principal Act, in sub-section (8), the following proviso shall be inserted, namely – "Provided that the Court may permit the victim to engage an advocate of his choice to assist the prosecution under this sub-section."'

31 *Code of Criminal Procedure (Amendment) Act 2008* (Ind): 'In section 26 of the Principal Act, in clause (a), the following proviso shall be inserted, namely – "Provided that any offence under section 376 and sections 376A to 376D of the Indian Penal Code shall be tried as far as practicable by a Court presided over by a woman."'

32 *Code of Criminal Procedure (Amendment) Act 2008* (Ind) Amendment of section 327: 'In section 327 of the principle Act, (a) in sub-section (2), after the proviso, the following proviso shall be inserted, namely – "Provided further that in camera trial shall be conducted as far as practicable by a woman Judge or Magistrate". (b) in sub-section (3), the following proviso shall be inserted, namely – "Provided that the ban on printing or publication of trial proceedings in relation to an offence of rape may be lifted, subject to maintaining confidentiality of name and address of the parties."'

33 *Code of Criminal Procedure (Amendment) Act 2008* (Ind) Insertion of new section 357A: 'After section 357 of the principal Act, the following section shall be inserted,

namely – "Victim Compensation Scheme 357A. (1) Every State Government in co-ordination with the Central Government shall prepare a scheme for providing funds for the purpose of compensation to the victim or his dependents who have suffered loss or injury as a result of the crime and who require rehabilitation. (2) Whenever a recommendation is made by the Court for compensation, the District Legal Service Authority or the State Legal Service Authority, as the case may be, shall decide the quantum of compensation to be awarded under the scheme referred to in sub-section (1). (3) If the trial Court, at the conclusion of the trial, is satisfied, that the compensation awarded under section 357 is not adequate for such rehabilitation, or where the cases end in acquittal or discharge and the victim has to be rehabilitated, it may make recommendation for compensation. (4) Where the offender is not traced or identified, but the victim is identified, and where no trial takes place, the victim or his dependents may make an application to the State or the District Legal Services Authority for award of compensation. (5) On receipt of such recommendations or on the application under sub-section (4), the State or the District Legal Services Authority shall, after due enquiry award adequate compensation by completing the enquiry within two months. (6) The State or the District Legal Services Authority, as the case may be, to alleviate the suffering of the victim, may order for immediate first-aid facility or medical benefits to be made available free of cost on the certificate of the police officer not below the rank of the officer in charge of the police station or a Magistrate of the area concerned, or any other interim relief as the appropriate authority deems fit." '

Part III
Victims in law and policy

Discord and debate

7   Victim rights in law and policy

Introduction

Recourse to legal frameworks that identify and provide rights or powers for victims of crime is made functional only by their relationship to a policy context that makes sense of and provides a means of accessing those rights, for all justice stakeholders. The complexity of victim rights for most jurisdictions results from the lack of a singular consolidating instrument, because victim rights and powers often necessarily span different sources of law and policy to account for different provisions and levels of access to justice depending on the harm suffered. Further complexity and ambiguity are added where victim rights manifest only in a policy context, because a particular member state or signatory has failed to ratify or provided only for partial ratification of the enforceable standard pursuant to the international convention. The context of victim rights operating through a particular legal and policy milieu at the local level of the individual jurisdiction is therefore significant to the operationalising of victim rights as they manifest across international and regional human rights discourses and norms down to the local, domestic level of the criminal justice system of each state.

The concepts of hard and soft law are relevant to international and regional law and procedure in that not all international or regional law is enforceable and much remains merely influential in a policy context. This distinction is a relevant one for victims of crime as increasingly, individual jurisdictions are influenced by discourses of human rights that manifest as victim rights and powers as spread across law and policy. Hard and soft law refers to those international and regional contexts that afford instruments full or quasi-legal status respectively. While hard and soft law does not always carry over to the domestic context, the regulation of the victim outside of the criminal law for administrative and policy contexts means that the victim has been largely governed through systems of soft law in order to leave the enforceable rights of criminal law and procedure for the state and accused. While this is truer of the common law, adversarial states compared to the European civil law states, the European approach has not always embraced victim participation in a uniform way either.

The rise of victimology as a discipline seeking to reposition the victim through renewed understanding of the plight of the victims in a heterogeneous context of stakeholders and agents of justice founded a promise of greater intervention in favour of the victims. While much can be said as to what this promise entails, and how supported the victim ought to be as an agent of welfare reform, the phases of the development of victimology identified in Chapter 1 reveal that the discipline has progressed towards the recognition of victim rights as human rights. Identified as the third phase of victimology, the emergence of the victim rights has become institutionalised into the fourth phase, through the convergence of key stakeholder roles that include reference to the powers of the victim. While the normative stakeholders of justice identified in Chapter 1 remain somewhat independent, increasingly out of international convergence of systems of justice, ratification of international and regional instruments, policy transfer, and law reform, the role of the victim is being further connected to that of the other stakeholders of justice. Victims are now institutionalised to the extent that the operation of the offices of those normative stakeholders includes, rather than excludes, the victim.

While the fourth phase of victim rights is more inclusive of the victim on an institutional level, this does not mean that all jurisdictions are converging towards the same set of standardised rights. Although there is evidence of global standardisation (cf. Hall, 2010), differences persist. Chapter 6 demonstrates how the international and regional norms of victim rights have been increasingly ratified on the domestic level in accordance with local politics, legal traditions, and the discrete needs of victims. This chapter brings together the legal issues traced in Chapters 1 through 6 to advance the argument that victim rights are offered on a legal and policy basis. The choice between hard and soft law, the desirability of law over policy, and the reluctance of engagement on the part of the normative stakeholders of justice are discussed. Points of resistance that emerge on the domestic basis and the option to progress victim rights through policy over law, or as non-enforceable against accused or state, will be assessed. The consequence for victims and the impact on normative stakeholder relations will also be considered.

International and regional instruments and the domestic reform process

International and regional sources of law and policy have provided important points of connection between the domestic jurisdictions discussed in this book. These supranational sources have established and significantly contributed to the normative framework of victim rights that most jurisdictions now draw upon in their ratification or transfer of rights to the domestic level. Chapter 2 presents these agreements in a normative context, indicating the constitutive role they have played setting the framework of normative rights and powers down to the domestic level. International and regional laws and policies are therefore increasingly guiding domestic jurisdictions towards a rights framework of substantive and enforceable rights based on the convergence of victim rights and policies on a global level. Although these supranational agreements are applied in local contexts, they do provide for the breaking down of traditional boundaries that otherwise provide for the isolated, disconnected analyses of victim issues on the individual jurisdictional level. The range of modes of transfer of law and policy – from direct ratification into law to policy transfer and law reform, to the organic breaking down of traditional boundaries of law between inquisitorial and adversarial – demonstrates how these international and regional norms may be significantly influential in the modern era. These supranational agreements therefore encourage a degree of transference of law and policy to those jurisdictions that are geographically isolated from dominant regional agreements, especially those of the Council of Europe, and that otherwise do not ratify international conventions in whole or part.

Chapter 3 covered those modes of transfer of law and policy that allow for the rapid transfer of victim rights, powers, and interests internationally. While this book has argued that international transfer is always sensitive to local contexts and domestic issues, certain trends do present. These trends tend to follow the normative discourse of victim rights that emerge from the international and regional instruments, which in turn develop out of trends dominant in certain domestic states or across justice traditions. Certain domestic instruments may also become influential, especially those that present victim rights and interests in a considered context of law and policy reform that another jurisdiction seeks to adapt for local purposes. The Japanese tradition of adopting aspects of German and American law and procedure provides a case in point (see Kodner, 2003; Albanese and Dammer, 2010). The fusion of adversarial processes with inquisitorial modes of inquiry in the European continental tradition, as further influenced by the ECHR and the jurisprudence of the ECtHR, indicates transference within international, regional, and domestic contexts. Certain trends – to access counsel, to support vulnerable witnesses and victims, to consult with the prosecution regarding decisions made, to challenge decisions that adversely affect the interests of the victim, and to have standing in court and during sentencing – are developed in international and regional conventions as influenced by a range of justice traditions. These trends have, however, found their way into domestic law reform processes in those states that may not be signatories to international and regional conventions that provide for the ratification of those trends. The development of substantive victim rights in the USA, India, Brazil, and, to a limited extent, Canada, Australia, and New Zealand provides evidence of adherence to the international normative discourse of victim rights and powers. However, variance between jurisdictions and the different approaches taken also indicate degrees of divergence between how each jurisdiction will adapt these normative trends to local contexts. In most instances, this means partial adoption or influence of local policy that does not afford a wholly enforceable right to victims. Access to counsel in limited pretrial contexts, to challenge evidence that has been subpoenaed or to consult with the prosecution, in Australia, Canada, and the USA provides examples as to victim rights in this context.

Hard law/soft law in domestic contexts

The distinction between hard and soft law as a means through which to suggest the differences between the authoritative sources of law from the policy context of the application of these laws is relevant to the development, organisation, and ratification of human rights instruments on a domestic level. As noted in Chapters 1 and 3, the inculcation of law and policy occurs in different ways according to the needs of domestic jurisdictions. While standardisation may be desirable as a matter of international and regional policy, as a convention seeking to unify practices to realise the rights of victims, domestic standardisation of laws and policies may not be possible out of recognition of the individual needs of victims, local politics, and the constraints otherwise provided by individual legal systems. However, this particularised context of the local turns us back to the important distinction between hard and soft law, and how that distinction operates on a functional level within local jurisdictions (see Groenhuijsen and Pemberton, 2009). The Netherlands, for instance, developed local policies in accordance with the CEU FD of 2001 prior to reform of the Code for Criminal Procedure in 2011, a decade after the framework decision was presented to the region (Ezendam and Wheldon, 2014: 63–64).

The relationship between law and policy or sources of hard and soft law is made relevant to the framework of international human rights as informing victim rights because victim rights are generally unenforceable and outside the scope of the traditional sources of criminal law and procedure (Rock, 2014). Much therefore rests on the distinction between law and policy for victim of crime. Although defendants and the state have rights dispersed between hard and soft law, the balance between the two types of laws, in terms of what may be a constitutive right to be enforced in court, varies fundamentally for each stakeholder. State rights may be required to be in hard law because such rights are constitutive of state power. Thus, state rights derive from authoritative instruments, constitutional or other stat-utes, on the domestic level. Defendant rights may also be more likely a matter of hard law out of the requirement of a fair trial, equality of arms, and the foundational rights of the accused recognised in common law, or as ratified under criminal procedural law. Although policy supports the rights of the accused to access, for instance, public funding for legal aid, such rights nonetheless may be recognised in hard law in so far as each state or jurisdiction consolidates such rights under statute, or in adversarial countries, under common law. Out of connection to internationalised standards of the fair trial, the accused is increasingly pos-sessed of rights in law rather than policy.

Victim interests remain largely secured and indeed standardised through policy, at least as an initial arena through which reluctant jurisdictions express a concern over the needs of victims as important to public policy. This does not mean that certain states have allowed victims to enjoy legal rights of standing in the criminal justice system for some time. How-ever, most adversarial, common law countries and even certain civil law states, such as the Netherlands, have been slow to provide victims with a set of rights that may be identified as enforceable against the state or accused. Clearly, continental European countries have made significant progress towards providing victims with rights in hard law, while common law countries have generally refrained from such measures. However, the movement towards hard law is not universal and much policy remains in support of victim rights and interest, even in continental European countries.

The rights of victims in hard law across continental European countries do follow the trend towards accessory and auxiliary prosecution, in addition to rights to state-funded support during the trial where victims are not participating alongside the state prosecu-tion. The amendment of the German Code of Criminal Procedure with regard to the rights of the private accessory prosecutor under sections 395 and 397, and the right to counsel for the purpose of support and general assistance under sections 397a and 406g, indicates how rights to legal counsel and legal assistance may be included as availing the victim of degrees of agency within the trial process. These rights are available as a mat-ter of authoritative procedure. French victims do not possess such far-reaching rights to join the state prosecution. Although French victims have a right to private prosecution under Articles 1 and 528-2, to insist upon police investigation under Articles 15–3 and 53–1, and to counsel or an advocate under Articles 113–2, they lack general party stand-ing before the court. However, a claim of compensation may be attached at trial under Articles 2 and 40–1. Both Germany and France offer alternative resolution and mediation that may include victims, at the discretion of the prosecution. Those countries that tend towards adversarial trial processes also afford a significant role for the victim. The move-ment away from purely inquisitorial processes for quasi-adversarial ones indicates a degree of convergence between systems of justice. The Swedish process of allowing for private prosecution so long as the offence has been reported, with rights to the aggrieved person where the state decides to prosecute, is provided for under the Code of Judicial Proce-dure. The role of the *målsägandebiträde*, for instance, is to safeguard the aggrieved person during the trial phases under chapter 20, section 15 of the Code of Judicial Procedure. The Netherlands, as mentioned earlier, has recently provided for accessory prosecution as an injured person under section 51a of the Code for Criminal Procedure. Access to the prosecution case file and to legal assistance is provided for under sections 51b and 51c respectively. Austria has also recently reformed its Code of Criminal Procedure with regard to substantive victim rights to join the prosecution and be heard in court. Sections 6 and 66 provide the rights of the victim to participate in hearings, and section 66 provides private party rights.

The rise of the victim in hard law is, however, gaining momentum in civil and common law jurisdiction. Despite moving at an uneven pace, even in European states under the CEU FD of 2001 and then the CEU DVC of 2012, progress is being made towards the promulgation of a series of rights to justice across Europe. Even England and Wales, as members of the EU, have progressed towards limited enforceable rights under the CEU DVC of 2012 (see *R v Killick* [2011] EWCA Crim 1608 and Article 11 of the CEU DVC of 2012). England and Wales have, however, substantial hurdles to overcome should they seek to reform their criminal procedure from an adversarial tradition to one that embraces a broad set of participatory rights for victims during the criminal trial process. Although this seems an unlikely goal for a country founded upon its adherence to adversarial processes, standing for victims in the English criminal trial may already be better realised compared to other common law countries. The criminal procedure of Scotland and Ireland demonstrates a movement towards legal standing for victims that affords victims access to legal counsel in the trial phase. The *Victims and Witnesses (Scotland) Act 2014* (Scot) provides a means for victims to access counsel in the criminal trial phase where a vulnerable witness so requires it. Although rather more limited, the *Criminal Justice (Victims of Crime) Bill 2015* (Ire) provides for counsel during the investigative phase, although the *Sex Offences Act 2001* (Ire) provides counsel during interlocutory applications for discovery of confidential evidence.

Other common law, adversarial jurisdictions not signatories to the EU or Council of Europe also demonstrate a movement towards enforceable rights. By virtue of their geographic location, these jurisdictions have tended towards a combination of identifying with international and regional human rights norms by way of policy intervention and transfer. These countries include the USA, Australia, Canada, New Zealand, and South Africa. These countries represent a significant degree of diversity between modes of law and policy reform with regard to the development of victim rights out of international human rights norms. This is because the instruments that provide for international and regional coherence may be seen as soft law in each country, influential but not necessarily binding. While the 1985 PJVC has been generally adopted across the common law world, the extent to which it has been ratified and provided for in sources of hard law is variable. Other international, mainly UN, instruments have also been ratified by these states, to varying degrees. The development of victim rights' frameworks, although a clear matter of public policy concern for each country, has emerged through different processes of law reform and policy transfer, in addition to the ratification of specific international conventions and treaties. The local context of the constraints provided by constitutional law and procedure and the general organisation of the legal system has also affected the extent to which each non-European common law system is directly comparable. However, like England and Wales, there has been a general reluctance to grant victims enforceable rights to participate in the criminal trial. Rather, declarations and charters of rights have been preferred, despite not being enforceable in court. Thus, with the exception of the USA and India, the emergence of victim rights has largely come about through soft law reform. This has led some to argue that victim rights are largely illusory (Beloof, 2005). The *Crime Victim Rights Act 2004* (US) provides a substantial point of departure by providing victims with enforceable, substantive rights to justice under 18 USC § 3771. India has recently followed by providing for private counsel under section 24(8) of the Code of Criminal Procedure. Progress towards consultative rights with the prosecution has followed in South Australia, but this right is largely unenforceable.

The mixed and hybrid jurisdictions have departed from the adversarial paradigm that would otherwise restrict greater support of the victim. Rights to victim participation are largely provided through hard law. Japan has embarked on a period of reform and transformation from 2000 onwards, culminating in the reform of the Code of Criminal Procedure of Japan, following introduction of the *Act to Amend Parts of the Code of Criminal Procedure and Others in Order to Protect Rights and Interests of Victims of Crime*, Law No. 95 of 2007 (Jpn). The changes to the Japanese criminal trial following the introduction of a lay, or Saiban-in, jury system in 2004, were further developed in 2007 by the provision of specific rights of participation for victims of crime. These rights extend to the power to seek review of a prosecution decision not to proceed with a matter. The *Keijisoshōhōtō no ichibu wo kaiseisuru hōritsu*, Law No. 62 of 2004 (Jpn), or Act to Revise the Code of Criminal Procedure of Japan, allows for a review where the public prosecutor refuses to bring charges in a case involving the death of the primary victim, such that a family member may appeal to the PRB. Article 292–2 of the Code of Criminal Procedure grants victims the benefit of providing a statement of their feelings to the court. Victims can seek assistance from legal counsel, who may assist the victim where they make a submission as to the charge, the evidence, or the conduct of proceedings. Complementary rights of protected trial participation are granted under the Victim Protection Act *(Higaisha no hogo ni kansuru hōritsu)*, Law No. 75 of 2000 (Jpn). Victims may seek preferential seating in court, and a support person may be present when the victim testifies in court. The support person may provide emotional assistance but cannot inform or influence the victim's testimony. Physical shields and barriers may screen the victim from the offender or gallery where they are distressed or intimidated, or of a frail mental condition. Out-of-court evidence may also be used if sought by the victim or prosecution. Brazil provides for several sources of hard law for victim rights and interests and is increasingly keen to intervene in justice policy to provide these rights where they are otherwise not granted under existing justice policies. Articles 23–24 of Federal Law No. 11,340 of 2006 (Brazil), for example, grant victims of domestic violence increased protections from the accused, and even extends to women of any 'sexual orientation', providing transgender victims with identifiable victim rights. Brazil's Code of Criminal Procedure provides various rights for victims in both the investigative and prosecution or trial phases, as developed out of the mixed legal traditions from which Brazil's modern justice system emerges. Article 32 of the Code of Criminal Procedure allows for private counsel, who may be state-funded, and who may join as accessory prosecutor in the main trial.

The recourse to hard law for the development and proliferation of victim rights is a trend internationally. Certain countries, specifically those non-European common law jurisdictions not bound to international or regional convention, demonstrate a lack of willingness to afford substantial rights through law. These states provide victim rights through sources of soft law, which mainly manifest across government policies that seek to provide victims a measure of access to justice that is non-enforceable against the state or accused. Countries that now ratify victim rights by processes of hard law also utilise soft law as a contextualising system of non-enforceable provisions that complement the system of rights that may be enforced. The main difference between countries that resort to hard law over soft law sources is that countries that give victims substantive recourse to hard law tend to do so out of a commitment to the right of the victim to participate and stand in the criminal process as an actual stakeholder of justice. Although their standing may be connected to other agents or institutions, or be exercised under assumptions that certain fundamental rights not be infringed (including the accused's right to a fair trial), victim rights in jurisdictions that gravitate towards hard law options allow access to the accused and state in a way that soft law countries do not.

The limits of public policy

The problem with a public policy approach to victim rights and powers is that soft law that is non-enforceable may be used to constrain and contain the victim within the justice process. Policy may liberate, and a soft law approach is arguably better than no law or policy whatsoever. However, policy may be used as a vehicle to give the appearance of victim rights where few exist. Furthermore, policy may disguise the rights of victims as important, substantive, and enforceable to the lay observer. The charters and declarations of victim rights across Australia, the Victims' Charter of England and Wales (see extracts in Chapter 2), and the Victims' Charter (SthA) are all non-enforceable charters that do not grant the victim substantive rights to access justice. Each is prefaced with a clause of non-enforceability against the state, and do not give rise to rights in criminal and even civil proceedings. These rights exist as a matter of public policy alone. Although they are a welcome addition compared to a system devoid of victim rights, and have the benefit of guiding public officials in support of the better treatment of victims in the justice process generally, such policies have the danger of misleading victims and the public into thinking that victims are subjects possessed of rights and powers in the first instance.

The danger of public policy as the means through which victim rights proceed is that lay victims identify no distinction between rights of policy as opposed to rights of law. Certainly, a plain reading of the Victims' Charter in England and Wales, for example, gives the impression that one is reading a declaratory instrument of law that has the force of law. However, this is just an impression, founded upon an oversight of the clause that precludes enforceability. Often, the clauses that preclude enforceability are in the authoritative statute that prescribes the declaration as an instrument of policy.[1] Victims and members of the public not prone to reading sources of law, including statutes, will be largely unaware that their rights lack substantive enforceability against the state or accused until the time comes when they choose to exercise such rights with an expectation that an infringement of those rights may be remedied with action. Alternatively, the enabling law may contain the excluding clause that phrases victim rights as a matter of policy alone. Indeed, one of the early criticisms of the *Canadian Victims Bill of Rights* was that it lacks any mechanism of enforcement. This clause is contained within the *Canadian Victims Bill of Rights* under clause 28, which provides that '[n]o cause of action or right to damages arises from an infringement or denial of a right under this Act'. This clause effectively limits any action against the accused or state because of the denial of rights contained under the *Canadian Victims Bill of Rights*. Arguably, this is to render the Bill as gesture only, ineffective in its ability to effect change. The victim is therefore denied access as a normative stakeholder of justice, possessed of rights and powers determinative in justice stakeholder relations. Furthermore, victims are denied the ability to access discrete remedies where rights as granted under the Bill are unfairly refused.

The ratification of victim rights and powers in policy over law, or where ratified in law, as non-enforceable laws, denies the momentum of the normative framework of victim rights identified in Chapter 2 (extracted in Chapter 2 at 5.1–5.9). While degrees of enforcement may characterise any domestic framework of victim rights, in that most domestic systems grant victims some rights that may be enforced while others may specify modes of treatment or access to information that is essentially non-enforceable, frameworks that are substantially or wholly non-enforceable risk exacerbating the tradition of not taking victims seriously. Such frameworks continue the tradition of placing victims at the periphery of justice. While all laws ought to be supported by appropriate policy to bring context to those laws, and while policy may fill gaps in justice processes where no directive otherwise exists, the use of law as a vehicle that houses a non-enforceable policy provides incentive to maintain past justice arrangements where victims are identified as being of lesser status than other normatively placed stakeholders.

While the use of policy as a vehicle through which victim rights come to be expressed is limited in a legal sense, the implication of the expression of rights through such policies lies far beyond the individual's right to access remedies. The consequence for victims is the continued containment and denial of their standing as justice stakeholders. Arguably, the greatest advantage achieved by the ratification of rights and powers of a substantive and enforceable character is that those powers will impress upon other justice stakeholders to the extent that they will take victims seriously in the decision-making processes that compose justice procedure, from arrest through to sentencing, appeal, and parole. Victims with substantive and enforceable rights have standing in their own right, even where this standing does not afford the right to present equally in court, thus preserving equality of arms between state and accused.

Victim rights and the reluctance of normative stakeholders

For victims of crime, policy through law is potentially deleterious and dangerous. This is because the use of statutory devices to provide victims with a rights framework may suggest that victim interests can be satisfied by reference to what ought to be done in best practice, as a courtesy to victims. Although policy or soft law may connect to hard law that can be enforced against state or accused, and may thus provide a necessary complement to the laws that grant rights of substantive participation, soft law on its own provides an arguably insufficient vehicle through which to regulate victim participation in internationalised systems of criminal justice. Although each jurisdiction will determine the extent to which victims ought to participate in accordance with local needs, the influence on international and regional conventions and the development of local laws and practices in accordance with international victim rights norms sees the gradual disassembly of barriers to substantive participation. While it is possible to resist the international trend to afford victim rights and advance interests through policy alone, jurisdictions which ignore the positive benefits of substantive and enforceable victim participation risk further excluding victims in domestic systems, while garnering criticism from the international community as to the detrimental effect that a lack of standing generally brings. Although advances in policy may bring some benefit, most jurisdictions, including those under the CEU DVC of 2012, have been required to make the necessary legal and policy changes to provide the range of rights to afford victims actual, comprehensive, and organised rights to services and processes as provided for under the CEU DVC. Although this accounts for European jurisdictions and states, and while civil law countries will likely afford victims greater levels of access to justice on a substantive level even prior to the CEU DVC of 2012, countries beyond the region are still likely to seek to regulate victim involvement in criminal justice through police arrangements. This is particularly so for countries adhering to a common law, adversarial tradition, removed from international obligations or treaties towards victims.

The consequence of the use of non-enforceable powers for victims of crime is that the normative stakeholders of justice identified in Chapter 1 will continue to identify victims as peripheral and removed from justice processes. This means that victims will continue to be dismissed as constituents of justice, a judgement of far-reaching consequences beyond the mistreatment of any one victim or crime. Although the movement to substantive and enforceable rights through law may be confronting to some victim groups who exercise caution with regard to the offering of substantive and enforceable rights (see, e.g., HVSG, 2016), the movement towards hard law options for victims will be of substantial benefit for a number of reasons. These benefits include greater consistency and coherence between victim rights in an international context. However, the local benefits are most desirable and meaningful to individual victims. Movement towards substantive rights to justice will grant victims the power to choose in a system that has otherwise relegated them to the sidelines of justice. While this choice is not mandatory, in that victims always have the power to not exercise a substantive right, the fact that victims have the option to participate on a substantive level achieves a measure of justice that far outweighs any decision exercised in an individual case.

The significant and long-lasting impact of the promulgation of victim rights on a substantive level will be cultural shifts invoked amongst normative justice stakeholders. We are already witnessing this shift, identified in Chapter 1, and as provided for under reform options covered in Chapter 3, in those jurisdictions that afford victims significant rights to justice. The European, civil law context and network of international tribunals already provide an example of systems that include rather than exclude the victim. Hybrid and mixed systems also provide evidence of the reconfiguration of justice systems to bring the victim within the framework of traditional stakeholders. Chapter 1 identified how the movement towards enforceable rights provides a means through which victims are becoming partly constitutive of the powers exercised by criminal justice agencies as constituents of justice. It is this process of bringing the victim within the scope of everyday criminal justice processes that will, arguably, change the standing of the victim from peripheral agent to justice stakeholder and valued participant. This does not mean that victims will be forced to participate. Rather, it means that victims will be empowered to make decisions in their own interest, and in an environment that better regards and supports their standing as important protagonists of justice.

The development of victims in victimology and victim rights frameworks will continue to press upon other normative stakeholders of justice until victim rights become at least partially constitutive of the powers exercised by the agencies of criminal justice. This process of development will not position victims as central agents of justice nor will it allow victims to take over the criminal process to the exclusion of other central interests, such as those of the community or state. Victim participation through substantive, enforceable laws and supportive policies will encourage a reflexive process of engagement on the local level. Increasingly, lessons will be taken from those international, regional, or domestic frameworks that already position victims as significant agents of justice. There will be a degree of globalisation witnessing the emergence of a normative framework of victim rights within the context of local law-and-order priorities and justice traditions. The reflexivity of victim participation will result in a power-sharing arrangement between stakeholders, with the offender and state continuing to exercise primacy under fair trial rights to justice. This power-sharing arrangement will, over time, reposition the victim as significant to the interests of justice, providing for significant restorative force by reshaping the normative assumptions about the virtues of victim participation.

Note

1 See, for example, section 34(1) of the *Domestic Violence, Crime and Victims Act 2004* (UK): 'Effect of non-compliance: (1) If a person fails to perform a duty imposed on him by a code issued under section 32, the failure does not of itself make him liable to criminal or civil proceedings. (2) But the code is admissible in evidence in criminal or civil proceedings and a court may take into account a failure to comply with the code in determining a question in the proceedings.'

8 Victim rights in the twenty-first century
Intervention and innovation

Introduction

Progression towards local victim frameworks in the context of the global movement towards normatively framed international discourses of victim rights characterises the twenty-first-century development of victimology and victim rights. The movement towards victim rights as human rights evident at the local level, not least in terms of substantive participation in justice decision-making processes, has occurred across all jurisdictions analysed in this book. This includes, albeit in a more nuanced or restrained way, and perhaps through channels of soft law or policy, those common law, adversarial countries that have not traditionally afforded a significant role for the victim. Increasingly, it is evident that common law, adversarial countries are learning from the international victim rights norms identified in Chapter 2, and as discussed in context in Chapters 4 and 5.

Working through international and regional approaches, this book has considered the local development of the normative context of victim rights as a significant influence on domestic law and policy. Despite influencing law and policy in a fragmented and uneven way, in accordance with the justice history and tradition of each jurisdiction considered, all states identified in this book have progressed towards internationally recognised victim rights and powers. States have achieved this by reference to the different instruments canvassed, brought about by numerous modes of inculcation of victim rights, many of which provide for law and policy reform other than by direct parliamentary ratification. This book has considered and set out the international and regional level of human rights law and procedure, together with the local inquisitorial systems of Germany and France, and mixed systems of Sweden, Austria, and the Netherlands, common law and developing systems, including England and Wales, Ireland, Scotland, USA, Australia, Canada, New Zealand, India, South Africa, and the hybrid or mixed systems of Japan and Brazil. Each jurisdiction identified the principal enforceable and substantive rights of victims, relevant aspects of trial participation, criminal justice processes that support trial rights for victims, and relevant aspects of reparative, restorative, and therapeutic justice, in the context of international human right discourse, as law and policy context. The influence of grassroots movements on jurisdictional law and policy and the legal and political conditions of each jurisdiction as relevant to the explanation of the adoption of international norms of victim rights have been canvassed.

While Chapter 1 identified the phases of victimology, it is the emergence of the third and fourth phases that suggests significant progression towards the recognition of victim rights as human rights as institutionalised on the local level of the office holders of justice stakeholders. In this context, chapter 8 will ask the important question of whether the promise of victimology as realising a movement towards victim rights as human rights into the latter part of the twentieth century is being actually realised into the fourth phase. Is the institutionalising of victim rights on the local level a manifestation of politics and soft law, or can we say that victims are increasingly apprised of rights that may be enforced against the state and accused, for the betterment of victims and victim empowerment generally?

The promise of victimology realised?

Victimology as a discipline informs us that victims are a heterogeneous and diverse group, who relate differently to justice processes and justice systems. Participation as a victim may mean that the original harms incurred may be resolved, restored, or repaired. Alternatively, participation, or a denial of such, may contribute to and exacerbate harm, which may or may not be identified by systemised justice responses. The criminal trial, for instance, does not readily recognise secondary victimisation, despite increased attempts to minimise its occurrence. The harms and injuries of victims, and the individual and collective voices that represent and construct that victimisation, are, however, subject to power relations that connect victims with justice stakeholders in dynamic ways. These relations, the focus of this book, have been significantly influenced by international victim rights norms as informed by international and regional discourses of human rights and procedure.

Law requires the making of discerning judgements and not all values will be relevant nor ought to be relevant to those judgements. However, international human rights law, and international criminal justice in particular, has been influential in challenging the conceptualisation of victims as subjects peripheral to the criminal trial, transitioning victims to stakeholders of justice relevant to various justice processes, in their own right. This goes to the transformative effect of international human rights discourses on the local level, reassessing criminal law as a singular instrument of state sovereignty for other benefits and purposes (see Mégret, 2015, 2016). Although international criminal justice has tended to occur at the local level of the sovereign state, which has been criticised as reducing international criminal justice to the level of the state trial familiar to localised criminal law and procedure, the transformative effect of international law and justice has arguably not been lost on the victim. For victims of crime, international human rights law has provided a means of transformation from passive to active participant of justice. The twenty-first century bears witness to the better integration of the victim across all justice systems despite degrees of uneven integration across the world. Continental European systems differ from common law systems in Europe, which differ further still from non-European common law systems elsewhere in the world. Some countries resort to soft law over hard law, or manifest victim rights frameworks in policy rather than law. Alternatively, law may house the policy, as seen in England and Wales, Australia, South Africa, and Canada, such that the chief victim rights instrument or declaration of rights gains the standing of law, albeit unenforceable law, or policy phrased in law. Developing justice systems have also realised the significance of victim rights and have been increasingly receptive to the international norms of victim rights presented in Chapter 2. Both India and Brazil as discussed in Chapter 6 indicate how developing countries may make a concerted effort to transform their justice system to one that caters to the needs of victims with a view to the actual empowerment of victims through enforceable rights and privileges. These developing countries, together with other states that demonstrate degrees of victim empowerment through enforceable, substantive rights, demonstrate how international human rights discourse is progressively transforming local criminal justice systems from their focus on state trials alone. This shift means that the trial is evolving to include interests and capacities that identify victims as stakeholders of justice. The virtues of international human rights law and procedure are therefore evidenced through the local level of the inclusion of normative victim rights interests, and the nature of localised justice is transforming accordingly.

The ways in which localised justice systems are transforming in accordance with international and regional human rights norms and discourses have been identified throughout this book. The types of changes evident across jurisdictions internationally indicate that there are degrees of convergence between systems internationally. The non-exhaustive ways in which international and regional norms come to be identified in local criminal justice practice include: duties to consult with victims during the investigation; the power of victims to inspect the case file; the victim's right to consult with the prosecution regarding key decisions made, including charges brought or plea deals made; the victim's input into mode of disposal or to proceed to trial with a requirement to present as a witness; to ask for a modified trial process to afford greater protection to victims, especially where they are vulnerable; the proliferation of forms of statement or out-of-court evidence; rules regarding the examination and cross-examination of victims, with limits on personal, insulting, or spurious questions; the availability of private counsel to represent the interests of the victim or to protect the victim in court; the availability of intermediaries or support officers to offer assistance to the victim when testifying; the victim's ability to participate as an accessory or subsidiary prosecutor (where available); to make submissions to the court; to tender evidence aside from the state; to address the court or the jury; to present a statement during sentencing on the impact of the crime on the victim; to request an appeal brought by the state; to participate in restorative justice and intervention in appropriate cases; to utilise problem-solving justice and alternative court mechanisms to invite victim participation; to allow victims to make submissions during parole hearings; and to seek compensation and reparations during trial or at some other time; and to allow for reparations proceedings for remedies other than, or in addition to, pecuniary compensation and reparations. The ways in which victim rights modify the criminal justice processes of individual states are clearly variable, and not all modes of reform may be evident to the same level across all states. However, all jurisdictions identified in this book have made at least some progress towards these rights, as informed by international and regional norms as identified in Chapter 2.

The forms of change through which international and regional human rights norms and discourses have come to transform local jurisdictions are equally as important. These modes of change, identified in Chapter 3, provide for a comparative basis for victim rights. While direct ratification of international or regional convention may be cited as one means of encouraging international convergence, other modes also prevail. Increasingly, and particularly where a country is geographically isolated from regional frameworks, such as the Council of Europe, alternative modes of law and policy development may occur through: policy transfer and experimental public policy; modes of law reform; inquiries into significant wrongdoing; and progression towards recognising the artificiality of traditional boundaries of adversarial versus inquisitorial justice, together with the benefits of hybridised or mixed systems. These processes demonstrate a diverse means by which international and regional norms may come to influence the arrangement of local justice systems. Arguably, all come to bear on individual systems even where they adhere more strongly to international and regional instruments, and ratify them directly into local law and policy. The recognition that the influence of international and regional norms may come to bear on individual systems of justice in these diverse ways is more significant in the case of the development of victim rights and interests because the victim is normatively excluded from most justice systems. Thus, inventive modes of reform are often considered where direct processes of change, including parliamentary reform or systems of court-based precedent, continuously fail victims and their right to access justice.

The role of the victim has clearly developed across the jurisdictions traced in this book. However, has this met the expectations of the promise of victimology as improving conditions for victims generally, through the offering of a rights-based framework? Victims in the twenty-first century are undoubtedly better placed as stakeholders of justice in a way that differentiates them from their past role as essentially passive and excluded. It is true that injustice remains in that not all victims are being heard and many are still silenced by unconcerned policymakers, lawyers, and others who fail to see the right of the victim to participate as a stakeholder of justice. For example, secondary victimisation and institutional abuse continue to be uncovered in the modern era. However, progress has been advanced by the manifestation of a normative victim rights framework as introduced and developed out of international and regional human rights instruments. The result of this normative framework of victim rights has been the further dismantling of resistant boundaries that sought to protect justice traditions that were assumed as incapable of accommodating the interests of the victim. While different justice traditions may have been more open to the victim of crime, even European, civil law states have since modified their criminal procedure to better accommodate the victim as subsidiary and adhesive prosecutor, or in associated trial processes generally (see Ezendam and Wheldon, 2014). The development of victim rights frameworks in adversarial, common law countries moreover suggests the influence and development of supranational victim rights on the local level. While adversarial states tended towards soft law options, most are increasingly offering victims modes of substantive enforcement, albeit in discrete and controlled ways. The development of the role of the Commission of Victim Rights, and its powers of dispute resolution, for example, attests to the partially integrative approach taken towards the offering of rights of substantive content.

The movement towards the enforcement of victim rights must be phrased in a critical context of what this offers victims as participants in the criminal justice system of nation states. The emergence of rights-based frameworks provides victims with levels of standing that reposition them as significant to justice processes generally. This includes the normative stakeholders of justice, who now take account of the needs and interests of victims with regard to key decisions made throughout pretrial and trial process. However, the character of enforceable rights as providing actual, substantive access to justice must be understood in the context of how those rights and powers transform the role of victim within existing power arrangements and structures. The emergence of the victim as the subject of enforceable and substantive rights does not permit the victim to take over the justice process, contrary to the general criticism that greater empowerment for victims will jeopardise the interests of the state or the fair trial rights of the accused. Instead, victims are being successfully reintegrated in accordance with a rebalancing of the interests of justice to include victim perspectives and interests. This is occurring incrementally and unevenly across various domestic jurisdictions, in accordance with diverse processes of legal and policy change as traced in Chapter 3.

The general separation of jurisdictions into international, regional, and domestic, and again into inquisitorial, adversarial, and mixed or hybrid systems, has allowed for the interrogation of the different ways in which victim interests are negotiated into a rights framework on each level. The interplay of local law-and-order politics and the appetite for law reform that empowers victims, at times in controversial ways, demonstrates that the realisation of victim rights as a set of human rights accessible for victims and justice stakeholders is not dependent on globalising rights under a universalised model. Rather, the reform of local frameworks to create meaningful opportunities for substantive participation for victims is more determinative. It is the local level that impacts the lives of the victim as participants in the criminal justice system of each state. Opportunities for participation take a different form between jurisdictions, despite providing points of connection through substantive provisions to access justice, allowing victims to participate in the decision-making processes of justice agencies. For example, the Austrian Code of Criminal Procedure allows for rights to justice at each stage of proceedings, as against the enforceable powers of the Crime Victim Rights Act in the USA, as further compared to the discrete reforms to encourage consultation with prosecutors in South Australia, as an example of a framework of limited substantive value. These differences indicate that despite variable processes and degrees of enforceability, victims are accessing justice around a range of comparable substantive issues and interests, offered in terms of the constraints of each system. For many jurisdictions, however, especially those adversarial jurisdictions that have a long history of exclusion and limited participation, victims' progress towards the realisation of victim rights as human rights continues. The terrain is uneven and contested, but progress is being made.

The ultimate issue of whether the promise of victimology has been realised is dependent on the scope of the promise and the threshold of what qualifies as success. As both promise and indicia of success are dependent on what is perceived to be in the interests of the victim, debate will ensue as to whether the victim in the twenty-first century has met success as a rights-bearing subject now taken seriously as a member of the criminal justice system. Alternatively, we may have progressed to the point where we take victims seriously, only to uncover decades of hidden abuse and harm, most of which is still yet to surface. Even where we take the latter as indicia of the development of victim rights into the twenty-first century, the fact that victims have recourse of justice, to tell their narrative as victims, and to seek a response from justice authorities, evidences an advancement from the mid-twentieth-century position of being relegated to the sidelines of justice.

While the nature and scope of the benefits that may accrue to victims are debated and debatable, the impact of victim rights on the normative stakeholders of justice suggests that some progress ought to be noted in the advancement of victims generally. The twenty-first-century victim is therefore more empowered out of recognition that victim rights impact on and modify the offices and positions held by other normative stakeholders of justice as identified in this book. Judges, lawyers, prosecutors, police, and other justice officials now take account of the victim, their needs and desires, in a way that positions victims as actual stakeholders of significance in the modern justice system. This is true of all jurisdictions covered in this book. While it may not be true of all jurisdictions worldwide, developing jurisdictions are increasingly positioning the victim in justice policy in a progressive way that adheres to those international norms of victim rights that have done much to raise the standing of victims generally.

References

Abass, A. (2006) 'The International Criminal Court and Universal Jurisdiction', *International Criminal Law Review*, 6, 3, 349–385.

Abdul Waheed v State of UP (2015) ILC-2015-SC-CRL-Sep-27.

Act concerning Participation of Lay Assessors in Criminal Trials (*Saiban'in no sanka suru keiji saiban ni kansuru hōritsu*), Law No. 63 of 2004 (Jpn).

Act to Amend Parts of the Code of Criminal Procedure and Others in Order to Protect Rights and Interests of Victims of Crime (*Hanzaihigaishatō no kenririeki no hogo wo hakarutame no keijisoshōhōtō no ichibu wo kaisesuru hōritsu*), Law No. 95 of 2007 (Jpn).

Act to Revise the Code of Criminal Procedure (*Keijisoshōhōtō no ichibu wo kaiseisuru hōritsu*), Law No. 62 of 2004 (Jpn)

Albanese, JS. and Dammer, HR. (2010) *Comparative Criminal Justice Systems*, Cengage Learning, Boston, MA.

Alston, P. and Mégret, F. (eds.) (2013) *The United Nations and Human Rights: A Critical Appraisal*, Oxford University Press, Oxford.

Ambos, K. (2003) 'International Criminal Procedure: "Adversarial", "Inquisitorial" or Mixed?', *International Criminal Law Review*, 3, 1, 1–37.

An Act respecting Victims of Crime (SO 1995, c 6) (Can).

Anderson, K. and Johnson, DT. (2010) 'Japan's New Criminal Trials: Origins, Operations and Implications', in Harding, A. and Nicholson, P. (eds.) *New Courts in Asia*, Routledge, Taylor and Francis, London, pp. 371–390.

Assange v The Swedish Prosecution Authority [2012] UKSC 22.

Attorney-General's Reference (No. 3 of 1999) [2000] UKHL 63.

Baegen v The Netherlands (1994) ECHR 16696/90.

Bail Act 1976 (UK).

Bail Act 1997 (Ire).

Bail Act 2000 (NZ).

Bail Act 2013 (NSW).

Bail Bill 2015 (Ire).

Bajpai, GS. (2006) Psycho-social Consequences of Victimization in Rape', *International Perspectives in Victimology*, 2, 1, 67–81.

Baldev Singh v State of Punjab (1996) AIR 1996 SC 372.

Balraj v State of UP (1994) SCC (Cr) 823.

Barton v The Queen (1980) 147 CLR 75.

Basisth Narayan Yadav v Kailash Rai and Ors (2015) ILC-2015-SC-CRL-Jul-9.

Bassiouni, MC. (1999) 'Negotiating the Treaty of Rome on the Establishment of the International Criminal Court', *Cornell International Law Journal*, 32, 3, 443–469.

Bassiouni, MC. (2006) 'International Recognition of Victims' Rights', *Human Rights Law Review*, 6, 2, 203–279.

Beccaria, C. (1764) *Dei dellitti e delle pene*, 1973 edn, Mursia, Minano.

Beigbeder, Y. (2011) *International Criminal Tribunals: Justice and Politics*, Palgrave Macmillan, Houndmills, UK.

Bellelli, R. (ed.) (2010) *International Criminal Justice: Law and Practice from the Rome Statute to Its Review*, Ashgate, Oxon, UK.

Beloof, DE. (2005) 'The Third Wave of Crime Victims' Rights: Standing, Remedy, and Review', *Brigham Young University Law Review*, 2, 1, 255–365.

Berger v France (2002) ECHR 48221/99.

Bill of Rights Act 1990 (NZ).

Bocos-Cuesta v The Netherlands (2005) ECHR 54789/00.

Bodhisattwa Gautam v Subhra Chakraborty (1996) AIR 1996 SC 922.

Bowden, P., Henning, T. and Plater, D. (2014) 'Balancing Fairness to Victims, Society and Defendants in the Cross-Examination of Vulnerable Witnesses: An Impossible Triangulation?', *Melbourne University Law Review*, 37, 3, 539–584.

Braithwaite, J. (2003) 'Principles of Restorative Justice', in von Hirsch, A., Roberts, JV., Bottoms, AE., Roach, K. and Schiff, M. (eds.) *Restorative Justice and Criminal Justice: Competing or Reconcilable Paradigm?* Hart, Oxford, pp. 1–20.

Braun, K. (2014) 'Legal Presentation for Sexual Assault Victims: Possibilities for Law Reform', *Current Issues in Criminal Justice*, 25, 3, 819–837.

Brienen, ME. and Hoegen, EH. (2000) *Victims of Crime in 22 European Criminal Justice Systems*, Wolf Legal, Nijmegen, the Netherlands.

Brooks v Police [2000] SASC 66.

Canada Evidence Act 1985 (Can) (RSC, 1985, c C-5).

Canadian Criminal Code (RSC 1985 C-46).

Cassel, PG. (2005) 'Recognizing Victims in the Federal Rules of Criminal Procedure: Proposed Amendments in Light of the Crime Victims' Rights Act', *Brigham Young University Law Review*, 4, 1, 835–925.Cassell, PG. (2009) 'In Defense of Victim Impact Statements', *Ohio State Journal of Criminal. Law*, 6, 611–648.

Cassell, PG. (2010) 'Protecting Crime Victims in Federal Appellate Courts: The Need to Broadly Construe the Crime Victims' Rights Act's Mandamus Provision', *Denver University Law Review*, 87, 3, 599–631.

Cassell, PG. (2012) 'The Victims' Rights Amendment: A Sympathetic, Clause-By-Clause Analysis of the Proposal', *Phoenix Law Review – Special Edition: A Proposed Victims' Rights Amendment to the Constitution*, 5, 301–348.

Cassell, PG. and Erez, E. (2011) 'Victim Impact Statements and Ancillary Harm: The American Perspective', *Canadian Criminal Law Review*, 15, 2, 150–204.

Cassell, PG., Marsh, JR. and Christiansen, JM. (2013) 'The Case for Full Restitution for Child Pornography Victims', *George Washington Law Review*, 82, 61–110.

Cassell, PG., Mitchell, NJ. and Edwards, BJ. (2014) 'Protecting Crime Victims' Rights before Charges Are Filed: The Need for Expansive Interpretation of the Crime Victims' Rights Act and Similar State Statutes', *Journal of Criminal Law and Criminology*, 104, 1, 59–103.

Chalmers, J. (2014) 'Independent Legal Representation for Complainers in Sexual Offence Cases', in Chalmers, J., Leverick, F. and Shaw, A. (eds.) *Post-Corroboration Safeguards Review Report of the Academic Expert Group*, The Scottish Government, Edinburgh, pp. 185–189.

Charter of Human Rights and Responsibilities Act 2006 (Vic).

Chen v R [2015] NSWCCA 277.

Chockalingam, K. (2000) 'Female Infanticide: A Victimological Perspective', in Friday, PC. and Kirchhoff, GF. (eds.), *Victimology at the Transition from the 20th to the 21st Century: Essays in Honor of Hans Joachim Schneider: Dedicated on the Occasion of the Xth International Symposium on Victimology in Montreal, Canada 6–11 August 2000*, Shaker Verlag, Aachen, in cooperation with WSVP Mönchengladbach, pp. 273–287.

Christie, N. (1986) 'Ideal Victim', in Fattah, EA. (ed.), *From Crime Policy to Victim Policy: Reorienting the Justice System*, St. Martin's Press, New York, pp. 17–30.

Christie, N. (2015) 'Widening the Net', *Restorative Justice: An International Journal*, 3, 1, 109–113.

CICA v First-tier Tribunal and CP (CIC) [2013] UKUT 0638.

CIRCA and BOCSAR (2008) *Evaluation of Circle Sentencing Program*, Report, NSW Department of Attorney-General, May 2008.

City of London Police (2015) *Victims' Right to Review Scheme*, UK.

Civil Claims Alien Tort Claims Act (28 USC § 1350).

Code for Criminal Procedure (*Codice di Procedura Penale*) 1988 (Italy).

Code of Criminal Procedure (Act No. 131 of 1948) (Jpn).

Code of Criminal Procedure (Amendment) Act 2008 (Ind).

Code of Criminal Procedure (Código de Processo), Decree-Law No. 3,689 of Oct. 3, 1941 (Brazil).

Code of Criminal Procedure (France).

Code of Criminal Procedure (Germany).

Code of Criminal Procedure (Jpn).

Code of Criminal Procedure Act 1973 (Ind).

Code of Criminal Procedure of 1838 (The Netherlands).

Code of Criminal Procedure of 1975 (Austria).

Code of Judicial Procedure (Sweden).

Codice di Procedura Penale (Code for Criminal Procedure) (Italy).

Commission to Inquire into Child Abuse (CICA) (2009) *CICA Investigation Committee Report Vols. I–V* (Ryan Report), CICA, Dublin, Ireland.

Complementary Law No. 132 of 2009 (Brazil).

Constitution of the Italian Republic.

Council of Europe, Preventing and Combating Violence against Women and Domestic Violence, Treaty No. 210, in force 1 August 2014.

Courts Act 2003 (UK).

Courts Legislation (Neighbourhood Justice Centre) Act 2006 (Vic).

Crime and Courts Act 2013 (UK).

Crime and Security Act 2010 (UK).

Crimes (Domestic and Personal Violence) Act 2007 (NSW).

Crimes (High Risk Offenders) Act 2006 (NSW).

Crime Victim Rights Act 2004 (US).

Crime Victims Bill of Rights (Georgia Code) 2010.

Crimes (Sentencing Procedure) Act 1999 (NSW).

Crimes (Sentencing Procedure) Amendment (Family Member Victim Impact Statement) Act 2014 (NSW).

Crimes (Sentencing Procedure) Amendment (Victim Impact Statements – Mandatory Consideration) Bill 2014 (NSW).

Crimes Act 1900 (NSW).

Crimes and Other Legislation Amendment (Assault and Intoxication) Act 2014 (NSW).

Criminal Code of 1998 (Germany).

Criminal Evidence Act 1992 (Ire).

Criminal Injuries Compensation Act 1995 (UK).

Criminal Justice (Drug Trafficking) Act 1996 (Ire).

Criminal Justice (Theft and Fraud Offences) Act 2001 (Ire).

Criminal Justice (Victims of Crime) Bill 2015 (Ire).

Criminal Justice Act 1964 (Ire).

Criminal Justice Act 1967 (UK).

Criminal Justice Act 1984 (Ire).

Criminal Justice Act 1988 (UK).

Criminal Justice Act 1993 (UK).

Criminal Justice Act 2003 (UK).

Criminal Justice Act 2006 (Ire).

Criminal Justice and Public Order Act 1994 (UK).

Criminal Law (Amendment) Act 2013 (Ind).

Criminal Law (Jurisdiction) Act 1976 (Ire).

Criminal Law (Rape) Act 1981 (Ire).

Criminal Law (Sentencing) Act 1988 (SA).

Criminal Law (Sexual Offences) Act 1993 (Ire).

Criminal Law (Sexual Offences) Act 2006 (Ire).

Criminal Law Act 1976 (Ire).

Criminal Law Act 1997 (Ire).

Criminal Practice Directions Amendment No. 2 [2014] EWCA Crim 1569.

Criminal Procedure (Scotland) Act 1995 (Scot).

Criminal Procedure Act 1967 (Ire).

Criminal Procedure Act 1977 (SthA).

Criminal Procedure Act 1986 (NSW).

Criminal Procedure Act 2011 (NZ).

Criminal Procedure Code for Kosovo 2012 (Criminal No. 04/L-123).

Criminal Procedure Rules 2010 (UK).

Criminal Proceedings against Magatte Gueye and Valentín Salmerón Sánchez [2011] EUECJ C-483/09 and C-1/10.

Criminal Proceedings against Maurizio Giovanardi and Others [2012] EUECJ C-79/11.

Criminal Proceedings against Pupino [2005] EUECJ C-105/03.

Crown Prosecution Service (CPS) (2013a) *Code for Crown Prosecutors*, CPS, UK.

Crown Prosecution Service (CPS) (2013b) *Code of Practice for Victims of Crime: CPS Legal Guidance*, CPS, UK.

Crown Prosecution Service (CPS) (2013c) *Directors Guidance on Charging*, 5th edn, CPS, UK.

Crown Prosecution Service (CPS) (2014) *Victims Right to Review Guidance*, July 2014, CPS, UK.

Crown Prosecution Service (CPS) (2015) *Community Impact Statement – Adult*, Legal Guidance, CPS, UK.

Dabas v High Court of Justice in Madrid, Spain [2007] 2 AC 31.

Daly, K. (2014) *Redressing Institutional Abuse of Children*, Palgrave Macmillan, Houndmills, Basingstoke, Hampshire, UK.

Damaška, M. (2009) 'The International Criminal Court between Aspiration and Achievement', *UCLA Journal of International Law and Foreign Affairs*, 14, 1, 19–35.

Dangerous Prisoners (Sexual Offenders) Act 2003 (Qld).

Dangerous Prisoners (Sexual Offenders) Amendment Bill 2007 (Qld).

Dangerous Prisoners (Sexual Offenders) Amendment Bill 2007, *Explanatory Notes for Amendments to Be Moved during Consideration in Detail by the Honourable Kerry Shine, Attorney-General and Minister for Justice and Minister Assisting the Premier in Western Queensland*, Queensland Parliament.

Das, J. and Unterlerchner, B. (2014) 'Developing Programs for Victims of Domestic Abuse', in McFarlane, MA. and Canton, R. (eds.) *Policy Transfer in Criminal Justice: Crossing Cultures, Breaking Barriers*, Palgrave Macmillan, Houndmills, Basingstoke, Hampshire, UK, pp. 233–249.

Decision on the Applications for Participation in the Proceedings of VPRS 1–6, Pretrial Chamber I (ICC 01/04, 17 January 2006)

Decree No. 33,648 of 1953 (Brazil).

Decree No. 4,388 of 2002 (Brazil).

Department of Children and Youth Affairs (Ireland) (DCYA) (2011) *Children First: National Guidance for the Protection and Welfare of Children*, Government Publications, Dublin.

Dickinson, LA. (2003) 'The Relationship between Hybrid Courts and International Courts: The Case of Kosovo', *New England Law Review*, 37, 4, 1059–1072.

Director of Public Prosecutions for England and Wales (2014) *Victims Right to Review Guidance*, Crown Prosecution Service, UK.

Director of Public Prosecutions, Gauteng v Pistorius (96/2015) [2015] ZASCA 204; [2016] 1 All SA 346.

DK Basu v State of West Bengal (1997) AIR 1997 SC 61.

Doak, J. (2008) *Victim Rights, Human Rights and Criminal Justice*, Hart, Oxford.

Doak, J. (2015) 'Enriching Trial Justice for Crime Victims in Common Law Systems: Lessons from Transitional Environments', *International Review of Victimology*, 21, 2, 139–160.

Dolowitz1, DP. and Marsh, D. (2002) 'Learning from Abroad: The Role of Policy Transfer in Contemporary Policy-Making', *Governance*, 13, 1, 5–23.

Domestic Violence, Crime and Victims Act 2004 (UK).

Dooson v The Netherlands (1996) ECHR 20524/92.

Dussich, J. (2013) 'Forty Days after the Great East Japan Earthquake: Field Research Investigating Community Engagement and Traumatic Stress Screening in a Post-Disaster Community Mental Health Training', *The International Journal of Psychiatry in Medicine*, 45, 2, 159–174.

Dussich, J. (2015) 'The Evolution of International Victimology and Its Current Status in the World Today', *Revista de Victimologia/Journal of Victimology*, 1, 1, 37–81.

Elias, R. (1985) 'Transcending Our Social Reality of Victimization: Toward a New Victimology of Human Rights', *Victimology: An International Journal*, 10, 1/4, 6–25.

Ellenberger, H. (1955) 'Relations Psychologiques entre le Criminel et la Victime', *Revue International de Criminologie et de Police Technique*, 8, 757–790.

Ellison, L. (2002) *The Adversarial Process and the Vulnerable Witness*, Oxford University Press, Oxford.

Erez, E. (2004) 'Victim Voice, Impact Statements and Sentencing: Integrating Restorative Justice and Therapeutic Jurisprudence Principles in Adversarial Proceedings', *Criminal Law Bulletin*, 40, 5, 483–500.

European Commission (2013) DG Justice Guidance Document related to the Transposition and Implementation of Directive 2012/29/EU of the European Parliament and of the Council of 25 October 2012 Establishing Minimum Standards on the Rights, Support and Protection of Victims of Crime, and Replacing Council Framework Decision 2001/220/JHA, European Commission, Parliament of Europe, 19 December.

European Union, Council Decision 2015/1523 of 14 September 2015 establishing provisional measures in the area of international protection for the benefit of Italy and of Greece.

European Union, Council Decision 2015/1601 of 22 September 2015 establishing provisional measures in the area of international protection for the benefit of Italy and Greece.

European Union, Directive of the European Parliament and of the Council 2003/9/EC of 27 January 2003 laying down minimum standards for the reception of asylum seekers.

European Union, Directive of the European Parliament and of the Council 2004/81/EC of 29 April 2004 on the residence permit issued to third-country nationals who are victims of trafficking in human beings or who have been the subject of an action to facilitate illegal immigration, who cooperate with the competent authorities.

European Union, Directive of the European Parliament and of the Council 2005/85/EC of 1 December 2005 on minimum standards on procedures in Member States for granting and withdrawing refugee status.

European Union, Directive of the European Parliament and of the Council 2011/36/EU of the European Parliament and of the Council of 5 April 2011 on preventing and combating trafficking in human beings and protecting its victims.

European Union, Directive of the European Parliament and of the Council 2011/93/EU on combating the sexual abuse and sexual exploitation of children and child pornography.

European Union, Directive of the European Parliament and of the Council 2011/99/EU of the European Parliament and of the Council of 13 December 2011 on the European protection order.

European Union, Directive of the European Parliament and of the Council 2012/13/EU of the European Parliament and of the Council of 22 May 2012 on the right to information in criminal proceedings.

European Union, Directive of the European Parliament and of the Council 2012/29/EU, 25 October 2012, Establishing minimum standards on the rights, support and protection of victims of crime, and replacing council framework decision 2001/220/JHA.

European Union, Directive of the European Parliament and of the Council 2013/33/EU of the European Parliament and of the Council of 26 June 2013 laying down standards for the reception of applicants for international protection.

European Union, European Council Framework Decision 2001/220/JHA, 15 March 2001, Standing of victims in criminal proceedings.

European Union, Proposal for a Directive of the European Parliament and of the Council 2011/0129 (COD), Establishing minimum standards on the rights, support and protection of victims of crime.

Evidence Act 1872 (Ind).

Evidence Act 2006 (NZ).

Extraordinary Chambers in the Courts of Cambodia (2015) *Internal Rules*, revised 16 January 2015.

Ezendam, H. and Wheldon, F. (2014) 'Recognition of Victims' Rights through EU Action: Latest Developments and Challenges', in Vanfrachem, I., Pemberton, A. and Ndahinda, F.M. (eds.) *Justice for Victims: Perspectives on Rights, Transition and Reconciliation*, Routledge, Oxon, pp. 51–65.

Federal Law No. 1,060 of 1950 (Brazil).

Federal Law No. 9,807 of 1999 (Brazil).

Federal Law No. 11,340 of 2006 (Brazil).Federal Rules of Evidence (28 USC Art. IV).

Fernández de Casadevante Romani, C. (2012) *International Law of Victims*, Springer, Heidelberg, New York.

Fernandez de Gurmendi, SA. (2001) 'The Elaboration of the Rules of Procedure and Evidence', in Lee, RS. (ed.), *The International Criminal Court: Elements of Crimes and Rules of Procedure and Evidence*, Transnational, Ardsley, NY, pp. 235–258.

Ferri, E. (1892) *Sociologia Criminale*, 3rd edn, Torino, Fratelli Bocca.

Finkensieper v The Netherlands (1995) ECHR 19525/92.

Friday, PC. and Kirchhoff, GF. (eds.) (2000) *Victimology at the Transition from the 20th to the 21st Century: Essays in Honor of Hans Joachim Schneider: Dedicated on the Occasion of the Xth International Symposium on Victimology in Montreal, Canada 6–11 August 2000*, Shaker Verlag, Aachen, in cooperation with WSVP Mönchengladbach.

Fukurai, H. (2013) 'Step in the Right Direction for Japan's Judicial Reform: Impact of the Justice System Reform Council Recommendations on Criminal Justice and Citizen Participation in Criminal, Civil, and Administrative Litigation', *Hastings International and Comparative Law Review*, 36, 2, 517–566.

Garófalo, R. (1885) *Criminologia*, Torino, Italia, Bocca.

Gaur, KD. (2011) *Textbook on the Indian Penal Code*, Universal Law, New Delhi, India.

Geneva Conventions (1864–1949) Geneva Convention for the Amelioration of the Condition of the Wounded and Sick in Armed Forces in the Field of 12 August 1949, 6 UST 3114, TIAS No. 3362, 75 UNTS 31; Geneva Convention for the Amelioration of the Condition of the Wounded, Sick and Shipwrecked Members of Armed Forces at Sea of 12 August 1949, 6 UST 3217, TIAS. No. 3363, 75 UNTS 85; Geneva Convention Relative to the Treatment of

Prisoners of War of 12 August 1949, 6 UST 3316, TIAS No. 3364, 75 UNTS 135; Geneva Convention Relative to the Protection of Civilian Persons in Time of War of 12 August 1949, 6 UST 3516, TIAS No. 3365, 75 UNTS 287.

Giani Ram v State of Haryana (1995) AIR 1995 SC 2452.

Goss, B. (2014) *Criminal Fair Trial Rights: Article 6 of the European Convention on Human Rights*, Hart, Oxon.

Government of India (2003) *Report on the Committee on Reforms of Criminal Justice System, Vol. 1*. Ministry of Home Affairs, New Delhi, India.

Gram Nyayalayas Act 2008 (Ind).

Greer, S. and Williams, A. (2009) 'Human Rights in the Council of Europe and the EU: Towards "Individual", "Constitutional" or "Institutional" Justice?', *European Law Journal: Review of European Law in Context*, 15, 4, 462–481.

Groenhuijsen, M. (2014) 'The Development of International Policy in Relation to Victims of Crime', *International Review of Victimology*, 20, 1, 31–48.

Groenhuijsen, M. and Pemberton, A. (2009) 'The EU Framework Decision for Victims of Crime: Does Hard Law Make a Difference?', *European Journal of Crime, Criminal Law and Criminal Justice*, 17, 1, 43–59.

Guinchard, S. and Buisson, J. (2011) *Criminal Procedural Law*, 7th edn, LexisNexis, Paris, France.

Gutsanovi v Bulgaria (2013) ECHR 34529/10.

György Katz v István Roland Sós [2008] EUECJ C-404/07.

Habitual Criminals Act 1957 (NSW).

Hall, M. (2009) *Victims of Crime: Policy and Practice in Criminal Justice*, Willan, Cullompton, UK.

Hall, M. (2010) *Victims and Policy Making: A Comparative Perspective*, Willan, Cullompton, UK.

Hans, VP. (2014) 'The Impact of Victim Participation in Saiban-in Trials in Japan: Insights from the American Jury Experience', *International Journal of Law, Crime and Justice*, 42, 2, 103–116.

Hardgrave, RL. and Kochanek, SA. (2008) *India: Government and Politics in a Developing Nation*, 7th edn, Thomson/Wadsworth, Boston, MA.

Hehir, A. (2010) 'Introduction: Kosovo and the International Community', in Hehir, A. (ed.) *Kosovo, Intervention and State Building: The International Community and the Transition to Independence*, Routledge, Oxon, pp. 1–17.

Henderson, E. (2014) 'All the Proper Protections: The Court of Appeal Rewrites the Rules for the Cross-Examination of Vulnerable Witnesses', *Criminal Law Review*, 2, 93–108.

Hill v Chief Constable of West Yorkshire Police [1999] AC 53.

Hinton, AL. (2014) 'The Transitional Justice Imaginary: Uncle San. Aunty Yan and Victim Participation in the Khmer Rouge Tribunal', in Vanfrachem, I., Pemberton, A., and Ndahinda, FM. (eds.) *Justice for Victims: Perspectives on Rights, Transition and Reconciliation*, Routledge, Oxon, pp. 247–261.

Holder, R. (2015) 'Satisfied? Exploring Victims' Justice Judgements', in Wilson, D. and Ross, S. (eds.) *Crime, Victims and Policy: International Contexts, Local Experiences*, Palgrave Macmillan, Houndmills, Basingstoke, Hampshire, UK, pp. 184–213.

Homicide Victim Support Group (NSW) (HVSG) (2016) Aims and Objectives of the Homicide Victims' Support Group (Aust.) Inc., online, http://hvsg.com.au/.

Hoyano, L. (2015) 'Reforming the Adversarial Trial for Vulnerable Witnesses and Defendants', *Criminal Law Review*, 2, 107–129.

Human Rights Act 1998 (UK).

In re Antrobus (2008) 519 F 3d 1123.

In re Dean (2008) 527 F 3d 39.

Indian Penal Code Act 1860 (Ind).

Isaacs, T. (2016) 'International Criminal Courts and Political Reconciliation', *Criminal Law and Philosophy*, 10, 1, 133–142.

Jackson, J. (2009) 'Finding the Best Epistemic Fit for International Criminal Tribunals: Beyond the Adversarial–Inquisitorial Dichotomy', *Journal of International Criminal Justice*, 7, 1, 17–39.

Jägervi, L. and Svensson, K. (2015) 'Conceptions of Gender and Age in Swedish Victim Support', *International Review of Victimology*, 21, 2, 217–231.

Jaishankar, K. (2014) 'Implementing Victim Rights in Newly Industrialized Countries', in Vanfrachem, I., Pemberton, A., and Ndahinda, FM. (eds.) *Justice for Victims: Perspectives on Rights, Transition and Reconciliation*, Routledge, Oxon, pp. 68–88.

James Wood v Fonds de Garantie des Victimes des Actes de Terrorisme et d'autres Infractions [2007] EUECJ C-164/07.

Johnson, DT. and Shinomiya, S. (2015) 'Judging Japan's New Criminal Trials: Early Returns from 2009', in Wolff, L., Nottage, L. and Anderson, K. (eds.) *Who Rules Japan? Popular Participation in the Japanese Legal Process*, Edward Elgar, Cheltenham, UK, pp. 18–44.

Johnson, ST. (2009) 'Neither Victims nor Executioners: The Dilemma of Victim Participation and the Defendant's Right to a Fair Trial at the International Criminal Court', ILSA *Journal of International and Comparative Law*, 16, 2, 489–496.

Joutsen, M. (1987) 'Listening to the Victim: The Victim's Role in European Criminal Justice Systems', *Wayne Law Review*, 34, 95–124.

Judicial Commission NSW (2003) *Circle Sentencing in New South Wales A Review and Evaluation*, NSW Government.

Juvenile Justice NSW (2010) *Guidelines for the Management of Conduct of Conferences*, Department of Juvenile Justice, NSW.

Kelkars, RV. (2014) *RV Kelkar's Criminal Procedure*, 6th edn, Eastern Book, Lucknow.

Keller, L. (2007) 'Seeking Justice at the International Criminal Court: Victim's Reparations', *Thomas Jefferson Law Review*, 29, 2, 189–218.

Kemp, G., Walker, S., Palmer, R., Baqwa, D., Gevers, C., Leslie, B. and Steynberg, A. (2012) *Criminal Law in South Africa*, Oxford, Southern Africa.

Killean, R. (2015) An Incomplete Narrative: Prosecuting Sexual Violence Crimes at the Extraordinary Chambers in the Courts of Cambodia', *Journal of International Criminal Justice*, 13, 2, 331–352.

Kirchhoff, GF. (2010) 'History and a Theoretical Structure of Victimology', in Shoham, SG., Knepper, P. and Kett, M. (eds.) *International Handbook of Victimology*, CRC Press, Boca Raton, pp. 95–123.

Klip, A. (2015) 'On Victim's Rights and Its Impact on the Rights of the Accused', *European Journal of Crime, Criminal Law and Criminal Justice*, 23, 3,177–189.

KM Nanavati v State of Maharashtra [1962] AIR 605.

Knoops, G-J. (2014) *An Introduction to the Law of International Criminal Tribunals: A Comparative Study*, Brill, Nijhoff, Leiden, the Netherlands.

Kodner, JJ. (2003) 'Re-Introducing Lay Participation to Japanese Criminal Cases: An Awkward Yet Necessary Step', *Washington University Global Studies Law Review*, 2, 1, 231–254.

Koss, MP. and Dinero, TE. (1989) 'Discriminant Analysis of Risk Factors for Sexual Victimisation among a National Sample of College Women', *Journal of Consulting and Clinical Psychology*, 57, 2, 242–250.

Kostovski v The Netherlands (1989) 12 EHRR 434.

KS v Veitch (No. 2) [2012] NSWCCA 266.

Kury, H. and Kichling, M. (2011) 'Accessory Prosecution in Germany: Legislation and Implementation', in Erez, E., Kilchling, M. and Wemmers, J-A. (eds.), *Therapeutic Jurisprudence and Victim Participation in Justice: International Perspectives*, Carolina Academic Press, Durham, NC, pp. 41–66.

Lai, B. (2005) 'The Alien Tort Claims Act: Temporary Stopgap Measure or Permanent Remedy', *Northwestern Journal of International Law and Business*, 26, 1, 139–165.

Latha, L. and Thilagaraj, R. (2013) 'Restorative Justice in India', *Asian Journal of Criminology*, 8, 4, 309–319.

Law Commission of India (1996) Victimology in 154th Report on the Code of Criminal Procedure 1973 (Act No. 2 of 1974) Chapter XV, Law Commission of India, New Delhi, India, pp. 57–65.

Law Enforcement (Powers and Responsibilities) Act 2002 (NSW).

Laxminarayan, M. (2015) 'Enhancing Trust in the Legal System through Victims' Rights Mechanisms', *International Review of Victimology*, 21, 3, 273–286.

Lens, KME., van Doorn, J., Lahlah, E., Pemberton, A. and Bogaerts, S. (2016) 'Observers' Reactions to Victim Impact Statements: A Preliminary Study into the Affective and Cognitive Responses', *International Review of Victimology*, 22, 1, 45–53.

Letschert, R. and Parmentier, S. (2014) 'Repairing the Impossible: Victimological Approaches to International Crimes', in Vanfrachem, I., Pemberton, A., and Ndahinda, FM. (eds.) *Justice for Victims: Perspectives on Rights, Transition and Reconciliation*, Routledge, Oxon, pp. 210–246.

Lomax, M. (2014) 'Developing Programmes for Victims of Sexual Violence', in McFarlane, MA. and Canton, R. (eds.) *Policy Transfer in Criminal Justice: Crossing Cultures, Breaking Barriers*, Palgrave Macmillan, Houndmills, Basingstoke, Hampshire, UK, pp. 250–270.

Lombroso, C. (1876) *L'Uomo Delinquente*. Torino, Fratelli Bocca.

LRM v Kastenberg (2013) 13–5006/AF (CAAF 2013).

Maintenance and Welfare of Parents and Senior Citizens Act 2007 (Ind).

Manco, N. (2015) 'The European Court of Human Rights: A "Culture of Bad Faith"?', *Global Policy*, 6, 4, 526–530.

Matsui, S. (2011) 'Justice for the Accused or Justice for Victims? The Protection of Victims' Rights in Japan', *Asian-Pacific Law and Policy Journal*, 31, 1, 54–95.

Maxwell v The Queen (1996) 184 CLR 501.

McAsey, B. (2011) 'Victim Participation at the International Criminal Court and Its Impact on Procedural Fairness', *Australian International Law Journal*, 18, 105–125.

McBride, J. (2009) *Human Rights and Criminal Procedure: The Case Law of the European Court of Human Rights*, Council of Europe, Strasbourg, France.

McCann and Ors v United Kingdom (1995) 21 EHRR 97.

McCarthy, C. (2012) *Reparations and Victim Support in the International Criminal Court*, Cambridge University Press, Cambridge.

McDonald v R [2014] NSWCCA 127.

McEwin, A. (2014) *Letter to the Honourable Brad Hazzard MP, Attorney General of NSW, First 12 Months of Victims Rights and Support Act 2013*, 16 June.

McFarlane, MA. and Canton, R. (eds.) (2014) *Policy Transfer in Criminal Justice: Crossing Cultures, Breaking Barriers*, Palgrave Macmillan, Houndmills, Basingstoke, Hampshire, UK.

McGarry, R. and Walklate, S. (2015) *Victims: Trauma, Testimony and Justice*, Routledge, Oxon.

McGee, H., Garavan, R., deBarra, M., Byrne, J., and Conroy, R. ('SAVI Report') (2002) *Sexual Abuse and Violence in Ireland: A National Study of Irish Experiences, Beliefs and Attitudes concerning Sexual Violence*, Liffey Press, Dublin, Ireland.

Mégret, F. (2014a) 'The Case of Collective Reparations before the International Criminal Court', in Wemmers, JA. (ed.) *Reparation for Victims of Crimes against Humanity: The Healing Role of Reparation*, Routledge, Oxon, pp. 171–189.

Mégret, F. (2014b) 'International Criminal Justice: A Critical Research Agenda', in Schwöbel, C. (ed.), *Critical Approaches to International Criminal Law*, Routledge, Milton Park, Abingdon, pp. 17–53.

Mégret, F. (2015) 'What Sort of Global Justice is "International Criminal Justice"?', *Journal of International Criminal Justice*, 13, 1, 77–96.

Mégret, F. (2016) 'The Anxieties of International Criminal Justice', *Leiden Journal of International Law*, 29, 1, 197–221.

Mendelsohn, B. (1937) 'Methods to Be Used by Counsel for the Defense in the Researches Made into the Personality of the Criminal', *Revue de Droit Penal et de Criminologie*, August–October, 877–883.

Mendelsohn, B. (1940) *Il Stupro dentro la Criminologia*, Giustizia Penale, Rome, Italy.

Mendelsohn, B. (1956) 'Une Nouvelle Branche de la Science Bio-Ssycho-Sociale, la Victimologie', *Etudes Internationales de Psycho-Sociologie Criminelle*, 11, 2, 95–109.

Miers, D. (1989) 'Positivist Victimology: A Critique Part 1', *International Review of Victimology*, 1, 1, 1–29.

Miers, D. (1990) 'Positivist Victimology: A Critique Part 2', *International Review of Victimology*, 1, 3, 219–230.

Miers. D. (2014a) 'Compensating Deserving Victims of Violent Crime: The Criminal Injuries Compensation Scheme 2012', *Legal Studies*, 34, 2, 242–278.

Miers, D. (2014b) 'Offender and State Compensation for Victims of Crime: Two Decades of Development and Change', *International Review of Victimology*, 20, 1, 145–168.

Ministry of Justice (2011a) *Achieving Best Evidence in Criminal Proceedings: Guidance on Interviewing Victims and Witnesses, and Guidance on Using Special Measures*, Ministry of Justice, UK.

Ministry of Justice (2011b) *Breaking the Cycle: Government Response*, UK Government, London.

Ministry of Justice (2012a) *The Criminal Injuries Compensation Scheme 2012*, UK Government, London.

Ministry of Justice (2012b) *Getting It Right for Victims and Witness*, UK Government, Consultation Paper CP3/2012, January 2012.

Ministry of Justice (2014) *Pre-Sentence Restorative Justice (RJ)*, UK Government, London.

Ministry of Justice (2015) *Code of Practice for Victims of Crime*, UK Government, London.

Misuse of Drugs Act 1977 (Ire).

Moffett, M. (2014) *Justice for Victims before the International Criminal Court*, Routledge, New York.

Mohid Jawad v The Queen [2013] EWCA Crim 644.

Morris, A. (2002) 'Critiquing the Critics: A Brief Response to Critics of Restorative Justice', *British Journal of Criminology*, 42, 3, 596–615.

Munro, M. (2014) 'Victims' Policy in Scotland: A Review', in Croall, H., Mooney, G. and Munro, M. (eds.) *Crime, Justice and Society in Scotland*, Routledge, Oxon, pp. 151–164.

Murray, S. (2009) 'Keeping It in the Neighbourhood? Neighbourhood Courts in the Australian Context', *Monash University Law Review*, 35, 1, 74–95.

Nagel, WH. (1949) *De criminaliteit van Oss. Antwerpen*, de Sikke, The Netherlands.

National Prosecuting Authority (NPA) (2014) *Prosecution Guidelines*, Pretoria, South Africa.

New South Wales Law Reform Commission (NSWLRC) (2013) *Sentencing*, Report 139.

Non-Fatal Offences Against the Person Act 1997 (Ire).

Nou, L. (2015) 'Elusive Retributive Justice in Post-Khmer Rouge Cambodia: Challenges of Using ECCC Victim Information Forms as a Victim Participatory Rights Mechanism', *Torture*, 25, 2, 61–84.

Ochoa, JC. (2013) *The Rights of Victims in Criminal Justice Proceedings for Serious Human Rights Violations*, Martinus Nijhoff, Leiden, the Netherlands.

Offences Against the Person Act 1861 (Ire).

Offences Against the Person Act 1861 (UK).

Offender Rehabilitation Act 2014 (UK).

O'Keeffe v Ireland (2014) ECHR 35810/09.

Opuz v Turkey (2009) ECHR 33401/02.

Osman v United Kingdom (1998) 29 EHRR 245.

Palmer, E. (2016) 'Localizing International Criminal Accountability in Cambodia', *International Relations of the Asia-Pacific*, 16, 1, 97–135.

Pemberton, A. (2014) 'Respecting Victims of Crime', in Vanfrachem, I., Pemberton, A. and Ndahinda, FM. (eds.) *Justice for Victims: Perspectives on Rights, Transition and Reconciliation*, Routledge, Oxon, pp. 32–50.

Pena, M. and Carayon, G. (2013) 'Is the ICC Making the Most of Victim Participation?' *The International Journal of Transitional Justice*, 7, 3, 518–535.

Penal Code (Código Penal), Decree-Law No. 2,848 of December 7, 1940 (Brazil).

Penal Code (*Keihō*), Law No. 45 of 1907 (Jpn).

Penal Code of 1810 (France).

Penal Code of 1881 (The Netherlands).

Penal Code of 1962 (Sweden).

Penal Code of 1974 (Austria).

Penal Code of the German Empire of 1871.

Perez v France (2004) ECHR 47287/99.

Perrin, B. (2014) 'Benjamin Perrin: Without Enforceability Provisions, Harper's "Canadian Victims Bill of Rights" Won't Do Much for Victims', *National Post*, online, http://news. nationalpost.com/full-comment/benjamin-perrin-without-enforceability-provisions-harpers-canadian-victims-bill-of-rights-wont-do-much-for-victims.

Police and Criminal Evidence Act 1984 (UK).

Powers of Criminal Courts (Sentencing) Act 2000 (UK).

PPC v Williams [2013] NSWCCA 286.

Pravin v The State of Maharashtra (2012) HC (Bombay) 249.

Prevention of Caste-Based Victimization and Protection for Victims: The Scheduled Castes and the Scheduled Tribes (Prevention of Atrocities) Act 1989 (Ind).

Prisoners of War of 12 August 1949, 6 UST 3316, TIAS No. 3364, 75 UNTS 135; Geneva Convention Relative to the Protection of Civilian Persons in Time of War of 12 August 1949, 6 UST 3516, TIAS No. 3365, 75 UNTS 287.

Privacy Act 1993 (NZ).

Prosecution Review Board Act (*Kensatsu shinsakaihō*), Law No. 147 of 1948 (Jpn).

The Prosecutor v Dario Kordić and Mario Čerkez (IT-95–14/2-A) Appeals Chamber, 17 December 2004.

The Prosecutor v Dragomir Milošević (IT-98–29/1-A) Appeals Chamber, 12 November 2009.

The Prosecutor v Du [Ko Tadi] (IT-94–1-A) Appeals Chamber, 15 July 1999.

The Prosecutor v Duško Tadic (IT-94–1-T) Trial Chamber, 7 May 1997.

The Prosecutor v Katanga and Chui (ICC-01/04–01/07 OA 11, 16 July 2010, Judgment on the Appeal of Mr Katanga against the Decision of Trial Chamber II of 22 January 2010 Entitled 'Decision on the Modalities of Victim Participation at Trial').

The Prosecutor v Katanga and Chui, Appeals Chamber (ICC- 01/04–01/07, 22 January 2010, Judgement Entitled 'Decision on the Modalities of Victim Participation at Trial').

The Prosecutor v Lubanga (ICC-01/04–01/06–1432, 11 July 2008, Judgment on the Appeals of the Prosecutor and the Defence against Trial Chamber I's Decision on Victims' Participation of 18 January 2008).

The Prosecutor v Thomas Lubanga Dyilo (ICC-01/04–01/06–2904, 7 August 2012, Decision Establishing the Principles and Procedures to Be Applied to Reparations).

The Prosecutor v Thomas Lubanga Dyilo, Trial Chamber I, (ICC-01/04–01/06, 14 December 2007).

The Prosecutor v Zdravko Tolimir (IT-05–88/2-A) Appeals Chamber, 8 April 2015.

Protecting Victoria's Vulnerable Children Inquiry (VVCI) (2012) *Report of the Protecting Victoria's Vulnerable Children Inquiry Vols. 1–3*, The Honourable Philip Cummins (Chair), Emeritus Professor Dorothy Scott OAM, Mr Bill Scales AO, January 2012.

R v Camberwell Green Youth Court [2005] 1 All ER 999.

R v DPP, Ex parte C [1995] 1 Cr App R 136.

R v Killick [2011] EWCA Crim 1608.

R v Loveridge [2014] NSWCCA 120.

R v Lubemba [2014] EWCA Crim 2064

R v Martin [2003] 2 Cr App R 21.

R v Previtera (1997) 94 A Crim R 76.

R v Sellick and Sellick [2005] 2 Cr App R 15.

Raitt, F. (2010) *Independent Legal Representation for Complainers in Sexual Office Trials*, Research Report for Rape Crisis, Glasgow, Scotland.

Raitt, F. (2013) 'Independent Legal Representation in Rape Cases: Meeting the Justice Deficit in Adversarial Proceedings', *Criminal Law Review*, 9, 729–749.

Razzakov v Russia (2015) ECHR 57519/09.

Re: Jewell Allen, et al. (2014) 12–40954 (5th Cir. 2014).

Reiger, C. and Wierda, M. (2006) *The Serious Crimes Process in Timor-Leste: In Retrospect*, International Center for Transitional Justice, New York.

Requa, M. (2010) 'Absent Witnesses and the UK Supreme Court: Judicial Deference as Judicial Dialogue?', *International Journal of Evidence and Proof*, 14, 3, 208–231.

Restorative Justice Council (2014) *Restorative Justice in the Magistrates' Court Information Pack*, December 2014.

Roberson, C. and Das, DK. (2016) *An Introduction to Comparative Legal Models of Criminal Justice*, 2nd edn, Taylor and Francis, Boca Raton, FL.

Rock, P. (2014) 'Victims Rights', in Vanfrachem, I., Pemberton, A. and Ndahinda, FM. (eds.) *Justice for Victims: Perspectives on Rights, Transition and Reconciliation*, Routledge, Oxon, pp. 11–31.

Rome Statute (Statute of the ICC) (A/Conf 183/9, 1998).

Rossner, M., Bruce, J. and Meher, M. (2013) *The Process and Dynamics on Restorative Justice: Research on Forum Sentencing*, University of Western Sydney, Sydney.

Royal Commission into Institutional Responses to Child Abuse (RCIRCA) (2015) *Advocacy and Support and Therapeutic Treatment Services*, Issues Paper 10, 1 October 2015.

Rudul Sah v State of Bihar (1983) AIR 1983 SC 1086.

Saeki, M. (2010) 'Victim Participation in Criminal Trials in Japan', *International Journal of Law, Crime and Justice* 38, 4, 149–165.

Safferling, C. (2011) 'The Role of the Victim in the Criminal Process – A Paradigm Shift in National German and International Law?', *International Criminal Law Review*, 11, 2, 183–215.

Saheli, a Women's Resources Centre through Mrs. Nalini Bhanot v Commissioner of Police, Delhi Police (1990) AIR 1990 SC 513.

Sandeep and Anr v State of Haryana (2015) ILC-2015-SC-CRL-May-17.

Schafer, S. (1968) *The Victim and His Criminal: A Study of Functional Responsibility*, Random House, New York.

Schwikkard, PJ. (2008) *Possibilities of Convergence: An Outside Perspective on the Convergence of Criminal Procedures in Europe*, Kluwer, Deventer, the Netherlands.

Sebba, L. (1982) 'The Victim's Role in the Penal Process: A Theoretical Orientation', *American Journal of Comparative Law*, 30, 2, 217–240.

Sebba, L. (1996) *Third Parties, Victims and the Criminal Justice System*, Ohio State University Press, Columbus.

Sebba, L. and Berenblum, T. (2014) 'Victimology and the Sociology of New Disciplines: A Research Agenda', *International Review of Victimology*, 20, 1, 7–30.

Sentencing Act 2002 (NZ).

Sex Offences Act 2001 (Ire).

Sexual Offences Act 2003 (UK).

Sexual Offences (Procedure and Evidence) (Scotland) Act 2002 (Scot).Singh, DR. (1985) 'Development of Victimology in India', *Indian Journal of Criminology*, 13, 2, 144–150.

Sithole, K. (2013) 'The Council of Europe, Rights and Political Authority', *European Review*, 21, 1, 118–134.

South African Government (2013) *National Development Plan 2030*, Republic of South Africa.

Starmer, K. (2014) 'Human Rights, Victims and the Prosecution of Crime in the 21st Century', *Criminal Law Review*, 11, 777–787.

Statutes Amendment (Victims of Crime) Act 2007 (SA).

Statutes Amendment (Victims of Crime) Act 2009 (SA).

Stivachtisa, YA. and Habeggera, M. (2011) 'The Council of Europe: The Institutional Limits of Contemporary European International Society?', *Journal of European Integration*, 33, 2, 159–177.

Sukhdev Singh v State of Punjab (1982) SCC (Cr) 467.

Summary Offences Act 1981 (NZ).

Summary Offences Act 1988 (NSW).

Summers, S. (2007) *Fair Trials: The European Criminal Procedural Tradition and the European Court of Human Rights*, Hart, Oxford.

Sutherland, EH. (1924) *Criminology*, JB Lippincott, Philadelphia, PA.

Theft Act 1968 (UK).

Theoneste Bagorora and Anatole Nsengiyumva v The Prosecutor (ICTR-98–41-A) Appeals Chamber, 14 December 2011.

Thornhill, C. (2012) 'The Formation of a European Constitution: An Approach from Historical-Political Sociology', *International Journal of Law in Context*, 8, 3, 354–393.

United Nations (CAT) (1984) Convention against Torture and Other Cruel, Inhuman or Degrading Treatment or Punishment, resolution GA/RES/39/46 of the General Assembly 10 December 1984, in force 26 June 1987.

United Nations (CEDAW) (1979) The Convention on the Elimination of All Forms of Discrimination against Women, resolution GA/RES/34/180 of the General Assembly 18 December 1979, and in force 3 September 1981.

United Nations (ICCPR) (1966) International Covenant on Economic, Social and Cultural Rights, International Covenant on Civil and Political Rights and Optional Protocol to the International Covenant on Civil and Political Rights, resolution GA/RES/2200(XXI)A-C of the General Assembly on 16 December 1966, and in force 23 March 1976.

United Nations (ICERD) (1965) The International Convention on the Elimination of All Forms of Racial Discrimination, resolution GA/RES/2106(XX)A-B of the General Assembly on 21 December 1965, in force 4 January 1969.

United Nations (ICMW) (1990) The International Convention on the Protection of the Rights of All Migrant Workers and Members of Their Families, resolution GA/RES/45/158 of the General Assembly on 18 December 1990, in force 1 July 2003.

United Nations (ICRPD) (2006) The International Convention on the Rights of Persons with Disabilities, resolution GA/RES/61/106 of the General Assembly on 13 December 2006, in force 3 May 2008.

United Nations (PJVC) (1985) The Declaration of Basic Principles of Justice for Victims of Crime and Abuse of Power, resolution GA/RES/40/34 of the General Assembly 29 November 1985.

United Nations (1992) The Declaration on the Protection of All Persons from Enforced Disappearance, General Assembly, resolution GA/RES/47/133 of the General Assembly on 18 December 1992.

United Nations (2005) Basic Principles and Guidelines on the Right to a Remedy and Reparation for Victims of Gross Violations of International Human Rights Law and Serious Violations of International Humanitarian Law, resolution GA/RES/60/147 of the UN General Assembly, 16 December 2005.

United Nations (2006) International Convention on the Protection of All Persons from Enforced Disappearance, resolution GA/RES/61/177 of the General Assembly on 20 December 2006, in force 23 December 2006.

United Nations Economic and Social Council (UNESC Guideline) (2005) Guidelines on Justice in Matters involving Child Victims and Witnesses of Crime, resolution 2005/20 of the Economic and Social Council on 22 July 2005.

United Nations Transitional Administration in East Timor (UNTAET) (2000a) Regulation No. 2000/11 on the Organization of Courts in East Timor, 6 March 2000.

United Nations Transitional Administration in East Timor (UNTAET) (2000b) Regulation No. 2000/15 on the Establishment of Panels with Exclusive Jurisdiction over Serious Criminal Offences, 6 June 2000.

United Nations Transitional Administration in East Timor (UNTAET) (2000c) Regulation No. 2000/30 On Transitional Rules of Criminal Procedure, 25 September 2000.

United States v Monzel (2011) 641 F 3d 528.

United States v Stamper (1991) 766 F Supp 1396 (WDNC 1991).

UP v Damodar and Anr (2015) ILC-2015-SC-CRL-May-2.

van Boven, T. (1999) 'The Perspective of the Victim', in Danieli, Y., Stamatopoulou, E. and Dias, C. (eds.) *The Universal Declaration of Human Rights: Fifty Years and Beyond*, Baywood, New York, pp. 13–26.

Van Camp, T. and Wemmers, J-A. (2013) 'Victims' Satisfaction with Restorative Justice: More Than Simply Procedural Justice', *International Review of Victimology*, 19, 2, 117–143.

van Dijk, J. (1988) 'Ideological Trends within the Victims Movement: An International Perspective', in Maguire, M. and Pointing, C. (eds.) *Victims of Crime: A New Deal?*, Open University Press, Milton Keynes, pp. 115–126.

van Dijk, J. (2009) 'Free the Victim: A Critique of the Western Conception of Victimhood', *International Review of Victimology*, 16, 1, 1–34.

van Dijk, J. (2013) Victim-Centred Restorative Justice', *Restorative Justice: An International Journal*, 3, 1, 426–429.

Van Mechelen v Netherlands (1997) 25 EHRR 647.

Van Ness, D. (2003) 'Proposed Basic Principles on the Use of Restorative Justice: Recognising the Limits and Aims of Restorative Justice', in von Hirsch, A., Roberts, JV., Bottoms, AE., Roach, K. and Schiff, M. (eds.) *Restorative Justice and Criminal Justice: Competing or Reconcilable Paradigm?* Hart: Oxford, pp. 157–176.

Vanscoy v Ontario [1999] OJ 1661 (QL).

Verdun-Jones SN. and Yijerino, AA. (2002) *Victim Participation in the Plea Negotiation Process in Canada: A Review of the Literature and Four Models for Reform*, Policy Centre for Victim Issues: Research Statistics Division, Canada.

Victim of Crime Act 2001 (SA).

Victim Protection Act (Higaisha no hogo ni kansuru hōritsu), Law No. 75 of 2000 (Jpn).

Victims and Witnesses (Scotland) Act 2014 (Scot).

Victims Bill of Rights Act 2015 (Can).

Victims of Crime (Commissioner for Victims' Rights) Amendment Act 2007 (SA).

Victims of Crime Act 2001 (SA).

Victims' Rights Act 2002 (NZ).

Victims' Rights and Restitution Act 1990 (US).

Victorian Law Reform Commission (VLRC) (2015a) *The Role of Victims of Crime in the Criminal Trial Process*, Consultation Paper, July.

Victorian Law Reform Commission (VLRC) (2015b) *Victims of Crime: Information Paper 3: The International Criminal Court*, Information Paper, May.

von Hentig, H. (1948) *The Criminal and His Victim: Studies in the Sociology of Crime*, New Haven, CT, Yale University Press.

Vulnerable Witnesses (Scotland) Act 2004 (Scot).

War Crimes Research Office (2007) *Victim Participation before the International Criminal Court*, International Criminal Court Legal Analysis and Education Project, American University, Washington College of Law.

War Crimes Research Office (2009) *Victim Participation at the Case Stage of Proceedings*, International Criminal Court Legal Analysis and Education Project, American University, Washington College of Law.

Wąsek-Wiaderek, M. (2000) *The Principle of 'Equality of Arms' in Criminal Procedure Under Article 6 of the European Convention on Human Rights and Its Functions in Criminal Justice of Selected European Countries: A Comparative View*, Leuven University Press, Belgium.

Wemmers, J-A. (2005) 'Victim Policy Transfer: Learning from Each Other', *European Journal on Criminal Policy and Research*, 11, 1, 121–133.

Wemmers, J-A. (2009) 'Where Do They Belong? Giving Victims A Place in the Criminal Justice Process', *Criminal Law Forum*, 20, 4, 395–416.

Wemmers, J-A. (2010) 'Victim Rights and the International Criminal Court: Perceptions within the Court regarding the Victims' Right to Participate', *Liden Journal of International Law*, 23, 3, 629–643.

Wemmers, J-A. (ed.) (2014a) *Reparation for Victims of Crimes against Humanity: The Healing Role of Reparation*, Routledge, Oxon.

Wemmers, J-A. (2014b) 'Restoring Justice for Victims of Crime against Humanity', in Wemmers, JA. (ed.) *Reparation for Victims of Crimes against Humanity: The Healing Role of Reparation*, Routledge, Oxon, pp. 38–50.

Wieczorek, I (2012) 'A Needed Balance between Security, Liberty and Justice: Positive Signals Arrive from the Field of Victims' Rights', *European Criminal Law Review*, 2, 2, 141–157.

Wilks, A. (2012) 'The International Bar Association in Brazil: Forging Partnerships', in Foley, C. (ed.) *Another System Is Possible: Reforming Brazilian Justice*, International Bar Association, London, UK, pp. 129–144.

Wilson, MJ. (2009) 'Japan's New Criminal Jury Trial System: In Need of More Transparency, More Access, and More Time', *Fordham International Law Journal*, 33, 2, 487–572.

Witzleb, N. (2016) *Translation of Selected Sections of the Austrian Code of Criminal Procedure*, Melbourne, VIC.

Wolfgang, M. (1958) *Patterns in Criminal Homicide*, University of Pennsylvania Press, Philadelphia.

Wyngaert, C. (2011) 'Victims before International Criminal Courts: Some Views and Concerns of an ICC Trial Judge', *Case Western Reserve Journal of International Law*, 44, 475–496.

Y v Slovenia (2015) ECHR 41107/10.

Young Offenders Act 1997 (NSW).

Youth Justice and Criminal Evidence Act 1999 (UK).

Zappala, S. (2010) 'The Rights of Victims v the Rights of the Accused', *Journal of International Criminal Justice*, 8, 1, 137–164.

Zila, J. (2006) 'The Prosecution Service within the Swedish Criminal Justice System', in Jehle, JM. and Wade, M. (eds.) *Coping with Overloaded Criminal Justice Systems: The Rise of Prosecutorial Power across Europe*, Springer, Berlin, Germany, pp. 285–311.

Index